St. Louis Community College

Library

5801 Wilson Avenue
St. Louis, Missouri 63110

This Well-Wooded Land

Thomas R. Cox,
Robert S. Maxwell,
Phillip Drennon Thomas,
and Joseph J. Malone

This Well-Wooded Land

Americans
and Their Forests
from Colonial Times
to the Present

UNIVERSITY OF NEBRASKA PRESS

LINCOLN AND LONDON

The Forest History Society, established in 1946,
is a nonprofit, educational institution dedicated
to the advancement of historical understanding of
human interaction with the North American forest
environment. Interpretations and conclusions in
FHS publications are those of the authors; the
institution takes responsibility for the selection
of topics, the competence of the authors, and
their freedom of inquiry.

The paper in this book meets the guidelines for
permanence and durability of the Committee
on Production Guidelines for Book Longevity of
the Council on Library Resources.

Publication of this book was assisted by a grant from
the National Endowment for the Humanities, a
federal agency that supports the study of such fields
as history, philosophy, literature, and languages.

Library of Congress Cataloging in Publication Data

Main entry under title:

This well-wooded land.

Bibliography: p.
Includes index.
1. Forests and forestry – United States – History.
I. Cox, Thomas R., 1933–
SD143.T44   1985   333.75'0973   85-1141
ISBN 0-8032-1426-X (alk. paper)

To Elwood R. "Woody" Maunder,
who blazed a trail through the
tall timber of forest history
for over a quarter of a century

Contents

Preface

In 1974 we set out to write a brief overview of the role of forests in American history. It seemed like a straightforward project that could quickly be brought to fruition, and we looked forward to having a manuscript in hand by the end of the nation's bicentennial year. How wrong we were! The secondary literature proved far more extensive than any of us had realized; no brief synthesis could possibly encompass it all. Moreover, despite the work already done — especially during the preceding two decades — huge gaps remained. Fresh research, not just synthesis, proved necessary. Inadvertently, we had taken on a major project. Now, years later, it is complete. We hope its product, this volume, will still meet the needs of those students in environmental history for whom it was originally envisioned. We hope, too, it will be of value to that larger audience of specialists and interested laymen for whom we have also come to intend it.

The forms of historical and literary collaboration are almost as numerous as are jointly written books themselves. Varying personalities, diverse talents, and other differences all shape the particular patterns of interaction. So it has been with this work. It is the product of very different people, living at great distances one from another, each with his own interests and period of specialization. We set out with a shared conviction of the centrality of forests in the American experience; but we did not pretend to agree on all historical questions — not even all those involving forests. We ended the same way. Although we present this as one book, not a series of essays, each part is primarily the product of a single author and bears his stamp. I have coordinated the work and edited all the contributions with an eye not toward homogenizing the whole, but toward making them compatible. I trust that major internal contradictions, if not all minor ones, have been excised. The late Joseph J. Malone was the primary author of chapters 1–3 and part of the Bibliographical Essay, Phillip Drennon Thomas of chapters 4–6, and Robert S. Maxwell of chapters 11–

13; I wrote the Introduction, chapters 7–10, most of the Bibliographical Essay, and small portions of other chapters.

Ronald J. Fahl put his unparalleled knowledge of the historiography of the field to the service of us all.

Since this work is intended largely, if not entirely, for nonspecialists, we have kept the notes to a minimum. Where secondary sources exist, we have indicated some of the more valuable, to aid readers in probing further. When key interpretations appear, we have sought to make their authorship clear. When there are no secondary sources focusing on a particular area of importance, we have tried to make that clear too. But we have eschewed citations of manuscript materials, even though they have been used, and long compendiums of relevant sources. We have also not given sources for the many quotations from explorers, early observers, and the like. For the audience this book is aimed at, we trust that the notes we have provided, together with the Bibliographical Essay, will suffice both as a guide to further reading and as an indication of the wealth of historical literature now available in the field of forest history.

Most authors incur numerous obligations in the course of writing their books. Certainly we have. Vital support of our research and writing came from the National Endowment for the Humanities in the form of a grant to the Forest History Society (RO-22783-75-631). The Forest History Society itself provided encouragement, matching funds, and other help. The American Conservation Association, the Laird, Norton Foundation, and John M. Musser, Thomas J. McHugh, and Gene C. Brewer all contributed funds to the society to support the project. Elwood R. Maunder, long the executive director of the Forest History Society, was an enthusiastic supporter during the planning stage and subsequently reviewed the manuscript for us. Harold K. Steen, the present executive director of the society, not only took a key part in planning but also provided ideas and steady, constructive guidance thereafter. San Diego State University, Wichita State University, and Stephen F. Austin State University contributed less extensive but still vital aid.

Numerous other individuals also helped. Douglas H. Strong, William D. Hagenstein, and Richard G. Lillard each read the entire manuscript and made useful suggestions. Peter A. Fritzell, David C. Smith, Richard W. Judd, Raymond G. Starr, and Robert C. Detweiler reviewed portions dealing with their individual fields. Judy Reardon, Stephanie Belt, and Lois Malone lent research and editorial assistance on the first three chapters. Others far too numerous to mention by name gave help on individual points and questions. An even larger number of people, both in and outside the academic world, have expressed interest in our project and an eagerness to see it completed. Such expressions were vital: as the project constantly expanded, threatening to overwhelm us, we needed reassurance that what we were engaged in would prove of interest and utility to others.

To all these supporters we offer our sincere thanks. That our book is not perfect, we readily acknowledge; that it is far better than it would have been without their help, we also gladly admit.

THOMAS R. COX

Introduction

San Diego sits on the far southwestern corner of the United States, snug against the Pacific Ocean on one side and the border with Mexico on another. Across the international boundary lies Tijuana. As the 1980s began, both cities were growing rapidly, each approaching one million in population. They rest on remarkably similar terrain—dry hills and benchlands originally covered with the scrub growth typical of that semiarid region. Sycamores and live oaks are scattered along the usually dry watercourses that dissect the landscape. Only on the higher ridges in the distant backcountry can forests be found; there open stands of oak and pine, once the scene of a number of small sawmill operations, now primarily serve recreation seekers and occasional herdsmen and woodcutters. San Diego long outstripped Tijuana in size, for it had one of the finest harbors on the Pacific Coast while its neighbor to the south was virtually inaccessible by sea. However, within recent decades Tijuana commenced growing rapidly, eventually passing its neighbor in population. In spite of changes in both total and relative size, the two cities remain tied in a close, symbiotic relationship.

But San Diego and Tijuana represent different worlds. Relative wealth provides the most readily apparent difference, but far more distinguishes them. Perhaps nowhere else on earth can so sharp a cultural gradient be found in so short a distance as that from downtown San Diego to downtown Tijuana—some twenty miles. One need not even be on the ground to detect the difference. LANDSAT photographs taken from orbiting satellites clearly reveal the border, for land-use patterns north and south of it are markedly different.

The greater availability of water north of the border is partly responsible for the contrasts, but cultural factors are also at work. In San Diego the basic building material for private dwellings, and for many commercial buildings as well, is wood. In Tijuana it was originally adobe and has more recently been concrete (often in the form of concrete blocks, adobe's modern replacement). One can stand at the international border and watch wooden houses dating from the 1920s, 1930s, and 1940s being hauled south from San Diego to Tijuana. There they will be set down, usually on the outskirts of the city, to furnish inexpensive dwellings for those unable to afford better quarters—that is, unable to afford a building of adobe or some modern equivalent. Others erect even more modest dwellings from salvaged lumber also brought from San Diego. Wooden houses are virtually uninsurable in Tijuana, where fire protection is geared to a city built of masonry and concrete, not wood. Mortgages cannot be obtained on them for the same reason. Residents of Tijuana live in wooden houses at their own peril. In San Diego, meanwhile, new dwellings being erected on the lots vacated by houses moved south across the border are in most cases built of wood—even when they have a stucco exterior—just as their predecessors were. Similarly, yards in San Diego are regularly fenced with wood—frequently redwood from northern California—whereas in Tijuana fences are normally of stone, concrete, wrought iron, or similar material. In these and a host of other ways, San Diegans depend on wood to a degree that is out of the question just a few miles to the south—and to a degree at odds with the natural surroundings of San Diego itself.[1]

San Diego's dependence on wood followed hard on the heels of American control of California, established in 1846. Before that it was an isolated, sleepy Mexican town, built of adobe and huddled about its dusty central plaza. The oldest extant building from the American period is the William Heath Davis house, a prefabricated two-story dwelling of pine that was shipped out from Maine and erected in 1851. Other wooden buildings followed, and Old Town with its adobe structures gradually fell into disrepair. Elegant Victorian houses, built of wood, sprang up on the hills overlooking San Diego Bay; the residences of the less affluent and the business structures closer to the waterfront were also largely wooden. By the 1880s one had to look closely to detect San Diego's Hispanic origins.

San Diego and its appetite for wood continued to grow, inducing Simon Benson, a leading lumberman from the Pacific Northwest, to build a large sawmill there in 1906. In the absence of nearby forests, he supplied his mill with logs towed twelve hundred miles from the Columbia River in huge oceangoing rafts. In spite of dire predictions, "Benson's folly" proved profitable and continued to operate for some forty years. San Diegans not only built with lumber from the Benson Lumber Company's saws, but also heated and cooked with the sawdust, slabs, and trimmings they generated. When the mill finally closed, it was because of problems of log supply; the demand for wood products was still growing in San Diego. By contrast, apparently no one ever considered erecting a large sawmill in Tijuana or of investing in other major enterprises to supply it with wood. The demand was simply not there.[2]

The contrast between San Diego and Tijuana reflects larger realities. Walter M. Kollmorgen has traced the clash of land-use patterns that occurred when Anglos from forested areas brought their agrarian values onto the relatively dry and treeless Great Plains (and regions beyond); there they collided with pastoralists—sheepmen and cattlemen who were not often Hispanic themselves, but whose methods of operation had roots that ran through Latin America to Spain. As the agriculturists triumphed over the pastoralists, they transplanted eastern traditions into a vast realm where they were an incongruous, exotic growth, spreading them even to distant San Diego. Viewed in this light, the border between San Diego and Tijuana is both a political and a cultural demarcation line, an indicator of the outer limit of a forest-based people.[3]

Other students of the American past have focused on environmental rather than cultural factors, emphasizing how ill suited to the West many eastern, agrarian concepts were. The problems that resulted from extending land and water laws developed in forested, well-watered realms to areas west of the one hundredth meridian, where rainfall is generally less than twenty inches a year, were immense. In time, legislators and bureaucrats made grudging adjustments to better fit these laws to the realities of arid and semiarid lands, but by then great environmental damage had already been done. Even so, cultural traditions remained strong: hundreds of miles from the nearest commercial forests, Americans continued to live wood-intensive lives.[4]

This mode of life was peculiarly American. To be sure, the origins of the land and water laws that were long applied in the West were largely English. But colonists from England came from a land where forests were in short supply to one where forests and woods were all around them.[5] As these settlers adjusted to the abundance of wood on the western side of the Atlantic, they developed new ways and different values. What they built would have been impossible in England. A British visitor warned his countrymen that if they were to travel to the United States they would have to resign themselves to "a Wooden Town in a Wooden Country & a wooden bred set of Tavern-keepers." He found it all a bit distasteful. Without realizing it, our nameless British visitor had supplied an answer to that often-quoted question of J. Hector St. Jean de Crèvecoeur: "What then is the American, this new man?" The American and his society were, above all else, products of the continent's forested plenty.[6]

Old ways seldom die without a struggle. Much of the study of the interaction between Americans and their forests is the story of conflict between imported (especially English) agrarian and pastoral concepts and indigenous ones more suited to the American environment. Just as transplanted eastern approaches were ill suited to the arid West but hung on stubbornly nonetheless, so too did transplanted English approaches prove inappropriate but persevering on the eastern seaboard. In each case the friction between the system being transferred and its new environment caused both natural disasters and human suffering. Such is, perhaps, the inevitable price when societies expand into new realms.

The contest between imported cultural baggage and the demands of the new environment in which immigrants found themselves may have buffeted them from the first, but the settlers' economic and political ties to Great Britain remained strong. Throughout the colonial period, powerful integrative forces were at work pulling them toward the mother country just as surely as disintegrative environmental forces pulled them away. Not the least of the former was the value that British policymakers saw in the forests of their New World colonies and the absorption of much of the forests' products by British markets. For Americans, the ships of the Royal Navy offered welcome assurance—even security—in an age when France, Spain, and Holland each presented a maritime threat and France represented, in addition, a threat by land from its base in Canada and through its Indian allies. It did not escape the notice of Americans that British naval vessels were often built of colonial timber, carried masts from colonial forests, and sometimes were caulked and had their lines tarred with colonial naval stores. Differences could be overlooked in such circumstances.

To fix the point at which disintegrative forces gained ascendancy over integrative ones would be difficult, if not impossible. The pace of development varied greatly from place to place. Indeed, in some locales the integrative forces proved remarkably durable. Not until after the War of 1812 did many New Englanders loosen their transatlantic ties sufficiently to make their region truly American rather than an overseas extension of England.[7]

A half-century and more later, a similar conflict of values and a similar pattern of mixed results developed west of the Mississippi. Converging interests pulled the transmississippi West toward the older parts of the nation, while environmental differences set them against one another on matters of resource policy and control. This time integrative forces triumphed; the West remained tied to the rest of the country in spite of differences and the efforts of advocates of the Pacific Republic (among others) to exploit them. American nationalism, improved transportation and communication, and geographic contiguity combined to keep East and West together. The continuing political connection helped keep cultural ties strong. For all Westerners' grumbling over the years about eastern manipulation of policies regarding western resources and about Easterners' failure to understand either the land or the people of the West, the fact remains that Westerners and Easterners have in common many attitudes toward resources. Not the least of these have to do with forests, for the two share a wood-intensive culture. It is thus natural that most San Diegans find their ideas toward forests and wood more widely shared east of the Appalachians than just a few miles to the south of them in Tijuana.[8]

Yet a picture painted in such broad strokes obscures as much as it reveals. For all the ties and differences between England and America in early times, and in spite of all that East and West have both shared and disagreed on since, far more than these elements must be incorporated if one is to trace the story of the interactions of Americans and their forests as fully as it deserves. Past or present, East or West, viewpoints have varied. Social and economic factors, as surely as regionalism and cultural baggage, have shaped attitudes and determined actions. Moreover, what has been viewed as true or desirable in one era has often been rejected in another. In short, the story of the American forest is as complex as the nation itself.

For all the complexity and differences, a basic point remains. Whether one looks at the broad picture or at the more intricate interrelations and crosscurrents that lie behind it, forests have had a central place in the American experience—far more central than is generally recognized. This book traces this centrality, demonstrating both the forest heritage of Americans and their continuing dependence on their forests. It is a long, sometimes tortuous story, yet one that can help Americans understand not only their past, but their present and future as well.

*Americans and Their Forests
in the Colonial Period*

Part One

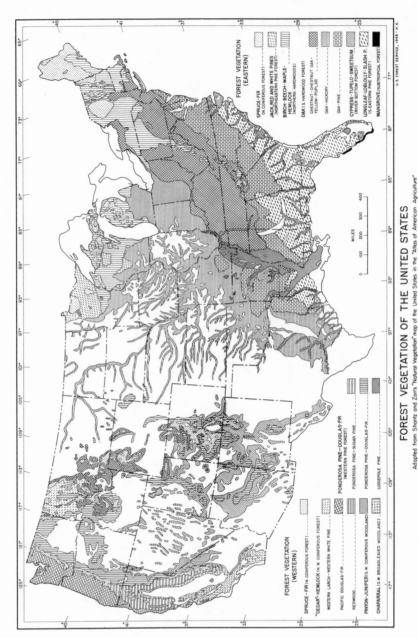

Forest Vegetation of the United States
Adapted from Shantz and Zon's "Natural Vegetation" map of the United
States in the *Atlas of American Agriculture*. U.S. Forest Service.

Landfall, Settlement, and Forest All Around

Chapter 1

Human use of North America's forests no doubt goes back nearly to that day when the first paleo-Indians worked their way across an ice or land bridge from Asia to Alaska. The stories of man and of the continent's forests have been intertwined ever since. Small wonder, for the continent's woodlands were as varied as they were vast.

Along the Atlantic, where the first Europeans were later to land, the forests were especially complex. Pine, fir, walnut, cedar, ash, mulberry, oak, chestnut, elm, locust, maple, cherry, laurel, spruce, birch, hemlock, hickory, beech—all were either mentioned by explorers and early settlers or described in a manner that has allowed subsequent identification. Perhaps as much as 90 percent of the English area of settlement, stretching from the Carolinas to the Maritimes, was covered by forest—a varied mantle of green that was in places open and parklike, in others barely penetrable.[1]

In Maine the early settlers encountered pine, spruce, balsam fir, and some maple, birch, beech, and hemlock. In the northern portion of what became the province of New Hampshire, a wide area of spruce forest grew intermingled with maple, birch, and other hardwoods. Farther south white pine dominated, although various hardwood trees were also found. This pine belt extended through Connecticut, where stands of spruce were also numerous. Northern New York was an area of dense forests with maple, birch, beech, and other deciduous trees intermingled with spruce and pine. To the west, broadleaf trees characteristic of the Mississippi basin dominated.

Much of New Jersey, or the Jerseys as they were known in early days, was covered by pitch pine forests—a fact hard to imagine today in urban areas, though elsewhere much of the state remains forested. Early settlers in Pennsylvania encountered white pine and hemlock forests, extending over enormous areas on both sides of the Allegheny Mountains. In the west, heavy growths of broadleaf trees intermingled with hemlocks and groves of pine.

Northern Delaware was blanketed by deciduous forests. In the sandy soil farther south in the colony, pitch pines made up as much as 50 percent of the forest growth. The Appalachian area of Maryland was covered with white pine, hemlock, spruce, birch, oak, and maples. In central Maryland, as far as Chesapeake Bay, oak, hickory, gum, and other deciduous trees proliferated. Maryland's Eastern Shore was a pitch pine region. Virginia possessed dense forests of pine, hemlock, oak, cherry, poplar, and other trees also found in the northern colonies. In the southwestern part of the colony, oak, chestnut, hickory, walnut, and cherry were the predominant varieties; the Eastern Shore of Virginia was a continuation of the pine belt that stretched south to Georgia and beyond.

The variety of the forests in the Carolinas and Georgia was unequaled. The coastal areas were covered with coniferous stands. The central region was dominated by a pine-oak forest with other hardwood trees intermingled; the Appalachians to the west were densely covered by hardwoods intermingled with pine, spruce, fir, and hemlock. South Carolina, as it would come to be known, had especially dense pine forests on the coast; Georgia possessed — along with its noted pines — firs, beeches, and a vast swampy area of cypress. Everywhere there were local variations to add further complexity to the scene — and to widen the range of options open to settlers.

Like the native Americans, when Europeans arrived in North America they turned almost as once to utilizing its trees. Long before Columbus set foot in the New World, cargoes of timber had already been dispatched from its shores. Norse sagas recount how Vikings cut trees in what they called Vinland to help meet the needs of settlements in Greenland. Ships sailed from Greenland expressly to obtain timber. Thorfinn Karlsefni left there for North America in A.D. 1010 with three ships and 160 people. He hoped to found a permanent settlement and apparently expected trade in timber to play an important role in its economy. In one of his first acts, he "ordered timber to be felled and cut into lengths for a cargo . . . and it was left on a rock to season." In the end Karlsefni's settlement failed; the settlements on Greenland also eventually perished, thanks to climatic changes and other factors. The Vikings' commerce in North American timber died with them, but the way had been pointed.[2]

Time after time, subsequent explorers were to see value in the forests of the continent; and settlers in the colonies of Sweden, Holland, France, and England all turned to felling and using trees almost as soon as they stepped ashore. Forests provided material for heating, cooking, and building shelters as well as items for commerce. Whatever they may have thought of the forests that surrounded them—and reactions on that score varied considerably—nearly everyone recognized that North America's forests could be remarkably useful. It is a judgment that has never been seriously challenged.

But the forest was a stage as well as a treasure chest. In it native Americans met whites, colonial empires clashed, and administrators and individual settlers sought to have their different—and often conflicting—ways. Frequently the nature of the stage shaped the course, or even the outcome, of the struggles waged upon it.

This juxtaposition of peoples in a wilderness environment suggests hardship, even privation, but the English colonies survived and, after initial trials, prospered. Although the patterns varied from area to area, taken as a whole the white population of the colonies soon came to enjoy a standard of nutrition superior to that of all but the wealthy classes in Europe. Sufficient food could be produced to supply local needs and still leave a surplus for export—largely because some 85 percent of the colonial work force was committed to agriculture.

After the rigors of settling in were behind the colonists, in about 1650—give or take five years—an appreciable rise in living standards began. The process continued for generations, encouraging a high rate of natural increase in the population. Joined to immigration and minimal involvement in major warfare over nearly two centuries before the Revolution, this increase gradually created a large as well as prosperous citizenry whose stake in the new society grew year by year. As the settlers' stake grew so too did conservative attitudes that probably did as much to drive the colonists apart from Great Britain as did those often-described British initiatives after 1763 that eventually led to open revolt.

When it came time to face the British, American recruits came from a vigorous population. They were the legacy of good, healthful living over many decades. Infant mortality, like disease in children and adults, was significantly lower than in England and continental Europe. Along with good nutrition, the relative warmth in winter of the American colonial home helped maintain a healthy population. In contrast to Europe, there was an ample supply of wood for fuel, gleaned from the clearing of agricultural land or obtained directly from the forest.[3] What Francis Higginson wrote of Massachusetts in 1630 applied elsewhere as well: "Though it bee here somewhat cold in the winter, yet here we have plenty of Fire to warme us, and that a great deal cheaper than they sel Billets and Faggots in *London*: nay, all *Europe* is not able to afford so great Fires as *New England*." Victory over the mother country can hardly be attributed to the availability of firewood, but that it contributed to that end, however indirectly, seems certain. And there were many other ways the American forest influenced the growth to nationhood of a few scattered settlements along the Atlantic shore, most more readily apparent than those related to demography, nutrition, and health.

Even before the Plymouth and Massachusetts Bay colonies, before Jamestown in Virginia and the Spanish settlements in Florida, preconceptions had been formed concerning the wilderness of the New World. These assumptions were shaped by the nature of European society at the time. In turn, they shaped what Europeans thought they perceived in the New World.

When Columbus brought news of his discovery to Spain in 1493, he was convinced that he had found Indians because that is what he wanted the inhabitants to be. Much else in his accounts was not so much what he saw as what he had concluded the land he had reached should be—an earthly Paradise. The bowers of that paradise were made from trees "of a thousand kind and tall." His was the first word, enthusiastically received and passed throughout Europe: the transatlantic wilderness stood welcoming, full of promise.[4]

The impression that there were resources enough for all soon grew suspect. As early as 1536, firewood had to be brought twelve miles across denuded areas to the Spanish settlement of Santo Domingo on the Caribbean island of Hispaniola. Yet at the same time a growing knowledge concerning the variety of trees, vegetables, and medicinal plants in the New World gave impetus to settlement, fortifying the arguments of those who sought to spur England to join in colonizing North America.

Most promoters of transatlantic settlement saw not an unruly wilderness that needed to be tamed, but the promise of good life on the Golden Shore.[5] Richard Hakluyt was one. Arthur Barlowe's account of his visit to Virginia 1584, which Hakluyt published as a promotional piece, described "valleys thick with fine cedar trees . . . the highest and reddest . . . in the world, far better than the cedar of the Azores, of the Indies, or of Lebanon." There were numerous other varieties "of excellent quality and fine fragrance," pine, cypress, and gum trees and of course the stately oak, "the same . . . as we have in England, but far larger and better."

Nonetheless, fruit trees and medicinal plants ranked higher than forestry in descriptions of opportunities to be exploited in the New World. Forestry was associated with hard labor and was therefore given short shrift in accounts of the bowers of Paradise. London's *Moderate Intelligencer* noted in 1649 that in America one was "plentifully fed and cloathed with the natural Commodities of the Country, which fall into your hands without labour or toyle, for in the obtaining of them you have a delightful recreation."

Reactions to the New World were far from uniform. Some writers depicted it as surreal and threatening. Buffon's *Historie naturelle* and Diderot's *Encyclopédie* expounded on the "woeful case" of America, with accounts of pygmies on the shore of Hudson Bay and of "monstrous birds." A contemporary account of America's woodlands asserted that "extensive marshes, great lakes, aged, decayed and crowded forests with the other circumstances that mark an uncultivated country are supposed to replentish the air with heavy and noxious vapours that will give a double asperity to the winter and . . . carry the inconvenience of the frigid zone far into the temperate."

Intimate knowledge was not a prerequisite for claiming to speak with authority on the New World. In the early sixteenth century, Verrazano sailed away with little more than the scent of pine trees off the Carolina coast to inform his judgments, but he wrote knowingly of "a land full of the largest forests, some thin and some dense, clothed with various sorts of trees, with as much beauty and delectable appearance as it would be possible to express." Buffon and Diderot did not even come within pine's scent of the new land.

Settlers had a different perspective. When the Pilgrim William Bradford wrote that the cedar swamps of Massachusetts in their natural state offered a "wild and savage view" and called the New England wilderness "hideous and desolate," he was describing what he knew close up and on a continuing basis. But his view too was shaped by presumptions and desires as much as by reality. His awestruck reaction to Massachusetts's cedars was an exclamation on the subject of how much had to be cut down, cleared away, and subdued before the New Jerusalem could rise on the Atlantic shore. The contrast between this new world and the gentle countryside left behind, and the conviction that there would be no returning, account for his vehemence. The title of the Reverend Samuel Danforth's election sermon of May 1, 1670—"A Brief Recognition of New England's Errand into the Wilderness"—is indicative of the spirit of the times.

For Puritans the forest became a metaphor for what America was, and for what had to be overcome were religious faith to endure and that "city upon a hill" to be built for all the world to behold. New England's towns, with houses and fields close-set, stood in stark contrast to the forests beyond. Roads seldom penetrated far into the forest, and most citizens avoided it whenever possible. As settlements developed and grew more ordered, the contrast became increasingly apparent. More than ever, wilderness seemed poised to engulf New

England's towns. To the Puritan mind the conclusion was obvious: the forest, the source of the threat, was the domain of Satan and his minions, a place to be avoided and condemned if it could not be changed. It was, Michael Wigglesworth wrote in 1662, "a waste & howling wilderness where none inhabited but hellish fiends & brutish men." Descriptions from such sources—as surely as those of Verrazano, Buffon, and Diderot—must be used with caution.[6]

Whatever the name given the distant star that attracted Europeans to America—religion, profits, liberty, philanthropy, or a vision of transatlantic empire—more basic requirements evoked the settlers' initial response to the woodlands. They needed food and shelter and turned to the woods to obtain them.

Even before the first tree was felled, it had been learned that the forest could sustain life for the newcomers. Walter Raleigh's party, exploring Roanoke Island in 1584, found food so plentiful in midsummer that the next expedition came inadequately provisioned. Deer, rabbits, and fowl abounded in the woods and were sources of clothing as well as food. Settlers reported stands of trees heavy with fruit and nuts. Subsequent arrivals extended their knowledge. No special skills, they found, were required in at least one branch of animal husbandry, raising hogs, since these creatures—forest dwellers before their domestication by man—could roam the woods feeding on acorns, nuts, roots, and herbs. Fish runs crowded northern streams. Maples yielded sap for sugar, and from spruce and other trees came medicinal juices. Bark was used in home tanneries. Colonial Americans drew heavily on this store of sustenance. Many, however, came unaware of the seasonality of much of the forest's largesse and thus for a time suffered great privation.

From the first, the forests also provided material for shelters. Initially these were crude huts and lean-tos of wood and bark—in some cases hardly more than piles of brush—but as time passed and housing became more elaborate, wood continued to be the primary building material. Conditioned by the scarcity of lumber in Europe, early English settlers built half-framed houses but soon abandoned them for full-framed, clapboard-covered structures. The Dutch introduced shingle covering for walls on Long Island sometime around 1650. Shingles required as much wood as clapboards but took less time and labor to produce. They caught on quickly and soon replaced slate, thatch, and bark in most roofing. The forest's abundance also made log cabins practical. Log construction techniques were introduced by Europeans from more heavily forested areas—Germans, Finns, and Swedes—and were promptly adopted by many Americans. Wood was also used for a greater part of the construction of finer dwellings when those appeared. North of New Spain, Americans of all social and economic strata became dwellers in wood—although masonry construction was never completely absent.[7]

But more than food and shelter was necessary if the settlements were to survive and prosper. Solid economic foundations had to be laid. Captain John Smith began the process at Jamestown by putting his untrained gentlemen—apprentice frontiersmen—to work clearing underbrush, felling trees, and making boards. They took the first, rudimentary steps in extracting "cash crops" from the woodlands—lumber, pitch, and potash—for shipment to the mother country. Smith's *General Historie of Virginia, New England, and the Summer Isles* proclaimed his hope for a balanced, mercantile society. It should be a market for the manufactured goods of England as well as a provider of raw materials.

Progress came slowly. During the first winter, not more than four acres of land were cleared. Most was planted to wheat, but it did poorly. The great fertility of the soil produced enormous plants with stunted heads; only a second crop balanced the size of stalk and grain. This problem and the great amount of land required combined to discourage wheat farming.

The rate at which agricultural land was brought into production rose sharply when Smith and his men learned from the Indians how to kill trees by girdling— cutting a ring around the trunk near its base so as to sever the life-sustaining layer that carries food to the roots. But plowing in a field studded with the dead snags and roots left by girdling was a difficult process that continued to discourage the would-be raisers of wheat.

Soon, however, it was determined that the still-arduous task of clearing land in Virginia was best rewarded when tobacco was given priority. This crop did well on new land from the first year, was adapted to cultivation by the hoe (which eased problems of raising it among girdled snags), and brought more return per acre. The rewards were so great that a "tobacco imperialism" quickly emerged from Maryland to the Carolinas. By 1688, John Clayton observed, the plantations of Virginians had grown vast, owners "each ambitioning to engross as much as they can that they may be sure [to] have enough to plant." Six hundred acres of tobacco fields "surrounded by 2400 Acres of Woods" was common, he wrote. By this time the attitude was widespread among settlers in Virginia that "the extermination of the forest" was a necessary and vital preliminary to economic progress. For the moment, the colony's economy seemed secure, but the same could hardly be said for its forests—or for the soil, which tobacco cultivation wore out with startling rapidity.[8]

Forest clearing was an initial concern everywhere, not just in the tobacco South, and everywhere it was an undertaking for which English settlers were ill

prepared. Land clearing had ceased to be a common need in England generations before. Haltingly they proceeded with the chore, borrowing techniques
from others as they did so. Pennsylvania's settlers not only learned girdling
from Virginians, but also adopted the use of fire and communal log-rolling
bees to open land for agriculture. The last two techniques were apparently introduced by Swedes, Finns, and Germans, who had used them in the old
country; were quickly adopted by the Scotch-Irish, who had been accustomed
to burning the moors to improve pasture; and were then picked up by English
settlers. Pennsylvanians also learned that leaving tall stumps gave better lever-
age two or three years later when they were ready to pry them from the ground
than did the short stumps preferred in wood-limited western Europe. With
their combination of techniques, Pennsylvania's colonists developed into the
finest land clearers of their age. They directed their efforts especially to stands
of hickory, beech, maple, and ash, for they found that the moist conditions
these required resulted in a rich, black, humus-laden soil ideal for farming.

In New England the need for farmland was also great, but the rocky terrain
and small valleys combined with the ideal of close-set communities to keep
fields small. Rocks were especially important: it simply required too much labor
to move them the distances required to make the large fields needed for extensive agriculture even if Puritan ideals had encouraged it. This combination discouraged certain land-clearing techniques used elsewhere—girdling, for example, was abandoned at an early date in favor of more thorough clearing of
limited acreage. Moreover, local conditions were such that far more land was
cleared for pasture than for crops. The result of all this was a landscape that
appeared more familiar to European visitors than the landscape of Virginia
and that was thus less criticized by them. In fact, of course, the pattern in New
England sprang from the interplay of economic, cultural, and environmental
forces as surely as did those that emerged farther south.[9]

Initially, the greatest impact of colonial Americans on the forest came when
they cleared land for settlement, crops, and pasture. Gradually their use of the
forest diversified. Whatever the settler's means of livelihood, the forest had to
be exploited or even laid waste. Transplanted Europeans may have marveled
at the beauty, variety, and immensity of the American forest or have been
moved by the aura of mystery, of the unknown, that emanated from its silent
depths, but they were almost as quick to regard the profusion of trees as so
much timber. Whether the eye of the beholder transformed a tree into a mast
or so many handspikes, furniture or planking, a barrel or a spar, depended on
the beholder and the options open to him.

Early writings from America reveal that the potential of naval stores was recognized as soon as the commercial value of the forests came under discussion. James Rosier, who briefly surveyed the Maine coast in 1605, was impressed by "oak very great & good" and by the dense stands of pine—which he identified as fir—"out of which issueth turpentine in so marvelous plenty, & so sweet, as our chirurgeon [surgeon] & others affirmed they never saw so good in England." Thomas Harriot's *Brief and True Report of the New Found Land of Virginia* (1587) gave emphasis to the potential for pitch tar, turpentine, and resin production and of trees well suited for use as masts and spars.[10] Naval stores seemed to promise steady employment for anyone in the cooper's trade as well.

It was perhaps inevitable that the forests' best use should have appeared thus. The concerns of the age were commercial—but for the most part it was commerce supported by a maritime rather than a settler society. To that society the Spanish, then Dutch and French, threats were just over the horizon when not actually within sight. Hence the supply of masts and naval stores—the muscles and sinews of naval supremacy—were the most compelling promise of the New World. Even in Puritan New England, where finding Canaan in the wilderness rather than commercial opportunity provided the initial impetus to settlement, such concerns could never be pushed completely from mind. And as commercial opportunities eroded the religious foundations of the community, they loomed larger and larger.[11]

Iron manufacturing also began at an early date. Harriot noted "the infinite stores of wood for smelting"—coal was to become important for the purpose only later. In 1657, writing from Virginia, Anthony Langston observed: "the only defect wee have to make us the most flourishing and profitable Plantation his Majesty hath . . . [is] want of Iron and Steele whereby the Smiths trade might go forward, wch is the foundation of all other Arts." To locate such resources, Langston thought, would require much time and "a great disbursement," which was why newcomers "have found quicker wayes to make profitable returns." If the basis for an iron and steel industry was to be provided, Virginia's leaders would have to be specific and selective about the skills of "new Transported people." Iron, it should be noted, ranked with masts and naval stores as a necessity in the struggle for naval and commercial superiority.[12]

The forest did more than give up wood to house the new settlers, land for them to farm, and products to enrich their commerce. It touched nearly every aspect of their lives. The settlers' simple furniture was made of wood, as were tools, utensils, containers (such as boxes and barrels), and means of transportation (wagons, ships, and carriages). Wood fires heated their homes and cooked their meals. So plentiful was it that ingenious early Americans even substituted wood for stone, iron, and leather.

The worm or Virginia rail fence illustrates the lavish use of wood in America. Apparently adopted from Scandinavia or middle Europe during the colonial period, these fences were built by interlocking sets of six to ten rails at alternating angles so that they zigzagged across the landscape. They required a prodigious quantity of timber—some 6,500 rails for every mile of fence—and took up considerable space, but they were cheap, durable, and easy to build and repair. An English visitor summed up the reasons for their widespread adoption (and for their continued use after the colonial period): "the fences are not as straight as in England, but a continual zig-zag. The reason for the difference is, timber and land are of comparatively little value in America, while their method requires less labor than ours." He had touched on the heart of the matter: in colonial America, nature provided on a scale unknown in the Old World, and settlers drew on that largesse to lay firm foundations for their settlements.

Colonists had not found gold or silver lying about free for the taking, or a paradise where the good life came without labor, as early publicists had promised. But they had found a land so richly endowed with forests—and the rich soils that moist hardwood forests helped build up—that they were able to survive and prosper. As they did, a new way of life came into being: wood, the most abundant of their resources, was a factor of greater significance in the development of colonial America, and then of the United States, than perhaps of any other country.[13]

The forest was a means of survival, and it seemed limitless. It was a deliverer from the privations of Europe and a liberator of attitudes as well. Necessarily restrictive Old World, husbandry-oriented attitudes regarding land and resources were gradually replaced by more expansive views.[14] Thus, even before the survival of England's North American colonies was assured, one of the earliest contributions to American folklore, the legend of the inexhaustibility of the forest, had begun to take shape. The forest could hardly have seemed otherwise to an Englishman, whose home country was built to a very different scale, where a wooded expanse of one hundred acres was a major forest and the bounty of the forest was unavailable to the common man. How different was America, where the forest environment made possible a conviction, less ambivalent than it might at first glance appear, that the forest was at once the source of subsistence and a wilderness whose conquest was the key to that future of plenty that early Americans sought for themselves and their descendants.

1. Frontiersmen using girdling and fire to clear the forest for agriculture. From *Harvey's Scenes in the Primeval Forests of America* (London, 1841). Courtesy American Philosophical Society.

2. Savannah, Georgia, and the surrounding pine forests as they appeared in 1734. Courtesy Library of Congress.

3

4

5

3. Collecting gum for naval stores in the southern pineries, a monthly task from March to November. From *Knights American Mechanical Dictionary*, vol. 3 (1884). Courtesy Sleepy Hollow Press.

4. Farm buildings and fence types in use in early America. From P. Campbell, *Travels in the Interior Parts of North America in the Years 1791 and 1792* (Edinburgh, 1793). Courtesy American Philosophical Society.

5. Woodcut of one of America's ubiquitous water-powered sawmills. Perhaps the oldest in Ohio, this one operated from 1789 to 1840. From *The American Pioneer* (1843).

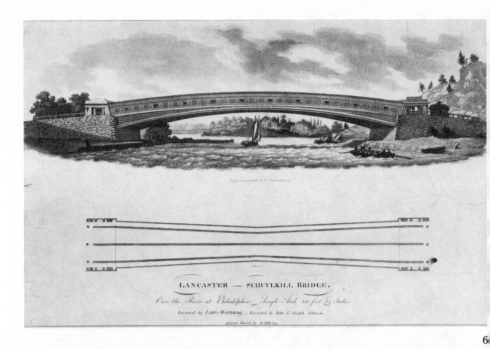

LANCASTER — SCHUYLKILL BRIDGE,

Over the River at Philadelphia. Single Arch 340 feet 3½ Inches.

Invented by Lewis Wernwag ... Executed by him & Joseph Johnson.

general finish by R. Mills Esq.

GRAND TURK

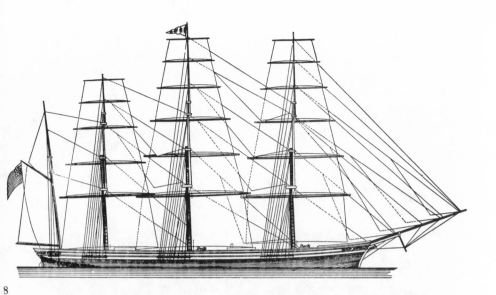

8

9

6. The Schuylkill River bridge in Philadelphia. A 340-foot single-arch span, this wooden masterpiece was completed in 1814. Courtesy Lee Nelson.

7. Steamboat taking on fuel wood at night, a familiar sight on western rivers. Courtesy St. Louis Art Museum.

8. The four-masted *Great Republic,* a 334-foot clipper ship built by Donald McKay in Boston in 1855. From Henry Hall, *The Ship-Building Industry of the United States* (1884).

9. Master builder (fifth from left) and crew in A. M. Simpson shipyard, North Bend, Oregon, ca. 1890. Courtesy National Maritime Museum, San Francisco.

10

11

2

0. The Susquehanna boom at Williams-
ort. When enlarged to its fullest, it had
lmost four hundred thirty-foot-high
tone-filled cribs, stretched for seven
iles above the city, and had a capacity of
hree hundred million feet of logs. Cour-
:sy Lycoming County Historical
Iuseum, Pennsylvania.

1. Sorting logs below the Susquehanna
oom for rafting to different mills.
:ourtesy Lycoming County Historical
Iuseum, Pennsylvania.

2. An abandoned plank road near Coos
ay, Oregon. Courtesy Bureau of Land
Ianagement.

13. The R. F. Learned mill at Natchez on the Mississippi River. Founded in 1828, the mill operated until the turn of the century. Courtesy American Forest Institute.

14. Rafting logs on the Kentucky River.
Courtesy Alice Lloyd College, Kentucky.

Woodlands, Trade, and Expansion

Chapter 2

The forests of America represented not only a challenge but such a remarkable catalog of opportunities that what emerged in British North America can be identified as a "timber-intensive" economy. The colonial era was a wooden age not only in terms of daily life, but also in terms of the commerce that lay at the heart of the economic order; from the first wood played a central role in colonial development.

Most evidence of expanding timber intensiveness in the colonial economy relates to the export trade. Exports represent only a part of forest utilization in America—and not the most important part in terms of volume of activity—but ubiquitous customs and tax collectors generated statistics not duplicated for local markets and local users. Still, statistics on trade suggest much about domestic colonial development. If, for example, North Carolina shipped 2.5 million cedar and cypress shingles in 1753 and tripled the export total by 1775 (as it did), the increase tells much about the pace of settlement and work-force expansion within the colony itself.

Even a small dwelling required several tons of timber. The scarcity of iron nails made it necessary to fasten house frames by means of notched joints secured by wooden pegs. Notching weakened the wood; hence very thick framing timber was deemed necessary. When grander or more substantial buildings were erected, the seemingly limitless supply of firewood for baking clay into bricks aided their construction. Pine was king in housing construction. Since pines sixty to seventy feet tall often had a uniform diameter of sixteen to eighteen inches for two-thirds of that length, they were ideally suited for such use. In Georgia, fully 80 percent of the houses were of pine, their roofs shingled with the originally despised cypress.

Building taxed the forests not only through the wood required but also through the space it took. Clearings for dwellings and commercial establishments, for the roads—however bad—that radiated from them and tied them together, and even for the skidways along which logs were removed from the woods all took their toll of timberland. Road construction ate away at the forest in another way too. Lopped brush and saplings were used to make temporarily muddy areas passable; more permanently marshy sections were kept usable by placing logs side by side across the roadway. These "corduroy" stretches were hard both on the forests and on the travelers who bounced over them in wagon or carriage.[1] However, the construction of dwellings and roads took only a small portion from America's forests. The population of Britain's North American colonies was small. The number of dwellings, the size of towns, and the miles of road the settlers required—or were capable of building—had far less impact than the various commercial activities through which colonists sought to fashion a viable economy.

Probably even more lumber went into exports than into colonial buildings. The lumber trade began with a small shipment of hand-sawn clapboards sent from the James River settlement to England in 1607. The water-powered saw-mill was introduced—in the autumn of 1611—near the site of Richmond. The expertise was Dutch or German and was reinforced before 1624 by additional groups of sawyers from those countries, as well as a few Poles. William Byrd of Westover imported saws and sawmill parts from Europe and boasted that his mills could rip two thousand board feet in five hours.

The most rapid proliferation of sawmills occurred initially in New Nether-land, which had three in operation by 1623. Shipments of timber to Holland began three years later. The Dutch had an advantage in developing sawmills because they were common in Holland at the time, whereas many had been destroyed across the Channel by English sawyers and others who feared for their jobs. By the time the English took over New Netherland in 1664, there were some forty sawmills already operating in the colony—more even than in heavily forested New Hampshire.

New England's combination of thick forests, good harbors, plentiful water-power, and—soon after the initial period of settlement—a thriving merchant marine made the proliferation of sawmills inevitable. At a conservative esti-mate, there were seventy-two mills active in Massachusetts Bay Colony at the end of the seventeenth century. The first, in all probability, was in operation on the Neponset River, near Dorchester, in the early 1630s. New Hampshire's citizens were lining the Piscataqua River with mills at the same time. At Scituate in Plymouth Colony, as elsewhere in New England, permission to build a mill for commercial use was granted only if logs brought in by townspeople were given first priority in sawing. Mills appeared not only where stream fall was sufficient to turn waterwheels, but also in locations where the tidal flow could be harnessed.

Sawmills also spread along the watercourses of New Jersey and Pennsylvania. Most of New Jersey's mills were erected and in operation early—by about 1680. They also appeared early in North Carolina's Cape Fear region—so early as to exert significant influence on the pattern of settlement there—and sawn pine became a staple export of the colony.[2]

Iron manufacturing also drew heavily on the forest. By the 1630s iron was being produced in Lynn, Massachusetts, in quantities sufficient to meet the needs of the New England colonies; and by 1650 small amounts of bar iron were being exported to England, an enterprise that would soon rouse the opposition of the London government. Two decades later an ironworks was established in New Jersey, and by 1720 others were present in Virginia, the Carolinas, and Pennsylvania. By the eve of the Revolution there were at least eighty-two charcoal blast furnaces busily at work in British North America.

Wherever it occurred in the colonies, iron production was an important factor in the destruction of forests, for it was extraordinarily timber intensive. William Byrd, journeying to Fredericksburg, Virginia, to observe the furnaces there, was amazed at the huge clear-cut area he passed through as he approached the town. An ironmaster explained to him that it took at least two square miles of forest to provide a continuing supply of fuel for a moderate-sized furnace. The estimate may well have been low. Some reports suggest that the average colonial furnace needed fifteen thousand acres of woodland to support its operations. Indeed, so great was the need that the presence of timber for charcoal was a major factor in locating iron manufactories. "Iron plantations" like Hopewell, Pennsylvania, evolved where wood supplies were ample. Legions of woodcutters labored to supply the smelters; nearer the furnaces and forges there developed whole communities, with stores, offices, and the entire range of eighteenth-century services.

Elsewhere operations were more limited and transient. An account of 1779 described the problems of one such enterprise in Virginia:

The Accakeek Iron Mines in Stafford County, belonging to a company in England whose property they will remain, were worked but discontinued upwards twenty years ago because they had larger & richer Banks of ore, with greater conveniencys of Wood & Water in Maryland, where all their Hands, stocks & utensils were removed. The Lands are said to have been offered for sale by the company's agent and probably from their being very broken without Timber and the soil excessive poor, have not been sold.

A migratory pattern was under way not unlike the one that had deforested England long before. However, in America the limited size of the work force and the extensiveness of the forest-clad area softened the impact of the production of charcoal iron.[3]

Potash and pearlash production were no less timber intensive than iron manufacturing. From three to five acres of timber had to be burned to yield a ton of potash. Potash and its refined derivative, pearlash, were so valuable as fertilizer and in industrial processes such as glassmaking that production was encouraged on both sides of the Atlantic. Customs accounts usually lumped both products under the heading potash.

The refinement of taste and improvement in living standards in colonial America reached a stage that made potash important for domestic use about the time, in 1751, that the demands of the British glass and textile industries encouraged Parliament to lift import duties and offer premiums for this valued chemical. Throughout the colonies, settlers also used it in making soap and gunpowder. Thus an export and domestic trade in potash that was worth millions flourished at the end of the colonial period.

Eventually production processes became more efficient, but for most of the colonial period they were crude. Trees were cut, piled, and burned, and the ashes were collected. These were then placed in barrels with holes in the bottom and leached by pouring water over them. The solution that drained off was boiled down in large iron kettles and then reheated in smaller ones to drive off impurities. The potash that resulted was usually less than 25 percent potassium carbonate, the chemical that gave it its valued properties, but that was sufficient to meet most needs of the day.

To reduce the labor required, whole sections of forest were sometimes fired and the resulting ashes gathered in from the blackened wastelands. Much was inevitably lost in the process. Moreover, this yielded a low-quality ash; hardwoods produced the best ashes, but all species were consumed in these fires. Yet there was reason behind this seemingly profligate practice. Wood ashes, even those from pines and other less desirable species, were close enough to potash to serve as fertilizer, so ashes left behind during collecting enriched the soil for agriculture. Indeed, most of the wood for potash production came from land being cleared for agriculture. In such cases what resulted was not devastated forests, but new farmland; potash production helped pay the costs of transformation.[4]

Of the various naval stores, pitch and tar were the first to be important in mercantile calculations. The most extensive tree-burning activity was the extraction of tar from pine trunks and branches. The general practice was to arrange the wood in conical piles, which were covered with dirt to intensify the heat once the piles had been set on fire. The liquefied tar that oozed from these primitive kilns was collected in depressions dug beside them. Pitch was a secondary product, secured by a simple distillation of tar.

Turpentine production was also important in the pineries. Trees were crudely boxed by chopping large cavities or a series of gashes in them. This caused turpentine gum (oleoresins) to flow into the cavities or into depressions dug in the soil at the bases of the trees. Laborers ladled the crude turpentine that collected into barrels. A single workman could care for three thousand boxes, one observer reported, and in peak periods during warm weather could fill fifteen to twenty barrels a day. During the winter, when the gum ceased to run, these same workers often turned to gathering wood to make tar.

Naval stores were an obvious priority. Both England's navy and her merchant marine were made up of wooden ships; both needed naval stores to operate, and both were essential to the empire. A seller's market was possible in England because of its dangerous dependence on Baltic supplies and the perennial threat of shortages. The production of naval stores could hardly have seemed more attractive to early settlers. The possibility of a rapid return for the slightest investment was more apparent than the long-run necessity of matching Baltic prices and quality. Only a year after the founding of Jamestown, authorities dispatched a team of eight men from England to begin producing tar, pitch, and resin. All other colonies soon entered upon naval-stores production too, encouraged initially at least by its barter value.

The production of both tar and turpentine was more wasteful of trees than it needed to be. The vast majority of those engaged in turning out naval stores had minimal skill. There had been no significant naval-stores operations in Great Britain for generations. Masters were nearly as lacking in knowledge of proper production techniques as were the African slaves who made up much of the work force in the southern pineries. Authorities tried to increase efficiency by sending knowledgeable Germans, Poles, and Scandinavians into the woods, but they were too few, and many of the European techniques they advocated were too labor intensive to be effective.

Techniques continued to be primitive and the quality of product low. Crudely boxed trees often died after only one or two seasons, when they might have yielded turpentine for many years. Ignorant workers, unable to recognize standing trees with enough pitch to make them suitable for tar kilns, frequently felled eight or ten pines for every one that proved usable. No doubt this inefficient use of scarce labor troubled people more than did the waste of trees, but the destructive impact on the woods was not always overlooked. Discarded trees were simply left on the ground, where they provided added fuel, encouraging the spread of forest fires. This too was sometimes noted, but solutions seemed beyond the reach of a labor- and capital-short colonial society that desperately needed the earnings that exports of naval stores could bring.[5]

In New England the timber trade, which offered swifter and greater economic returns, soon took precedence over tar burning and turpentine production. The cod, beaver, and West Indies markets also beckoned, drawing people away from the production of naval stores. Ironically, this decline in interest in naval stores began in New England even as the London government was concluding that naval-stores production was a means by which Massachusetts, New Hampshire, and New York could become more useful units in the empire.

In spite of the expectations of policymakers, it was on the otherwise unpromising Carolina coastal plain that the naval-stores industry flourished. The longleaf and slash pines of the South were extremely resinous. Moreover, in the Carolinas turpentine as well as tar and pitch could be turned out—the one largely in summer, the other in winter. This resulted in a better balance in naval-stores production than existed elsewhere in North America (at least until Georgia became a major producer considerably later). In these circumstances it was nonsensical for New Englanders to try to compete; they could find more profitable ways to utilize their own pines.

Slave labor and year-round production assured a cost effectiveness in the Carolinas that was unequaled elsewhere. The importation of slave labor was to some degree accelerated because of a widespread belief that whites were unable to resist diseases—real or imagined—in the pine barrens and swampy areas. More important, slave labor was cheap labor, whether the end product was naval stores, rice, or indigo, all of which became important exports from the southern colonies.[6] Quality was another matter. The Royal Navy's preference for the Baltic naval stores remained unaltered throughout the colonial period, and always for the same reason: Baltic products were better. Nonetheless, there was a good market for Carolina's naval stores. By 1768 North Carolina was producing 60 percent of all North American naval stores, with a record production of 70,729 barrels of pitch, tar, and turpentine.

Georgia was settled much later than the colonies to the north. Its reluctance to devote scarce manpower to naval-stores production was based to some degree upon an assumption that the market for tar and pitch would weaken. Nonetheless, the tempo of forest-based activity quickened after the colony's ban on slavery was lifted in 1749. But the English premium or bounty for naval stores had been significantly reduced by the time the colony was established; lumbering soon became much more important in Georgia than naval-stores production. It retained that standing throughout the colonial period. Turning out naval stores was to a great extent only a wintertime, income-supplementing activity in the colony.[7]

By 1768 the Carolinas and Virginia were the only major naval-stores producers. Most of what exports there were from New England were reexports of products from the South. On balance, Pennsylvania, in terms of both its local and its export markets, was the closest rival to the front-runners, but its output was less than 10 percent that of North Carolina, barely a quarter of Virginia's, and less than half of South Carolina's.

Other timber-related exports were also pouring from the southern colonies. Staves, shingles, boards and planks, and firewood joined potash and naval stores in outbound cargoes. North Carolina was the largest exporter of boards and planks among the southern colonies; Virginia shipped the most shingles and staves. Even after tobacco came to dominate its economy, exports of forest products from Virginia remained important, as did those from neighboring Maryland. A good portion went to Barbados, Antigua, and St. Christopher in exchange for rum, sugar, and cash. It was largely a direct trade carried in small sloops from the James River and Maryland's Eastern Shore. The firewood trade, which provided fuel for the ever-hungry boilers of Caribbean sugar refineries, was essential but little noticed, either at the time or by historians since. Firewood poured from all the southern colonies, much of it a by-product of land clearing.

The forest-based trade of the Carolinas was especially extensive. Indeed, opportunities there were such as to encourage some migration from New England, especially during the economic stagnation that beset the northern colonies in the 1730s. Beaufort, North Carolina, for example, boasted not only a shipbuilding industry based on easy access to mast pines, cedar, and oak ("excellent for Ship Timber being crooked and very lasting"), but also a nascent whaling industry. These assets combined with the port's role as an assembly point for the region's agricultural and forest production to make Beaufort and its environs extremely attractive to those in search of opportunity.

Moreover, one of the most important triangular trades was New England–the Carolinas–the West Indies. In New Bern, North Carolina, New Englanders picked up staves and other cooperage components together with naval stores, shingles, pine boards, pork, and herring for shipment to the West Indies. The impact of this commerce was felt well into the hinterland. Merchants from New Bern bought large quantities of naval stores from tar burners and turpentine gatherers in Craven, Carteret, Beaufort, and other nearby counties. By 1765 sawmills "dotted the countryside" wherever there was a stream large enough to drive the vital waterwheel. Shipments of forest products were supplemented with salt pork, hams, furs, and beeswax from Moravian settlements in the interior: so much icing on the mercantile cake.

Yankees purchased goods at southern ports in exchange for West Indian molasses, rum, and English and northern manufactured goods (including some bar iron and cabinetry originating in the middle colonies and perhaps secured on runs down the coast). The specter of competition from a direct North Carolina trade with the mother country arose when the market price for naval stores rose significantly. But the British West Indies were supportive of the New England–Carolinas trading combination. A number of other profitable, but illegal, trades also flourished; hence business was never really depressed. Until the Revolution, demand continued to outpace supply.

English economic growth caused a surge of expansion in the English Caribbean colonies from about 1745 to 1760. This was mirrored in the French Caribbean and served to increase the volume of West Indian imports from the continental colonies. Thanks to the cultivation of sugarcane and the production of rum and molasses, the West Indian market for wooden containers provided an expanded outlet for the North American timber industry.

The multiplier effect this trade had upon employment can be seen in the impact of a typical three-hundred-ton ship departing New Bern for the Caribbean in the mid-eighteenth century. The vessel had provided work in port for thirty-three different trades, including joiners, carvers, cabinetmakers, blockmakers, small-boat builders, coopers, painters, sailmakers, smiths, and ropemakers. Ten ship chandlers were called upon to supply nails, bolts, and a variety of naval stores. And then there was the ship's crew. All hands, ashore or afloat, and the merchants who underwrote their work, relied on the West Indian market. Similarly, as New Bern and its commerce grew not only did cordwainers, coopers, and carpenters appear in the town, but so did a tailor, weaver, skinner and glover, tanner and currier, turner and cabinetmaker, baker, barber, hatter, and even a "perukier."[8]

In addition to the West Indies market, other valuable outlets for the hogsheads, pipes, barrels, and staves of the cooper's trade were the wine ports of deforested Spain and Portugal and of the "Wine Islands"—Madeira, the Canaries, and the Azores. The requirements of the whaling and fishing industry were also growing. Nearly all commodities shipped in the coastal and transatlantic trades—New England's whale oil and fish, the wheat and flour of the middle colonies, and the rice, tobacco, and naval stores of the South—added to the requirement for wooden containers. From Maryland to Georgia, nearly a quarter-million casks of all types were used annually in the early eighteenth century. By the eve of the Revolution the figure had risen about three hundred thousand, and cooperage had come to employ more craftsmen than any other activity in the South.[9]

Maritime industries were another major source of employment. The men employed in fisheries were tied to forest utilization through the ships they manned, the containers their catch was stored and shipped in, and the wood expended in evaporating brine into the salt that preserved their catch. The story was similar for whaling.

As New England and the middle Atlantic colonies turned to the sea and the mercantile arts and the South turned to exploiting nature's bounty on land, pragmatic responses to market opportunities ensured that links between coastal regions would be more significant than tidewater-hinterland relationships. In time this would be of political importance, but for most of the colonial period only the economic ramifications were understood. The interior Carolinas had commercially significant ties with the Virginia and Pennsylvania backcountries, while the Cape Fear–Albemarle Sound region continued to look to the sea for markets and to New England for the ships to reach them.

Pennsylvania's exploitation of a rich woodland heritage was nearly as comprehensive as that of the southern colonies. If forest-related activities seem less impressive in its export statistics, the explanation lies with the strength of the colony's domestic market. Pennsylvania's export statistics are more indicative of a prosperous economy than of any particular emphasis in economic activities. The colony founded by William Penn became the most self-sufficient of all the colonies, achieving by the mid-eighteenth century a virtual economic independence that prepared it to make the most of political independence when it was achieved.[10]

It could have been otherwise. The short-lived Swedish settlement on the Delaware River, had it survived and spread into what became Pennsylvania, would surely have been more oriented toward timber and naval-stores production than the one that did develop there. Governor Johan Printz's instructions in 1643 included attending to "the culling of choice woods." In any case, Swedish settlers turned early to the type of work they had engaged in along the shores of the Gulf of Bothnia. Waterfalls and fast-moving watercourses encouraged some to install sawmills; the availability of compass timber—the curving oak trunks and branches so valuable for ship construction—induced others to commence shipbuilding, while the unending stands of trees led still others to embark on the cooper's trade or the production of pitch, tar, and turpentine.[11]

Later Pennsylvanians were encouraged to enter these occupations too, but there were so many other ways to turn a profit that forest industries never gained pride of place. Lumbering was a major industry, but the growth rate of

Philadelphia and other settlements was so rapid that there was a demand for all the lumber produced and thus little was exported. The influx of a heterogeneous population ensured a diversified economy. In the mid-1700s traveler Peter Kalm noted that many German immigrants to New York quickly moved on to Pennsylvania, whose population soon was greater than that of Virginia, Maryland, and New York combined. Kalm's explanation was "the generous privileges which the sagacious Penn wrote into his wise laws and constitution." He was correct, of course, but the variety of economic opportunities was also a magnet. Pennsylvania was, a contemporary claimed, "the best poor man's country." These factors combine with the terror and suffering of a Europe torn asunder by the wars of the late seventeenth and eighteenth centuries to account for Pennsylvania's pace of development and population growth.

The expansion of urban settlement throughout the eighteenth century was led by Philadelphia, with New York and Boston close behind. Not long after independence the total population of the three cities exceeded that of all the continental colonies combined in 1700. Ships were built to export agricultural produce from rural Pennsylvania and New York as well as from the southern colonies. Philadelphia's timber hunger seemed insatiable. Nearly nine hundred ships were launched there between Penn's arrival in 1681 and the Revolution. It was there that shipwrights founded the White Oak Society, one of the many colonial groupings—coopers and carpenters were others—that were not structured enough to be considered guilds but nonetheless bespoke the trend to subdivide wood-based industry by crafts.[12]

As elsewhere in the middle colonies, New Jersey's timber products were important but not the foundation of its export economy. Especially after 1750, stands of white cedar yielded vast quantities of wood for New Jerseyans to export to the West Indies and to use at home. Most of this timber was made into shingles. New Jersey's exports also included staves, bar iron, corn, wheat, flour, cheese, butter, and meat.[13]

Staple exports from New York—mostly food before New Netherland was seized by the English—were supplemented thereafter by staves and, in the words of a colonial official, "Timber and Lumber of all kinds." Shipments went to the traditional markets in the mother country, to southern Europe, and to the West Indies. Very soon there was overcutting of accessible white pine, but newcomers were on the way to exploiting the more isolated tracts, even the spruce and hardwoods, of the Adirondacks and Catskills. As elsewhere, exports created a demand for coopers. In 1701, of the 101 men granted freedom of the city in New York—that is, permission to ply a trade—10 were coopers.[14]

Nowhere along the Atlantic coast was the "timber economy" more developed than in New England. Much legend is based upon the cod and the beaver, to say nothing of the Bible, but by the 1630s lumbering ranked in importance with fishing and the fur trade. In time it would overshadow both. That distinction was achieved by shipments of staves and planking, boards and hoops, headings and posts, handspikes and oars to the West Indies and to the wine ports. The mast trade, about which much more has been written, was a cream-skimming operation—but the cream was exceedingly rich.[15]

As in the South, the cooper's trade was important in New England. Massachusetts used fifteen thousand hogsheads annually for the shipment of rum. Inevitably, the cooper's trade was widespread in colonial Boston. By 1648 the coopers of New England had already formed a corporation to protect their interests—the earliest American labor association. It was the combined effect of the diverse and growing sources of demand, however, not the organizing of coopers, that led to a steady rise in prices for staves, hogsheads, and the like.

By the mid-eighteenth century, lumbering had become so profitable and widespread that farming was sometimes neglected. Indeed, as early as 1701, when the population of Massachusetts Bay Colony reached seventy thousand, there was not enough cleared agricultural land to support its needs. Such developments made New England excessively dependent upon supplies from the middle and southern colonies and on "carriage trade" shipments from England.

Taking all the continental colonies together, lumber and wood products (excluding masts, spars, and bowsprits) ranked fifth in value among exports a decade before the Revolution. The returns were handsomest in New England. Only tobacco, rice, fish, and the combination of bread, flour, and wheat outranked forest products. And the bounty of the woods was even more extensive than statistics indicate. Many forest-related activities, such as boiling sap into sugar and converting marble into lime, are largely unremarked aspects of the forest economy.

Then there was shipbuilding. As early as 1676, Boston had thirty master shipwrights. A half-century later, most of the town's artisans were involved in building ships for local use or for sale abroad, though many applied their skills to other jobs too. Almost everywhere that shipwrights could be assembled and a keel laid down, but especially along the banks of the Mystic River in Massachusetts and in Bath, Maine, shipyards prospered. The Boston registry of 193 ships prompted the colony's governor, Lord Bellomont, to remark in 1693 that there were "more good vessels belonging to the town of Boston than to all Scotland and Ireland." Even two decades of Indian wars at the end of the seventeenth century could not deter the shipbuilders of Kittery and York, in Maine; 47 vessels were launched during the period of hostilities.

Whether they worked in New England, the middle colonies, or the South, easy access to ship timber gave America's shipbuilders an important advantage over those in Europe. The cost per ton for oak-timbered vessels built in England, France, or Holland was over twice that of those from North America. Shipbuilding strengthened the colonial economy, but so did manning the vessels. An idea of the important place of seamen in the occupational distribution in coastal towns is gained from statistics from New York in the mid-eighteenth century. The number of New York port's seamen rose from 755 in 1747 to 3,552 (out of a population of only 13,000) fifteen years later.[16]

As cities grew and plantations flourished, a measure of affluence was achieved that created a market for more than the rough carpentry that was a sure source of income during the first phases of settlement. A rising standard of living was reflected in refinement of taste, and finer goods were now sought. To the more mundane occupations—joinery, wood turning, coffin-making, and wagon manufacture—were added "fancier" skills: cabinetmaking, coach-making, and carving wood for clock cases and musical instruments. Furniture manufacture became one of the largest urban crafts, especially in Boston and Philadelphia. Throughout the eighteenth century, furniture imports declined as the volume and quality of local manufacture improved, eventually reaching a level of excellence still admired. There were, as skilled colonial handicraft attests, many ways to declare independence.[17]

Trade is one matter, British regulation of it another. The ways the latter helped bring on the American Revolution have been extensively chronicled, but the place of forests and forest products in these regulations has not. In fact, so important were colonial forests in British mercantile thinking and in the troubled web of events spun from it, that no discussion of the impact of colonial forests would be complete without careful consideration of their role in bringing about the final rupture.

To many British officials, almost any independent colonial economic activity—from the West Indies trade to cabinetmaking—was, in terms of the mother country's interest, diversionary. Reports by colonial officials, sent to tighten the London government's control over Massachusetts and New Hampshire after Cromwell's years in power, emphasized the potential for producing masts and naval stores. A mass of legislation and directives aimed toward this goal resulted, but in the end these efforts—which were only a part of Britain's larger mercantile policy—had more political than strategic significance, generating conflicts between colonists and the mother country and spawning much illegal trade.[18]

The shipment of large masts from the colonies to England began in the middle of the seventeenth century. Felling huge "sticks," transporting them through dense woods by teams of oxen, and shepherding them past jagged rocks and down the rivers of New England to the mast ponds were processes as costly as they were arduous. So were loading them on specially constructed ships and the transatlantic voyage itself. But a mast three feet in diameter brought £150 or more, and a standard shipment of ninety masts, requiring three transport vessels, was valued on the average at £6,000. A few colonists could make money on such a low-volume enterprise, but most lacked the requisite capital and the political connections necessary to obtain a contract. For most who drew upon the forests for their livelihood, turning the large pines into planks, shingles, and the like was the only viable route to profits. Such conversion of trees reserved for the Royal Navy by the surveyor-general's "broad arrow" mark was an illegal encroachment on "the king's woods," but many a New Englander disputed, or ignored, the royal status of the forests and made good money in the process.

One of the responsibilities of Jonathan Bridger, who arrived from England in 1706 to become surveyor-general of the woods, was to instruct in proper methods of producing naval stores. He never had any significant opportunity to demonstrate a practical application of his "book learning," if only because he was stationed in the wrong place. In New England his time was taken up in fruitless attempts to prevent "the king's trees" from being put to uses not on the agenda of the Lords Commissioners of Trade and Plantations (commonly known as the Board of Trade), the body created toward the end of the seventeenth century to supervise colonial affairs. Whether Bridger would have been effective in the southern colonies, one can only speculate.

The broad arrow policy was only one cog in a restrictive machinery that began to take shape before the attempted sequestration of white pines and continued long after the post of surveyor-general of the woods had become an ineffectual sinecure. Indeed, the most obvious cultivator of an independent spirit before the Proclamation of 1763 and a last flurry of draconian measures broadened the revolutionary constituency was the regulatory system imposed by the London government. Democracy may not have grown out of the forest, but it did grow, in part at least, out of English attempts to give direction to the evolution of a timber economy.[19]

The chief importance of the colonies to the mother country was commercial. English economic policy was grounded on the mercantilist principle that gold, secured by trade or other means, was the basis of a country's wealth and power. In practice this dictated expanding commerce and maintaining a balance of trade favoring England. Since the strength of the mother country was the goal, all trade, whether originating from home or from colonial ports, had to be kept out of the hands of European rivals—or enemies, as they were much of the time. Moreover, products imported into England must not compete with goods produced at home. The common official position was that all finished goods must be produced in England. The role of the colonies was to be complementary: supplying raw materials to English manufacturers and purchasing finished goods. In sum, the colonies were to be kept in a subordinate position, channeling their energies to serve England's needs by helping to increase her wealth. The mercantile system theoretically operated for the mutual benefit of the colonies and the mother country; but when applied to American commerce, theory and practice did not converge.

England's policies regarding colonial America's forests developed against a background of depleted English forests as well as mercantile theory. England had once been covered with woodland, but by the sixteenth century the exhaustion of stands had become a matter of concern. Population increase with its attendant demand for cleared, arable land, the heavy dependence of the populace upon timber products of all kinds, and inefficient administration of the royal forests all contributed to a timber-supply crisis.

By the end of the seventeenth century, only one-eighth of England's original forest remained. A good index to the extent of the problem was the price of timber, which rose dramatically in the sixteenth and early seventeenth centuries. The costs of transportation from less accessible areas exacerbated the difficulties posed by a waning supply. Between about 1540 and 1570 the price of firewood doubled, and by about 1630 it had doubled again, and then tripled. Some attempts at conservation and reforestation were made, but they were halting and sporadic. The crisis was felt by all social classes. For the common people, perhaps the worst effect was the severe shortage of fuel for heating. Moreover, because England's security and authority were increasingly based upon command of the sea and on maritime trade, the rising cost of shipbuilding was a dire threat.[20]

As early as the Middle Ages, the Baltic countries were exporting timber to England; by the American colonial period, great quantities of naval stores and wood were arriving from that region. Obtaining forest products from the Baltic created an imbalance of trade against England, because the northern countries bought few of the manufactured goods with which England hoped to pay for timber. The first official acknowledgment that England was dependent upon foreign supplies (and that such dependence violated a cardinal principle of mercantilism) came in 1668. Concern grew thereafter.

England's dependency created acute problems in the late seventeenth and early eighteenth centuries, when Sweden set up a variety of restrictions on trade. This fostered a desire to be rid of dependence on the Baltic; more important, war with Louis XIV and the exacerbation of England's rivalry with the Dutch made alternative sources a desperate necessity. By the mid-seventeenth century the Dutch had a virtual monopoly of the Atlantic carrying trade and were even acting as agents for the distribution of American and West Indian goods. The largely deforested Netherlands also drew heavily on the Baltic countries for timber and forest products, thereby creating another source of rivalry with England. In the face of this competition, British policymakers believed they had no choice but to challenge Dutch control of the carrying trade.[21]

The colonies became a pawn in the struggle. Starting in the mid-seventeenth century, a series of laws were passed whose basic intent was to eliminate the Dutch as carriers of foreign trade. The Navigation Act of 1651 required that all goods imported or exported by the colonies be carried in English-built vessels manned by predominantly English crews. The term "English" obviously included the settlers in Britain's North American colonies. When practical considerations superseded this ideal, as would often happen, a further anti-Dutch stipulation took effect: foreign goods could be brought into the colonies only in ships of the country of origin.

With the end of Cromwell's regime in 1659 the law became invalid, but pressure from London merchants, who complained of competition from Massachusetts shippers, resulted in the formulation of a new Navigation Act. Passed in 1660, it was largely a duplication of the original. The system was completed three years later with the addition of further restrictions. All foreign goods brought into the colonies had to pass through an English port before they could be reexported to America. Colonial goods were with few exceptions also required to enter English ports before reexport to foreign destinations.

Colonial merchants largely ignored the Navigation Acts, continuing to trade directly with Europe and the foreign (French and Dutch) West Indies. Supplementary laws of 1669, 1673, and 1696 set up more stringent means of enforcement but only served to define the scope of evasion. New England's commerce expanded greatly during the second half of the seventeenth century, and it has been estimated that virtually all of Massachusetts's trade in the period 1660 to 1675 was carried on in violation of the acts. But if the Navigation Acts did not produce the desired results, they made explicit the colonies' mercantilist subordination to the mother country, at least from the standpoint of Parliament and, eventually, the Board of Trade.

The means used to execute the laws reinforced this relationship. Colonial governors were required to obtain pledges of obedience, in the form of bonds, from all ships' masters, who also had to furnish detailed information on their vessels and cargoes. Under the provisions of the last of the enforcement acts, customs officials could enter without a search warrant and forcibly seize goods in warehouses and aboard ships.

Expansion of colonial shipbuilding and increased production of naval stores were unintended effects of the Navigation Acts. This expansion resulted from the requirement that all ships be English built. Colonial construction met the requirement and, as has been noted, was highly competitive in price with ships constructed in the mother country.

But forest products were more directly and specifically affected via the "enumeration" clause of the Navigation Act of 1660. To ensure that the supply of raw materials was secure and to eliminate dependence on foreign sources, Parliament stipulated that certain goods produced by the colonies could be shipped only to England's ports. This proviso closed off continental Europe and many West Indian markets for the "enumerated" commodities. Initially the list included only sugar, tobacco, cotton, indigo, ginger, and certain dyewoods, but it was gradually lengthened until by the time of the Revolution it included almost every commodity the colonies produced.

The decision not to list forest products in the first enumeration was hardly a gesture of goodwill. England still relied on domestic supplies of lumber, while the absence of naval stores from the enumeration suggests that dependence on the Baltic countries had not yet reached the critical stage. Moreover, American naval stores were considered inferior in quality, and the cost of transportation from the colonies worsened their competitive position. Pitch, tar, and turpentine were not enumerated until the beginning of the eighteenth century; not until 1764 were potash and pearlash, iron, and lumber added to the list.

The enumeration of colonial naval stores in 1706 was a direct result of the War of the Spanish Succession, which threatened to bring France, Spain, and the low countries together in anti-English hands when their continental rivals sought to pull Sweden into their circle. Parliament determined once and for all to become independent of the Swedish Tar Company's monopoly. Incentives were offered to the colonists. The Naval Stores Bounty Act of 1705 (and two subsequent acts) granted subsidies for the production of tar, pitch, turpentine, rosin, hemp, and masts. The bounties were intended as compensation for the high freight charges that had discouraged trade in colonial naval stores in the past. From 1706 to 1776, £330,000 (or about $1,650,000) in bounties were paid, over half to residents of the southern colonies, and production increased significantly as a result. But despite bounties and a secure market in England, Americans chafed under the restrictions on their trade.

The procurement of naval supplies from North America had been a concern of English authorities from the first years of settlement, not solely for strategic reasons. King James I complained that the economy of Virginia was "wholly built on smoke" (i.e., tobacco) and attempted to persuade the colonists to diversify their plantation-based economy by producing naval stores as well as lumber, potash, iron, and other commodities. A similar plea came from Charles II after the Restoration. Between 1664 and 1669, authorities lifted the duties on naval stores originating in Maryland and Virginia in order to encourage production there. The dispatch of several thousand Palatinate Germans to New York in the early part of the eighteenth century had the same goal—and even less success. The hopes of English policymakers were undone by the fertile soil of the Mohawk Valley. The Germans were too skilled as farmers and husbandmen to be interested in retraining themselves to produce pitch, tar, and turpentine.[22]

King James II shared his forebears' concern. He instructed the Lords of Trade, forerunner of the Board of Trade, to make naval stores a top priority. "You are instructed," he wrote, "to inform yourselves what Navall Stores may be furnished from Our plantations, and in what Quantities, and by what methods Our Royall purpose of having our Kingdom supplied with Navall Stores from thence may be practicable and promoted."

The importance to England of colonial forest products, especially naval stores, created interest in providing positive incentives—bounties or a secure market—for these goods. But because England's interests were the prime concern of policymakers, it was only by sheer chance that laws, regulations, and American interests converged. For example, a technicality in the act of 1663 defined the Canary Islands as African rather than European; so trade in American wheat and barrel staves was inadvertently permitted to continue there, as it did with Madeira and the Azores, which belonged to Portugal, England's ally.

More portentous problems arose as the American colonies grew to the point where the British West Indies could no longer absorb all that their northern neighbors offered for sale. As a result, a trade totally contrary to the spirit of mercantilist philosophy developed with the sugar islands that were under the flags of Spain, Denmark, the Netherlands, and—more important and ominous—England's principal rival, France. The trade was stimulated by the low prices at which the French sold their sugar; this in turn exacerbated economic decline in the British West Indies, whose planters and investors petitioned Parliament for relief.

The efforts of the English sugar barons led to the introduction in Commons in 1731 of a bill to regulate the sugar trade by prohibiting the importation of foreign sugar, rum, and molasses into America and forbidding the export of lumber and horses from there to foreign ports. Debate over the proposed bill was extensive, and great indignation was expressed at the enrichment of the French at the expense of English commerce. Various speakers asserted that great cargoes of lumber, and ships as well, were being sent from Boston to be sold in the French islands. One colonial official complained, "Great quantities of oak timber, and lumber, are exported from Boston, and the most part of it is cut out of the king's woods for the French trade." He added that "there has been so great a destruction of the king's finest and best pine trees, by this trade, that if a stop be not put to it, the king's woods must be ruined."

The bill called forth a rash of protest from the colonies. The London agents of Massachusetts, Connecticut, Rhode Island, Pennsylvania, New York, New Jersey, Virginia, and South Carolina, as well as several London merchants trading with America, informed Parliament that the proposal would mean the ruin of colonial trade. Further remonstrances were heard in colonial legislatures, and petitions were sent to the Board of Trade insisting on the dire consequences of such legislation. Happily for colonial merchants and seamen, the bill failed to pass the House of Lords.

The fears of the colonists were realized two years later with passage of the infamous Molasses Act. Although absolute prohibitions against imports and exports were omitted, high import duties were placed upon the most important West Indian cargoes: molasses, rum, and sugar. The ostensible aim of the act was to halt the decline of the British West Indies, but its effect was to make it more difficult for the continental colonies to sell fish, lumber, and provisions in the foreign sugar islands. Like other British trade regulations, the Molasses Act was widely evaded, often by ingenious means. It remained virtually a dead letter for thirty years.

The end of the French and Indian (or Seven Years) War in 1763 marked the advent of British hegemony in North America. A new era in the relationship of the colonies to the mother country began. Up to this time, England's motive in regulating the colonies had been primarily commercial and largely independent of political considerations. After 1763, England's motives became more explicitly political and resulted in the assertion of more direct control over the colonies. The era of salutary neglect had ended.[23]

Renewal of the Sugar Act in 1764 was part of the London government's new program. The objective was twofold: to make the colonies bear a portion of the cost of their defense and to give practical expression to resentment over the commerce of the colonials with the French West Indies during the war. The legislation of 1764 continued duties on sugar and molasses from the foreign

West Indies but differed from the earlier version in placing an outright prohibition on the importation of rum and spirits from all foreign islands except
the Portuguese ones, Madeira and the Azores.

The act was declared to be law "in perpetuity." If the foreign West Indies
could no longer sell their rum to America, and if their sugar and molasses were
barred by high duties, they in turn could not buy the fish, lumber, and provisions of British North America. The sugar trade was given some relief the following year with passage of an act lowering duties, but any benefits were canceled out by the addition of lumber to the list of enumerated commodities.

Reaction in the colonies was more vocal than ever before. The interests of
the Massachusetts trading community were heavily at stake. The general conclusion in Boston, Salem, and other ports was that sugar duties were so high as
to amount to an absolute prohibition. The result would be either an end of the
West India trade (and thereby of the colony's ability to buy British manufactured goods) or smuggling on an unprecedented scale. Grave concern over the
effects of the act on fisheries and the lumber trade impelled the Massachusetts
legislature to petition the royal governor and the House of Commons. Fully
two-thirds of the fish caught in New England waters were sold to the foreign
West Indies. It was a question not only of planks and boards, but of barrels and
hogsheads for fish, rum, sugar, molasses, and a whole range of staples.

The remonstrances of the Massachusetts General Court (its legislature)
underscored the importance of lumber to the economy and the devastating
effect of cutting off West Indian trade. In its instructions to its London agent,
the General Court explained: "The Exportation of Timber, Boards, Staves,
Hoops and other Articles of Lumber, tends greatly to promote the clearing and
cultivating of our unimproved lands, and is a great Incouragement [*sic*] to our
Infant Settlements; it improves a great Number of Hands to cut the Lumber,
and prepare it suitable for a Market; it employs more than an hundred Sail of
Vessels in this Province." Shipbuilding was "a considerable Branch of Business" threatened by the act's ban on the sale of vessels to the West Indies; the
requirement that bonds and certificates be posted to guarantee that cargoes
enter only English ports was a costly inconvenience; and the closing of foreign
ports to the extensive trade in staves made little sense, because it was not a trade
in competition with the mother country.

Other objections were also raised. One colonial official wrote to Lord Hali-
fax, head of the Board of Trade from 1748 to 1761 and now secretary of state:

That any difficulties should be put on the Sale of American Lumber is unaccountable,
when that country is covered with Timber, and cannot be cultivated untill that is cut

down and disposed of . . . this is stunting the growth of the Colonies, by the growth of which only we can reap advantage of an Accession of Territorys.

Rather open all the Markets that can be found for American Timber as well as the whole produce of that Continent and allow a Bounty for importing it into Great Britain, who now pays large sums of money for Timber from the North.

Which is the interest of Great Britain? To pay a Bounty to her own subjects in America or the whole value of the timber we have to Foreigners?

However cogent such arguments might have sounded to colonial ears, they fell on deaf ones in London.

The threat to the timber-intensive West Indies trade began the portentous process of intercolonial correspondence and coordination. Pennsylvania had a special motivation to collaborate. Its balance of trade with England was very adverse, since it imported £700,000 worth of British manufactures but sent back only £300,000 worth of its own produce. However, it had developed an extensive trade with the foreign West Indies. Debts to British merchants could be paid only by means of trade with foreign ports. John Dickinson's pamphlet of 1765 expressed the view of Pennsylvanians: "We already *suffer*. Trade is decaying; and all credit is expiring." Money was scarce, he continued, bankruptcies were frequent, and the "late regulations" had made the supply of money in Pennsylvania decline still further, thus making it more difficult to buy goods from England.

The barrage of colonial protest led to a reduction on sugar and molasses duties in 1766, but the punitive and coercive machinery remained in place. The impulse to think of England as the mother country was being rapidly eroded. Colonials had become the colonized. At this juncture politics mingled with economics as never before. Typically, the Massachusetts General Court advised its London agent that the Sugar Act would have "dangerous consequences" because accepting it would "be conceeding to the Parliaments having a Right to Tax our trade which we can't by any means think of admiting; as it wou'd be contrary to a fundamental Principall of our Constitution vizt That all Taxes ought to originate with the people."

Hard lines, those. And they were triggered as much by British interference with the timber trade as with the sugar trade. They give emphasis to the importance the timber economy had to a people who had come to understand that a forest was not a fearsome place, but the sine qua non of development and optimism—and, perhaps, the building of a very different New Jerusalem from the one that the Puritan fathers had envisioned.

Inexhaustibility
and Forest Conservation
in Colonial America

Chapter 3

The concept of the forest as both a source of livelihood and a wilderness whose challenge had to be met persisted from the first to the last of the colonial era — and into America's national period. But in the nearly two centuries before independence from Great Britain, conservation too had some significance in Britain's American colonies. Initial measures failed to halt wasteful practices, but beginnings were made—beginnings that have all too frequently been overlooked.

Vast tracts of forest fell to the ax during the colonial period. As deforestation proceeded, it both created problems and spurred responses. Incompatible ideas began to conflict. The results of this clash determined the extent and limits of conservation during the period.

Settlers came to build a new life in a new land. They were consciously building not only for themselves, but also for their children and their children's children. Although forests could supply the needs of the moment, they would also have to meet those of future generations. English common law, which formed the basis of the colonial legal system, recognized the conflicting demands of present and future. The doctrine of waste, a part of this system of law, held that a landholder was responsible for maintaining his land's productive capacity. Only a limited quantity of wood could be removed, and that only for certain purposes. There was an absolute prohibition against cutting some species. Under this doctrine, even clearing woodland to convert it to more valuable agricultural land could be defined as waste. Clearly, English common law was more suited to sustaining a developed order than to building a new one.

Gradually Americans modified this legal system to serve the needs of their new land. Common sense suggested that there was little value in rigid restrictions on cutting trees and clearing woodlands when there was obvious social and economic need for more cleared land and more products of the forest.

This view made its way into the law. The doctrine of waste remained available as a potential restraint against destructive practices, but courts in Britain's American colonies came to interpret it more liberally than did those in England. American courts were especially lenient when land was being cleared for cultivation; the removal of timber had only to be beneficial to the estate. The absence of prudent husbandry became the new test of waste. New England's courts departed from English common law more slowly than did those in other jurisdictions, but Americans everywhere were gradually freed to build as they never could have under the legal system of the mother country. And whatever the law held, trees were felled with abandon. In settled areas where courts held sway, the doctrine of waste was seldom called upon. In hinterlands where the hand of the law touched lightly, if at all, it was simply ignored, for the need to cut seemed manifest to everyone.[1]

Economic considerations, even more than legal ones, shaped the patterns of colonial forest and land use. Colonial Americans liked to boast that they were engaged in taming a wilderness; in fact they were doing far more. They were tying North America to Europe's rapidly growing market economy and its insatiable hunger for commodities. Exports of tobacco, naval stores, iron, potash, and the like provided the basic link. As the new order evolved, Indian patterns, with their relatively fixed demands on the land, gave way before the greater concentrations of population, the fixed settlements, and the more intensive forms of land use that were hallmarks of white society. Land became a form of capital. This, perhaps more than anything else, lay behind the changes that swept through and reshaped, when they did not eliminate, the American forest.

Capital and labor were in short supply in Britain's North American colonies; only land (and the assets associated therewith, such as forests) was plentiful. In these circumstances it was wise—even essential—to carefully husband those factors of production that were scarce by substituting, whenever possible, those that were abundant. Clearing ground for a rude log cabin and for subsistence farming was the initial task of most settlers; there was no way of totally avoiding that difficult, time-consuming task, but settlers did their best to reduce its requirements to a minimum. They sowed their first crops in natural openings or old Indian clearings when they could, eagerly adopted girdling to open up land for farming with a minimum of labor, and planted crops that could flourish under the conditions that resulted from such an approach—crops such as tobacco and maize.

Once the initial stages of settlement were past, agriculture became more commercial. But the basic problem of labor shortage remained, continually pushing farmers to adopt laborsaving strategies. The result was the emergence nearly everywhere of patterns of agriculture that made extravagant demands upon the land. Only in those places where settlers anticipated staying in the same spot year after year, generation after generation—as in the settlements of conservative Germans in Pennsylvania—did husbanding the land become an important consideration in day-to-day farm management.

The cultivation of tobacco was especially hard on the land. Virginians turned to tobacco early because it yielded a better return on investment than did alternative crops; it did so largely because it required less labor input. But in a few years tobacco wore out the soil, continually forcing plantation owners to open new land for planting. They did so by girdling and by limited rather than full-scale clearing. To do more on a tract that they would soon be abandoning seemed ill advised. For the same reason, they also hesitated to invest heavily in houses and outbuildings, satisfying themselves with simple, utilitarian structures that usually bore little resemblance to the plantation buildings of a later age's romantic imaginings. To be sure, the land left behind when tobacco planters moved on seldom remained idle for long. After a season or more it was put to use again, often by new, poorer settlers who raised wheat rather than tobacco. Living as they did on impoverished soil, this new wave of farmers seldom prospered, but they did manage to wear out the soil even further. The result of all this was that by the middle of the seventeenth century Virginia had already taken on a scraggly, worn-out appearance that European and New England observers believed resulted from the sloth and negligence of its residents and for which they roundly condemned them.

Tobacco's toll on the land might have been lessened had fertilizers been utilized. Potash and manure were available but seldom applied. The increasing demand for potash in manufacturing pushed up its price and made it an important export—an earner of desperately needed exchange—thus discouraging its use in agriculture. On the other hand, laborsaving animal-husbandry practices adopted in the South allowed cattle and hogs to roam free much of the time. This reduced the quantities of manure retrievable for use as fertilizer. Taste as well as limited supplies seems to have dissuaded planters from manuring tobacco lands. As one contemporary explained, manured land "produces a strong sort of Tobacco in wch the Smoakers say they can plainly taste the fullsomeness of the dungg." In any case, it was cheaper to buy and open new land than to repeatedly fertilize old.

Thus the economics of tobacco culture led to a form of "tobacco imperialism" that wreaked havoc with forests and soils from Maryland to the Carolinas. Looking back in 1833, John Craven put it bluntly: his forerunners in Virginia had "butchered" the land. Had it been realized from the beginning how rapidly tobacco exhausted the soil, some other economic strategy might have been adopted—but it seems unlikely. Colonial options were so limited that even outside the tobacco belt it had appeared necessary to most settlers to adopt agricultural practices that taxed the land heavily. Maize, the crop best suited for replacing tobacco in the South (and often planted in its wake), brought smaller returns and was almost as hard on the soil.[2]

Not all—perhaps not even most—of the timber felled during land clearing was wasted. It provided materials for houses, barns, fences, and market as well as fuel for homes and industries. As has been noted, potash, a major by-product of land clearing, was a significant source of income for settlers in many parts of the colonies. Indeed, as the author of *American Husbandry* reported in 1775, in colony after colony the products yielded up in clearing the land could bring a sufficient return to cover the costs of doing so. By providing the means to pay the costs of clearing, forests thus aided in the spread of agriculture and in many places helped seal their own doom.[3]

Agricultural demands for and on land were not the basic problem, although they were the direct cause of most tree felling. In some areas tapping the forest was an end in itself. The early settlers of Georgia rejoiced, as had Carolinians before them, at the prospect of profits from the thick stands of pine trees that constituted their overwhelming first impression of the land. In some such places agriculture, when it developed at all, was something of an afterthought. But regardless of the product being yielded up, production processes nearly everywhere were resource intensive. The producers of naval stores, charcoal iron, staves, lumber, and a host of other products sought as desperately as did farmers to save scarce labor. Toward this end, they adopted modes of production that took a heavy toll of natural resources, and especially of the forests.

Yet there is another side to all this. The sales of products wrung from the land resulted in a gradual accumulation of capital—albeit not always by those who actually produced the goods. As settlers turned fixed assets of land into more fluid capital assets, the transformation enabled Americans to build a stronger, more diversified economy. In other words, colonists disinvested the capital latent in their land and forests and invested it in assets that had greater value or greater foreseeable potential for returns. Savings and investment rates were remarkably high throughout the colonial period, so that what resulted from this "mining" of land and forests was seldom wasted—instead, it fueled the remarkable economic expansion that was the hallmark of American society for years. Later generations might wish that early Americans had "despoiled" fewer acres, but if they had, the comforts of the highly developed economy that critics have often taken for granted would have been fewer and would have come more slowly. However dimly understood at the time, colonists had engaged in an economic trade-off. In their own eyes, they were simply pursuing the only practical approach open to them.[4]

Still, not all tree cutting was a result of social and economic needs. Attitudes were at work that sometimes led to felling when there was no good reason for it. Jared Eliot observed in 1747 that the first settlers of New England "tho't themselves obligated to stubb all Staddle, and cut down or Lop all great trees; in which they expended much cost and time, to the prejudice of the Crop and impoverishing the land." Although he recognized their folly, Eliot was nonetheless sympathetic: "When we consider the small Number of the first Settlers, and coming from an old Cultivated Country, to thick Woods, rough unimproved Lands; where all their former Experience and Knowledge was now of very little service to them; They were destitute of Beasts of Burthen or Carriage; Unskilled in every Part of Service to be done: It may be said, That in a Sort, *they began the World a New.*" As they built, they sought to construct what they had known in their "old Cultivated Country." Having no other models, they innocently assumed that achieving their goals meant eliminating the forests that had no place in their vision.

Eliot was not alone in what he saw. In 1749 Scandinavian visitor Peter Kalm reported: "We can hardly be more hostile to our woods in Sweden and Finland than they are here." A few years later, a visitor to the mid-Atlantic states echoed the charge: "at the beginning in the nearer, and latterly in the farther reaches of America, wood has been everywhere in the way of the new planter [and] . . . people have grown accustomed to regard forests anywhere as the most troublesome of growths." In some areas, not even a tree that promised shade for the settler's cabin during the heat of summer was spared.

More than pastoral mental images may have been behind this often-observed behavior. In a land where labor and capital were in desperately short supply, huge tracts of timber near at hand must frequently have seemed not an indication of opportunity but a psychologically depressing sight that constantly reminded colonists of how much work there was to do and how inadequate to the tasks were the resources at their disposal. Felling such trees not only removed the reminders, it subconsciously assured settlers that they were indeed equal to the challenge of the new land—that they were capable of shaping their own destinies. That the forest was home for the Indian, providing him with an environment in which he was supposedly invincible, added further incentive for its removal. Could one ever feel truly safe with woods nearby?[5]

God-fearing Puritans had reasons of their own for hostility to the forest: it was the domain of satanic forces and a place to which, Cotton Mather complained, libertines swarmed "to find elbowe-room for phanatick Doctrines and practices." Moreover, as New England prospered the forest grew ever more alien and unfamiliar to the residents of the well-ordered, close-knit communities that developed. Many Puritans who entered the woods shared the fate of the group of Massachusetts militiamen who took a shortcut through the woodlot of their own town one night "and in them woods . . . got most confusedly lost."

Not everyone reacted in these ways, of course. Eventually the forests began to appear less ominous even to the Puritans, perhaps because the woods came to seem more a part of God's legacy to his people than a wild and desolate testing ground. The path to Canaan might be arduous, but once there, one should be able to live in comfort. If rising sales of timber and other forest products yielded profits to the faithful, as they increasingly did, it must be a part of God's plan. He may well have intended the forest not so much as a place to be feared as one to be utilized—perhaps even carefully husbanded.[6]

The Puritans were not alone. Throughout the colonies there were those not wedded to the relatively secure and regulated life of tidewater areas who came to view the forest as a place of opportunity, not just of danger and hardship. Indeed, the food supplies of the forests helped make possible the move inland and westward. But mixed feelings were widespread even on the frontier—as is revealed in the account by a member of a transappalachian expedition of 1671 who reported that "it was a pleasing tho' dreadfull sight to see the Mountains and Hills as if piled one upon another . . . rich ground but stony curious rising hills and brave meadows with grass above man's height, and many Rivers."

Certain others were less ambivalent. Migrants from the more heavily forested areas of Europe seem from the first to have been appreciative and sparing of America's abundance. German settlers in Pennsylvania were especially careful to cut and clear only what they needed. From experience they knew the value of woodlands as settlers from long-cleared areas of England never had. Pennsylvanian Benjamin Rush, one of the leading scientists of the late colonial period, observed with approval that "German farmers are great economists of their wood."[7]

Varied though reactions to the land were, one thing was constant: wherever white settlers established themselves, the land was changed. The clearing of cropland brought the most obvious alterations. Regardless of whether they used girdling and associated techniques, as in the tobacco South, or the more thorough methods of clearing favored to the north, the activities of early settlers inexorably led to a less stable and varied environment than they had found upon their arrival. Settlers sought to prosper by producing a relatively few crops and other commodities. Toward this end, they cleared the forest and introduced forms of land use far more intensive than those of the Indians, who had moved from place to place in a regular cycle, seeking to take advantage of the seasonal abundances and rich variety that nature offered. This sufficed. Indian populations had been relatively small, their commercial intercourse restricted, and their technology adapted to the needs of personal rather than market-oriented production. They had neither the need nor the wherewithal to remake the landscape as thoroughly as the English were to do.

To be sure, Indians cleared land for agriculture in many areas that the English would subsequently colonize, and they raised a long list of crops that Europeans adopted to their profit. But for most native Americans agriculture was subordinated to other concerns. It seemed natural and practical to burn the forests, easing the hunter's task and opening areas for the grass and other growth that game could feed on. The Indians and, more transiently, the game benefited. If the repeated burning added ash that enriched the soil, it was a matter of no particular interest to the Indians.

Historians of colonial Virginia have, for whatever reason, emphasized the "serious inroads on the primeval growth of timber" made by the native inhabitants. The extent of destruction has no doubt been exaggerated. Underbrush was removed, forests were made more open, and occasional clearings were created, but such actions involved modification of the forest rather than its eradication. Whites used fire as a tool to aid in clearing the way for domesticated plants and animals from Europe; Indians used fire to encourage certain wild native species that they favored over others they found less useful. Indian fires, which primarily burned in the understory, were less hot and thus did less damage to the soil than those of the land clearers, which frequently consumed much of the organic matter in the upper layer of soil, damaging its capacity to hold water or resist erosion. The tool was the same, but the effect was different: Indian use of fire did little to jeopardize the natural variety of the land or its capacity for self-renewal.

Indians, moreover, used relatively little timber. They built dugout canoes and used bark for lighter ones. They lived in shelters built of reeds, bark, and a few saplings and gathered dead or fallen branches for firewood. Before the advent of trade goods, their technology had not advanced much beyond the stone ax. The white man's tools, once available, might have made more difference had the natives' need to split wood or saw planks been greater, but reflecting the traditional Indian economy, their impact stayed small.

Perhaps even more important in limiting the Indians' elimination of forest

was the fact that they did not perceive the woods as the antithesis of civilization—and never knew the release from privation that was so much a part of the
initial experience of whites in the New World. They neither saw wilderness as
something that needed to be "conquered" to ensure prosperity and abundance
nor considered the forest in its natural state something to be feared.

The widely divergent Indian and white approaches to land use resulted as
much from different opportunities as from different social and environmental
outlooks. Whites had access to the commodity markets of Europe. What they
produced could go to feed not only themselves and their neighbors, but distant
peoples they would never know. The land could enrich them in ways it never
could enrich those operating within the more narrowly circumscribed world of
the traditional Indian economy. When Europeans gave them partial access to
the larger world through the fur trade, the Indians responded by slaughtering
furbearers with such a vengeance that various animal populations were decimated throughout vast stretches of their natural range. White technology—
most notably firearms—speeded the process of self-aggrandizement. Some
scholars have suggested more complex socioreligious reasons for the burst of
Indian trapping, but human greed—and sudden access to the markets of Europe—is enough to explain it. Clearing worked in the same direction. It destroyed the habitat of forest animals, undermining the traditional base of the
Indian economy and thus speeding arrival of the new order.[8]

The sweeping changes in land use that European settlement brought—the
clearing for crops and pastures, the harvesting of trees for timber, the manufacturing of naval stores, charcoal iron, and potash, and the rest of that complex of activities that colonization introduced—had inadvertent as well as intended results. The assault on the woodlands, from whatever corner it came,
reduced the forests' capacity to contain annual spring flooding. Creeks began
to run dry. The phenomenon was described in southeastern Pennsylvania in
1753: "Our runs dry up apace; several which formerly wou'd turn a fulling
Mill, are now scarce sufficient for The Use of a Farm, the Reason of which is,
when the Country was cover'd with Woods and the Swamps with Brush, the
Rain that fell was detain'd by These Interruptions." In the first seventy years of
European settlement in Pennsylvania, some waterways ceased to be navigable,
apparently for this reason. The same thing was occurring elsewhere. By the
late eighteenth century, a number of observers had detected it. For example,
Samuel Williams reported that many mills in Vermont "which at the first settlement of the country, were plentifully supplied with water from small rivers,
have ceased to be useful."

Erosion was the consequence of rapid runoff. Soil cleared of forest cover and loosened by hoe and plow washed away with startling rapidity if preventive steps were not taken—as they usually were not. Without forests to restore it naturally, the organic content of the soil gradually declined, making it both more susceptible to erosion and less useful for crops. Close-cropped grazing land was nearly as vulnerable as cropland. In these circumstances, huge quantities of silt washed downstream to clog waterways and harbors. In combination with slackened streamflow during the dry months, this made water transportation to the interior increasingly difficult, widening the already great divide between backcountry folk and inhabitants of the tidewater region.

There were other problems too. Fires set by land clearers sometimes got out of control and burned fields and structures. Sawdust from mills and silt from erosion polluted streams and caused fish runs to dwindle, as did dams built by mill operators. The list goes on and on; throughout the colonies, problems spawned by the patterns of land use introduced by European settlers were readily apparent.[9]

Although concern was not widespread, resource-intensive economic patterns did lead at an early date to scattered warnings. In 1701 an English official in New York noted with alarm the large number of sawmills the Dutch had erected there. The Dutchman, he wrote, is "an extraordinary artist at these mills"; one mill even had twelve saws! He expressed a fear that "a few such mills will quickly destroy all the woods in the province at a reasonable distance from them."

The primitive sawmills of the colonial period, whether Dutch-built or not, were wasteful of both wood and human energy. It took much hand labor to wrestle logs into place and move them between cuts; the saws took wide kerfs, turning much of each log to sawdust in the process of making boards. But inefficient though they were, these mills were adequate to meet demand, and the worried English official in New York was the exception. For most it was the waste of human labor, not of wood, by inefficient sawmills that was troubling. There seemed a plentitude of established forest trees; besides, one Virginian noted, "Wood grows at every Man's Door so fast, that after it has been cut down, it will in Seven Years time, grow up again from Seed, to substantial Fire-Wood; and in Eighteen or Twenty years 'twill come to be very good Board-Timber." Under such conditions, neither the number of colonial mills nor the quantity of sawdust they generated caused much comment.

Much of the timber shortage in the early period was due to transportation problems that limited access to trees. Still, there were signs that the inexhaustibility of the forest was a fiction. A traveler in New Jersey in 1750 noted that many of the swamps were "quite destitute of cedars, having only young shoots left." Similarly, by the American Revolution, even before the advent of large-scale manufacturing based upon forest products, the accessible woods of North Carolina were reportedly much diminished. Annual growth far exceeded annual cut, but if the trees could not be reached it made little practical difference.[10]

Excessive agricultural inroads upon the forest, and the misuse of land that exacerbated it, drew special criticism. As early as 1688 John Clayton was arguing that Virginians ought to be manuring and enriching their fields and draining lowland swamps rather than clearing upland forests that would have only fleeting value for tobacco. A generation later Robert Beverley, one of the wealthiest of Virginia's planters and owner of at least thirty-seven thousand acres, expressed similar concern over the demands made on the land by tobacco cultivation. Another American observed pointedly: "the emulation [i.e., competition] that takes place among the present generation is not who shall put his estate in the most beautiful order, who shall manage it with most skill and judgment for posterity, but who shall bring the largest crop to market." In his words, the unwritten land-use policy was based on the notion, "let the children provide for themselves." Peter Kalm agreed; colonial eyes, he wrote, "are fixed upon present gain, and they are blind to the future."

Not all reactions were utilitarian. Jonathan Edwards, a leading Puritan minister of the mid-eighteenth century, had as a child sought solitary places in the woods to communicate with God in prayer, and in his later life he wrote passages praising the beauties of nature. "When we are delighted with flowery meadows and gentle breezes . . . we see only the emanation of the sweet benevolence of Jesus Christ," Edwards proclaimed, adding that there are "many things wherein we may behold His awful majesty; in the Sun in His strength, in comets, in thunder, in the hovering thunderclouds, in ragged rocks and the brows of mountains." For all his stern Calvinist background, Edwards was displaying a side that was harbinger of the nature-loving transcendentalist who would spring from New England's womb in a later time and help shape the course of conservation and forest use.

In spite of Edwards's presence, concern for the quality of life—for the aesthetic dimension of conservation—was more often manifested than articulated as the first rigorous decades in the New World ended. The tradition of the village common survived first in the town square, then in public parks. As early as 1641 the legislature of the Massachusetts Bay Colony passed an ordinance setting aside "Great ponds"—bodies of fresh water ten acres or more in size—as reserves for fishing and hunting. In this case concern seems to have been more with recreation and domestic food supplies than with economic returns. Though the spirit was willing, the enforcement was weak. All the same, it was a beginning. Elsewhere in the thirteen colonies land was also set aside, in large settlements or small, for the enjoyment of the people.

Urban expansion in Philadelphia, New York, and Boston eliminated many open areas. Nonetheless, room for a stroll, or for quiet contemplation, could be found by those who had time to enjoy it. That more than a few did is attested by the repeated efforts of authorities in Massachusetts to prohibit residents from "uncivilly walking in the streets and fields" on the Lord's day. In spite of such regulations, the practices continued, especially during hot weather. Some even sought to profit from the lure of the outdoors. An announcement in the *Boston News-Letter* of July 10–17, 1735, read: "Any Person that has a mind to take a walk in the Garden at the Bottom of the Common, to eat Currants, shall be Kindly Welcome for Six Pence a piece." Whether turned to a profit or not, saving places for walks and leisure—and the practice of taking them—represented a small, unsung step toward that appreciation of nature from which parks programs would later spring. Although the aesthetic qualities of the forest were sometimes remarked upon, the all-enclosing, barrierlike woods on the perimeter of settlement were as yet little valued for the recreational opportunities they presented. Recreation was taken in such safer, more civilized arenas as the village common—or perhaps a tavern or coffeehouse.[11]

More frequent, more important, and far more often noted than this appreciation of nature as a source of inspiration and recreation were the numerous regulations on resource use that emanated from authorities both in England and in the colonies. References to "the king's trees" recurred frequently in correspondence between the London government and colonial authorities. Such terms and the broad arrow, ubiquitous in New England's woods, bespoke colonialism—attempts at authoritarian rule—and were manifestations of an unqualified mercantilist conviction. No less were they the results of a struggle for survival in the intense maritime rivalries that would attain global dimensions before America's colonial era came to its dramatic conclusion. Emphasis on "the king's trees" and obedience to the act of sequestration that the mark of the broad arrow signified was, more generally—and thus less clearly understood—an inarticulate expression of concerns aroused by the depleted state of English forests.

But more important were developments in North America. The prospect of abundance, fostering legends of inexhaustibility, soon rendered meaningless in the settled areas of Atlantic America those concerns about deforestation derived from the mother country. This shift by no means suggests that there was no sense of responsibility in the colonies for the "state of the woods." Colonial legislatures were fully involved in regulating the use of the forests and by the time of the War of Independence had produced a considerable body of legislation directed toward that end.

The lead in establishing a regulatory domain, with conservation aspects, was taken in New England. Motives were both commercial and communitarian: the regulations sought to prevent the destruction and waste of valuable resources as well as to ensure that community members, not outsiders, profited from them.[12] A law passed in Plymouth Colony in 1626 sought to prevent "such inconveniences as do and may befall the plantation by the want of timber." Shipment of timber outside the colony's narrow confines, "how little soever the quantity may be," was subject to licensing. A subsequent Plymouth law, noting that "several Townes in this Collonie are already much straightened for building timber," called for better-supplied settlements to share with those less blessed. Plymouth's early action should come as no surprise: it was never well endowed with timber stands of quality.

The American forest was to the settlers first and foremost a source of wealth. Conservation began to be a viable concern in the colonial era as timber near waterways that were both navigable and accessible approached depletion. Especially in New England, observers perceived dwindling stands as a threat to the means of sustaining the colonial experiment. A mid-seventeenth-century Connecticut law restricted times and areas for the felling of timber, and ordinances of Kittery and Dover, Maine, limited the number of trees one person could legally fell. The laws found emulation elsewhere in the colonies. Much regulation had a "waste not, want not" tone consistent with the Americanized version of the doctrine of waste. To clear land for grazing, planting, and settlement was meritorious only if felled trees were fashioned into something usable or salable — planks, clapboards, or staves, for example.[13]

From regulating the cutting and shipping of timber, Massachusetts and New Hampshire turned to prolonging the life of "turpentine trees," stipulating that extraction — "boxing" — should be limited to one part of a tree's trunk. The preamble of an act passed by the Massachusetts General Court in 1715 spelled out its fear for the future of naval-stores production: "there has been greate waste and stroy [i.e., destruction] made of pine trees and other timber within this province." The act sought to end them. Similar legislation was appearing elsewhere as well.

At the same time that legislative bodies were regulating forest use, they were also encouraging its exploitation. In 1637 export-intensive Virginia sought to foster shipbuilding by offering premiums in kind — the kind, of course, being tobacco. Massachusetts Bay Colony exempted shipbuilders from military obligations. South Carolina granted generous exemptions from export duties to vessels built there, and a variety of provisions for tax relief and land grants encouraged New Jersey's sawmill operators to expand their activities.

The inconsistency is more apparent than real. Legislators were seeking to strike a balance between present and future need. It was toward this end that they modified the doctrine of waste to allow more extensive clearing and harvesting. In any case, more than an embryonic conservationist ethic guided the hands of legislators as they imposed duties (anything but onerous) on exports of boards, planks, hogsheads, and other timber products. Legislatures seek revenues where they can find them, and seventeenth-century options were decidedly limited.

A corollary of ensured supply was quality control. A laissez-faire philosophy would take hold in the federal era, but colonial legislation prescribed in detail standards for the manufacture and trading of forest products. Such regulations came easily to policymakers steeped in the mercantilist thought of the day. Naval-stores shortweighting and slipshod processing were the unwritten rule until supplanted by exceedingly specific prescriptions by colonial assemblies. Inspection was routinely provided at specified sites. Each barrel of pitch or turpentine, for example, had to contain thirty-one and a half gallons, be free from foreign matter, and be in a cask bound by twelve hoops. Tar production and export were subject to similar provisions. North Carolina took the lead in setting standards, but the results seldom measured up to the intent of the enactments there or elsewhere in America.

Similarly, standards and inspection requirements were set for wood products ranging from shingles to boards to firewood. The goal was to build a domestic economic base from which competition in the world market could be launched. Hence the processes of resource management and economic development were linked from the very beginnings of European settlement.

The body of legislation surrounding the harvesting and sale of forest products was sizable, but that regarding replenishment was another matter. Reforestation is at a far remove from a policy of allowing trees to mature before "harvesting"—yet in colonial America there was nothing nearer. To be sure, at the beginning of the eighteenth century householders in Philadelphia, New Castle, and Chester were called upon to plant and preserve one or more trees in front of their homes, but this was an exception more apparent than real. It did not supply a beginning for ideas on reforestation. On the other hand, regulations on harvesting were widespread. Even these, however, were a far cry from what was to come. A penalty was authorized in Connecticut in 1702 for felling small trees, but only at the end of the colonial era—with the exception of pine trees reserved for the Royal Navy under the broad arrow policy—were precise definitions of size written into law. A New York act of 1772 stated that firewood could not be cut from pine trees under six inches in diameter or other trees under four inches. More typical was a subsequent Pennsylvania act requiring "that in clearing the Ground, Care be taken to leave One Acre of Trees for Every Five Acres clear'd, especially to preserve Oak and Mulberries, for Silk & Shipping." Thus came the first small, but not insignificant, glimmerings of silviculture.

Quite another matter was the well-founded fear of forest fires. The Indians were convenient scapegoats, but more timber areas were seared by the settler-applied torch than by native Americans in search of game. At first, legislation sought to limit the burning season. The authorities of Plymouth Colony noted in 1633 that "many have sustayned great damage by the indiscreet fyring of the woods." Restrictions were thus placed on the times when such methods of land clearing were allowed. Modest as it was, the act was America's first forest fire prevention legislation. Much similar legislation was subsequently enacted up and down the Atlantic coast. Usually the period from March to May was designated for burning because fires were least likely to get beyond control during those months. Heavy fines were imposed for out-of-season firing and for fires that damaged a neighbor's property, and citizens in some communities were obliged to serve as firemen when blazes erupted.[14]

Not just use but even access to land was—in some colonies—controlled. The social structure of medieval England was largely left behind, but the penchant for enacting laws concerning trespass was not. In England the royal hunting rights were sacrosanct. Their legacy of a forest surrounded by regulations crossed the Atlantic, even if the stylized royal or aristocratic hunt was a much later importation. The regulations were in fact trespass laws against felling timber not only on the property of others but also on common or undivided land. Penalties were stiff—treble damages, imprisonment, or both were not uncommon—and they increased in severity throughout the colonial era in a series of frustrated responses to continuing violations. New Jersey legislation of 1666, 1714, and 1771 charted the course toward greater harshness in trespass laws. The motivation for flouting the regulations is obvious—the potential for monetary advantage made the risk worth taking. Trespass laws, then, were an imperfect mechanism employed in the search for balance between exploitation and conservation.[15]

It was a short step from trespass laws to monopoly legislation. Plymouth Colony passed a law in 1670 that set the pattern in fixing the price of tar and regulating to whom it could be sold. The Massachusetts Bay Colony followed a year later, extending the monopoly to pitch, turpentine, and resin. Such measures were perhaps most important for the antiegalitarianism, the exclusivity, they fostered. It was enough to make a man long to move on, to escape regulation, and to do with the forests what he wished.

As settlement expanded "down east" from the Massachusetts Bay Colony to Maine after 1650, access to forest resources was limited—at least in theory—to a small group of timber merchants. The spread of the colony's authority has been ascribed to a desire to ensure religious conformity north of the Merrimack River. Every bit as important was the availability there of vast tracts of timber. Colonial merchants were aware that if Maine could be brought under Boston's jurisdiction, a stable government could be fostered under conditions favorable to their commercial interests. The commissioners empowered to extend the authority of Massachusetts northward were chosen from merchants of fur, fish, and lumber who were active in the area. They obtained huge land grants and soon monopolized the distribution of English manufactured goods there, selling at artificially high prices. In what was to become a distressingly familiar and long-lived practice in America's frontiers, they extended credit to settlers on confiscatory terms.[16]

The small-scale empires of resource monopoly, in colony after colony, intensified the existing circumstances of economic deprivation. Even at this early stage of American history, control of resources had become a political matter. It might be argued that a good measure of the seeds of democracy was planted in the American forest in response to such blatant monopolism. Certainly the forest harbored major implications for the course of America's relationship with England and for the relations of Americans with one another.

Colonial America's economic history is an account of remarkable acceleration in the processes of resource utilization. Yet there were many detours and delays. At the time of independence it was England, not America, that was well advanced toward becoming the workshop of the world, and some Americans pondered the wisdom of severing ties with such a vigorous economy. But the foundation for the challenge to Europe's economic dominance was in place, based in no small measure on the exploitation of the new nations's greatest resource—the American forest. First steps had been taken toward a utilitarian brand of conservation, and a faint glimmer of an aesthetic appreciation of nature had appeared. Anything beyond that would have to wait much, much longer.

The War of Independence would help develop new attitudes toward the bounty, promised, and challenge of the American forest. Further development—because of the rapidity of population and agricultural expansion—and the prohibitory threat of the Proclamation of 1763, which barred land-hungry colonists from land west of the Appalachians, had already started to shape such new attitudes. Fighting the war added to Americans' knowledge of the land, a land that had already become their patrimony. Conflict, as always, tore people from their roots and fostered a restless, adventurous, even rebellious spirit. For those who imbibed that spirit, the remedy was most often the land beyond the edge of the forest—the frontier. And the winning of independence, most of all, made the frontier accessible. As increasing numbers of Americans turned their backs on the sea in the years following the Revolution, the frontier—and the trees found there—became of greater and greater importance. In time this chain of events would lead to a second, fuller flowering of the conservationist impulse. But for the time being that was set aside: development of the new nation was the all-consuming order of the day.

*The New Nation and
Its Forests, 1776–1850*

Part Two

The New Nation Confronts Its Forests

Chapter 4

When Americans at last faced Britain in their war for independence, they were a healthy, well-housed people with a solid economy. Both the people and the economy had been well nurtured by the legacy of North America's forests. And the Americans fought the mother country in new ways. Even as the forests had forced European colonists to develop new methods and tools for clearing woodlands, so did Indians and forest conditions require them to adjust their tactics and techniques in warfare. Gradually they had learned. A reluctance to fight in massed formation, a concern for terrain, and a greater emphasis upon the accuracy of one's aim were hard-won lessons that were applied against the British with great effect during the Revolution.[1]

Independence not only freed Americans from a host of mercantilist controls, it also swept aside the hated Proclamation Line of 1763. From the War of Independence until the mid-nineteenth century, America's use of her forests and their resources grew rapidly as the new nation's population surged into the now-open West. The forest itself both nurtured and hindered this expansion: while it provided the raw material for many necessities of frontier life, its seemingly impenetrable vastness was a physical and psychological challenge to those who confronted it. The perils of the forest were real, but forest skills that had been acquired slowly through two centuries of experience in the New World now enabled settlers of the forest frontier to successfully confront these dangers. The impact of the newcomers was immense. The vast majority of them came, after all, to transform the forest into farms.

Both Thomas Jefferson and Benjamin Franklin fervently espoused the value of agriculture, believing that the citizen farmer was endowed with special virtues that would strengthen the fiber of the nation. Jefferson contended: "those who labor in the earth are the chosen people of God, if he ever had a chosen people." Franklin was more prosaic; agriculture, he maintained, was the "great Business of the Continent."[2]

To obtain more land for cultivation, the American people had to fell trees during the national period just as they had earlier. Reactions were mixed. Some settlers, although viewing the forests as impediments to progress, also recognized the majesty of what they were destroying. William Nowlin described the clearing of his family's farm in Michigan: "The grand old forest was melting away. . . . Beautiful workmanship of nature was displayed in that timber." Yet he welcomed the change. "Now finally I thought we had quite a clearing. . . . I could look to the east and there, joining ours was the clearing of Mr. Asa Blare. . . . Then it began to seem as if others were living in Michigan, for we could see them. The light of civilization began to dawn on us. We had cleared up what was a few years before, the lair of the wolf and the hunting ground of the red man."

Others shared these mixed feelings. U. P. Hedrick wrote that the "mainspring in my father's life was a desire to subdue wild lands. His triumphs were those of man over nature. He loved to transform prairies and forests into smiling fields of growing grain and grazing herds." And yet this frontiersman—who had moved from Virginia to northern Indiana, to Illinois, to Iowa, to Michigan, each time carving out a new life—"had a rare eye for natural beauty." And when John Parsons traveled through Indiana in 1840 he found a variety of leaders who were both knowledgeable about forests and appreciative of their beauty.[3]

But there were also those less sympathetic. Caroline Kirkland—a perceptive, well-educated New Yorker who moved with her husband to frontier Michigan—noted of her new neighbors that "whatever cannot evidently be turned to account *to-day* is rejected as worthless." As she explained,

The Western settler looks upon these earth-born columns and verdant roofs and towers which they support as "heavy timber,"—nothing more. He sees in them only obstacles which must be removed, at whatever sacrifice, to make way for mills, stores, blacksmith's shops,—perhaps churchs—certainly taverns. "Clearing" is his daily thought and nightly dream; and so literally does he act upon this guiding idea, that not one tree, not so much as a bush, of natural growth, must be suffered to cumber the ground, or he fancies his work incomplete. The very notion of advancement, or civilization, or prosperity, seems inseparably connected with the total extirpation of the forest.

When the Kirklands lent a neighbor a piece of land on which stood a giant oak that they had carefully saved, the man girdled it and "expected our thanks, observing pithily 'nothing wouldn't never grow under sich a great mountain as that!'"

The attitude was widespread. Visitors to frontier communities often met early settlers who boasted that they had cut the first tree felled in their region. Among those combating this outlook was Henry Ward Beecher, a well-known cleric, who was distressed that all the fine trees on the squares and along the thoroughfares of Indianapolis had been felled when the city was being laid out; he unsuccessfully sought to have "specimens of all our best forest trees planted in the city" to replace them.[4]

The contrast between those who treasured the noneconomic values of forests and those who did not seems to have sprung in part from their different educational and economic levels. The gulf between Caroline Kirkland and Henry Ward Beecher and many of their neighbors was huge, however much Kirkland (if not Beecher) may have admired some of the latter's homely virtues.

But other factors were involved as well. Timothy Flint, a Congregational minister who spent years traveling and preaching in the West and became a leading interpreter of the region to the rest of the country, noted a wide divergence between the land-use practices of frontiersmen from Kentucky and of those who had moved west from New England. "To the eye of a Kentuckian," Flint wrote, "the lofty skeletons of dead trees [that had been girdled], the huge stumps that remain after cultivation had commenced, are pleasant. . . . They are, doubtless, associated in his mind with remembrances of this own country, and with the virgin freshness and exuberance of the soil." Flint liked and defended frontiersmen, but to his New England sensibilities this pattern of land use was clearly distasteful. What Flint was observing was not new. In colonial times girdling had been widely practiced in the South and on the frontier but had not been common in New England — or in the German-settled areas.[5]

When Isaac Weld, an English visitor to the American shores from 1795 to 1797, wrote that Americans "have an unconquerable aversion to trees . . . not one is spared; all share the same fate, and all are involved in the same general havoc," he was generalizing far too broadly. The description may have fit a host of frontiersmen, but there was also a large body of Americans whose outlook was very different. He was nonetheless expressing a widely shared judgment.

Numerous European travelers — who were neither involved in the arduous task of winning a living from an often inhospitable wilderness nor particularly close to the people whose attitudes they purported to describe — marveled at American indifference to the beauties of the forest. Alexis de Tocqueville expressed the common view when he wrote that "Europeans think a lot about the wild, open spaces of America, but the Americans themselves hardly give it a thought. The wonders of inanimate nature leave them cold, and one may almost say they did not see the marvelous forests surrounding them until they began to fall beneath the ax." The comments of such observers must be used with caution. They saw what their European prejudices allowed them to see, extending to all Americans the attitudes of a particular segment of frontier society.

The accuracy of foreign assessments did not go unchallenged. J. Hector St. Jean de Crèvecoeur, the famous Frenchman-turned-American, wrote, "I have heard many Europeans blame us for many of our operations. Alas! They censured us before they knew anything of our climate, of our seasons, and of the scarcity and dearness of labourers." Benjamin Vaughan developed the idea more fully: "Wood is too abundant & labor too scarce in a new country, to admit of other than coarse operations for clearing lands from the woods with which the early hand of nature had almost constantly clothed them. . . . *A foreigner may judge the system* [of clearing] *improvident;* but were he transported to the scene of it, he would in a short time cease to wonder. . . . Everything in short depends upon circumstances." The circumstances, he made clear, were as much economic as attitudinal.[6]

Actually, the views that pioneer settlers had of the forests were compounded of a mixture of elements. There was indeed a widespread hostility to trees, an attitude that they should be eliminated as soon as possible. At the same time, there existed a hardheaded materialism that encouraged forest clearing not because of any distaste for the woods but because economic necessity—survival—dictated that money had to be earned from crops raised in forest clearings, from the sale of woodland products, or from a combination of the two.

Yet the idea that trees ought to be felled regardless of whether a profit resulted does seem to have been widespread on the frontier. Most people holding such views left no written records, but their attitudes show through from time to time in accounts by others. Caroline Kirkland told of "fine oaks" set aside to grace the "grand esplanade" of a new townsite in Michigan that were, for no apparent reason, among the first trees felled when settlers moved in and commenced clearing. Part of the reason in fact was probably a hostility, however subconscious, to anything preserved for nonutilitarian purposes: such things smacked of eastern (or European) upper-class affectations against which frontiersmen felt a deep antagonism. Kirkland noted that "an angry battle must be fought for every tree. Pretended blunders—accidents—all stratagems will be resorted to in order to get rid of those marked for preservation." Half a continent away, John C. Frémont told of searching for a lone tree that "had been a beacon" on the Oregon Trail for many years. His party watched for it in vain until they found it at last "stretched on the ground . . . felled by some inconsiderate emigrant axe." The tree had not been used; it had simply been destroyed.[7]

For the poor settler, seeking to support a family while clearing a farm in the timber, the presence of a towering forest was more than an impediment; it was a threat to survival. In a society short on both labor and capital, an abundance of trees was an asset that few could capitalize on. Farmland, by contrast, was something that could be turned to profit with a rudimentary knowledge of husbandry and an abundance of hard work. Small wonder that many pioneers looked upon clearing the forest as freeing them from an alien, hostile environment. One frontier resident wrote of the "everlasting sound of falling trees" that accompanied life in a region freshly opened to settlement and was "a relief to the dreary silence of these wilds." A sense of freeing oneself from danger and deprivation appears to have contributed to such statements, and to the "senseless" destruction of trees that troubled Kirkland, Frémont, and others.

Even those who did not share this hostility to trees chopped away at the woods. They had a living to make, and though there might be beauty in the wilds there were also responsibilities and opportunities. William Nowlin's father, who let "stand as monarch of the clearing" a giant oak that grew on their homestead, also welcomed the approach of the railroad. "Now," he said, "our best wood is worth something": it could be sold as cordwood to the railroad to fuel its engines.

Growing recognition of the commercial value of timber resulted in more husbanding of forestlands in the early national period than has generally been recognized. Benjamin Vaughan reported that individual trees left to shade the house, farmyard, or orchard had a tendency to die or fall victim to windthrow, which "led to the expedient of preserving valuable timber, by suffering select pieces of the original woods to remain entire." Similarly, while in the United States as a commercial agent, Talleyrand—more perceptive than most European observers—noted that "one finds . . . on the best plantations reserves of woods which have never been cut down although the land is very fertile and as suitable for cultivation as the adjacent land which has been cleared." Stands were left because owners found them convenient and profitable; forestlands, he said, did not sell any cheaper than adjacent farmlands "whose value they increase by reason of their pleasantness and utility; indeed there is never too much wood on land."

Tench Coxe, a leading American political economist of the time, went even further. He noted that the country's *"immense and unequalled magazine"* of timber invited its commercial use, adding that the *"unavoidable deficiencies of Euro-*

pean wood and timber can only be supplied from America." In these circumstances, it "would be unwise . . . [for] the United States to neglect the due preservation" of its timber, for it is important to "maintain an abundant stock." Fortunately, he observed, "the present redundance and cheapness of American lands enables us to effect the *preservation and reproduction of our forests* with less inconvenience and expense, than any other civilized nation."

Thomas Jefferson, George Washington, John Quincy Adams, and others shared Coxe's concern that the nation's store of wood not be wasted or willfully destroyed. In Philadelphia in 1787, the Society for Promoting Agriculture called for tree planting on farms. Two years later Nicholas Collin published a plea for forest preservation that marshaled all the basic arguments that would be used by conservationists a hundred and more years later. In short, there was present during early national period a utilitarian concern for forest conservation that both contemporary and subsequent American critics have ignored and obscured.

But not everyone shared in this concern—nor did opposition come only from unlettered frontiersmen and grasping, shortsighted materialists. Benjamin Franklin, for one, was little moved by pleas for forest conservation. He believed that clearing farmland would in the long run yield more to society than would forest preservation; in any case, the United States had so much forest that continued clearing would make only small inroads into it. Jeremy Belknap agreed; he described lumbering as "a risky business to be encouraged only insofar as it does not interfere with cultivation." Even Jefferson and Coxe had mixed feelings. They did not want trees wasted or the country denuded, but they also did not want preservation to stand in the way of economic growth. That it could do so was manifest. As Talleyrand put it in speaking of Maine, "Your great uncultivated forests repulse . . . [investment capital] more than they attract it; it is necessary to have something more manageable, more disposable to the European [investor] to awaken his interest and solicit his confidence. . . . In a word, the province of *Maine* is not agricultural enough and work not divided enough [to attract capital from abroad]." Forest conservation would do nothing to overcome this.[8]

Forest harvests and forestlands, once cleared, offered economic opportunities to many an American. Those who sought to turn the forest to their own use while still valuing forest beauty did not believe they had to choose utility over aesthetics. Neither did those who recognized both present and future needs believe they had to make a choice between them. With the unexploited wealth of the continent before them, no one saw a need to cease taking the land's treasures. Forest beauty and forest harvests would remain even after all the good farmland had been cleared—or so it appeared.

Religion and nationalism sanctioned the processes at work. Jacksonian Americans, Whig and Democrat alike, glorified economic development, seeing in it a means of fulfilling America's mission to lead the world to a better life. Andrew Jackson himself stated this position clearly in a presidential message delivered on December 6, 1830:

Philanthropy could not wish to see this continent restored to the condition [in] which it was found by our forefathers. What good man would prefer a country covered with forests and ranged by a few thousand savages to our extensive Republic, studded with cities, towns, and prosperous farms, embellished with all the improvements which art can devise or industry execute, occupied by more than 12,000,000 happy people, and filled with all the blessings of liberty, civilization, and religion?

Similarly, a frontier preacher reflected the spirit of the time when he recorded: "Preached again two sermons in the old log courthouse. . . . The text was Neh. ii, 20: 'The God of Heaven will prosper us, therefore, we his servants will arise and build.'" They built with wood, of course, on what had once been forestland.[9]

The attitudes toward the forest held by frontiersmen and by those who followed them differed in a variety of ways. The former lived closer to the forest and, seeing themselves less as builders, were not so intent on destroying (or converting) it. For that reason, as well as simply because of their much larger numbers, it was the later arrivals who most changed America's forestland. Still, the frontiersmen opened the gateway to the woods. If they did not shape the values of those who followed, at least they gave them room for expression in action.[10]

Frontiersmen were notoriously mobile, but so were other Americans. Timothy Flint detected that behind this lay a "restless hope of finding in a new country, and in new views and combinations of things, something we crave but have not." Unfortunately, in the new country "every thing visionary and unreal gradually gives way to truth and reality"; unhappiness sets in and the frontiersman is soon on the move again. But there was also, Flint noted, a practical, hardheaded motivation behind the westward migrations. The "general motive for coming here is to be a freeholder, to have plenty of rich land, and to be able to settle his children around him. It is a most virtuous motive."

This restless quest for something better may have sprung from virtuous motives, but it had its unfortunate side effects. "The general inclination here [in the West], is too much like the Tartars," Flint wrote. People "only make such improvements as they can leave without reluctance and without loss. I have every where noted the operation of this impediment in the way of those permanent and noble improvements which grow out of a love for that appropriated spot where we were born, and where we expect to die." Such actions as "the planting of artificial forests, which on the wide prairies would be so beautiful and useful . . . will not become general for many years." At another point he noted that "people are too busy, too much occupied in making farms and speculations, to think of literature." Other nonutilitarian activities suffered too. Even what had a practical use had to be of value in the short rather than the long run or it would be ignored—or even derided.

Yet, as has been shown, not everyone in the West—to say nothing of the country as a whole—was equally wedded to such views. German settlers preferred to stay and improve their holdings rather than move on. People who appreciated forest beauty and sought to husband parts of it were also a part of the scene. Caroline Kirkland's neighbor may have frustrated her with his narrow views; but not many miles away was William Nowlin, whose father saved a giant oak "on account of its greatness, and its having so nice a body" and who described trees as "our most beautiful and best antiquities."[11]

Not all—or even most—Americans lived on or near the frontier. However, even those remote from the new settlements often shared in the vision of Americans as a people marching through the wilderness, draining marshes, diverting rivers, peopling the wilds, and subduing nature. Expansion and settlement were altering the landscape and shaping Americans' views of themselves in the process. An early indication of this came in 1792 when Jeremy Belknap wrote a satirical history of the United States. Britain—the nation of shopkeepers—was represented in the person of "John Bull, the tailor"; Americans, on the other hand, were simply "The Foresters." Belknap clearly believed that Americans were products of the forest environment and of natural forces against which they had to contend as they built homes in the wilderness; they were a new people, distinct from those from whom they had sprung.

In the older, settled sections of the country, remote from the realities of life in a new land, people were often hostile to the frontiersman. But as the momentum and complexity of American life grew, people began to write and to read romances of the backwoodsmen who enjoyed freedom of the forests. A work of 1842 entitled *The Forest Rangers* celebrated the abilities of the frontiersman and revealed the distinction seen between the existence of those who enjoyed the life of the forests and those who resided in settled communities. A backwoods hunter explained to an admiring visitor how he had acquired his skills:

> I'm no bookish scollard,
> Caze all my life the woods I follered;
> But yit a heap of things I larns,
> 'Bout Ingins and backwoods concarns.
> That painter what up yander howls,
> And bears, and deers, and wolves, and owls,
> And snakes, and Ingins, is the books,
> Where I for larnin always looks.

His listener applauded such knowledge.

> Your close, attentive observation,
> Affords a fund of information.
> Of greater value in this wood
> Than all the intellectual food
> That e'er was gleaned from books or schools,
> Or journals writ by traveled fools.

James Fenimore Cooper's Leatherstocking Tales provide the classic example of the romantic view of forest pioneers in nineteenth-century literature. In *The Pioneers* (1823) Cooper put forth the idea that man should use the resources of nature so as to conserve them. Page after page deals with the waste of natural resources. Observing the slaughter of passenger pigeons, Leatherstocking comments that "the Lord won't see the waste of his creatures for nothing, and right will be done to the pigeons, as well as others, by and by." Cooper appealed especially to woodsmen, who cut "as if no end could be found to their treasures, nor any limits to their extent. If we go on this way, twenty years hence we shall want fuel." Cooper's concern was not simply utilitarian. Natty Bumppo speaks for him: "how should a man who has lived in towns and schools know anything about the wonders of the woods? . . . [N]one know how often the hand of God is seen in the wilderness, but them that rove it for a man's life."

Such works served in a variety of subtle and often indistinct ways to shape the attitudes and actions of Americans as they dealt with the nation's resources in the years that followed. The dichotomy between the romantic West of literature and the pioneer West of reality was such that Americans ever after tended to approach questions of land use in general—and wild land in particular—with mixed emotions and divided views.[12]

Perhaps nothing dramatized these differences as much as did the American

Indian. European settlement led to the destruction of traditional Indian hunting grounds, bringing conflict between cultures that used the land in distinctly different ways. When the Indians did not peacefully accept the steady intrusion of white settlers onto lands upon which they had dwelled for centuries, conflict arose.

Americans may have learned much from the Indians, but until the emergence of romantic literature they only rarely questioned whether the displacement of Indian tribes was justified. Tocqueville relates that he was frequently informed by "honest citizens" that "God, in refusing the first inhabitants the capacity to become civilized, has destined them in advance to inevitable destruction. The true owners of this continent are those who know how to take advantage of its riches." And take advantage they did. Forestlands were cleared, stumps removed, fields cultivated, and new communities of roughhewn cabins erected. Romantic literature helped to soften judgments on American Indians and generate some genuine sympathy for them, but it did little to change the basic American conviction that had been given voice by Tocqueville's informants: progress was not only inevitable, it was good, and what happened to the Indian—or to the forest—in the process should be encouraged, for it was a mark of that progress.[13]

The practical knowledge of the forests that settlers had been amassing was augmented in the early years of independence by scientific assessment of the nation's arboreal wealth. In the late 1780s and early 1790s, André Michaux began investigating the forests of America. After neglecting her own forests for centuries, France now wished to replenish them with American species. Supported by the French government and aided by his son François André, Michaux searched for trees, especially oaks, that would grow in France. In 1801 he published his treatise on the oaks of America, *Histoire des chênes d'Amérique*, which established his reputation as a talented student of American forests. A year after his death in 1802, his *Flora boreali-americana* was published in Paris. This work is justly praised as the first North American flora, but it is unfortunately limited by its focus upon eastern America and by the inclusion of only those species that Michaux had personally collected or at least seen.

After the death of his father, the younger Michaux continued their work. Noting the decline of forests between his visits in 1802 and 1807, he tried to alert Americans to the consequences of "an alarming destruction of the trees proper for civil or naval construction." Without the protection of federal or state governments, Michaux maintained, this destruction would surely increase as the population grew.

In 1817 Michaux published his three-volume *North American Sylva,* the first systematic survey of American flora. There were still gaps in the work, but this culmination of the father's and son's investigations of American trees was a significant contribution to the growth of dendrology—the study of trees—and to the development of forestry in America. It was not only a systematic survey of the trees of much of North America, but also a source of encouragement for the wise use of the country's forests. Michaux stated in his introduction:

I have . . . endeavoured to impress on the American farmers the importance and pecuniary advantages which would result to them and to their families from the preservation of different species of timber of which they ought to insure growth, and on the contrary I have noted those which ought to be destroyed, for I am of the opinion that a bad tree ought not to be suffered to exist where a better tree could grow; and there is no country where it is more important to make a choice than in America.

The younger Michaux's contributions to American forestry were not just scholarly. He bequeathed twelve thousand dollars to the American Philosophical Society and eight thousand to the Massachusetts Society of Arts and Agriculture for "the extension and progress of agriculture and more especially silviculture."[14]

André and François Michaux were not alone. In 1792 Jeremy Belknap had observed that few people in the United States had studied natural history "and of those who have a taste for inquiries of this kind, none have had leisure to pursue them." Gradually the situation changed. In 1807 the University of Pennsylvania established a botanical garden "for the improvement of the science of botany." Robert Owen's utopian community of New Harmony, Indiana, became a center for the study of natural history. As one twentieth-century authority has put it, "In this [frontier] society there burgeoned most improbably a group of eminent naturalists, and the cause of theoretical science . . . flowered exotically on the banks of the sluggish Wabash. . . . It was the most brilliant assemblage of original intellects in the field of natural history that the western Hemisphere has ever witnessed." Perhaps. Certainly what occurred there was impressive. So too was the work of Amos Eaton, who (first at Williams College and then at Rensselaer Polytechnic Institute) pushed forward the study of botany, seeking always to make it available and relevant to laymen rather than something cloistered in the hallowed halls of pure science.

Unlike the two Michaux and many of those at New Harmony, Eaton was American born. But from wherever they came, the rising number of naturalists in the United States, and botanists in particular, helped pave the way for later work in forest management. For the time being their efforts were nearly all purely descriptive—ecological understanding and concerns were still far in the future. But by insisting that the work of scientists needed to be made comprehensible and available to the general public, Eaton in particular helped ensure that it would not always remain descriptive and isolated from the concerns of the nation's citizenry.[15]

In spite of Michaux's admonitions and the work of Eaton and others, few Americans in the first half of the nineteenth century believed that the nation's forests could be exhausted. Much colonial legislation was discarded after independence, and the body of new legislation protecting the forests grew slowly. Moreover, what regulations there were were largely ignored. Regardless of scattered calls for conservation, most Americans simply did not believe that a resource as abundant as timber could become scarce.

Indeed, the forests of North America had a profusion and variety unequaled in the temperate zone. This combination provided a readily exploitable natural resource that could be found almost everywhere east of the Mississippi River and in much of the Far West. It was a resource that could be inexpensively transformed into useful objects by a society lacking the wealth and skilled labor necessary for the development of a more complex energy- or capital-intensive technology. Americans could select from a diverse assortment of trees that wood that possessed the particular color, flexibility, weight, warp or rot resistance, and texture needed for a given task. Wood could be shaped, carved, bent, or hewn and thus turned into a host of products and uses. It became in effect the plastic of the period.

Wood was also the principal fuel for heating in Jacksonian America; it remained so until America began to use fossil fuels extensively in the latter half of the nineteenth century. Approximately half of all trees that were cut for purposes other than land clearing were used for fuel. Seeking savings in time and labor rather than in wood, Americans built large fireplaces that would hold logs up to five feet long so that wood need not be cut into small sizes. With such a fireplace, a family in the North might use from ten to fifteen cords of firewood a year to heat its home. These fireplaces were prodigiously wasteful of energy, some allowing as much as 80 percent of the heat generated to escape up the chimney.

For small farmers living near urban areas, firewood was an important cash crop. However, even before the Revolution, firewood was becoming difficult to obtain in Philadelphia; it was even suggested that coal might have to be imported from England to alleviate the city's fuel shortage. George Washington appreciated the value of firewood. In the letter to the manager of his Mount

Vernon estate, Washington observed: "if the trees which have been fallen in all parts of my land, and only a small part of them used, were corded for fire wood instead of lying to rot on the ground . . . they would sell for many hundreds of pounds." As wood for fuel had to be brought from greater distances, its price rose. Throughout the last half of the eighteenth century and into the early decades of the nineteenth, the price of firewood climbed—and complaints increased.

The pressing need for firewood in eastern cities was a powerful stimulus to inventors to create more efficient fireplaces and stoves. In his first scientific paper, published in 1744, Benjamin Franklin had described his design for a free-standing iron stove—the Pennsylvania fireplace, more commonly known as the Franklin stove. Franklin predicted that with "the help of this saving invention our wood may grow as fast as we can consume it, and out posterity may warm themselves at a moderate rate, without being obliged to fetch their fuel over the Atlantic." Throughout his life, Franklin continued his search for more efficient stoves, fireplaces, and chimneys. Since he never patented his stove, his design was widely used by stove-makers.

Other inventors followed Franklin's lead. From 1790 to 1845, the United States Patent Office granted more than eight hundred patents for improved stoves and fireplaces. Up to 1846, stoves were the most commonly recorded invention at the Patent Office. But the new stoves were not without their critics. Since they prevented large amounts of air from escaping up the chimney, one champion of the traditional open fireplace maintained, poisonous gases were left in the rooms they heated. This, he claimed, was the true national poison, not slavery, socialism, Mormonism, tobacco, coffee, or patent medicine. However, inertia and a lack of concern for saving wood were probably more responsible than such fears for the failure to adopt stoves more widely at an early date. One of the things Benjamin Rush found to applaud in Pennsylvania's German population was their economy in burning wood in stoves instead of in the fireplaces preferred by most of their neighbors.

Even if they had been generally adopted, stoves such as Franklin's could not have substantially reduced the need for firewood in the continually growing urban areas. But the 1820s the demand for—and cost of—firewood had become so critical in Philadelphia that a Fuel Saving Society was organized to help the poor. It became an accepted form of charity in that city to give free firewood to "respectable, poor female housekeepers."

Some Americans sought other fuels to replace wood. Coal had been used with varying degrees of success since before the Revolutionary War, but most stoves and fireplace grates were poorly designed for its use. In the 1820s Americans began to seriously investigate the use of coal as a heating and cooking fuel, designing stoves and fireplaces for that purpose. Anthracite coal sales increased from 365 tons in 1820 to 181,000 tons a decade later. Nevertheless, wood remained far more important. As late as 1850 it still supplied approximately 90 percent of the nation's fuel.[16]

Even as technology began to affect the way wood was used as fuel, it also altered the ways trees were felled, milled, and transformed into wood products. Early settlers felled trees with techniques little changed since the Middle Ages. Human labor played the essential role. Lumbering was labor intensive, placing great demands upon the human body. Americans felled trees with axes and split them into planks with wedges or sawed them into boards using whipsaws. The ax was a crucial tool in harvesting the forests. American craftsmen made important improvements on it; during the first half of the eighteenth century they refined the awkward European felling ax into a heavier, better-balanced, and sharper implement. The poll, or back of the axhead, was made thick and flat so it was heavier than the bit. The axhead, which sometimes weighed more than seven pounds, was attached to a three- or four-foot hickory handle carefully shaped for grasping. With such an ax, a skilled woodsman could fell three times as many trees in a day as was possible with the earlier type.[17]

Sawpits for the production of boards had appeared in the colonies early. Accomplished by two men, pit (or whip) sawing was done in two ways. The log to be cut was suspended above a pit deep enough to hold one man; alternatively, the log was supported on a frame high enough above the ground for a man to work under it. The top sawyer would mount the log and pull the long saw on the upstroke. Below, the pit sawyer (or pit man) would pull the saw back down. The thick, heavy blade was usually designed to cut on the downstroke, though on occasion blades were made to cut on both strokes. The saw blade was sometimes enclosed in a wooden frame to prevent it from warping from side to side as it was pulled through the log. This simple innovation permitted straighter cuts. But with or without the addition of a frame, pit saws were clearly inadequate. Even the best sawyers could produce only a few boards a day.

Attaching the frame, or sash, saw to a waterwheel brought more efficiency to the production of lumber. Water-powered sawmills could produce lumber of relatively uniform quality more quickly, in larger quantities, and with less human labor than their predecessors. Such sawmills spread rapidly; they were in the vanguard of settlement in almost every new region. The Sixth Census of the United States reveals that by 1840 there were 31,650 water-powered sawmills in the country.

Alone or in combination with gristmills, sawmills frequently provided the nucleus around which settlement clustered: there, throughout the nineteenth century, one could obtain lumber, the basic building material for home, farm, transportation, and industry. Sawmills often preceded saloons, general stores, schools, and churches in a community. In 1850 the commissioner of patents observed that not until a sawmill was established could frame dwellings and villages arise; the water-powered mill was "civilization's pioneer machine: the precursor of the carpenter, wheelwright and turner, the painter, joiner, and legions of other professions." Moreover, the presence of sawmills enabled settlers to abandon the crude comforts of a dirt-floored log cabin for the more refined pleasures of a wood-floored frame house. By 1855 in New York State frame houses outnumbered log cabins eight to one. Frame structures were appraised at an average of eight hundred dollars per dwelling, while log cabins averaged only fifty dollars. At this same time, New York had almost five thousand sawmills, approximately one mill for every seven hundred people.[18]

Waterpower spurred a number of innovations in sawing operations. One of the earliest mechanical saws to appear was the water-powered, vertically reciprocating sash saw. First used in the seventeenth century, it operated slowly and required little supervision once the log was placed on the carriage that carried it to the blade. But the heavy weight of the frame required considerable energy just to begin its action. Indeed, such saws operated so slowly that it was facetiously claimed that a man could load a log in the morning, begin the cut, and go squirrel hunting while the saw gradually worked its way through the length of the log. One of these early mills might produce five hundred feet of one-inch boards in a day; most produced less. While this represented a significant saving of human labor from the arduous task of cutting board after board with whipsaws, such sawmills were far from ideal.

Until the 1840s, water-powered sash mills were standard in America, but they were gradually replaced by saws promising greater efficiency—an efficiency accomplished by connecting several parallel blades to a frame, creating a gang of saws. With a gang saw, several boards could be cut at the same time. More and more blades were added until, using such a saw, an entire log could be cut in one passage through the mill. Once the edges were trimmed, the lumber was ready for market. With this innovation, production leaped ahead.

Initially, most saw blades used in American mills were imported from France or England; but about 1840 American foundries and machine shops commenced producing mill equipment and blades. In the same period, American sawyers (apparently copying German designs) created the muley saw, which eliminated the heavy frame of the sash saw and instead held the blade or blades by light crossheads. With less weight to move, more energy could be devoted to the cutting action. This new mechanism cut much faster; the output of a mill could be doubled by installing a muley saw of the same size as the sash saw used previously. Greater portability as well as efficiency soon gave the muley saw widespread popularity.

As it became more and more difficult to increase the efficiency of the reciprocal, sash, gang, and muley saws, people began to look for a saw with a continuous cutting action. The circular saw fit their needs. While the precise origins of this saw are unclear, English sawyers were apparently experimenting with it as early as the 1770s. In the 1790s, the noted engineer Sir Marc Isambard Brunel refined the circular saw and other woodworking machines for use in British naval yards. Although there are references to circular saws in America in the late eighteenth and early nineteenth centuries, the date and place of their initial appearance in the United States remain unknown. Newspaper accounts indicate that circular saws were being imported from England in the 1820s and 1830s, and in 1820 an American patent was issued for a "Circular Saw" for making clapboards. Such a saw was excellent for cutting boards for flooring, lath, and other specialized mill products that had formerly required much hand labor.

The high-speed continuous operation of circular saws had drawbacks when used in lumber production, however. As the saw ran, the heat created by the friction of cutting caused the blade to warp, bow, and begin to wobble, making it difficult to cut a straight line. This wobble, and the thickness required to give the blade strength for high-speed sawing, meant that early circular saws took an even wider kerf than had their predecessors. Almost one-third of every thousand feet of logs cut was wasted—much of it transformed into sawdust which was simply discarded. But to most, production, not conservation of raw materials, was the order of the day. There seemed a sufficient supply of softwoods to last indefinitely, and softwood lumber was, after all, the principal commodity demanded by America's builders.

Furniture-makers and cabinetmakers working with expensive walnut, cherry, maple, and oak faced rather different circumstances. They led the search for an efficient continuous-action saw that took a smaller kerf than did the circular saw. The band saw met their needs. It was composed of a flexible, saw-toothed band of steel mounted on flywheels above and below the log to be cut. Its steel blade could be reduced to a width of no more than one-twelfth of an inch, so the band saw cut a much narrower kerf and thus reduced by 25 to 60 percent the amount of wood turned to sawdust.

An Englishman had developed the principles of the band saw as early as 1808, but the technical problems involved in creating a continuous band of steel that could withstand the torsional stresses during sawing kept band saws small and prevented their use in the manufacturing of softwood lumber until the 1870s. Until then, circular saws dominated the nation's lumber industry.[19]

Circular saws were for the most part powered by steam engines, a more reliable source of power than water and one more appropriate for high-speed cutting. Water-powered sawmills were operable only when there was a sufficient head of water to turn their cumbersome wooden wheels, so they were restricted to sites where sufficient streamflow and fall were available. In addition, they suffered from seasonal changes: spring floods often washed them away; summer drought could bring them to a standstill; and in the North, the harsh winters that allowed lumbermen to skid logs in the woods also froze the rivers and streams that provided the mills with power. Most water mills spent as much time idle as running.

Steam-powered mills had few such limitations. They were not dependent upon streams and rivers for power; and most important, they could operate through dry spells when streams were low. In 1802 a New Jersey newspaper suggested that steam sawmills "will be carried to the timber, instead of the timber being at so great an expense of cartage . . . carried to the mills." Logs were bulky and transporting them was expensive and time comsuming—particularly if there were no waterways on which to float them to the sawmills. By moving steam-powered sawmills nearer to the timber than the older water mills, savings were possible. Logs could be cut into lumber and the exterior slabs, sawdust, edgings, and trim could be disposed of before shipment, thus reducing costs of transportation. As the newspaper observed, fuel for the engine would not be a problem. "The limbs of trees, rough slabs, butts of logs, and refuse stuff will serve for fuel, and perhaps no better manure for your lands can be found than the ashes which remain from the fuel so employed." When a steam sawmill was demonstrated in New York, a visitor described it as the "wonder of New York . . . a handsome price of machinery" that would "soon make a fortune for the owner" by allowing him to clear thirty dollars in each twenty-four hours.

But early steam engines had inherent limitations. Small, primitive engines could be purchased in the early 1800s for as little as five hundred dollars; but larger, more efficient ones required capital outlays too great for many individuals and small companies, and their operating costs were high. Larger engines were heavy: a five-horsepower engine might only weigh one and a half tons, but a sixty-horsepower engine would weigh sixteen tons. Moreover, the crude boilers of these high-pressure engines frequently exploded, and sparks from their engines often caused destructive fires.

In spite of these drawbacks, the use of steam engines spread from 1803 on. By 1838 the Treasury Department reported that two thousand were in operation in the United States, many employed in sawmills. These steam engines averaged only twenty horsepower, but each one provided five to ten times as much power as a traditional water-powered mill and could thus run larger mills and more saws.

The capital costs and high operating expenses of steam-powered facilities encouraged centralization, specialization, and consolidation of smaller operations. Steam-powered sawmills could be located almost anywhere. Although the prediction had been that mills would now move closer to their sources of timber, and some owners in fact moved into the woods, many found it advantageous instead to open sawmill operations closer to their main markets. Many mills— especially resaw mills that utilized large-dimension lumber, not logs, for their raw material—appeared in urban centers. Furniture manufacturing, sash and door production, and a variety of other secondary processing industries grew up in Boston, Baltimore, New York, Philadelphia, Pittsburgh, Cincinnati, Louisville, and Charleston.[20]

Railroads, powered by steam and fueled by wood, were also putting in an appearance, but their main impact lay in the future. For the moment, riverboats were more important and made greater inroads into the forest. The high-pressure steam engines of western riverboats burned vast quantities of firewood. Steamboats required as many as 529 cords for the passage from Louisville to New Orleans; they seemed always in the market for wood for their boilers. Many itinerant "woodhawks" labored along the Ohio, Mississippi, and Missouri rivers to provide it. They received from $1.25 to $6.00 for each cord sold, maintaining themselves by cutting trees that they seldom owned.

These woodcutters were the subjects of frequent comment in the travel narratives of the period. A British observer in 1833 described them as outcasts who had "fled for crimes, to a region where the arm of the law cannot reach them" or else were "men of broken characters, hopes, and fortunes who fly not from justice, but contempt." However, not everyone who provided fuel for steamboats was a so-called woodhawk. Many respectable small farmers along major western rivers found that cutting and selling firewood provided a valuable opportunity to augment their incomes, just as many colonial farmers had found profits in the sale of potash and other by-products of land clearing.[21]

Wood played an essential role in other phases of the nation's transportation system too. Ever since the colonial era, marshy lands had been made passable by crude corduroy roads, which provided a rough and bumpy surface upon which frontier commerce could move, however slowly. One frontier resident recalled the road building that his father had engaged in to make their farm accessible:

[Father] crosswayed the lowest spots and across the black ash swales. He cut logs twelve feet long and laid them side by side across the center of the road. Some of the logs, that he put into the road on the lowest ground, were more than a foot through; of course smaller poles answered where the ground was higher. We called this our corduroy road. . . . When it was still I could hear a cart or wagon, coming or going, rattling and pounding over the logs for nearly a mile. But it was so much better than water and mud that we thought it quite passable.

Sometimes logs were split or dirt was put on top of them to smooth the surface a bit, but these were only limited improvements. Countless western travelers bemoaned the "shaking and drubbing" they received from what one of their number despairingly referred to as "the eternal cordiroy." Such roads at least allowed traffic to get through—and in a region where, as Timothy Flint put it, "few of the roads are much wrought or kept in good repair," this was no small factor.

Plank roads were less bumpy than corduroy. Techniques for building roads surfaced with rough-sawn lumber apparently were first developed in Russia and then, in 1834, brought to Canada. Their use quickly spread to the United States, for they seemed to promise better land transportation than anything then available. In 1840 the National Road across Indiana was leased to private interests that converted it to a plank toll road. Chicago, because of its marshy location, became a center of plank roads in the late 1840s. In Alabama twenty-four separate plank road companies won charters between 1848 and 1850 alone. Plank roads were also built elsewhere. Unfortunately, the warping and fracturing of the boards used in them necessitated frequent maintenance, and plank roads almost invariably proved poor investments for their builders. Indeed, neither these enterprises nor the more primitive—and less expensive—corduroy roads were adequate for the nation's needs.

But timber did make possible gradual improvement in transport. In the 1830s and 1840s, travel in America was made easier by the development of stronger wooden bridges. High labor costs and a lack of technical skills restricted the development of stone and steel bridges in the United States, but intricately designed trussed timber bridges permitted the spanning of most streams, rivers, and chasms.[22]

Shipbuilding continued to be one of the most important and wood-intensive industries of America. Just as in colonial times, its success from 1783 to the 1850s was based on an abundance of raw materials. The peace of 1783 encouraged Americans to expand old shipbuilding yards and open new ones; they were quick to respond. Although labor costs were generally higher than in European yards, the quality, availability, and moderate cost of ship timbers enabled American shipwrights to launch vessels that were less expensive, more sturdily built, and longer-lived than most of those from abroad.

Shipbuilding flourished along the coast of Maine and down the Atlantic shore to the Virginia Capes, encouraged by the ready availability of oak for keels and ribs and straight, smooth pine for decks and masts. Shortly after 1783 there were ten shipbuilders at Bath on the Kennebec River, and by 1813 flourishing yards had appeared on the Penobscot. Initially, Maine's yards produced small schooners, brigs, and barks; but by 1825 they were turning out larger, full-rigged ships. In 1840 the tonnage coming from the state's yards reached 52,000; in 1845 it was 110,000 tons; and a decade later it reached 215,000 tons. Theodore Winthrop observed in the early nineteenth century that the state

has two classes of warriors among its sons—fighters of forests and fighters of sea. Braves must join one or the other army. The two are close allies. Only by the aid of the woodmen can the watermen build their engines of victory. The seamen in return purvey the needful luxuries for the lumber camps. Foresters float down timber that seamen may build ships and go to the saccharine islands of the South for molasses: for without molasses no lumberman could be happy in the unsweetened wilderness. Pork lubricates his joints; molasses gives tenacity to his muscles.

Maine was not alone in turning to the sea. New York, which by 1830 had fourteen yards, also was a significant center for shipbuilding, as were Boston and Philadelphia. Although the South was an important source for live-oak timbers and naval stores, and ships were turned out at Baltimore, Norfolk, and Charleston, the region lagged behind the North in developing this important industry.

The demand placed on American forests to supply maritime building materials increased between 1830 and 1860. The tonnage of the ruggedly built American whaling fleet rose from some 40,000 tons in 1830 to nearly 200,000 in 1858. Yankee whalers circled the globe in short-rigged barks of American live oak, moving into the earth's most dangerous seas. In this year the overall tonnage of American vessels increased fivefold, a level not surpassed until the twentieth century. This was the great age of sail in America, a period that witnessed a trebling in the size of wooden ships, with numerous vessels of over a thousand tons launched. From 1831 to 1858, 4,338 vessels of this size joined the nation's merchant fleet. They carried grain during the Irish famine, transported cargoes of tea from Canton and Shanghai, served the burgeoning cotton trade of the South, and rushed Forty-niners to California. To supply the needed vessels, shipyards increased in size, expanding in some instances to the point where they could build up to six full-rigged vessels at one time. By the 1850s Americans had the largest merchant fleet in the world.[23]

The growth of America's maritime fleet sprang from the growth of the nation's commerce. Down to the middle of the nineteenth century, most American cities were mercantile rather than industrial centers; trade and related activities stood at the heart of the economic order. John Jacob Astor was the most spectacularly successful participant. He arrived in the United States as a poor immigrant lad in 1780, but by the time of his death in 1848 he was the richest man in the country, having accumulated a fortune of more than twenty million dollars through the fur trade and foreign commerce—a commerce carried out in a host of wooden ships.

Not just wealthy merchants like Astor took part in international trade. So did many others, especially young men from New England and New York. As one maritime historian has noted, more of the youth of New England had visited the coast of China at mid-century than had seen Cincinnati or St. Louis; many of those who had not been to the Orient dreamed of going; and houses in Salem, Boston, and other ports of the region were filled with items brought back from Canton and Hong Kong. The old China trade was not only the most romantic but at times the most lucrative sector of the commercial-mercantile order. And nothing spoke of the China trade so clearly as clipper ships, those fast, graceful vessels developed to meet its needs.[24]

American designers had gradually grown more proficient until finally, to satisfy a real or imagined need for more speed, they sacrificed carrying capacity to swiftness to produce the clipper. The short-lived clipper era was born with the launching at New York in 1845 of *Rainbow*, a swift ship of 752 tons built for the China trade. Her lofty masts and long, graceful spars enabled her to carry enough canvas to reach speeds of fourteen to eighteen knots. *Rainbow* became a model for other vessels involved in this trade as well as that with California and still later, Australia.

Most of the great clippers were launched from shipyards on Boston Harbor or the East River in New York. From a yard in East Boston, Donald McKay in 1851 launched *Flying Cloud*, a clipper that claimed two of the three eighty-nine-day runs from New York to San Francisco. As historian Samuel Eliot Morison observed, "for perfection and beauty of design, weatherliness and consistent speed under every condition," *Flying Cloud* was unsurpassed. "She was the fastest vessel on long voyages that ever sailed under the American flag." But there were a host of other fine clippers, too; collectively they came to dominate major commercial routes, including the lucrative tea trade between China and London.[25]

Americans not only developed new ship designs in the first half of the nineteenth century, they also created new techniques in wood construction that enabled them to solve complex structural problems ashore. They erected impressive three-story wooden buildings that could carry the massive weight of textile equipment, and the long trussed wooden bridges of this period had no peers. But there are perhaps no better compliments to the resourceful talents of American builders than the graceful wood-trussed roofs that covered the spacious vaults of churches and railroad stations in the three decades before the Civil War. American builders were accomplishing with wood what Europeans did with masonry and iron.

The construction of simpler buildings also changed during the nineteenth century. In the colonial and revolutionary periods, Americans, following the tradition of late medieval Europe, had used a heavy, braced timber-frame construction for most of their permanent buildings. Heavy timber frames were more than adequate for the stresses and loads imposed upon the floors and roof of the average house, barn, or shop; but the large timbers were awkward to work with, and mortising these frames required much skilled labor, reducing the speed with which even small buildings could be erected. Americans needed a cheaper, more labor-efficient method of building.

The need was soon met. In 1833 builders employed a new system of construction in erecting a church in Chicago. Instead of building the walls and roof with a heavy timber frame, they used lighter milled lumber to form a skeletal frame of sills, joists, studs, and rafters. The walls of this "balloon frame" structure—so called because critics considered it as insubstantial as a balloon—were reinforced with diagonal members to confront wind loads and were then covered with sheathing and clapboard siding.

Balloon-frame construction was a radical departure from earlier practices. The utility of this design, the rapidity with which it could be erected, and the consequent reduction in building costs led to its immediate acceptance across the nation. It answered a need for an inexpensive form of building that could assume a variety of shapes, using materials that were easily transportable and that could be erected by men possessing limited skill as carpenters. With the use of milled lumber rather than heavy timber beams, transportation costs for housing materials fell, making the design ideal for the treeless prairies west of the Mississippi River. Many a prairie family poignantly remembered the day it moved from its crude sod house into its new frame dwelling. The balloon frame quickly became the principal form of construction for private dwellings and small buildings, a position it has maintained to the present. Critics soon learned that it could withstand high winds, and the pejorative "balloon" dropped from common use.[26]

The frame house could not have gained popularity so rapidly without the development of inexpensive nails. When nails were hand wrought, and usually imported, they were expensive. Their utility encouraged American artisans to seek less expensive methods of producing them. By the beginning of the nineteenth century, twenty-three American patents had been granted for nail-making machines. One machine from this period was reportedly capable of producing two hundred thousand nails a day. By 1842 increased efficiency in production had lowered the cost of nails from twenty-five to three cents a pound. A decline in the expense of constructing wooden structures naturally followed. The demand for nails rose so quickly that by 1849 they had become the nation's leading use of iron.

Building with wood was also aided by the development of mechanical planers. Once a log had been sawn, the rough surfaces of the lumber had to be smoothed to make it fit for many uses. Before the advent of planing mills, carpenters and joiners laboriously handplaned flooring, paneling, molding, and other lumber used for finishing. The development of planing machinery in the first half of the nineteenth century sharply reduced this labor, again making it less costly to build with wood.[27]

In the three-quarters of a century after the Declaration of Independence, the continuing process of western settlement steadily forced Americans to confront the forests that covered much of their nation. Technological advances helped them do so successfully. More sophisticated saws and sawmills enabled them to transform logs into lumber with ever greater efficiency. Per capita purchases of lumber rose by more than 400 percent from 1799 to 1859. This often led to waste, for Americans made the same economic trade-off of substituting an abundant timber resource for scarce labor and capital as had their colonial forebears. But as their woodworking skills increased, Americans built wooden bridges, ships, and houses that had no equals. The new nation had confronted its forests and in the process developed a culture that was more wood dependent than any other advanced society. The period was indeed America's wooden age.

Chapter 5

As Americans developed new skills in working wood and new uses for lumber in almost every facet of their lives, commercial demands upon the country's forests increased. In New England, and especially in the southwestern section of Maine, stood some of the largest and most accessible stands of white pine—a resource waiting to be harvested. More and more, Maine's residents turned to doing so. By 1820 Maine had assumed leadership in the young nation's lumber industry. As more pines were felled for markets beyond Maine's borders, its timber industry became the backbone of an entire region's economy.

Geography suggested that much of the future for Maine's settlers lay within the towering forests around them. Such proved to be the case. Because a substantial part of Maine was forestland unsuitable for agriculture, timber became a major incentive for settlement. Initially, most of the harvest of the Maine woods went to satisfy local needs; but production from the great virgin stands easily met these and created a surplus that cried out for greater markets. Blessed by proximity to the growing urban centers of eastern America, Maine's loggers had an opportunity to develop a flourishing export industry. With some of Maine's ports only 225 miles from Boston, Massachusetts early became a major outlet for its white pine. Other markets developed along the Atlantic seaboard. The ease of transportation by water and the relatively short distances involved ensured that Maine's lumber was a convenient and inexpensive building material in all of them.[1]

Unlike Massachusetts, Maine was penetrated by broad, swift rivers flowing to the coast from deep within the interior. These rivers not only provided power for sawmills but also were arteries of inexpensive transportation to carry logs to the mills and the products of the mills to the sea en route to market. In addition, Maine was aided in the development of its forest industry by major forest fires that destroyed large stands in New Hampshire in 1761 and 1762. New

Hampshire residents who had maintained themselves as woodsmen soon moved to Maine, stimulating lumbering there.

Before an agricultural base could develop in Maine, forestlands had to be cleared for cultivation. The "lumberers" to whom this task fell in the 1790s and after were frequently viewed by contemporaries as among the most dissolute, profane, unreliable, and indolent members of society. Timothy Dwight, president of Yale College from 1795 to 1817, was one such critic. He observed that it was to the "foresters" that the task of preparing the wilderness for settlement had been given: "the business of these persons is no other than to cut down trees, build log houses, lay open forest grounds to cultivation and prepare the way for those who come after them." Although woodsmen provided a valuable and necessary service,

These men cannot live in regular society. They are too idle, too talkative, too passionate, too prodigal, and too shiftless to acquire either property or character. They are impatient of the restraints of law, religion, and morality; grumble about the taxes by which rulers, ministers, and schoolmasters are supported; and complain incessantly, as well as bitterly, of the extortions of mechanics, farmers, merchants, and physicians to who they are always indebted.

By the 1790s, many men of this sort could be found in the Maine woods; with the decline of the fur trade and fishing, the forests provided the next opportunity to be seized by capital-poor settlers.

Traveling through Maine in 1807 and 1808, Edward Augustus Kendall observed the men who participated in small-scale logging. According to Kendall, "wood in all its forms, is marketable, and to the settlers is therefore equivalent to furs or fish; and the settlers have consequently degenerated, not into hunters or fishermen, but into *lumberers.*" These men lived "upon the bounty of nature" and consequently always lived in poverty. Kendall's critique was unrestrained. The lumberer wandered through the forest "making spoil in his turn of the wealth of nature. Unlike the husband-man, whose toil is always for the future." In words that could have been uttered by some modern environmentalists, Kendall remarked that "the lumberer toils only for the moment that is passing, and provides for that moment only by preying on the future one: what nature has planted he enjoys, but he plants nothing for himself." Such men were averse neither to felling trees that belonged to others nor to appropriating others' logs from the rivers.

Salvation from such a life, Timothy Dwight predicted, would come through the eventual decline of lumbering and growth of farming. When this occurred, industry would succeed "to sloth, regularity to dissoluteness, thrift to poverty, and comfort and reputation to suffering and shame." Nevertheless, Dwight recognized that the efforts of the lumberers produced the cleared ground and lumber necessary for settlement and future growth.[2]

Maine was the northeastern frontier of Massachusetts until 1820, and disposing of the lands the white pines grew on was the responsibility of the latter. From the 1780s until Maine acquired statehood in 1820, timberlands were granted to the veterans of the Revolution and the War of 1812, to colleges and academies, and to others. Many speculated in Maine's forestlands. Land titles became confused in the south and along the coast to the Kennebec River, the areas then being tapped. As early as the 1780s, unscrupulous lumbermen were cutting timber from public lands, and by 1784 the Massachusetts legislature had responded by levying a fine of one hundred dollars on those found guilty of cutting there.

Maine's lumbermen exploited the tree-covered river drainages. Working progressively north and east, they felled stands along the Saco, Presumscott, Androscoggin, Kennebec, Penobscot, Union, and Narraguagus. Lumber from these was sold not only in the growing metropolitan areas of Boston and New York but also in markets abroad. By 1800, François André Michaux noted, Maine was exporting three-quarters of the pine shipped from the United States. As foreign shipments became important, the ports of Bath, Portland, and Bangor rose to prominence, and shipbuilding as well as lumbering prospered.

Bangor in particular played a key role in the evolution of Maine's forest industries. The port was on the west bank of the Penobscot River well inland from the coast. A tidal rise of seventeen feet enabled seagoing vessels to reach the city to take on the products of its mills for transport to the markets of the world. Bangor was settled in 1769 and within three years had the first of its many sawmills. Briefly occupied by the British in 1814, it prospered throughout the century as the center for the state's forest enterprises. In 1816, the first year for which there is statistical information, Bangor milled some one million board feet of timber; by 1832, mills along the Penobscot River at Bangor and nearby Orono and Old Town were producing almost thirty million feet annually. In 1833 the *Bangor Republican* noted the city's preeminence with justifiable pride: "Maine furnishes about three-quarters of all the white pine exported from the United States, and the Penobscot River is the centre of this trade, and hereafter must furnish the main supply in the timber market." Not unexpectedly, Bangor was often a center for speculation in timberlands. In 1834 and 1835 the city was filled with investors, speculators, timber cruisers, and gamblers who gathered there to pay as much as ten dollars an acre for timberland that a decade earlier had sold for as little as six cents an acre.[3]

Henry David Thoreau noted in 1837 that there were more than 250 saws operating in mills upstream from Bangor. Large quantities of lumber were still being produced on the Androscoggin and Kennebec, and production had also risen "down east" along the coast on the Machias and St. Croix rivers and inland on the St. John, but the Penobscot was the center of Maine's timber industry. Ever suspicious of the price of progress, Thoreau commented that the mission of men on the Penobscot "seems to be, like so many busy demons, to drive the forest all out of the country, from every solitary beaver swamp and mountain-side, as soon as possible."

In 1846 Thoreau again recorded his impressions of Bangor. It was, he said, "the principal lumber depot on this continent, with a population of twelve thousand, like a star on the edge of night, still hewing at the forest of which it is built, already overflowing with the luxuries and refinements of Europe and sending its vessels to Spain, to England, and to the West-Indies for its groceries—and yet only a few axe men have gone 'up river' into the howling wilderness which feeds it." In the years that followed, larger numbers penetrated Bangor's hinterlands, and production continued to rise. In 1850 its mills sawed more than two hundred million board feet of lumber.[4]

It was white pine that beckoned lumbermen into the "howling wilderness" of Maine. The white pine was widely distributed in North America from west of the Great Lakes to the Atlantic coast and southward from central Canada to northern Illinois, eastern Ohio, and Pennsylvania. A broad extension of this northern forest plunged south along the Appalachian Mountains to Georgia. It has been estimated that the great primeval stand of white pine once contained more than one hundred billion board feet of commercial timber. White pines reached reported heights of over 150 feet, providing the most majestic specimens among the eastern conifers. A mature white pine has remarkable reproductive capacity; it can distribute tens of thousands of seeds when its cones open in the fall. The species can, as a result, compete successfully with other growth in abandoned fields or partially timbered areas, but its intolerance to shade leads it gradually to give way in many areas to a mixed climax forest of hemlock and deciduous trees. Because of this, stands of white pine were neither solid nor omnipresent in Maine or elsewhere in its range.[5]

Michaux indicated that the wood of white pines "is employed in greater quantities and for more diverse uses than that of any other American pine." He further commented that "throughout the Northern States, except in the larger capitals, seven-tenths of the houses are of wood, of which three quarters estimated at about 500,000 are almost wholly of White Pine: even the suburbs of the cities are built of wood. The principal beams of the churches and the other large edifices are of White Pine." To Michaux and other nineteenth-century Europeans, used as they were to masonry construction, this seemed odd indeed.

The wood of white pines is light, strong, and durable, and lumber from old growth is relatively free of knots. With its soft, smooth-flowing grain, it can be readily cut and carved. Long trunks that tapered gradually from base to crown provided excellent spars for ships. With masts, yards, and bowsprits of New England pine, Yankee whalers plowed the seas of the world in pursuit of the great whales. The bows of American and English vessels were often graced by elegant figureheads carved from this versatile wood. Boxes, barrels, clapboards, shingles, and paneling were made from it, as were children's toys, cradles, piano keys, butter paddles, matchsticks, sleighs, windmills, and furniture. It was the preferred wood for millwork. When bored out, it even served on occasion as a durable water pipe. The picturesque covered bridges of the period were constructed partially, and often wholly, from it. Timber from this tree formed the long bridges over the Schuylkill River at Philadelphia and the Delaware River at Trenton. The lamp that signaled Paul Revere that the British were coming hung from a belfry made of white pine. In a cabin of white pine logs felled by his own hands near Walden Pond, Thoreau began to articulate his thoughts on man's relation to nature, becoming in the process "more the friend than the foe of the pine." The buoyancy of white pine enabled logs to be floated to mill and market on the streams, lakes, and rivers of America. For more than two and a half centuries, white pine was the premier timber tree in America.

Aggressive expansion northward in search of untouched white pine stands led woodsmen to the Aroostook Valley along the ill-defined border between Maine and New Brunswick. This touched off friction that for a time seemed likely to precipitate a major conflict between the United States and Britain. Although there were heated debates and minor skirmishes between timbermen from Maine and New Brunswick in early 1839, ten thousand of Maine's militia, the presence nearby of British and American regulars, and the wise negotiations of General Winfield Scott prevented this border issue from exploding into military action. The formal settlement of the "Aroostook War" came with the Webster-Ashburton Treaty of 1842, which delineated the international boundary and specified the American lumbermen's privileges on the St. John River. Thoreau trenchantly remarked that "the white pine tree was at the bottom or further end of all this." The only real Aroostook or Penobscot war, he wrote, was the "war against the pines."

The operations that led to this border conflict yielded not sawn lumber, but what was known as "ton timber"—long squared pine timbers hewn by hand in the woods and then transported out of the woods and across the Atlantic to British ports, where they underwent further manufacturing. It was a high-value commerce, much depended upon by British maritime interests. In the early nineteenth century, the only other significant forest product being shipped from the area was cedar shingles.[6] Elsewhere in Maine the standard logging and milling operations that were the hallmark of the period developed and were pursued. It is these activities that most of the literature of the period (and since) discusses.

Before logging of this more standard sort could begin, stands of timber had to be located, winter quarters erected and provisioned, and crews hired. The land to be logged was selected either by the lumberman himself or by a timber cruiser who went into the virgin forest seeking stands that could be felled in the winter and floated to sawmills on the spring flood. Once the land was selected, it had to be purchased or the right to cut the trees upon it obtained. Then the building of facilities could commence.

Ground had to be cleared of debris and underbrush and crudely leveled before a building could be erected to shelter the crew. The walls of these "camps," as the buildings were known, were of interlocking logs with the spaces between them caulked with moss. Spruce logs were preferred because they were light, straight, and relatively free of sap. The roof was of split shingles, often covered with boughs of fir, spruce, or hemlock to provide insulation. The floor was of compacted earth.

Within these crude buildings, the cook ruled supreme over the cooking and eating areas. His authority was such that should he wish it (and he often did), he could forbid talking during meals. Food was ample but varied little, consisting of whatever creative variations the cook could make of such staples as beans, bread, and pork.

Arranged along one wall of the cabin were the beds. Boughs of hemlock, cedar, or fir placed on crude wooden bunks provided what comfort the workers got. In some camps one large and frequently patched blanket covered the entire sleeping area. Exhausted by their labors, few seem to have found such spartan arrangements unacceptable.

At the foot of the bed was the deacon's seat, a long bench composed of a smooth-hewn plank twelve to fourteen inches wide and eighteen to twenty inches off the ground. Here the crew spent their evenings, sitting before the fire exchanging stories, playing cards, mending clothes, or dreaming of home and perhaps family. Since the bunkhouse was imperfectly warmed by a large open firepit, constant care was required to see that the fire was maintained safely. Fires were a persistent danger, and many a camp was set ablaze by an errant spark.

The health of the livestock required careful attention, for they were essential to logging operations. From the beginning, oxen were the preferred draft animals. Although slower than horses, they were stronger and more reliable when pulling heavy loads. They also were better foragers and could survive on meadow grasses harvested and dried in the fall before logging operations began; horses required oats, often difficult to obtain in remote areas. In 1792 Jeremy Belknap wrote that a large breed of "yellow" cattle had been sent from Denmark to New Hampshire by John Mason in 1633 and had been raised there so long as "getting lumber was the chief employment of the people." Maine's oxen apparently traced both to this stock and to later importations.

The oxen were stabled in a low, roofed log structure known as the hovel; unlike the crew's quarters, the hovel had a floor of smooth timbers, for it was important that the oxen's hooves dry out after a day's hauling. Next to the ox hovel was a small shed for fodder. John S. Springer, an early Maine lumberman and author of a vivid contemporary account of logging in the north woods, recorded that "no little pains are bestowed upon the conveniences designed for the team. With the exception of sporting horses, never have I witnessed more untiring devotion to any creature than is bestowed upon the ox when under the care of a good teamster." The teamster was important, but, with the possible exception of the cook, no one had longer hours. He had to feed and harness his teams before sunrise and then, after an arduous day skidding tons of logs, had to groom and care for his animals before he could attend to his own needs.

Once established, the logger's camp became part of the forest setting. Thoreau, who had seen many such habitations during his trips into the north woods of Maine, commented that the "logger's camp is as completely in the woods as a fungus at the foot of a pine in a swamp; no outlook but to the sky over head; no more clearing than is made by cutting down the trees of which it is built, and those which are necessary for fuel." The logger asked only that a camp "be well sheltered and convenient to his work, and near a spring."[7]

After the camp was set up, workers began "swamping" out logging roads from the pine stands to the yards, or landings, at streamside where the logs would be held until the spring thaw. Trees had to be cut from the path, underbrush cleared, and inclines prepared that could be safely managed by oxen pulling log-laden sleds.

There was a definite hierarchy in a logging camp based upon individuals' assigned tasks. Springer, who had been a member of such crews, outlined their social structure.

First . . . comes the "boss," or the principal in charge. Then the choppers, meaning those who select, fell, and cut the logs, one of whom is a master chopper. Next the swampers, who cut and clear the roads through the forest to the fallen trees, one of whom is a master swamper. Then comes the barker and loader, the man who hews off the bark from that part of the log which is to drag on the snow, and assists the team in loading. Then we have the captain of the goad, or teamster, and finally the cook, whose duty is too generally known to require any particular description.

Choppers used four- to seven-pound felling axes rather than saws to down trees in the decades before the Civil War. A skilled chopper could fell a tree with remarkable accuracy. To display their expertise, fallers would sometimes stand a stake some distance from a tree and then fell the tree so that it drove the stake into the ground as it landed. Unfortunately, not all choppers had this skill; and when a tree did not fall as expected, serious accidents could occur. It was also important that a towering pine be felled in a preselected position because its trunk would shatter if it fell across rocks or other logs and because it could be moved only with great difficulty, if at all, from some locations.

Once the tree was on the forest floor, branches had to be removed and part of the bark peeled off. The front end was then loaded on a crude sled for skidding to a site where it could be cut into logs fourteen to thirty feet long. These logs were next moved on sleighs to streamside over the swamped-out "roads," which were continually watered so that a thick layer of ice would build up to reduce friction, enabling the oxen to pull the heavy sleds. With the coming of the spring thaw, the streamside piles of logs were rolled into the water to commence the drive downstream to waiting sawmills.

Pines that grew along the banks of streams, rivers, and lakes were the first cut. Once these were gone, loggers moved progressively away from the waterways, always seeking the tallest and soundest trees. A nineteenth-century observer acknowledged the zeal with which the best trees were sought out. "Not all trees were worthy of the axe. A Maine forest after a lumber campaign is like France after a coup d'etat; the bourgeoisie are prosperous as ever, but the great men are all gone." After the most easily reached trees were cut, loggers sought to fell the isolated pockets of great pines that stood in more difficult locations. Springer observed that it would be a match for "Dame Nature" to locate a handsome Pine-tree beyond the grasp of the logmen. Where the Eastern hunter pursues the mountain goat, the logger would pursue the stately Pine. We have seen them in the deep ravine, or on the abrupt hilltop, and far up the rugged mountain side, or peering down from some lofty cliff upon the insignificant animal at its base who it contemplating its sacrifice; a few minutes, and the crash of its giddy plunge is heard "and wells along the echoing crag," causing the earth to tremble under the stroke of its massive trunk; and if it does not break in pieces, as is sometimes the case, in falling, it will in time find its way to the slip of the sawmill.

Getting such trees off the steep side of a mountain was a formidable task, and a variety of expedients were developed to move them where they could be skidded to a yard.[8]

When the spring thaw made it impossible to haul logs, the loggers stopped work in the woods and awaited the breakup of the ice on the river and streams. As the waters began to flow, preparations were made to drive the winter's labors to the sawmills. It was a time of joy, for woodsmen knew they would soon be with their families and friends. Their songs captured the excitement of their return to civilization.

> When winter's snows are melted
> And the icebound streams are free,
> We'll run our logs to market,
> Then hasten our friends to see,
> How kindly true hearts welcome us,
> Our wives and children too,
> We will spend with these the summer,
> And once more a lumbering go.

Not everyone participated in the drives, for they required fewer men than did felling trees. All watched with interest, however, in part because the men normally were not paid until the drives were in.

As soon as the spring breakup commenced, the men set to work clearing the landings of logs. It was an exacting and perilous task, for a logger was never sure when a whole pile might give way and crush him as the logs rolled toward the stream. But excitement was mixed with danger; once the logs were in the water the long-awaited drive was under way. Thoreau dramatically described the moment when the lumberman

stands on the bank, and whistles for Rain and Thaw, ready to wring the perspiration out of his shirt to swell the tide, till suddenly, with a whoop and halloo from him, shutting his eyes as if to bid farewell to the existing state of things, a fair proportion of his winter's work goes scrambling down the country, followed by his faithful dogs, Thaw, and Rain, and Freshet, and Wind, the whole pack in full cry, toward the Orono Mills.

From a hundred tributaries, logs were soon converging to form the main drives down the Penobscot, the Kennebec, and other major rivers.

The image of the drivers daringly riding logs is firmly fixed in the public imagination, but in fact most of their work was done from batteaux, specially designed flat-bottomed boats. As boatmen, log drivers were unsurpassed. When a log caught in the brush or on a rock, the logger would come close in his batteau and attempt to push it off with his pike. If that failed, he had to enter the icy water to free it. A supply raft, called a wanigan, floated along somewhere behind the drive, catching up each night to provide hot food and other essentials.[9]

On watercourses where the flow was small, splash or holding dams were frequently built to retain every gift of melting snow and passing shower. Once the sides of the stream had been cleared of brush and obstacles and sufficient water had been stored, the dam was opened. In an avalanche of water, logs were flushed downstream.[10]

In some operations logs were stored on the surface of frozen lakes. Booms of logs chained together surrounded the log piles so that when the thaw came they were held in one mass. If there was no current in the lake, the raft of logs was warped along with capstan and windlass. A rowboat carried forward an anchor attached to the raft and lowered it into the water. As the anchor was hauled in, the raft was maneuvered inch by inch toward its destination. This work was usually done at night when the wind had died down. It was often said that the men of these rafts could walk the capstan in their sleep. In calm weather this system was useful, but a sudden storm could snap the boom and scatter the logs, and working a raft against the wind was impossible. With the advent of steam, the exhausting and tedious work of warping a raft of logs was taken over by steamboats. They caught on quickly: by 1849 a raft covering twenty-one acres had been towed by a steamboat in Maine.[11]

Once the logs cut by various crews floated out of smaller tributaries into the major rivers, they mixed with logs being driven by other camps. With more than one camp driving the same river, confusion and conflict often resulted. Beginning in the 1820s, lumbermen formed voluntary associations to supervise this critical operation. Master drivers were selected to oversee the downstream passage and to make the numerous daily decisions that increased or lessened the profit of a winter's labor in the woods. By the 1840s participation in these drives had become mandatory on many streams.

To prevent theft and to avoid confusion over the ownership of logs mixed together in a drive, Maine's loggers introduced a system of chopping brands into logs. These marks were as important to lumbermen as the brands burned into the hides of cattle were to the owners of herds driven along western trails. As more and more brands appeared, the logger's ingenuity in inventing new designs was challenged—and so was his skill with an ax. Eventually the ax was replaced in branding, and marks were stamped into the ends of logs with a special hammer; this step led to even more imaginative combinations of letters, numerals, and symbols.

The system of branding had been devised to bring order to the sorting of the thousands of logs that floated to the mills each spring, but the system was occasionally thwarted by unscrupulous men who altered brands and claimed others' logs. If they lacked the talent or means to alter a brand, they could pull the log ashore and cut it into nontraceable shingles or simply cut off a few inches of the branded end and restamp it with their own mark. Log rustling was to remain a problem as the industry migrated westward. Eternal vigilance was the price of profit.[12]

As more and more logs were floated down the major rivers each spring, log-jams became more frequent. Log-driving associations removed many obstructions, but jams still occurred. Jams could bring a drive to a halt and prevent an entire winter's cut from reaching the mills that year. A jam on the Kennebec River in 1854 reportedly covered forty to fifty acres with some twenty-five thousand logs stacked from two to ten feet deep. To attempt to break such a jam was to risk one's life; loggers had to go out on the jam itself to pry loose the logs that held it together. When human strength applied to pikes and cant hooks failed to dislodge a jam, logs were chopped loose or blasted apart with gunpowder. Days and even weeks could be lost in attempts to break a large jam.

To make the hazardous task of freeing a jam somewhat safer, a logger might be lowered onto the logs by rope from a cliff or other high place. When the logs seemed on the verge of breaking loose, his companions would quickly pull him up so he would not be caught. Logs a foot thick snapped like matchsticks when a jam came loose.

In spite of precautions, many lives were lost in river drives and in clearing jams. When death occurred upon a river remote from civilization, a logger's coffin was sometimes constructed from empty flour barrels fetched from the wanigan—that is, if his body was found once the churning mass of logs had passed. A pair of boots hung on a streamside bush or tree marked many a place where a woodsman had met his fate.[13]

When logs arrived at the sawmills, they had to be corralled before they could float past. In the eighteenth century, before too many logs were in the river at one time, boatmen stationed in the river stopped them as they came by. When larger numbers began to come down the rivers, booms were stretched across to capture them; previously booms had been used only for storing logs. As early as 1789, a boom was chartered for the Penobscot; six years later the Kennebec Boom Corporation was established. However, the boom that led to a real revolution, ushering in full-fledged drives and large-scale milling, came considerably later. It was the Penobscot Boom, chartered in 1825.

Conflict was frequent between loggers and nontimber interests who did not want passage on the river blocked by booms, and legislatures were often called upon to regulate the operation of the booms. Other difficulties arose too. Booms sometimes broke, and logs that escaped downriver had to be regathered; even more frequently, disputes erupted over log ownership or boom management.

If the spring thaw arrived late, the number of days when logs could be floated was reduced. Drought and subsequent low water also shortened the period when logs could be collected at a boom. In the decade from 1842 to 1852, the great boom on the Penobscot River operated between 68 and 122 days per year. Beginning operations about the first of May whenever possible, this boom handled anywhere from 3,133 to 5,814 logs a day during the period.

The expense of erecting and maintaining a boom almost two miles long, holding up to six hundred acres of logs piled three feet or more deep and employing 150 to 300 workers, was substantial. The toll levied at the Penobscot Boom in 1825 was twenty cents per thousand board feet; by 1832 it was thirty-eight cents, and by 1854 it had risen to fifty-three cents. Finding the toll costs increasingly difficult to bear, the loggers formed a corporation to operate the boom. This corporation assumed responsibility for maintenance and new construction, paid the taxes, performed its own rafting, and paid a fee of ten cents a thousand to the Penobscot Boom Corporation, which continued to hold title to the property and booming rights. These payments were subsequently reduced, but as long as logs were driven down the river the basic arrangement remained.[14]

The romance of the logger's life in the forest and on the rivers was often told. Authors sought to capture the rough life of the lumber camp and the sense of community among men who shared the dangers of fire, falling trees, subzero temperatures, and swift streams. Viewed as frontiersmen of the forest, they were portrayed as men apart from civilized society. The songs of loggers helped popularize their image as dauntless knights of the woods who lived by a code of sylvan chivalry. "The Loggers' Boast" contained these proud verses:

> Come, all ye sons of freedom throughout
> the State of Maine
> Come, all ye gallant lumbermen, and
> listen to my strain

On the banks of the Penobscot, where
   the rapid waters flow,
O! we'll range the wild woods over
   while a lumbering we go. . . .

When you pass through the dense city,
   and pity all you meet,
To hear their teeth chattering as they
   hurry down the street.
In the red frost-proof flannel we're
   incased from top to toe,
While we range the wild woods over,
   and a lumbering we go.

You may boast of your gay parties,
   your pleasures and your plays,
And pity us poor lumbermen while
   dashing in your sleighs;
We want no better pastime than to
   chase the buck and doe
While we range the wild woods over
   and a lumbering we go. . . .[15]

Clearly, loggers contributed to the growing myth of their own profession—but
their camaraderie was not a myth.

John Greenleaf Whittier was no logger, but his brother was an itinerant mis-
sionary to woodsmen "down east" in Maine. The Quaker Poet celebrated their
annual travail in his poem "The Lumbermen" and thus contributed to the im-
agery of their life in the woods.

Comrades! round our woodland quarters
   Sad-voiced autumn grieves;
Thickly down these swelling waters
   Fall his fallen leaves
Through the tall and naked timber
   Column-like and old,
Gleam the sunsets of November
   With their skies of gold.

O'er us, to the South-land heading,
   Screams the gray wild goose;
On the night-frost sounds the treading
   Of the stately moose.

Fast the streams with ice are closing,
 Colder grows the sky,
Soon, on lake and river frozen,
 Shall our log-piles lie.

When, with sounds of smother'd thunder,
 On some night of rain,
Lake and river break asunder
 Winter's weakened chain
Down the wild March-flood shall bear them
 To the saw-mill's wheel,
Or, where Steam, the slave, shall tear them
 With his teeth of steel. . . .

Such a romantic view of the logger's season in the woods ignored the agony of long, hard days of labor performed in biting cold, of poor accommodations, and of long months of isolation. Nevertheless, the romantic myth of lumberjack was in the making, although in Maine in the nineteenth century the term lumberjack was not used. Indeed, the term was seldom used by loggers in other regions either, but nonwoodsmen used it to refer to the larger-than-life stereotype of woods workers. The real life of the logger was a harsh departure from the romantic popular image of the lumberjack. With the possible exception of whaling, there was no more hazardous profession that could attract a son of the New England soil.

The realities of financing, transportation, and marketing in the lumber industry neither lent themselves to romantic, literary treatment nor captured the attention of the general public. Yet they are critically important in assessing the nation's, and Maine's, interaction with its forests. Until the 1830s, the lumber industry in Maine was financed locally and generally with limited funds. From colonial times ambitious individuals had marshaled their resources, kept close watch on their operating expenses, and gone out to cut the pines or build sawmills, optimistically believing that their fortunes lay with the tall trees that rose around them. Less fortunate souls turned to logging simply because they had been unable to make a living by farming. But as the lumber industry grew and began to mature, greater capital investment in mills and equipment was needed. Consequently, in the late 1830s lumbermen increasingly turned to small companies and partnerships to increase their capital. While few records from the early decades of the nineteenth century reveal much about the financing of Maine's pioneer lumber industry, it seems that the limited external capital backing this endeavor came primarily from Massachusetts. Significant corporate financing for the industry did not become common until after the Civil War.

Once logs had been turned into lumber, inexpensive transportation was needed to get it to market. Until the development of the railroads, the least expensive method of shipping lumber was in rafts. The success of lumber rafts in carrying bulky mill products encouraged entrepreneurs on the Kennebec to dream of sailing large timber and lumber rafts shaped like ships' hulls across the Atlantic Ocean to Europe. Beginning in 1792, three such rafts were constructed in Maine. One failed off the coast of Maine; two successfully crossed the Atlantic only to founder off the coast of England.[16]

In areas where waterways were absent or inadequate, primitive railroads were constructed to carry lumber. A railroad between Bangor and nearby Old Town was chartered in 1832. Cars carried clapboards, shingles, and lath from the mills at Milford, Old Town, and Stillwater to Bangor over wooden rails covered with scrap iron. By 1840 the Whitneyville and Machias Railroad had begun a half-century of operation. Its early locomotives, the *Lion* and the *Tiger*, carried lumber from Whitneyville to Machias Port. Later the railway between Calais and Baring was active in hauling timber products. Logging railroads made it possible to cut hardwood—birch, maple, beech, ash, cherry, and oak— on a larger scale; their lack of buoyancy when green made it difficult to float them to sawmills.[17]

The demand for the products of Maine's forests was strong in the 1840s. Foreign commerce continued to contribute to the state's prosperity. Through the early decades of the nineteenth century, trade with the West Indies experienced many vicissitudes as the United States and Britain sought to define the economic privileges that would exist for each nation in that area. Despite difficulties, Maine's shippers persisted in entering this trade even when told in 1813 not to bring any more lumber to the British West Indies, since the British Empire's own vessels could do that now. Many British merchantmen were in fact carrying cargoes of wood products from New Brunswick and elsewhere, but vessels from Maine continued to sail for the West Indies, returning with holds filled with rum, molasses, and sugar; and Cuba, with its need for sugar boxes, became an important market for Maine's lumber. Other lumber markets also attracted enterprising Maine merchants. Vessels exhausted by years of service were loaded with white pine and sailed to La Plata in South America, where the lumber could be sold and the vessels dismantled for sale as firewood. Cargoes of Maine lumber were carried to other markets in South America, in Europe, and on at least one occasion to Australia.

Closer to home, Maine's lumber coasters sailed almost daily for Boston,

Salem, New Bedford, Portsmouth, Providence, and other eastern cities and through the Straits of Florida to ports as far west on the Gulf of Mexico as New Orleans and Galveston. With their holds full, their decks stacked high, and their scuppers barely above water, the small schooners of this trade could carry up to one hundred thousand board feet of lumber on a single passage. Such ships became familiar sights in the nation's ports.

In addition to Atlantic, Gulf, and foreign demand, the discovery of gold in the millrace of a California sawmill in 1848 added a western market for lumber from the Pine Tree State. Following the discovery at Sutter's mill, thirty-nine ships sailed from Bangor in 1849 carrying five million board feet of lumber to California.[18]

Maine's limited population meant that it could easily satisfy local demands for lumber and thus, unlike many other eastern regions, devote its mills primarily to producing for export. Blessed with large stands of pine and spruce that could be conveniently cut, with swift rivers and connecting lakes to carry logs to mills, with abundant waterpower to run large gangs of saws, and with ports that had good access to the ocean, Maine had the physical prerequisites to develop an efficient and profitable large-scale export industry.

But for all the prosperity and burgeoning activity in Maine during its heyday of white pine lumbering, changes were in the offing. As the nation's population moved westward, new forest areas began to echo with the sound of the lumberman's ax. As they did, Maine's timber production encountered increasing competition from New York, Pennsylvania, the Lake States, and the South. Maine did not cease to harvest the wealth of its woodlands, but its national leadership in the lumber industry was being challenged and would eventually be lost to more westerly states where unexploited tracts of white pine still stood. Although costs of transportation were frequently higher in these regions, the wealth of their forests and their proximity to developing markets enabled them to compete successfully with lumber from Maine.

Moreover, a decline in Maine's virgin stands of white pine was being noticed by the 1840s. In 1861 spruce would pass pine as the primary commercial timber in the state. Yankee loggers who had earlier spurned this tree now began a relentless quest for it. As before, the products of this activity were primarily exported. But though forests were to long remain the backbone of Maine's economy, after the Civil War its markets became more regional. With its industry concentrating more and more upon spruce, timber production actually increased; more timber was felled after 1861 than before. But though the last years of the nineteenth century witnessed new levels of productivity, the heyday of Maine's lumber industry had passed.[19]

Foundations West and South

Chapter 6

The growth and westward march of the nation in the first half of the nineteenth century created demands for forest products that could not be economically met from Maine. The expense of transportation forced settlers and urban areas that were growing inland from the Atlantic coast to develop timber resources closer to hand. Lumbering operations developed in the interior of New York and Pennsylvania. As emerging forest industry in the Lake States contributed both to the needs of settlement and to the economic stability of that region. Meanwhile, the southern states began a more sustained commercial development of their forests. In all these areas, water transportation was critical to the nascent lumber industry.

Commercial logging entered a new phase in the late eighteenth and early nineteenth centuries when lumbermen began to fell pines along the Delaware and the North Branch of the Susquehanna. Boards and timbers from these watersheds went to market in rafts and arks; those on the Delaware often floated all the way to Philadelphia. Rafts from the North Branch helped supply the timber and lumber Baltimore needed. Only in Maine had significant American lumbering previously been undertaken so far from the markets being served.

New York State was blessed with major stands of white pine, especially in and around the Adirondacks and along the upper reaches of the Delaware, Susquehanna, Allegheny, and Genesee rivers. Commercial logging came early to the Adirondack Mountains. The area's many streams, rivers, and lakes provided convenient arteries of transportation. As elsewhere, logs were at first floated downstream in rafts, but organized drives began on the upper Hudson River drainage about 1813, paving the way for large sawmills that subsequently appeared at Glens Falls, Sandy Hill, and Fort Edward. However, the growth of mills in the area was hampered by the difficulties of corralling logs from boats or with temporary booms erected at their destinations. The real flowering of production on the upper Hudson would not take place until a huge permanent boom went into operation near Glens Falls in 1851, eliminating much loss and substantially reducing costs.[1]

As in Maine, when the more accessible stands of pine adjacent to the rivers had been cut, New York's loggers began to fell trees on the steeper slopes and smaller drainages. To get logs from such locations to a river down which they might be floated to a sawmill, splash dams were often used to sluice logs out to larger waterways. Deforestation proceeded so rapidly in the Adirondacks that as early as 1820 Governor De Witt Clinton, concerned to protect watersheds vital to the operation of the Erie Canal, asked the legislature to cease the sale of state lands in the mountains. Sixty-five years later it finally acted, establishing the Adirondack Forest Preserve and bringing nearly all lumbering there to an end.[2]

Not all timber removal was the result of industrial operations. Indeed, until well after 1850 most was not. In New York as in most states, the seasonal and economic harmony between farming and logging encouraged settlers to pursue both. Work in the woods could be performed in the winter when the demands of agriculture were down. The value of land increased once it had been cleared of trees, and selling timber products that came from clearing provided a cash income, enabling settlers to obtain commodities and services.

Small sawmills sprang up in nearly every corner of the state to handle logs produced by these farmer-loggers. In 1825 New York had 4,321 sawmills, almost six times as many as Maine. By 1845 there were 7,406 in the state. Unlike the sawmills of Maine, few of these were commercial mills producing lumber for distant markets; rather, they were small operations satisfying demand in their immediate vicinities. The millowner, like the logger, often augmented his income by farming and not infrequently thought of himself primarily as a farmer rather than a lumberman.[3]

Gradually sawmills appeared that served larger, more distant markets. Such operations required inexpensive transportation to the main centers of population. Rivers supplied it in the era before canals and railroads. At New Madrid, Missouri, in 1815 Timothy Flint saw numerous flatboats en route to New Orleans with pine lumber that had been floated from southwestern New York. Even larger quantities of lumber and associated products made their way down eastern streams, especially the Susquehanna, Delaware, and Hudson.

Most shipments went in lumber rafts. A description of rafting on the upper Hudson appears in Anne Grant's *Memoirs of an American Lady,* first published in 1808.

The settlers . . . set up sawmills on every stream, for the purpose of turning to account the fine timber which they cleared in great quantities off the new lands. The planks they drew in sledges to the side of the great river; and when the season arrived that swelled the stream to its great height, a whole neighborhood assembled and made their joint stock into a large raft, which was floated down the river with a man or two on it, who with long poles, were always ready to steer it clear of those islands or shallows which might impede its course. There is something serenely majestic in the easy progress of those large bodies on the full stream of this copious river. Sometimes one sees a whole family transported on this simple conveyance; the mother calmly spinning, the children sporting about her, and the father fishing at one end and watching its safety at the same time. These rafts were taken down to Albany, and put on board vessels there for conveyance to New York; sometimes, however, it happened that, as they proceeded very slowly, dry weather came on by the time they reached the Flats, and it became impossible to carry them further; in that case they were deposited in great triangular piles opposite our door.

Rafts could be over 100 feet wide and up to 1,500 feet long. They moved to market not only the lumber and timbers of which they were made, but also deckloads of potash, staves, and agricultural commodities. In 1824 one observer counted over 150 rafts passing his home on the Delaware in a single day. So crowded did streams sometimes become that navigation was impaired and it was hard to find mooring space at night.

Some farmer-lumbermen claimed an added advantage for lumber that was rafted, maintaining that exposing boards to water drew sap and resin from the wood and caused it to season better. Mill operators and carpenters took a more jaundiced view, for logs or lumber that had been rafted were usually covered with mud that dulled the blades of their saws and planers.

When hardwoods were cut, arks often carried the timber and lumber. Occasionally pine was shipped in these craft too. Arks were crudely constructed squarish boats ranging from sixty to ninety feet long and sixteen to twenty feet wide. Roughly built hulls some four to five feet deep were built from heavy timbers and planks, cracks on the bottom and sides were caulked, a white oak bow was positioned, and a large sweep was installed. The result was a functional vessel for carrying to market wood that had little buoyancy, as well as other products. With a small shanty erected on the stacked timbers to shelter the six crewmen from the elements, the ark was ready to float downstream.[4]

These craft and much of the cargo they carried were the products of a host of sawmills, nearly all quite small, and of individuals hewing timbers, splitting shingles, and cutting spars in the forested backcountry. By 1850 New York had more sawmills and more capital invested in its lumber industry than any other state. It produced, according to the Census of 1850, over thirteen million dollars worth of timber products—surpassing Pennsylvania, its nearest rival, by more than five million dollars. The figures no doubt understate real production, for materials turned out for on-site or local use often went unreported.

For its part, Pennsylvania had abundant and diverse forests and a lengthy tradition of utilizing the wealth of her woodlands. When the British burned Washington during the War of 1812, white pine and hardwood from Pennsylvania went to help rebuild the nation's capital. Pennsylvania's lumber industry developed first in the forests of the eastern portions of the state, drained by the Delaware, Lehigh, and Schuylkill and the North Branch of the Susquehanna. By 1800 Philadelphia was a prominent center for the lumber trade. Indeed, it even imported mahogany from Honduras for its mills. By the 1840s, Philadelphia had many water-powered sawmills with capacities of from two thousand to five thousand board feet a day.[5]

As in New York, much of the production in Pennsylvania was by farmers operating little water-powered mills as adjuncts to their agricultural undertakings. They logged in the winter, sawed lumber as streamflow allowed, and rafted their cut to market on the spring (and occasionally fall) freshets.

By 1840 it was estimated that in Clearfield County, in the heart of the Allegheny Plateau, there were some four hundred small mills, most of whose cut was rafted down the West Branch of the Susquehanna River for sale. The local newspaper editor, like many Americans convinced that agriculture was the source of lasting prosperity, lamented that so much time was devoted to lumbering that crops were often planted late, fields left uncleared, and the economic foundations of the county thus kept insecure and transient. In fact the area was largely submarginal for agriculture. Timber operations combined with agriculture to make possible a population and prosperity that could not otherwise have been sustained.

The construction of a sawmill at Williamsport in 1838 encouraged cutting along the West Branch of the Susquehanna River; and when the Susquehanna Boom Company began operating there in 1850, the city's future as a lumber center was assured. Ultimately, fifty sizable mills arose in and around Williamsport to cut logs from the huge drainage of the West Branch.

Other cities in Pennsylvania also gained prominence in the lumber industry. Access to the Allegheny, Monongahela, and Ohio rivers helped make Pittsburgh a major center. Large rafts of timber, lumber, and logs both reached that city and left it on their way to the new communities arising in America's heartland. Rafts of pine and a mixture of hard- and softwoods went from it to Wheeling, West Virginia, Cincinnati, Ohio, Louisville, Kentucky, St. Louis, Missouri, and even, on occasion, New Orleans.[6]

While the pineries of Maine, New York, and Pennsylvania were being rapidly felled, the South still had extensive virgin stands. In 1800 the Bureau of the Census estimated that there was more than twice as much pine standing in the southern states as in any other region. Much of this was longleaf pine, which was to become the South's most important commercial species. Flourishing in dry, sandy soils from southeastern Virginia southward to Florida and westward to eastern Texas, longleaf pine yielded a hard, resinous, decay-resistant wood that was highly esteemed for maritime use, framing, flooring, and pilings, and later for railway ties and telegraph and telephone poles. The sandy, infertile pine barrens where it grew were less suitable for agriculture than were many other parts of the South. In C. F. C. Volney's words, the "perpetual verdure" of southern forests "is only a cover for sterility, except in those spots which the course of rivers and alluvial depositions have fertilized." As a result, little had been felled in the process of clearing farms and plantations. Lumbermen eventually more than made up for the oversight.

The abundance of good timber in the South ensured that, from an early date, wood rather than brick or stone was the region's primary building material. As time passed, this abundance led also to increasingly large commercial lumbering operations serving both local and growing export (especially Caribbean) markets. As earlier, much of this export trade was in naval stores, masts, spars, ship timbers, and packing boxes for sugar.[7]

Lumbering had been widespread on plantations and along coastal waterways from colonial times on, but the situation was often different only a few miles inland. Cutting in the interior had been restricted to narrow strips along the waterways, usually in areas where agriculture flourished. Away from the watercourses and in places poorly suited for crops, the forests remained virtually untouched by commercial operations. However, as production mounted, timber along the coast and near the plantations became depleted, and loggers were forced to turn to new stands.

Much of the land in southern Mississippi and Alabama was too poor for cotton. Before the 1840s local residents depended for their livelihood on cattle grazing, hunting, and limited subsistence agriculture. As Timothy Flint put it, they were "poor and indolent, devoted to raising cattle, hunting, and drinking whiskey," but it was more healthful there than in the alluvial lowlands where plantations flourished, and "nothing can be easier than subsistence in the pine woods."[8] In time the forces of change undermined this pastoral life. The deleterious effects of repeated fires set to improve grazing combined with overstocked range and a growing population to drive more and more Piney Woods residents to turn to the expanding lumber industry for employment. In 1850 mills in Harrison County, on Mississippi's Gulf Coast, sawed over eighty-six thousand logs — nearly all floated to them on the area's waterways. One observer reported the Biloxi River filled with logs en route to sawmills, while rafts of logs were so numerous on the Pascagoula River that for miles inland from the coast raft crews were seldom out of sight of one another.[9]

A similar shift away from grazing, hunting, and subsistence agriculture took place in East Texas, especially after independence from Mexico in 1836. Frame buildings replaced earlier log and half-timbered structures (used during the Mexican period because the area was too humid for adobe). Plantation agriculture appeared; wagons and steamboats linked the region to the larger commercial world. By 1846 Nacogdoches, the area's main community, had become a typical southern farming center dependent upon slaves and cotton. Sawmills supported its growth. The transition from a pastoral-hunting economy to an agricultural one had brought sweeping changes in the patterns of use of the surrounding forests and had opened the way for the greatly increased lumbering that would follow once railroads brought needed improvements in transportation.[10]

The transition was less noticeable where the production of naval stores dominated economic activity in the woods. In the Jacksonian period, the naval-stores industry continued to be an important component of North Carolina's economy. Other southern states enjoyed to a lesser degree the financial advantages that came from this forest activity. As America's merchant fleet grew ever larger, its ships consumed increasing quantities of tar and pitch. New uses also added to demand. Spirits of turpentine began to be utilized as a solvent by firms that produced rubber products, varnish, and illuminating fluids for lamps. Moreover, whales were becoming scarcer in the traditional Atlantic whaling grounds, and whale oil grew more costly. Camphene, a highly flammable mixture of alcohol and spirits of turpentine, came to be used as a lamp oil. Its clear, smokeless flame rivaled that of the finest oil from the sperm whale. In response to rising demand, improved methods of distillation were developed in the 1830s.

The pines growing on the large areas of poor soil in North Carolina offered small farmers a welcome opportunity to earn much-needed cash by collecting naval stores. Elsewhere tar and turpentine were often produced to keep slaves employed during farming's slack seasons. Throughout the two and one-half decades before the Civil War, the naval-stores industry was an important component of the South's economy, a handmaiden if not rival to King Cotton.[11]

In addition to the various species of pine that could be utilized for lumber and naval stores, southern loggers eagerly cut bald cypress. This nonevergreen conifer grew abundantly in southern swamps. Its "knees" (actually extensions of the roots) protruded above the water, letting it grow in a watery environment where most trees could not survive. The cypress, with a life span of one thousand years and more, frequently reached a height of 120 feet. Throughout the eighteenth and nineteenth centuries, there was always a market for it. Its light, reddish brown wood was highly prized. It was termite resistant and, unlike southern pines, free from resin and thus not very flammable. Like white pine, cypress has a long, straight grain, so it can be worked easily with hand tools. Because it is also highly resistant to rot and mildew, builders sought it both for structures (especially in warm humid areas) and for ship construction.

Cypress logging tested the ingenuity of lumbermen. Since this tree grew in swamps, bayous, and shallow lakes, choppers could not fell it as they did most trees. To make matters worse, green cypress logs would not float. Therefore, a year or more before a tree was to be felled, it was girdled so that it would die, dry out, and become buoyant. Realizing that it was impractical to fell large cypress trees from boats, loggers cut a notch above the swollen base and inserted a springboard they could stand on while chopping. In the dry season dead trees were felled and cut into logs. A skilled two-man team could fell, trim, and cut into logs two to four trees a day. When the rains came, workmen floated the dried logs to the sawmills. Afterward, rice was frequently planted where the trees had grown. Once again, trees gave way to agriculture.[12]

Southern forests also yielded the live oak. This southern evergreen was an important commercial timber in the colonial, revolutionary, and antebellum eras. Its hard, durable, close-grained wood was sought in the 1790s for warships for the young American nation. Its strong angular roots and limbs were ideal for the curved frames and knees needed in building a ship's hull. Experience demonstrated that live oak timbers could withstand the sea for forty to fifty years. A hull of southern live oak repelled the iron shot from the British frigate *Guerrière* in the War of 1812 and gave the U.S.S. *Constitution* the revered nickname "Old Ironsides." Launched from a Boston shipyard in 1797, the *Constitution* was one of the first frigates built for the United States Navy. Her keel was of New Jersey white oak; pine, cedar, and live oak provided the materials for her decks and hull. The copper sheathing on her bottom was attached with copper bolts made by Paul Revere. This proud ship, carrying fifty guns and constructed of the best American timbers, won fame for herself and glory for the nation.[13]

Scores of other naval and merchant vessels went down the ways. Observing the large quantities of live oak consumed in the shipyards of Boston, New York, Philadelphia, and Baltimore and the large exports of it to England in the early

1800s, François André Michaux predicted "its disappearance throughout the United States within fifty years." Scarcity of live oak, which so admirably served the demands of marine architecture, became a subject of national concern.

The first three laws pertaining to forests that the American Congress passed were aimed at protecting this tree. Encouraged by John Jay and others, Congress in 1799 passed the Timber Act, which appropriated two hundred thousand dollars for the purchase of live oak timbers and the acquisition of land where these trees grew. The War of 1812 underscored the importance of preserving live oak stands; but protection remained inadequate, and their decline continued. In 1827 the secretary of the navy reported that almost half the live oaks had been removed from coastal lands in the South, with up to two million cubic feet "consumed abroad." Exports were important to the young nation, for they brought desperately needed foreign exchange, but exports of live oak — vital for national defense — were another matter. Both the secretary and President John Quincy Adams urged Congress to take action.

Adams had a sustained interest in botany and silviculture. In a letter to a son he said, "I am observing the operations of nature, with a view to ascertaining some of her laws, and the ultimate object is to preserve the precious plants native to our country from the certain destruction to which they are tending." One of his goals was to produce trees that could serve the nation. He wrote another son, "My passion is for hard, heavy, long-lived wood, to be raised from the nut or seed requiring a century to come to maturity and then to shelter, shade or bear Columbia's thunder o'er the deep for one or more centuries more."[14]

Spain had generally ignored the timber resources of Florida; and although Britain had sought to develop them during the Revolution, not until after 1819, when West Florida became part of the United States, did an embryonic lumber industry begin to develop there. The live oak resources of West Florida were not apt to be long ignored by a maritime nation facing possible confrontations at sea. In 1828 Congress established a plantation to ensure a continued supply of the valuable tree. A tract of sixty thousand acres on Santa Rosa Sound near Pensacola, Florida, was selected. Much of this land belonged to the navy, but approximately three thousand acres was private property.

Judge Henry Marie Brackenridge, who had gained distinction in the Missouri fur trade, owned some of the site. Brackenridge's interest in botany had been aroused in 1811 when he joined John Bradbury and Thomas Nuttall in observing and collecting specimens on the upper Missouri River. Appointed a district judge for West Florida by President James Monroe, Brackenridge devoted his leisure time on his Santa Rosa estate to a tree nursery through which he sought to demonstrate that the barren coastal lands could be made fertile and productive. While being considered for the position of superintendent of the government's live oak plantation, Brackenridge sought to strengthen his candidacy by immodestly asserting that "there is no tree or shrub in this country with whose history, properties, and habits I have not an acquaintance." Officials seemingly were impressed; he received the appointment. Brackenridge believed that "no forest tree improves more rapidly by attention and care than the live oak." As superintendent of the plantation, he became not only the first United States forester but also the first director of a national forest research station—even if neither term had yet come into official use.

Unfortunately for the plantation, Adams's support came near the end of his presidency. The vitriolic presidential campaign of 1828 and subsequent election of Andrew Jackson cast the live oak program into disarray. Adams's administration was charged with exceeding its authority in planting young live oaks, and support was withdrawn. The Santa Rosa plantation drifted in limbo and was eventually abandoned.[15]

Although the federal plantation came to naught, the South still possessed great forest resources, and New Orleans was a developing market. In 1788 and 1794, fires destroyed whole sections of the city. Large quantities of lumber were required for rebuilding. The Louisiana Purchase of 1803 and the city's subsequent growth further contributed to its importance to the southern lumber industry. By the early 1820s, the growing prosperity of the lower Mississippi Valley led to domestic demands on the forest that rivaled those of the long-important foreign markets. The continued prosperity of New Orleans in the three decades preceding the outbreak of hostilities between North and South led to more and more utilization of the region's forests.

Illustrative of the growth of the industry in the South was the firm founded by Scottish architect Andrew Brown. Beginning with a small sawmill on the Mississippi at Natchez about 1828, Brown played a prominent role in the evolution of commercial logging in Louisiana from then until the Civil War. Brown was an ambitious entrepreneur sensitive to market conditions, technological changes, and the availability of timber resources. Alert to the advantages of circular saws, he installed a fifty-inch circular saw at his mill. By 1847 the plant was cutting up to fifteen thousand board feet of cypress lumber a day. Because of the shortage of white mill hands, Brown and most other southern millowners primarily employed slaves hired from local plantations. Logs for his mill were obtained in the 1840s and 1850s from the Yazoo-Mississippi delta and rafted to Natchez. Financial success was ensured by his operation's proximity to the flourishing market of New Orleans.[16]

Growing demand in the South was answered by the rapid adoption of steam-powered sawmills. Although the South was abundantly graced with rivers and streams, the languid flow of most made them inefficient for running water-powered sawmills. The advent of steam-powered sawmills significantly altered the pattern of logging and, in the South as elsewhere, allowed the cutting of trees that heretofore had escaped the ax. In 1803 two New Orleans entrepreneurs installed a high-pressure steam engine designed and built by Oliver Evans of Philadelphia. The engine had originally been purchased for a steamboat destined for use on the Mississippi, but before the boat could be put into operation an unexpected rise in the river tore it from its mooring and left it grounded in a nearby swamp. Perceiving the futility of attempting to move the vessel, the owners had the steam engine removed and installed in a nearby sawmill. The result was a mill capable of cutting three thousand board feet of lumber during a twelve-hour shift, easily more than the water-powered mills in the area.

This mill burned in 1806, but its profitable operation before then and its advantages over water-powered mills persuaded other lumbermen to turn to steam. Improved designs for steam engines led to ever greater efficiency in operation. Other engines were used to power both sawmills and gristmills. An Evans steam engine installed in a sawmill at Manchac, near New Orleans, in 1807 reduced the cost of production from fifty to forty dollars per thousand board feet.

By 1817 steam engines for sawmills and gristmills were being manufactured in Pittsburgh, Cincinnati, and Louisville, and by 1820 eight steam-powered sawmills were operating in Louisiana, primarily cutting cypress. They caught on elsewhere in the South too, though more slowly in Georgia than in other parts of the region, largely because of the availability there of choice sites for water mills. The early steam sawmills that did appear in the state were usually at or near seaports, locations that offered markets but lacked good sites for water-powered mills.

Growing use of steam-powered mills revolutionized the lumber business in the Old South. Such mills could be operated year round. In such circumstances, full-time employees and supplies of timber were needed, and logging was moving from a seasonal to a year-round occupation. Greater skills could be developed using full-time employees, but the small farmer's opportunities to augment his income by seasonal employment and the slave owner's chance to keep his hands busy during the slack agricultural seasons declined.[17]

Pressure grew to provide logs to met the insatiable demands of the steam sawmills. Theft was one expedient often used. In the spring of 1812, fifteen large rafts of cypress were stolen from public lands and driven down the Mississippi River. Rafts themselves were regularly stolen on southern waterways, and the piracy of log rafts on the Mississippi became a problem of some magnitude.

In sawmills, fuel for steam engines usually came from slabs, sawdust, and wood scraps produced during the manufacture of lumber. Fires were a persistent danger; accumulations of sawdust and sparks from boiler fires were a dangerous combination. Indeed, so many steam-powered sawmills burned that insurance firms were reluctant to cover them.

The relatively large capital investment of a steam-powered sawmill and the constant threat of fire created circumstances demanding a quick return on investment. Large profits could be made by operating efficiently. To this end the mills were kept running day after day, and lands were logged in the fastest, least expensive manner, without thought for the future.

Trained labor was always in demand. Sawmill owners generally employed white foremen and sawyers. Mill crews were a mixture of whites, black freedmen, and slaves. Pay varied according to the skills workers possessed and the particular conditions of supply and demand, but it equaled or surpassed that of other manual laborers. Ordinary hands usually earned slightly more than a dollar a day; a sawyer, shingle-maker, or carpenter received considerably more.

Most choppers also earned more than the basic wage. A capable chopper could fell as many as twenty mature trees a day in the pine barrens, although they averaged less. Once down, trees were bucked into logs before removal from the forest. Lacking snow over which to skid large logs to yards or riverbanks, the southern logger had to extract his fallen timber on carts or wagons pulled by teams of oxen. Whenever watercourses permitted, they were used in moving logs. But the sluggishness of many streams ruled out drives and resulted instead in extensive use of rafts, which were frequently pulled, paddled, or poled along. At times small ditches were dug across level terrain and strings of logs pulled along them by animal power.[18]

Where large stands of trees were far removed from convenient streams and rivers, such expendients were inadequate. Stands thus situated remained largely untapped until after 1840, when the spread of railroads began to permit their harvesting. In the South as elsewhere, railroads had a dual impact upon forests. They not only made it easier to ship logs to the mills and lumber to market but also used enormous quantities of timber themselves. Wood was required for ties and for constructing cars, water towers, stations, and bridges. Early railroad engines consumed up to 140 cords of firewood per track mile per year. With over two thousand miles of track in place in the South by 1850 and scores of engines in use, railroads were becoming a significant consumer of the region's timber.[19]

Cutting trees and producing lumber was fast becoming one of the South's leading industrial activities as midcentury approached. The South's 2,523 mills were producing over $9,800,000 worth of lumber products a year. The long-established bias of consumers against southern timber was slowly being overcome, and lumber from the South was entering northern (especially coastal) markets.

Progress had its price, however. The extensive cutting of this period, continued and expanded in the years that followed, led finally to widespread erosion that scarred southern lands and polluted rivers and streams. A great deal has been written about the disastrous effects of cotton farming on the topsoil of the South, but deforestation may well have been as responsible as cotton for the erosion that came to plague the region.[20]

Even as longleaf pine, live oak, and cypress were being felled in the southern states, lumbermen began to turn their attention to the forests around the upper Great Lakes. Michigan, Wisconsin, and Minnesota were lavishly endowed with the same species of white pine that grew so bountifully in New England, their stands being part of that great forest that stretched westward from New England. In that region's sandy soils, deposited by glacial action during the Ice Age, white pine grew with unsurpassed vitality. An acre of such land frequently yielded forty thousand board feet; one in Minnesota reportedly produced ninety-four thousand feet of white pine. Yields of from ten thousand to twenty-five thousand feet an acre were considered satisfactory. The same glaciers that prepared the soil of these states for their luxuriant growth of forests also left the land strewn with lakes, streams, and rivers upon which the fallen giants could be floated to the mills.

The northeastern states sent men, capital, and technology westward to fell these trees. To obtain a job in the forests of the Lake States, it was credential enough to say, "I'm from Maine," for conditions in the two areas were remarkably similar. As Maine's white pine forests dwindled, many woodsmen moved on to Michigan, Wisconsin, or Minnesota. Maine's congressman T. J. D. Fuller lamented over "the stalwart sons of Maine marching away by scores and hundreds to the piney woods of the Northwest." While regretting New England's loss, he observed with evident pride, "most fortunate that state or territory which shall receive the largest accession of them, for like the renowned men of olden times, '*they are famous for lifting up the axes upon thick trees.*'"[21]

This first great migration of the lumber industry was spread over a considerable period. Its beginnings can be dated from 1836, when Charles Merrill of Lincoln, Maine, purchased a large tract of sawtimber along Michigan's St. Clair River. Other lumbermen followed. In 1845 Isaac Stephenson, destined to become one of the greatest timber barons, moved from Bangor to Wisconsin. Hosts of loggers from Maine traveled westward over the Erie Canal to populate Bay City and Saginaw, the rising sawmilling centers of Michigan, and to spread north and west from there to every major lumber district in the Lake States. They brought with them knowledge built up over the years. The methods of felling, bucking, skidding, and driving logs used in the Lake States were essentially those of Maine. Getting pine out to the sawmills was something these migrants knew how to do—and get it out they did.

But men from Maine were never alone in the woods. Large numbers from Canada, especially the maritime provinces, and from Pennsylvania and New York were also present. Immigrants from Europe further swelled the woodsmen's ranks. Each group clustered where their earlier experience and established contacts could be put to best use.[22]

Wherever they came from, lumbermen found ready markets for their cut. The opening of the Erie Canal in 1825 led to a huge influx of people into the Ohio Valley, people who—like other Americans—were soon building with wood. At first most drew upon nearby forests. Indeed, in 1840 Ohio ranked behind only New York and Pennsylvania in number of sawmills. The Census of 1840 further reported that although Ohio had 2,883 sawmills, twice Maine's number, Maine nevertheless produced $1,808,683 in lumber products to Ohio's $262,821. Clearly Ohio's mills were small, erected to fill the needs of a frontier community.

Logging was complementary to farming in much of the Ohio Valley. It was a seasonal activity that could be undertaken when farming and clearing fields were made difficult by weather. In time-honored fashion, it provided frontier farmer-loggers with both a cash income and materials necessary for building homes, barns, and other structures. Timber products were produced for local consumption rather than distant markets—except for flatboats, constructed to float farm produce downstream and then be dismantled and sold, like their cargoes, at their destinations. One observer reported in 1840 that each fall about one thousand flatboats descended the Wabash River in Indiana, carrying some one million dollars' worth of produce. Easy to build from the readily available tulip poplar and other woods, these primitive craft provided an essential link to markets during the area's early years. But the scattered, mixed stands of the area could not long supply demand, especially as more and more of them gave way to farms. Pine forests to the north were soon being drawn upon.[23]

What was happening in Ohio, Indiana, and neighboring areas was the last major phase of the story of the farmer-lumberman, which reached back to colonial times. Henceforth farmers increasingly moved onto lands so lightly forested that from the first they had to draw on outside sources to meet their own needs, while lumbermen less and less often were farmers as well. A conservative estimate has placed the amount of forest cleared for agriculture by 1860 at 153 million acres, over twelve times the amount cleared as a result of industrial lumbering, mining, and urban development. After 1860 the rate of clearing for farms declined sharply, while the rate of cutting by industrial lumbering rose. The shift was already becoming apparent in 1850. As Ohio's forests gave way to crops, the end of the old system was already in sight.

As the older semiwooded sections filled up, settlers pushed out onto the prairies of Indiana, Illinois, Iowa, Michigan, Wisconsin, and Nebraska, thus exacerbating the need for lumber from the north. The heavy sod of the prairies made the land extremely difficult to bring under cultivation until the introduction of the steel plow in the late 1840s. Purchasing the necessary equipment was but one of many expenses facing the would-be farmer of the prairies. Wood for fences, buildings, and fuel had to be hauled from scattered groves that became ever more distant as cutting proceeded, or else it had to be purchased. Frequently the land required drainage, which was both difficult and expensive. But the prairie soil was worth the effort. High in organic content, it was superbly fertile. Wheat, which could bring returns more quickly than other crops and with a smaller initial investment, was from the first the region's staple. As one farm journal put it, wheat "pays debts, buys groceries, clothing and lands, and answers more emphatically the purposes of trade . . . than any other crop." It also paid for the vast quantities of lumber that flowed into the area as building proceeded and nearby sources of supply declined.[24]

The prairie farmers' demand for lumber and other forest products led to the emergence of suppliers who drew upon forests far to the north. Frederick Weyerhaeuser, Orrin H. Ingram, and many other timbermen laid the foundation for their industrial empires by catering to just such a demand. In so doing they helped tie together the economies of the prairies and the forests to the north.[25]

Nowhere was the trade linking the two regions more evident than in Chicago. In 1834 Captain John Carver opened a lumberyard in the then-embryonic city and began running a small schooner, the *General Harrison,* to ports on the Great Lakes for lumber. Others followed, and within a few years cargoes of white pine were arriving in Chicago from Saginaw, Muskegon, and Bay City in Michigan, from Green Bay and Menominee in Wisconsin, and from elsewhere as well.

Completion in 1847 of the Illinois-Michigan Canal, linking the Illinois and Chicago rivers, gave a tremendous stimulus to Chicago's lumber trade. Using the canal, Chicago wholesalers could sell lumber from Michigan to buyers in the prairie regions to the south—buyers who had previously been supplied from western New York and Pennsylvania by floating lumber down the Ohio River and then up the Illinois. Overnight the price of lumber was halved and a great deterrent to settlement of the prairies eliminated. In 1848 about sixty million board feet of lumber arrived in Chicago, much of it destined to be shipped southward. By 1856 the city was to supplant Albany, New York, as the nation's leading wholesale lumber market.[26]

The upper Mississippi, with its numerous navigable tributaries, also served to link forest and prairie. Increasing numbers of rafts of logs and lumber were soon floating southward on it. The rafting of logs was a colorful enterprise using techniques developed in Europe and then first adapted to American conditions on the waterways of New York and Pennsylvania. Logs were assembled at booms or sorting works on the upper reaches of the Mississippi, or on tributary streams, and there formed into rafts. As in Maine, each log carried the owner's brand. Crews collected logs bearing the same mark, arranged them side by side and placed cross poles over them, then bound them together by passing a rope over the cross poles and through paired holes drilled through the outside logs. Wooden plugs driven into the holes secured the rope and bound the whole into a "string," usually about sixteen feet wide. Several strings formed a raft.

Until the 1850s, rafts were carried downstream by the current and steered by the sweep of long oars. Crews had to struggle to keep these cumbersome aggregations out of trouble. Floods, sandbars, rapids, and bridge piers made passage a constant challenge. Crewmen erected a small shanty on the raft where they could store their possessions, sleep, and find shelter from rain. Whenever possible the raft was tied up at night near a town so that the crew could enjoy the delights of the boisterous riverfront taverns.

Stopping a raft required both care and skill. Men would jump ashore with a hawser and snub it around a tree or piling. They would then slowly stop the raft by playing off the hawser around a capstan on the raft. To prevent friction from setting fire to the heavy line, water would be poured on it as it skidded around the capstan. If the hawser broke or the crew was unsuccessful in snubbing it around a tree or piling, the raft would drift downstream until the crew found another site for stopping.

As more and more rafts floated downstream, railroad and steamboat interests grew more hostile. Rafts frequently broke up against the narrow piers of railroad bridges, often damaging them. Steamboat operators cursed the unwieldy rafts both for the difficulties their mere presence posed and because logs sometimes broke free from them to lie half-submerged, ready to smash through the hulls of vessels unlucky enough to strike them.

Regardless of protests, log rafts continued to run. Mills downriver demanded raw material to meet the need for lumber in the largely unforested lands they served, and rafts were the only practical method of supplying them. In the era before the Civil War, rafts were also the most economical means of moving lumber to distant markets. Besides, rafting provided employment for many men. Authorities were loath to interfere with so obviously useful a commerce.[27]

Although transportation was not an impediment to the growth of logging in the Lake States, Indian title to much of the timberland was. Treaties negotiated in the 1830s began the process of dispossessing the Winnebagos, Chippewas, and Sioux from tribal lands. The paper promises of the treaties salved the conscience of Jacksonian America while opening the way for development. Speculation in timberlands quickly followed. Daniel Webster, Edward Everett, Caleb Cushing, and Ralph Waldo Emerson joined countless others as investors in Wisconsin pine lands. The speculative euphoria vanished in the Panic of 1837, but logging became increasingly important in the region nevertheless.

Minnesota had more land covered with forests than either Michigan or Wisconsin. The finest pineries, however, grew in Michigan. The first two decades after Michigan gained statehood in 1837 saw much speculation in its timberlands. Encouraged by various federal land grants and by prices seldom more than a dollar and a quarter an acre, speculators eagerly sought title to pine lands. Fortunes could be made quickly, but there was intense competition for choice stands. Wealth could come either by reaping this bark-covered bullion or by selling it to others at a handsome profit.

Over the first several decades of Michigan's lumber industry, its rivers and streams carried the harvest of the forest to the mills. Woods along the Muskegon, Manistee, Au Sable, Tittabawassee, Menominee, Escanaba, and Manistique rivers resounded each spring with the cries of lumbermen herding thousands of pitching logs down the flooding water. Sawmills arose near the mouths of these rivers and encouraged the rise of the cities of Saginaw, Bay City, Muskegon, Manistee, and Menominee. It has been estimated that, computed at the then-common wholesale price of thirteen dollars per thousand board feet, Michigan's "green gold" surpassed in value the "yellow gold" production of California by more than a billion dollars.[28]

In Wisconsin as in Michigan, rivers played a vital role in lumbering. Sawmills were built along many a river, creating one of the state's first industries. In the 1830s the harvesting of pine began along the Wisconsin River; by 1847 there were twenty-four mills along its banks, producing over nineteen million board feet of lumber each year.

In the first half of the nineteenth century, forest industries in Wisconsin had been largely nourished by local settlement; but exportation to Chicago and down the Mississippi was well under way by 1850. A shift in settlement patterns accompanied this change. Before 1840, population and investment were concentrated in Wisconsin's southern and eastern counties where fertile prairies and open stands of mixed forests were found. A diversified economy emerged there. The area's timber harvest went for fuel, fencing, farm buildings, and such manufactures as furniture, barrels, and wagons. By 1850 settlement had pushed north to where good farmland was scarce. In places like Eau Claire County, foundations were laid for a manufacturing economy based exclusively on lumbering to supply purchasers outside the immediate area. Although its greatest growth was still ahead, by midcentury lumber production ranked only behind flour milling as a manufacturing activity in Wisconsin. The industry employed almost one-quarter of the state's industrial workers and produced more than $1,200,000 worth of products each year.[29]

North and west of Wisconsin lay the forests, rivers, and lakes of Minnesota, the last large stands of eastern white pine in the United States. In 1838 the St. Croix Valley in the Northwest Territory was purchased from the Chippewas. Within a year a sawmill was cutting on the St. Croix River. In 1843 Stillwater—founded on the St. Croix by a Maine man, named for his hometown in the Pine Tree State, and heavily populated in its early years with men from Maine—began its evolution into one of the most important mill towns anywhere.

Minnesota was to grow rapidly in the late 1850s, but in the 1840s its population was still small. In 1850 the territory had a mere 6,000 inhabitants, and laborers were too few to meet demand. However, seven years later the census for the statehood-enabling act would record a population of over 150,000. Increased settlement provided more laborers for Minnesota's forests and more markets for their products. Statistics from the St. Croix Boom bear witness to the rapid expansion of the state's logging industry. Five million board feet of logs were scaled at the boom in 1840, ninety million feet in 1850.

A fortunate accident introduced the loggers and raftsmen on the St. Croix to new opportunities. Until 1843 only lumber had been rafted down the St.

Croix to the Mississippi River; but in that year the St. Croix Boom broke and a winter's labor of some four hundred thousand logs surged downstream. An adventurous entrepreneur, John B. Page, gathered up the logs, formed a raft, and shepherded it to St. Louis, where he erected a mill to saw the timber. His profits were substantial. Log rafting soon became as common as lumber rafting in the upper Mississippi drainage.[30]

In the late 1840s Minneapolis began its own development as a lumber center. Situated at the Falls of St. Anthony, it was ideally placed for prominence in the timber industry. To the north and northwest, along the Rum River and elsewhere, stood large virgin stands of white pine. Abundant waterpower was available at the falls. Below them the Mississippi was navigable to the Gulf of Mexico, and thus many markets could be reached.

As early as 1822, the United States government erected a sawmill near the falls to cut lumber for Fort Snelling. Others soon recognized the potential of this site. In 1837 Franklin Steele, a Pennsylvanian, placed a claim for lands on the east bank of the Mississippi immediately above and below the falls—a claim that ultimately gave him the rights to waterpower generated from the middle of the main channel of the river to the east bank. Upon completion of the government's survey in 1848, Steele purchased his claim for $1.25 an acre. With the aid of men from Maine and sawmill machinery imported from Bangor, Steele erected the first commercial mill at the falls. It began operation on September 1, 1848, with two up-and-down saws that could produce up to fifteen thousand board feet of lumber a day. It turned out over five hundred thousand feet of lumber in its first year. The *Minnesota Pioneer* saluted Steele's accomplishments: "the saws went into operation last autumn, and have had no rest since, night or day, except on Sundays, and the demand for lumber at the Falls and at St. Paul had not nearly been supplied. There will not be a sufficient supply for years, however many mills may be built, to keep pace with the growth of Minnesota and our wants for building and fencing materials." It was a sound prediction.

To expand his operations, Steele sought eastern capital, and investors from Massachusetts joined in his enterprises. Other men also sensed the potential of the falls. In 1849 a gristmill and two sawmills appeared. Steele continued to develop his interests, and in 1851 he joined in two separate partnerships—the Mississippi Boom Company and the St. Anthony Boom Company—to handle and sort the increasing quantities of logs that were coming to the mills at the falls. As its lumber industry developed, the small community there would prosper, first as St. Anthony and then as Minneapolis. Indeed, its sawmills contributed more to its eventual growth than did agriculture and flour milling.

A solid foundation for the state's logging industry had been laid by the middle of the nineteenth century, but its greatest days still lay ahead.[31]

Not just in Minneapolis but elsewhere too the future of the lumber industry was bright. Between 1800 and 1850 it had established the foundation it was to build on in the years that followed. It had marched through New York and Pennsylvania, pursuing the white pine westward into the Lake States. In the South other species were harvested and other markets found.

This spread of the lumber industry can be statistically demonstrated. Adequate data for earlier years are unavailable, but in 1839 New York accounted for 30 percent of the lumber production in the United States, Maine 14 percent, the rest of New England 10 percent, Pennsylvania just under 9 percent, and New Jersey not quite 2 percent. In other words, the Northeast accounted for over two-thirds of the nation's total production of lumber. In 1849 New York reached its peak output, and production remained high elsewhere in the Northeast, but increases had been so great in other parts of the country that the states in the northeastern corner now produced only half the total. By 1859 the continuation of the shifts involved would reduce the Northeast's share to one-third. The movement reflected in these figures was a manifestation of changes that were to shape the lumber industry for decades to come.

The geographical shifts were, of course, no more important than the technological shifts that accompanied them and to a large extent were made possible by them. Especially in the South, the application of steam engines to milling operations permitted the cutting of stands that had been previously neglected and suggested the scope of activity and technologies yet to come. Improvements in transportation, as well as the adoption of improved methods of sawing lumber, created recognizable efficiencies.

The scale of the lumber industry had begun to change. The farmer-lumberman was falling by the wayside, and small mills producing for local and regional markets were being replaced by fewer but larger, more capital intensive sawmills serving greater and more distant markets. The stage was set for the transition to a modern industry.

The Great Transition, 1850–1909

Part 3

Watershed Years

Chapter 7

Wood had played a central role in the life of Americans from the time of the first European settlements. Its ready availability affected technology, economy, settlement patterns, and everyday life. The period down to the mid-nineteenth century was indeed America's wooden age. But gradually the situation changed. Forests increasingly appeared finite; and as they assumed a less central place in the nation's life, attitudes toward forests—and the larger world of nature of which forests were a part—underwent revision.

Although America's wooden age was coming to an end, in the nineteenth century forests were still of tremendous importance, and they would continue to be so in the years that followed. In 1850 lumber production ranked first among the various branches of manufacturing in the United States when measured in value added by manufacture, the most useful test of an industry's contribution to the economy. According to the Census Bureau, the lumber industry produced 6.7 percent of the national aggregate. By 1860 lumbering had dropped to 6.4 percent and second place (behind cotton textiles), but lumber output still had twice the value of all the machinery produced.

Even these figures understate the industry's importance. Loggers—fallers, buckers, river hogs, and all the others associated with getting logs out of the woods to the mills—and those distributing the end products of the mills were not considered by the Census Bureau to be part of the industry. Only those who worked in sawmills or planing mills qualified.

Nor was 1850 the peak year. Although lumbering's percentage of the national aggregate had dropped slightly by 1860, production was actually higher. It continued to rise in the years that followed, not reaching its maximum until 1909, when the industry turned out 44.5 billion board feet of lumber—to say nothing of enormous quantities of railroad ties, shingles, poles, and other wood products. The importance of America's forests at the time was

graphically described by Bernhard Eduard Fernow, the first major scientifical-
ly trained forester in the United States. In 1906 he wrote:

One thousand million dollars a year is the wood bill of the people of the United States. . . .
About one half of this value represents the cost of firewood, fencing, and other smaller
materials . . . while the other half is for lumber and other material that requires bolt or
log size. . . . We hear much about the mining industry, the coal fields, the importance of
the iron and steel industry, and about gold or silver. . . . And yet the value of these last
two products is not one-tenth in their annual output of what the forest furnishes; the iron
and steel industry furnishes hardly one-half the values of the forest; and if we put all the
mineral products, coal, metal, petroleum, and every other material together, they fall
forty percent below the value of the forest products. . . . With such a showing we are jus-
tified in placing our forest products as second only in importance to agriculture; wood
crops next to food crops, both equally indispensable.

Even Fernow's statistics are conservative. His calculations do not include the
value of forests in grazing, watershed protection, and recreation.

But Fernow wrote when production was near its zenith. Wood had been
central in American life during the early years and had a major, if somewhat
different, role in the industrialization and modernizing processes of the second
half of the nineteenth century. The system was not yet complete, but the
framework for a new order was firmly in place by the early twentieth century.
Forests had become less obviously important to most Americans and more distant from them in their everyday lives. For all the value of wood when Fernow
wrote, many items once made of it were now being made of glass, metal, or
other substitutes; many artisans who had earned their living in one form of
woodworking or another had disappeared. Ironically, while lumber production and per capita commercial consumption were still rising, wood was becoming less ubiquitous in American life.

The period from 1850 to 1908 was the bridge across which the United States
moved from the wooden age to the intricacies of a mature industrial society.
Appropriately enough, forest products played a key role in the transition: the
bridge was in large part made of wood. If the outlines of today's America were
determined during this transmutation, so too were many attitudes toward the
forest and its uses that continue today, long after the great transition was completed.

Railroads had a key role in transforming the United States.[1] Between 1850 and
the late 1870s, railroad building provided the primary impetus to business innovation. It created a huge demand for iron and steel rails, rolling stock, labor,
and investment capital. These demands wrought changes both within the rail-

road firms themselves and in the larger world they touched. The simple proprietorships and partnerships that had previously dominated American business were inadequate for these, the first of the nation's big businesses. The corporate form of organization, with all its advantages, was first adopted in a major way in the United States by railroad leaders. Older local and regional economic structures began to give way to larger, even national, ones as rail lines both opened new markets and gave access to the resources of more extensive hinterlands.

In spite of the dissenting works of some econometricians, the importance of railroads in setting in motion the economic boom of 1850 to 1870 still seems evident.[2] What has not generally been evident is the extent to which the nation's forest resources helped make possible the growth of the rail net—and the extent to which, in turn, railroad construction contributed to the first major wave of fear over a coming "timber famine."

One historian has noted that "the railroad, known in most languages as 'the iron road,' might as easily be called 'the wooden road.'" Indeed it might. More wood than steel went into its construction. Railroads consumed perhaps as much as one-fourth of each year's timber cut and, in spite of the relative cheapness of wood, spent more for forest products than for rails. An estimated 195,000 acres of timberland were required to supply the thirty-nine million crossties used by railroads in 1870, and the need grew as more lines were built. By 1890 demand for ties had more than doubled. Additional wood went into bridges and trestles, into station houses, platforms, and other structures, and into cars. With the exception of engines, rolling stock contained far more wood than metal. So great was the demand for wood that one official of the Union Pacific referred to railroads as the "insatiable juggernaut of the vegetable world."[3]

The plentitude of America's forest resources encouraged the burst of railroad building that commenced in the 1850s. In Europe bridges had tended to be of masonry, but in the United States they were usually of wood, which was cheaper, faster, and easier to use than stone or brick. In a labor-short nation, seeking to open vast areas quickly with limited investment capital, wood's advantages were vital. Just as the balloon-frame house had speeded the development of western regions, so too did methods developed for fast, inexpensive railroad construction. As a result, lightly built lines were pushed across the prairies more rapidly and in greater numbers during the 1870s than would have been possible earlier. As the area grew in population and as income from traffic mounted, the lines were rebuilt and improved, again using prodigious quantities of wood.

Nor were railroads the only consumers of wood. As new areas were opened to agriculture, the building of farmhouses, barns, and fences created increasing demand for lumber. Unlike earlier settlement, when most such wood had come from one's own farm or nearby sources, the bulk now came from commercial outlets and distant mills. Sawmill operators who serviced rural areas learned to watch weather reports carefully, for drought and resultant crop failures meant that farmers would have less money—which in turn would mean falling demand and lower prices for lumber.

Urban as well as rural development required enormous quantities of forest products, as did the growth of other industries besides the railroads. The tanning industry, which expanded rapidly during the period, was a major consumer. Its demand for tannin-yielding bark, used in curing leather, led to extensive operations in the vast hemlock stands of the East and in the oak stands of the Far West and elsewhere.[4] Other industries, too, placed their demands on the forests, though not always in such obvious fashion.

But if the nation's extensive forest resources in many ways encouraged growth, in other ways they had a restraining influence. As noted earlier, the cheapness and availability of wood helped encourage American iron manufacturers to cling to old-fashioned charcoal-fired smelting techniques that produced iron easily worked by local blacksmiths. Meanwhile, producers in Europe and especially in England (which had to turn to coal because of a shortage of wood) were moving on to new methods that yielded types of iron and steel more suited for industrial purposes. When a drive to build a modern navy of steel-hulled, steam-powered vessels began to develop during the administration of President Chester A. Arthur, one complicating factor was that American steel mills did not produce the high-quality steel plate needed to sheathe the hulls of the proposed vessels. New mills would have to be built using imported technology, or the steel would have to be purchased abroad. Americans were paying the price for their long dependence of wood—or more accurately charcoal—in smelting. Not until it turned its back on wood did America's iron and steel industry begin to catch up and then surge ahead.[5]

The presence of forests had an even greater impact on the nation's merchant marine. If railroads were symbolic of the new economic order that developed with a rush during the second half of the nineteenth century, perhaps nothing had symbolized the old as well as the clipper ships. But as conditions of trade changed during and after the 1850s, speed gradually became less vital and carrying capacity became more so. In response, American builders developed the down easter, a sturdy and capacious type that, though less speedy than the clipper, was still fast. Indeed, in some ways the down easter was superior to the clipper. The huge expanse of sail carried by the latter, and the speed that resulted, put great strain on the hull. Within a few years this stress literally tore the clippers apart, while the sturdy down easters went on at their more deliberate pace year after year, continuing to bring returns to their owners.

Unable to match the fine wooden-built American ships, British and French builders experimented with iron or steel hulls and with steam power. Government subsidies encouraged the process. But Americans, having had great success with wooden-hulled sailing ships and having accumulated technological expertise in their construction, continued to build them long after the superiority of steel and steam should have been apparent. As a result, the American merchant fleet, the world's largest and finest in the 1850s, declined precipitously; by the end of the nineteenth century it was a poor also-ran, and foreign-flag vessels were carrying the bulk of the nation's overseas commerce.[6]

The rise of railroads at a time when the merchant marine was stagnating was hardly coincidental. Many American entrepreneurs were transferring profits earned in the China trade, where some of their families had been doing business for three generations, to western railroads. They now saw less chance of profit in overseas trade than in internal development. It has been said that what England found east of Suez, the United States found west of the Mississippi. So it did, and the structure of American business adjusted accordingly. The older commercial-mercantile leaders, epitomized by John Jacob Astor, were replaced as the dominant businessmen by industrialists and their allies: people like Andrew Carnegie, Frederick Weyerhaeuser, John D. Rockefeller, and James J. Hill. By speeding the building of western railroads and thus helping to create an aura of great internal opportunity, American forests aided the shift.[7]

Lumbermen had no reason to lament the new order. The ships that had been the backbone of the old commercial-mercantile system had been made of wood, but the internal expansion that accompanied the new order required even more. Thanks to rising industrial use, per capita consumption of commercial wood products quadrupled between 1850 and 1909. Abundant, inexpensive forest resources had helped usher in a new order that in turn created unprecedented demands for wood products and resulted in the opening of new areas of production.

The surge of railroad building that commenced about 1850 was not the only factor that caused the period to appear as a watershed in the history of America—and of the American forest. Undoubtedly the most spectacular event of the time was the California gold rush, which had begun in 1848 with James Marshall's discovery of gold in the millrace of Captain John Sutter's sawmill in the foothills of the Sierra Nevada. Neither California nor the country was ever to be the same again.

Almost overnight the gold rush created a major American settlement on the Pacific shore. The existing sawpits and mills on the West Coast were incapable of providing sufficient lumber to build El Dorado's instant cities. A lumber industry quickly sprang up in the Far West, first in California's more accessible stands but soon along the coast of Oregon and around Puget Sound in Washington Territory as well. Andrew Jackson Pope and Frederic Talbot, who came around Cape Horn from Maine in 1849, were among the first to make a systematic attempt to supply the region's new need for lumber. Gold had provided the catalyst for the spectacular growth in California and tributary areas, but the building itself was done with wood — and done again and again as fires repeatedly leveled San Francisco and other cities. Cheap, abundant, and easily worked, wood enabled the Far West to develop at a rate that would otherwise have been impossible.[8]

Less spectacular developments were also changing the face of the nation about 1850. The movement onto the tallgrass prairies of Indiana, Illinois, Iowa, and southern Wisconsin, which had begun earlier, accelerated. There was still a tendency to settle near the forested fringe. In 1854 a Pennsylvanian who started a farm well out on the prairie of Livingston County, Illinois, was, according to a local historian, "generally pronounced a lunatic." But the fertility of most prairie soils was by this time clear to any who could look beyond inherited folk wisdom. The absence of trees for fencing, firewood, and a host of other rural uses had made settling on the prairies seem risky, but by this time sufficient supplies of lumber and other wood products were available commercially to supply what one's farmstead could not. Farmers on the prairies were less self-sufficient than earlier settlers along the edges of open land had been, but the richness of the prairie soil, and the fact that it cost less to get it ready for planting than to clear forested land, more than made up for this handicap.

Encouraged by successes to the east, farmers pushed onto the shortgrass prairies of Kansas and Nebraska—the beginnings of the Great Plains. Here there were cottonwoods along the streams, but few other trees. Distant from abundant sources of timber, settlers in Kansas developed the sod house in the 1850s. The soddy may have been cheap and picturesque, but it was only a stopgap; it had little if any lasting effect in reducing the need for wood in Kansas, Nebraska, and neighboring states and territories. The trickle of people into this area became a flood after midcentury, and commercial demand for lumber grew. Production around the Great Lakes—and distribution centers such as Chicago—burgeoned in response.[9]

The railroad boom of the 1850s played a major role in Chicago's ascent. The Chicago & North Western, Rock Island, Chicago, Milwaukee & St. Paul, Green

Bay, Milwaukee & Chicago, Illinois Central, and lesser lines formed a web tying Chicago to an expanding hinterland. Much of the wood used in their construction was supplied through Chicago; much of that consumed by the farms and towns along the lines came from the same source. Moreover, Chicago itself tripled in size between 1860 and 1870, which generated further demand, as did rebuilding following the burning of more than half the city in the great fire of 1871. During the period, eighty to one hundred schooners were sometimes jammed into the mouth of the Chicago River, while scores of others waited in Lake Michigan for a berth along the river where they could unload. By 1872 yards and docks for lumber lined the Chicago River for twelve miles.[10]

Other centers emerged, too. Milwaukee supplied an extensive area, and a number of marketing hubs sprang up along the middle Mississippi: Rock Island, Illinois, Davenport and Dubuque, Iowa, Hannibal and St. Louis, Missouri, and others. Some Mississippi River towns, lacking large sawmills, served primarily as distribution points for lumber cut to the north and then rafted downstream to wholesalers. Others had sawmills and depended on the river to bring them not sawn lumber but logs. In either case those centers with the more extensive westward-reaching rail nets, and thus the larger service areas, were the ones that moved ahead.[11]

Log rafting to supply the downriver mills was an extensive operation. In 1859 almost half of the white pine that left Minnesota did so as logs — that is, it was floated downriver to supply mills on the middle Mississippi. By 1868 the figure had climbed to 68.5 percent.

In 1850 total lumber production in the United States was over five billion board feet. New York produced the most, followed in order by Pennsylvania, Maine, and Ohio. With the exception of Ohio's relatively recent high production, this pattern had apparently long been present.[12] Although Maine was generally associated in the public mind with lumbering because there was so little other industry there to overshadow it, New York and Pennsylvania had no doubt led the Pine Tree State for some time.

Patterns were to shift dramatically over the next two decades, but not all changes came in the newer sections of the country. The urbanization and growth of manufacturing in the Northeast generated a growing demand for lumber. New York City — which mushroomed after the opening of the Erie Canal in 1825 — greatly extended its economic hinterland and was the biggest city and the greatest single market for lumber in the United States. At first nearby sources met demand, especially Glens Falls and other centers that drew on the timber of the Adirondack Mountains and floated their cut down the Hudson River, but these soon proved inadequate. Lumber dealers began to tap more distant sources. Middlemen at Albany soon began using the Erie Canal to bring white pine from Chemung and Allegheny counties in the southwestern part of the state; Albany was on its way to becoming one of the nation's two great lumber emporiums. For the next several years only Chicago was able to challenge its primacy, even though Albany's main source of supply shifted first to southern Ontario and then to the Lake States. The lumber trade at Albany grew so rapidly that as early as 1846, while the trade with Ontario was still on the ascendancy, dealers in the city were reaching out to Port Huron and Saginaw, Michigan, for additional supplies of white pine.

Buffalo as well as Albany prospered as a result of the trade through the Erie Canal. From about 1853 Buffalo was the point where lumber arriving from southern Ontario and Michigan was transferred to canal boats for the trip to Albany. For years it was chiefly a forwarding center, although as the forests of western New York became depleted it also became a wholesale distribution center serving an area of its own. By 1874 there were forty-three firms and individuals in the city dealing in white pine, hemlock, or hardwood. Collectively they handled over 300 million board feet a year. The nearby towns of Tonawanda and North Tonawanda had also emerged as major centers forwarding lumber to Albany. In 1875 Buffalo and the Tonawandas together received 189 million board feet from mills on Michigan's Saginaw River; Chicago received only 32 million.

The spectacular growth of the lumber industry in the Lake States after about 1850 was thus not just the result of the building of railroads, the opening of the prairies, and the general development of the Midwest. It was also a consequence of the great expansion of New York City and the markets that were reached through Buffalo and Albany. The importance of canals in this development cannot be overemphasized. One lumber dealer—noting that lumber reached New York's capital city by canal, was sorted in the city's waterfront lumberyards, and was then dispatched down the Hudson to reach the ultimate consumers—put it succinctly: "We are all water fowl in Albany."[13]

The growing lumber production of the Lake States required men, capital, and expertise. Much of all three came from Maine. By the 1850s migration from the Pine Tree State had reached its peak, but it continued through the sixties. Other sources contributed to the influx into the Lake States. In 1863 the Appleton (Wisconsin) *Crescent* compared the "Crusade into the pineries" to the Pike's Peak gold rush. By 1870 Michigan had passed Pennsylvania and New York to become the nation's leading lumber producer; in 1872 Michigan's mills cut more lumber than the two former leaders combined.

Investors and speculators led the way, but workers soon followed. Their labor and skill made possible the massive shipments to Chicago and Albany and, through them, the Lake States' newfound primacy. Yet large as the shipments through the Erie Canal were, they alone could not meet the Northeast's huge— and expanding—demand for wood products. Burlington, Vermont, and Williamsport, Pennsylvania, also emerged at midcentury as major sources of supply.

Burlington had been an early center for the lumber trade; but since its stands were depleted, the trade seemed almost over. Then in 1849 the Rutland and Burlington laid track to the city's waterfront. Rail connections gave Burlington's lumbermen access not only to New England's major centers but, through Boston, to many of the world's premier markets. They supplied these markets by importing from the very place they had once depended upon for sales: Canada. Lumber from Quebec first reached Burlington in 1850. A substantial trade soon developed, led by Lawrence Barnes, who in 1857 established the first planing mill in Burlington. Barnes found that by finishing the rough lumber received from Canada he could save 12.5 percent on freight charges and make a profit from the additional manufacturing he carried out. Others quickly followed suit.

The growth of Burlington's lumber business was spectacular. By 1860 lumber sheds, yards, and planing mills covered the waterfront; sales had grown to forty million board feet annually and were still rising. One firm, Shepard and Morse, had four thousand feet of dock frontage, sufficient to berth thirty to thirty-five vessels at a time. At one point over four hundred steamers and barges were active on the waters of Lake Champlain, carrying lumber to the planing mills that supplied the rail trade out of Burlington. By 1868 the city had become the nation's third largest wholesale lumber market, behind only Chicago and Albany.[14]

Midcentury was a turning point for Pennsylvania too, and for the same basic reasons as elsewhere in the Northeast: rapid development associated with industrialization and urbanization. Building required lumber, and central Pennsylvania still had large stands of white pine, especially in the 2,100 square miles that made up the drainage of the West Branch of the Susquehanna River. The opening of these stands to large-scale utilization was heralded in 1850 by the beginning of operation of the Susquehanna Boom at Williamsport. In the years that followed, the boom was repeatedly enlarged and improved. At its largest, it could hold some three hundred million feet of logs. Other nearby booms added further capacity. From 1850 to 1875, the area turned out an estimated six billion board feet of lumber. In the process, Williamsport for a time became the world's leading lumber-producing center.

The Susquehanna Boom brought problems as well as opportunities, threatening the livelihood of raftsmen who had long operated on the West Branch. The boom could be used to corral rafts, but its most efficient mode of operation was as a receptacle for free-floating logs driven downstream on the spring runoff. Drives were a cheaper means of moving logs than were rafts, but rafting in a river being used for a log drive was difficult and dangerous if not downright impossible.

Predictably, friction soon developed between rafters and "floaters." Public opinion tended to side with the former, who were skilled local residents engaged in an art long practiced on the streams of Pennsylvania; log drivers, by contrast, were usually men from Maine or southeastern Canada, and their method was unfamiliar to local residents. The conflict reached its peak in 1857 on Clearfield Creek, in the upper reaches of the West Branch drainage. There a group of armed rafters took to the woods to run off loggers who were felling timber for a drive. In spite of the raftsmen's success in forcing the abandonment of driving on Clearfield Creek, rafts were too inefficient, and their use on the upper West Branch declined rapidly after booms went into operation on the river. Rafts of long timbers continued to make their way downstream, but mill operators in Williamsport, Lock Haven, and the lesser centers of lumber manufacture on the West Branch depended upon drives to supply them with logs—and it was mills like theirs that represented the wave of the future.

Maine's patterns and techniques were replacing Pennsylvania's on the West Branch. Williamsport came to resemble Bangor more than it did the earlier, smaller sawmill centers of Pennsylvania that had depended upon rafts and supplied local markets. Like the city in Maine, it had large mills with the latest equipment, drew on distant timber supplies, and furnished markets even more distant from the point of production. Williamsport's millmen sold their cut in Philadelphia, Baltimore, and New York—all of which, like Bangor's principal markets, could be reached by water. But unlike Bangor's operators, those in Williamsport also dispatched a significant quantity by rail; moreover, they neither were served by sailing ships (canal barges carried most of the Pennsylvania city's waterborne cut) nor sold significant quantities abroad.[15]

The Susquehanna Boom was not the only large boom opened near midcentury. On the Hudson River about four miles above Glens Falls, the Hudson River Boom Association put into operation in 1851 what was known locally as the Big Boom. In its first year it handled over 130,000 logs; the next year, over 345,000. It continued at roughly that level through the Civil War years and then spurted to over 500,000 logs yearly for the next decade. In 1872 the Big Boom handled 1,069,000 logs. Lumbering in the vicinity of Glens Falls flourished and mill capacity increased; downstream, rapidly growing New York City furnished a ready market for the output of the mills at Glens Falls. Supply and demand surged forward together. Glens Falls would long remain one of New York State's leading lumber-producing centers.[16]

Similar if less spectacularly successful developments were taking place elsewhere. In Minnesota, lumbermen incorporated the St. Croix Boom Company in 1851 and began operation before the year was out. The venture was not financially successful, and it was soon replaced by others better located. In spite of such individual failures, it was clear to millmen in the Lake States that booms opened the way for vastly increased production. There was a rush to add others. Between 1851 and 1873, the Wisconsin legislature alone authorized some seventy-five companies to construct and operate booms on various streams in the state.

In 1862 Levi W. Pond invented the sheer (or fin) boom and installed one on the Chippewa. Pond's device was made up of a movable extension or wing that protruded from a solidly constructed fixed boom behind which logs could be stored. The extension was equipped with a series of fins or rudders that could be manipulated so that the force of the river would move the wing. When a drive approached, the wing would be extended to the opposite bank, and logs could thus be easily collected; at other times it could be withdrawn to leave a wide channel open for river traffic. Pond's invention was a major improvement and gave impetus to the expansion of booming, which was to be a key element in the tremendous growth of lumbering during the decades that followed.[17]

Two other basic—and interrelated—changes were under way at midcentury. In Maine lumber production was rising, owing in part to the widespread adoption of gang saws at this time, but another change of even greater importance was also taking place. White pine had provided the backbone of Maine's lumber industry since colonial times, but pine stands were rapidly vanishing and spruce was becoming the primary commercial tree there. Maine's first spruce lumber was sawed in 1845. The spruce cut rose rapidly; fifty million board feet were produced in 1851. In the Penobscot district, the leading area of production, spruce had passed pine by 1861. Hemlock lumber was also being sawed in considerable quantities, though, as with spruce, lumbermen had disdained it earlier. Spruce was generally knottier than pine, had a greater tendency to warp, and was weaker, and hemlock lumber was coarse grained and, being rather brittle, tended to split. As Maine's sawmills turned to spruce and hemlock, the way was opened for others to penetrate the state's old markets. These included not only the producers of white pine lumber around Williamsport and in the Lake States but also producers in the yellow pine forests of the South.[18]

The South had turned out lumber since colonial times, but for a variety of reasons the industry had not grown there as it had in the Northeast. However, by midcentury railroads were opening the interior of the South in a major way, and the lumber industry was responding. As southern lumber producers moved into untapped stands, output rose sharply. To market the cut, commission merchants began shipping more and more yellow pine lumber to New York and other northern ports. During the 1850s the production of lumber in the South more than doubled.

This increase was partly in response to increased consumption in the West Indies as a result of the expansion of plantation agriculture, most notably the production of sugarcane. In the early 1850s, commission houses in Savannah, Pensacola, Mobile, and Charleston shipped large quantities to the islands, especially Cuba. Of these cities, Pensacola was the most dependent on the lumber trade, for it had little else to ship. Charleston also benefited to an unusual degree. The overworked cotton lands nearby were becoming less and less profitable, and many planters were moving their main agricultural operations to newer lands to the west, lands tributary to other ports. By offering an opportunity for increasing profits on the older plantations, lumbering helped slow the exodus and buttress the sagging economy of the port.

The South's export trade in lumber suffered from the mid-1850s on. Shipping costs were being driven upward as a result of the burgeoning cotton trade's demand for cargo space, but domestic markets, carried along by the expanding cotton economy, were becoming major consumers. Millmen with plants located where they could economically ship to New Orleans or other internal markets continued to prosper; those elsewhere struggled on as best they could, sometimes by dispatching maritime shipments northward to markets once securely controlled by Maine.[19]

The sum of all these developments was dramatic. From New England to California, from Michigan to the Gulf of Mexico, changes were transforming the lumber industry. Buoyed by the general prosperity, by the economic growth in old areas and new, producers were increasing their cut at an unprecedented rate. But more than rising production was involved. The very thrust of the industry was changing. Urbanization and industrialization—as well as other factors such as the settlement of prairies and railroad construction—were creating demands that small, locally oriented mills could not fill. To meet the new demand, lumbermen erected larger and larger plants. The industry remained decentralized, as its resource base demanded, but in other ways it was rapidly assuming new forms.

The lumber industry was not alone. Midcentury was a transition point for the American business world as a whole. Previously, manufacturers had been relatively weak; power rested with commission merchants and others who dominated marketing in the nation's commercial-mercantile centers. Capital was the key. Under the old system, when manufacturers needed money for expansion or other major expenditures, they usually turned to the merchants who marketed their products for them. Manufacturers operated on too small a scale to generate the needed capital internally or through the sale of stocks or bonds to outsiders. But as the size of manufacturing enterprises grew, so did their independence. After 1850 more and more producers began to assume control over the marketing of their own products; and as their enterprises grew, increasing numbers found it possible to finance expansion through profits or by taking in new partners, and eventually by offering stock or issuing bonds.

The lumber industry that was evolving from the changes of midcentury fit the pattern perfectly. Whereas sawmill operators in Bangor had been wont to repair to Boston's merchants in search of funds, the new breed of lumbermen that was coming to the fore—men like Frederick Weyerhaeuser, Philetus Sawyer, and Henry W. Sage—had no such need. Indeed, others were coming to them, and so their holdings gradually became diversified. In the new America that was to appear during the second half of the nineteenth century, manufacturers held a position of strength; for manufacturers such as lumbermen, who produced a basic material needed for continuing growth, it was a strength that grew as time passed.[20]

If forests were inextricably intertwined with the growth processes that were building modern America, they remained at the same time very much a part of the everyday life of the population. Frederick Starr commented that the things most fundamental to national growth were "cheap bread, cheap houses, cheap fuel, and cheap transportation" and that wood was intimately involved in each of these.

Be that as it may, the relationships were changing, as the case of furniture demonstrates. Every home had furniture. Almost without exception, this was made of wood. However, in the second half of the nineteenth century furniture was increasingly becoming a standardized product of urban factories rather than the handcrafted work of local artisans. The change perhaps showed up the most clearly in central and eastern Texas.

This part of Texas was both isolated and fragmented during the mid-nineteenth century. It was difficult to enter the area either overland or from the coast. Its export-based economy tied the region financially to the outside world, but it depended on local production for the bulk of its durable goods. These came from centers such as Round Top, which served the surrounding areas and were sometimes separated by wide expanses of virtually uninhabited prairie and forest. Local cabinetmakers met the demand for furniture.

As urban centers grew and increased mechanization came into furniture manufacture, the centers of production became increasingly urban. Thus Galveston and Austin became furniture-making centers. Because of the difficulties of overland transportation, manufacturers in Galveston did not use wood from Texas but instead depended upon shipments from Alabama, Florida, and Maine. Gradually the old centers of furniture-making declined. Their artisans lacked the skill to match the machine-made products from the cities or to satisfy the taste of Victorian Americans for ornate pieces.

When railroads at last made transportation to the outside easy during the 1870s, the process was complete. Much of the furniture sold in Texas thereafter was shipped in from centers beyond its borders. As the authors of *Texas Furniture* put it, "Almost without noticing, the Texas craftsman [who made furniture] became first a repairman and then a curiosity." But if the mode of production had changed, the raw material had not. Texans—and other Americans—continued to use furniture, and that furniture continued to be made of wood.[21]

Long before the mid-nineteenth century, American roads had earned a reputation as the worst in Christendom. Their wretched condition was partially because waterways provided alternative transportation, partly because political power and wealth were concentrated in the seaboard commercial-mercantile centers so roads in the interior could easily be overlooked, and partly because there was not enough social overhead capital to build an extensive system of roads in any case. But farmers needed roads if their goods were to get to market, or at least to railroad sidings and riverboat landings, and merchants of the interior needed roads if goods were to reach them so they could supply their customers. Railroads could not reach every hamlet and farm, nor could waterways meet everyone's needs. In many an area, plank roads seemed a satisfactory alternative.

As already noted, roads "paved" with planks had begun to appear in the 1840s. Such roads increased in number and length during the 1850s. No center was more fully served by plank roads than Milwaukee. Mayor Byron Kilbourn declared in 1848, "with a good system of plank roads extending in all directions into the interior, and a railroad to the Mississippi, the foundations of the prosperity of our city would be laid deep and strong." Construction quickly followed. By the end of 1852, Milwaukee had 150 miles of wood-surfaced roads reaching into its hinterlands. Others followed, not only in the vicinity of Milwaukee but elsewhere in the state as well. By 1857 there were over a thousand miles of plank roads in Wisconsin.

Although plank roads were made of wood, they were less important to the infant lumber industry as consumers of wood than as contributors to the general economic growth that led to rising demand. The roads themselves were usually surfaced with oak, cut by portable sawmills erected to service the needs of road builders rather than as continuing enterprises. In spite of their effect on the larger economy, most plank roads failed to return satisfactory profits to their builders, and many were soon abandoned.

The plank road built to connect Portland, Oregon, with the agriculturally rich Tualatin Plains provides a classic example. At midcentury Portland was but one of a number of towns near the confluence of the Willamette and Columbia rivers contending for commercial supremacy in Oregon. In 1851 Portland's business leaders obtained a charter from the territorial legislature for the Portland and Valley Plank Road Company. Before it ran out of money and had to halt construction later that year, the company had managed to complete ten miles of plank road through Tanner Creek Canyon. The company was reorganized several times, but the road itself left much to be desired until the 1880s. In spite of its shortcomings, it was adequate to make Portland the main outlet for the produce of the Tualatin Plains. With this advantage, Portland forged ahead of its rivals, seizing the leadership that it has held ever since.[22]

Whether or not they lived in a city served by plank roads, in 1870 Americans were still dependent upon wood to an extraordinary degree. Most people, rural and urban alike, lived in wooden buildings. But behind even this element of continuity, change lurked. Shingles, with which the overwhelming majority of houses were roofed, had once been almost exclusively a product of farmers intent upon earning extra cash while clearing their lands. After 1860 shingles came primarily from commercial shingle mills. And shingles are but one example. Potash, firewood, hewn timbers, and similar items had long been important sources of income for farmers; now they were inconsequential for nearly all but the most isolated and backward. Forests were still a source of materials that farmers needed, but more and more frequently they had to buy them from others. Like urbanites, by 1870 farmers were buying far more forest products than they were producing. Wood may have still been ubiquitous in the everyday life of Americans, but those who supplied it were, like America as a whole, steadily becoming more commercial and industrialized.

The mid-nineteenth century was a watershed for the American forest in general and the lumber industry in particular. But this does not mean that thereafter forest utilization proceeded steadily in the new directions. Economic, political, and social developments made exploitation of the forests a halting process. Indeed, during the second half of the nineteenth century the lumber industry was one of the most volatile, erratic components of American industrial enterprise—as it would continue to be in the twentieth century.

Undergirding the changes that were sweeping the lumber industry at midcentury was a prolonged period of general prosperity. For most of the country, prosperous times continued until 1857, when financial panic brought building to a virtual standstill. On the West Coast the bubble burst in 1854. Lumbermen who had expanded operations during the gold rush years now suddenly found their industry badly overbuilt. Closures and bankruptcies followed. Millmen desperately sought alternative markets beyond those in California, which had sustained them since the discovery of gold at Sutter's mill. New outlets in Hawaii, Australia, China, and Latin America not only helped carry them through the crisis, but also continued to provide vital markets in the years that followed. Through the rest of the century the Pacific Coast's lumber industry stood with one foot in domestic markets and one foot overseas and helped to tie the Far West to the Pacific basin more closely in some ways than to the rest of the United States.[23]

The Panic of 1857 did not affect all areas—or mills—equally. Where continued railroad construction was the basis of demand,the impact on lumbermen was immediate. A cessation of construction meant a cessation of orders. But on the prairies and plains, the flood of immigration during the immediately preceding years resulted in continued demand even after the panic struck. The owners of established farms might be able to forgo building until the return of prosperity, but good times or bad, recent arrivals had to build barns, fences, and houses. Moreover, immigration did not cease at once; not until 1858 did it begin to fall off as the grim economic news from America reached potential migrants in Europe. Lumbermen who produced for newly opened agricultural areas thus had a partial immunity from the effects of the panic. To be sure, the price they obtained for their cut fell, but the costs of labor and logs were down too. Millmen such as Orrin Ingram, who sold primarily in the agricultural areas west of the Mississippi, continued to find buyers while others, dependent upon the railroads for purchases, closed. Some were even less affected than Ingram. Andrew Brown, who sawed cypress for the New Orleans market, was one. His sales, which had been rising steadily in value, leveled off in 1857, but real depression struck neither Brown nor New Orleans until fears generated by the approach of secession brought business almost to a standstill in 1860.[24]

The effects of the Civil War were much deeper than those of the Panic of 1857. The Union blockade cut Charleston, Pensacola, Mobile, and other southern ports off from the export markets on which they depended, and production in these areas ceased. Northern exporters were affected too. Confederate raiders made maritime shipments risky; freight and insurance rates soared, and obtaining crews became difficult and costly. Inevitably, American lumber became more expensive to foreign buyers, and as a result many turned to Canada and elsewhere rather than continuing to purchase from the United States.

The war did far more to the lumber industry of the North than interrupt its maritime trade. Not the least of its effects were psychological: the coming of the war added an element of uncertainty that was especially unwelcome to the host of sawmill operators just getting established in the Lake States pineries. Their feelings were not unwarranted. As the war drew off young men to the armed forces, construction on midwestern farms slowed, and lumbermen quickly felt the pinch. Moreover, it became increasingly difficult to find laborers for sawmill and woods work. But gradually the situation changed. The war brought better prices to farmers. By 1863 many had managed to pay off their debts and were undertaking improvements; agrarian demand for lumber revived, and this time sellers founds it less difficult to collect from buyers. An eagerness to pay and be done with it sprang in part from a distrust of the wartime currency; many considered it wise to turn greenbacks into fixed assets as quickly as possible. Wartime conditions also resulted in substantial expansion of various manufacturing enterprises, if not of the whole economy. The government itself purchased much lumber for military use. From both developments, lumbermen benefited.

Northern lumbermen received other benefits from the war. One of the most direct stemmed from the Union blockade of the South. Just before the war, some nine million board feet of southern pine entered Boston harbor each year, and considerable quantities arrived in other northern ports as well. Once the war started, these shipments almost completely ceased. In the year from September 30, 1862, to September 30, 1863, shipments of southern pine to Boston totaled a mere 47,904 feet. Northern producers now met that part of the demand that southerners had serviced before the war.

After the initial doldrums had passed, reduced competition and brisk wartime demand resulted in rising prices. Grades of white pine that had sold in Philadelphia for twenty-two dollars a thousand in 1855 were bringing forty-eight dollars in 1865. Part of the increase was a reflection of the depreciated wartime currency, but a significant rise in real price was also involved.

Like farmers, northern lumber manufacturers found in the solid demand and good prices that had developed by 1863 opportunities to retire old debts and strengthen their financial underpinnings. At the same time many were able to improve their plants. Orrin Ingram provides an example: his sawmill company had gone into the war an uncertain fledgling but emerged a sound, solid enterprise ready to grow apace during the period of rampant expansion that followed the war. The process was not limited to lumbering. Manufacturers as a whole had been weak and financially dependent upon the merchant class before the war but emerged from it stronger and more independent. A new day was coming in American business, and the Civil War had speeded its arrival.

Secession also broke the long stalemate over rival rail routes to the Pacific Coast. With the South out of Congress, it was at last possible to get legislation passed for a federal land grant and subsidies for the construction of a line along the central route to California. With completion of the Union Pacific–Central Pacific line in 1869, transcontinental rail connections were finally a reality. This line, like the prairie lines of the 1850s, required a great quantity of wood, but this had little lasting effect. Much of the wood for the railroad came from temporary mills that closed once construction was complete. The eastern portions of the line extended the area that lumber producers in the Lake States could supply at a reasonable cost, thus aiding the push westward onto the plains, but this too was hardly a major change.

More important was the psychological stimulus that the Central Pacific–Union Pacific line provided. Its completion spurred growth in the Far West. No longer did the area seem hopelessly distant to potential settlers or investors. From this attitudinal change came growth in the Rocky Mountain area and beyond—growth that would eventually have the most far reaching of effects. That, however, was still decades away as the Civil War ended.

Perhaps the greatest effect of the Civil War on business was the one least susceptible to measurement. Before the conflict lumbering, and nearly every other business enterprise except the railroads, was conducted on a relatively small and localized scale. But if entrepreneurs had a limited vision before the war, the war itself appears to have opened the eyes of many to grander possibilities. Millions of men and masses of material, North and South, were mobilized for the war effort. Surely not all who engaged in, or observed, such activity were oblivious to its implications for business. It seems more than coincidence that the same mobilization of vast resources, the same intricacy of management, and the same quest for broad, general goals through careful planning that had characterized the war effort should appear rather abruptly in American business soon after the war was over. The lumber industry, among many others, may simply have evolved to a point where these new patterns would have appeared in any case, but the suddenness of the change suggests that the war speeded and helped shape the course of events. Frederick Weyerhaeuser, as surely as John D. Rockefeller and Andrew Carnegie, appears to have been a beneficiary of lessons learned at the feet of the god of war.

If northern lumbermen generally came out of the war in better shape than they had entered it, the same clearly could not be said of those in the South. When General Braxton Bragg abandoned Pensacola, he burned the sawmills to prevent their falling into federal hands. Numerous other southern mills were also razed during the conflict, either by design or by accident. Not just mills were destroyed, but also the railroads upon which many of them depended for log transportation. So too were the system of slave labor on which many southern lumbermen depended and much of the investment capital with which the wartime damage might have been repaired. In these circumstances, southerners emerged from the war in no position to quickly recapture markets lost to northern lumbermen during the war.[25]

Once the war was over, rebuilding was slowed by a shortage of machinery, capital, and skilled workers. In Florida, where the industry quickly adjusted to the use of freedmen, something approximating the old levels of production was fairly promptly restored; but even there little expansion took place. Southern wealth did not tend to go into lumbering. As a leading historian has observed, one of the tragedies of the post–Civil War era was the failure of southerners "to see that their vast timber resources offered a high degree of economic security in perpetuity." Not until the 1880s, when northerners who were running short of timber in their own section began making large investments in the southern pineries, did the lumber industry of the South finally enjoy a period of expansion eclipsing that of the 1850s. When it came, it was largely instigated by outsiders, not by southerners themselves.[26]

Burgeoning demand during the fifties and sixties put pressure on producers. In part it was met by opening new plants in previously untapped or lightly tapped areas such as the Pacific Coast and Lake States, but it also stimulated a series of changes in production and marketing that affected new and old regions alike. As was to be true in following decades, sawmill operations proved more susceptible to change than operations in the woods. Suppliers of sawmill equipment, such as E. P. Allis and Company of Milwaukee, offered devices to drag logs to their main saws or headrigs, to turn the logs for cutting, and to move logs back and forth past the headrig. Previously much of this work had been done by sweat and muscle; now steam power was speeding and easing the tasks.

Sawing was also changing. Neither circular nor gang saws were new, of course, but between 1850 and 1870 mill after mill adopted them in place of the old up-and-down sash or muley saws. Only in the most isolated locations or the smallest operations did the older technology remain common. Genuinely new devices were also appearing; perhaps the most important was the gang edger. In 1856 Orrin Ingram adapted the principles of the gang saw to the edging and trimming of boards to improve their rectangularity. With a gang edger, both sides of a board could be squared simultaneously and automatically. Ingram's invention eliminated a major bottleneck in the production process, but he failed to patent it. His only profit from the gang edger came as a millman, not as an inventor.[27]

The many improvements installed to increase production and keep mills competitive with rivals made sawmilling increasingly complex. Managerial change resulted. Owner-operators, who had dominated from the beginning of the industry, gave way to hired managers who possessed the technical skills needed to run the new plants. Many of the industry's old guard, staunchly conservative and reluctant to allow outsiders into key positions, resisted the trend, but they could neither reverse it nor, in the long run, keep from joining in it if they wished to be successful.

Improvements encouraged other changes too. Only large mills could efficiently use much of the new equipment, and only financially sound ones could afford it. Frequently this led to the consolidation of small, formerly competing operations. These consolidations took various forms, with new partnerships frequently superimposed on old. The result was an industry with an increasingly complex web of control.[28]

The managers of these large mills had to range widely to secure an adequate supply of logs. In moving to tap fresh sources, the new combinations sometimes found themselves in sharp competition with mills already established near the timber. This sometimes led to clashes similar to those between raftsmen and log drivers in Clearfield County, Pennsylvania. And, as there, victory usually went to the better-financed forces of the rising new order.

As the productive capacity of mills rose during the 1850s and 1860s, more and more men had to go into the woods to provide the logs to keep them running. Many were immigrants from Canada or Europe. Woods crews were becoming an ethnic mix different not only from much of the rest of American society, but from the sawmill crews too. French-Canadians, for example, were common in the woods but were less frequently seen in the mills. Although the size and number of logging camps were increasing in the fifties and sixties and continued to increase in the decades that followed, logging operations themselves were changing relatively little. The basic means of cutting, skidding, and driving logs that had been developed in Maine continued to be used in the Lake States, the new Valhalla of loggers.

Yet however slowly, changes also appeared in the woods. Perhaps the most famous innovation of the period came in 1858 when an obscure Maine blacksmith named Joseph Peavey invented a new type of cant hook, the hand-operated pole-and-hook device loggers used in manipulating logs both ashore and during river drives. Peavey modified the method of attaching the hook to the handle, making it more rigid and thus less apt to slip during use. He added graduated collars of iron to give added strength to the handle and put a sharp iron spike in its end. Known to loggers simply as the peavey, the invention was a vast improvement over its predecessors. At about the same time, loggers from Pennsylvania introduced double-bitted axes into the woods, an innovation Mainers looked upon with suspicion when they moved into the Keystone State following the building of the Susquehanna Boom but soon adopted as they discovered its advantages. Both tools quickly became standard implements in the woods from coast to coast and have remained so ever since.

More noticeable to most observers were changes in the transportation of logs and lumber. The replacement of rafting by booms and log drives on the West Branch of the Susquehanna was only one such change. Steamboat-propelled rafts replaced free-floating ones as the prime means of moving logs down the Mississippi. Steamboats were faster and more dependable and created fewer hazards, an important factor on the increasingly crowded river.

Steamboats also came into use on Lake Erie and thus led to major adjustments in the growing lumber trade through the Erie Canal. Before 1866 most lumber to be shipped through the canal went by cargo ship or barge to Buffalo, where it was transferred to canal barges. With the use of steamboats, rafts of lumber could easily be towed past Buffalo and down the Niagara River to Tonawanda and North Tonawanda, situated on a quiet river harbor where the Erie Canal first reached the waters of the Great Lakes. The Tonawandas were closer to the eventual destination than was their rival Buffalo; thus shipments via the Tonawandas traveled a maximum distance in the less expensive steamboat-driven rafts and a lesser distance by canal barge. In addition, land cost less in the Tonawandas than in the growing city of Buffalo, making lumberyards and other facilities for sorting and transshipping lumber less expensive. After

1866 the Tonawandas outstripped Buffalo as the major lumber-forwarding center at the western end of the canal.[29]

Changes in production, marketing, and organization did not proceed at a uniform pace throughout the period 1850 to 1870. They were slowed by the Panic of 1857 and the advent of the Civil War and then were speeded, at least in the North, by developments during the later years of the war and after. From 1863 until depression struck a decade later, they proceeded at a rapid, if not breakneck, pace.

Out of it all, a dual industry had emerged. On the one hand there were large, modern mills serving the needs of an expanding, industrializing economy, and on the other hand there was a larger number of crude little plants serving the needs of more isolated communities. One historian had used manuscript census returns to map the pattern in the Pacific Northwest. He found that where inexpensive water transportation was available for moving lumber from mills to major markets, large plants developed; but in landlocked areas or at the poorer ports, where only the inefficient smaller cargo vessels could enter, operations remained small and primitive. A similar pattern could be found in nearly every corner of the nation. Change was coming to the lumber industry, but not all mills and not all localities were being affected in the same way.[30]

Midcentury was a turning point for American forests—and forest industries—just as it was for much of the rest of society. At first many of the changes went largely unnoticed, but by the end of the sixties it was readily apparent to perceptive viewers that there was no turning back to the simpler ways of the wooden age. Almost everywhere, it seemed, economic expansion was plunging ahead, and wood was playing a key role in the process.

The period 1870 to 1910 was to see the full flowering of Lake States lumbering, that segment of the industry most clearly attuned to the emerging new order, but by the end of the sixties what was coming was already clear. A huge industry was to emerge that would tap—and, the more prescient realized, eventually strip—old-growth stands in the farthest reaches of Michigan, Wisconsin, and Minnesota. Shortly before 1850 Henry David Thoreau had written: "You have only to travel for a few days into the interior and back parts even of many of the old States to come to that very America which the Northmen, and Cabot, and Gosnold, and Raleigh visited." By 1870 this was no longer true in a number of places, and it was evident that it soon would be true in far fewer.

15. Driving spruce logs down a river in Maine. These logs are for pulp; earlier drives of pine for lumber involved much longer logs. Courtesy American Forest Institute.

1

1

6. Loading pulpwood at Grand Marais, Minnesota, for shipment to the mill. Courtesy American Forest Institute.

7. Big wheels and early log loaders in use in Michigan. Courtesy U.S. Forest Service.

8. Bandsaw in operation. Courtesy Forest History Society.

19. Loggers in the Pacific Northwest fe
ing a Douglas fir from springboards.
Courtesy Forest History Society.

20. John Muir at his desk about 1897.
Courtesy of Forest History Society.

21. President Theodore Roosevelt and
Forest Service chief Gifford Pinchot dur-
ing the Inland Waterways Commission
Mississippi River excursion in 1907.
Courtesy U.S. Forest Service.

22. President Franklin D. Roosevelt and
Secretary of the Interior Harold C. Ickes
visiting a Civilian Conservation Corps
camp. Roosevelt Library Photo.

23. Douglas fir regeneration on land
clearcut a decade earlier. Courtesy Forest
History Society.

24. Actor William Boyd (Hopalong Cas-
sidy) lends his help to the Smokey Bear
publicity campaign against forest fires.
Courtesy U.S. Forest Service.

25. President Richard M. Nixon, with other dignitaries, dedicating Lady Bird Johnson Grove in Redwood National Park on August 27, 1969. Courtesy Nixon Library Service.

Attitudes and Perceptions

Chapter 8

The attitudes of Americans toward their country's natural resources were widely disparate as the second half of the nineteenth century began. They continued to be so in the years that followed. Past experiences and present realities, the preachments of diverse taste makers, and personal, regional, and class differences combined to create a kaleidoscopic mix of views. For all these differences, certain trends can nonetheless be discerned from 1850 to the early 1900s. Americans' attitudes toward and perceptions of their forests were assuming new forms, and changing patterns of use were appearing that were both a cause and a reflection of this.

The romantic movement, which reached its peak in the United States about 1850, was a major force shaping the outlook of educated Americans. Increasing numbers, caught up in its currents, turned for enjoyment and uplift to outdoor scenes. Classical European canons of taste had held that, to be truly moving, scenery had to have historical and human associations—the added mystery that comes from having been long lived in or the site of great events. Few American scenes could meet such standards, and as a result travelers in the United States had been more apt to describe what they saw as monotonous and frightful than as picturesque or beautiful.

Gradually, concepts of the American landscape had changed—at least in part. Washington Irving's immensely popular tales of Rip van Winkle and Sleepy Hollow gave the Catskill Mountains legendary associations formerly lacking. In addition, Irving, Thomas Cole, and others discovered that the Hudson River Highlands, with their battlements and other echoes of the Revolutionary War, had the historical associations deemed requisite for classification as great scenery. Both the Catskills and the Highlands became popular destinations for midcentury excursionists. Even some Europeans conceded their beauty.

The works of William Wordsworth, popular on both sides of the Atlantic, encouraged the rising acceptability of American scenes. The Lake poets and their successors preached that in the presence of nature one was closer to God. Nature, Wordsworth maintained, should be the poet's main source of inspiration; he should present it with fidelity and insight. Americans as well as Europeans were affected by these ideas; the poet William Cullen Bryant, the novelist James Fenimore Cooper, and Cole and other artists of the Hudson River school were all influenced by them. Even after it had passed its peak as an intellectual movement, romanticism continued to mold the outlook of educated Americans. Textbooks used in the burgeoning school systems of the late nineteenth and early twentieth centuries featured the works of Wordsworth and authors of similar outlook and helped shape what young Americans saw in nature.

The transcendentalist movement strengthened the trend initiated by romanticism. Writers such as Ralph Waldo Emerson and his one-time protégé Henry David Thoreau sought to bridge the gap between man and nature by underscoring the universal forces, the spark of divinity, present in both: rather than abhor nature or stand aloof from it, the wise man should contemplate and savor it.

Americans, sensitive to European (especially English) criticism that the scenery of the United States lacked the proper associations to be truly uplifting, found an answer in the works of romantic and transcendentalist thinkers. The American landscape might not boast ancient castles or ruins left by the Caesars, but its unsullied wildness could show the hand of God more clearly than the much-lived-in, man-shaped scenery of Europe. American scenery, short of human and historical associations, was assigned divine ones. Nationalistic sensitivities were assuaged.[1]

Yet European standards of taste continued to have a pervasive effect in shaping Americans' reactions to their land. The "nature" of Wordsworth was hardly the awesome wilderness of an unconquered continent. England's Lake District, which Wordsworth lovingly depicted, had been settled for centuries. Quiet pastoral scenes, not primeval forests, informed his aesthetic tastes. Others followed his lead. Capability Brown and Humphrey Repton, pioneers of landscape architecture in England, and Frederick Law Olmsted, their counterpart on the United States, were among them. Central Park, Olmsted's most famous project, was an attempt not to recapture the truly natural but to create an idealized rural landscape in the center of New York City.[2]

Such ideas died hard. In 1904 Andrew Dickson White, a leading American educator and statesman, gave voice to aesthetic judgments that Wordsworth and Olmsted would surely have shared. He described how, while serving in the 1880s as ambassador to the court of Kaiser Wilhelm II, he had observed the young emperor's efforts to renovate the Tiergarten. Earlier efforts of "improve" this large park in the center of Berlin had met uncompromising opposition from the public and had been abandoned. White was perplexed by the desire of Berliners for untamed woodland, replete with swamps and tangled undergrowth:

This [opposition to the renovation of the park] seemed a great pity, for while there were some fine trees, a great majority of them were so crowded together that there was no chance of broad, free growth either for trees or for shrubbery. There was nothing of that exquisitely beautiful play, upon expanses of green turf, of light and shade through the wide-expanded boughs and broad masses of foliage, which gives such delight in any of the finer English or American parks.

White, like many others both before and after, based his aesthetic judgments on a pastoral ideal. Expanses of grass sprinkled with occasional trees for contrast were preferred to wilder scenes. Americans imbued with such tastes were not apt (at least not on aesthetic grounds) to protest the rapid felling of forests and the destruction of the wilderness that a later generation would cherish.

The pastoral ideal encouraged a tendency to avoid nature in the raw. Thoreau provides a case in point. Like others who sprang from the transcendentalist movement, Thoreau rejected the materialism of most of his contemporaries. Seeking harmony and beauty through an appreciation of nature, he left Concord, Massachusetts, in 1845 to reside in a small cabin in the forest by Walden Pond. For two years Thoreau lived a simple, rustic life there. He enjoyed the stillness of the woods, the opportunity to study nature quietly and to write, but he was no hermit. Thoreau liked people; he had many visitors and frequently walked to town to take odd jobs, make a few purchases, or see friends. In 1846 he left Walden briefly for his first trip into true wilderness, the woods of northern Maine. He was surprised by his reactions. Unlike the soothing, gentle environment at Walden Pond, the unbroken wilds of Maine were to Thoreau "savage and dreary." He found himself irritated by insects and Indians rather than uplifted by nature.[3]

Yet Thoreau's life at Walden Pond was primitive indeed compared with that of most midcentury visitors to the out-of-doors, who sought pleasure resorts with broad verandas and attractive walkways rather than unmanicured retreats. On the eve of the Civil War, most who traveled for pleasure could afford to frequent such places as the posh Mountain House in the Catskills or exclusive spas like Saratoga Springs, New York, and White Sulphur Springs, in present-day West Virginia. Such pleasures were hardly an American invention. In Europe "taking the waters" was common among the well-to-do, and upper-class Americans were simply aping European practices. For such people, roughing it was likely to mean little more than going to the Jersey shore or some other place slightly less opulent than Saratoga Springs.

In 1869 William H. H. Murray published *Adventures in the Wilderness; or, Camp Life in the Adirondacks.* Encouraged by it and similar works, increasing numbers actually began camping out in the "wilds." However, most who did so were loath to lay aside urban comforts and complained bitterly when deprived of them. Hunting and fishing for sport also began to become popular among the well-to-do, and an elaborate sportsman's code developed that defined proper behavior for field and stream. In time many of these sportsmen became active in conservation work through organizations such as the Boone and Crockett Club. However, initially their main interest in sport stemmed from a desire to pursue activities that helped define them as gentlemen. They may have looked with disdain on their pampered fellow patricians who frequented Saratoga Springs, but they shared more of the latter's outlook than most of them cared to admit. They were wont to despise common rural folk for their coarse ways, for hunting and fishing for meat rather than sport, and for being spiritually unmoved by the natural beauty around them. Such people might serve as guides and other outdoor servants, but they could never be true companions even in the wilderness.[4]

During the last decades of the nineteenth century, national parks became popular destinations for the still-elite tourist traffic. Hotels catering to such visitors appeared at Yellowstone's Mammoth Hot Springs, on the south rim of Grand Canyon, and on the floor of the main valley of Yosemite. In 1903 Ray Stannard Baker depicted the clientele of such places when he described a visit to Yellowstone: "most of the tourists remain pretty snugly in their coach-seats or near the hotels. One meets them in great loads, some wrapped in long linen coats, some wearing black glasses, some broad green-brimmed hats. . . . Occasionally one sees them devouring their guidebooks and checking off the sights as they whirl by [in tourist coaches], so that they will be sure not to miss anything or see anything twice." Olmsted and others lauded national parks as preserving scenic sites for the people, but in fact until after the First World War nonurban parks in general and national parks in particular were primarily retreats for the wealthy. The *San Francisco Chronicle* attacked them on precisely those grounds: "Places like Yosemite and Yellowstone Park in the Rocky Mountains are seldom visited by the common people, and never from any distance by the poor. The rich—foreign and native—enjoy a monopoly of these pleasure grounds. It is wrong in principle and oppressive in practice for any government to tax the common people and the poor for the exclusive benefit of the rich." Development of Yosemite, the paper argued, would cost "many thousands of dollars in the shape of taxes on the property of the great masses of people who never can and never expect to see the Valley or derive the slightest benefit from its beauty and sublimity."[5]

Although trees graced the grounds of Central Park and the resort hotels and clothed the slopes of the Catskills and much of the acreage in the early national parks, the presence of forests was not in itself the reason such places were deemed worthy retreats. In Central Park and other products of landscape architects, trees were decorative adjuncts to the walks, waterways, and lawns that served to focus attention and activity. At the spas it was the mineral springs and at Mountain House the scenic vista of the fabled Catskills that provided a raison d'être. Trees helped to make such places attractive, but if nature failed to supply them man could readily do so. Developers did precisely that around the Hotel Raymond and Hotel del Coronado, plush hostelries built on treeless tracts in southern California when the arrival of railroads in the 1880s made that area (and its climate) readily accessible to those wealthy enough to take their leisure there.[6] To the gentlemen sportsmen, trees were at first important only in that they provided habitat for game and protected watersheds for fish. Later some, such as Madison Grant, were to become active in forest conservation, but it would take years before such concerns became common in patrician circles.

Niagara Falls and most of the early national parks, on the other hand, were preserved as natural curiosities or wonders. Monumentalism, as one historian has labeled the movement to preserve such sites, was an outgrowth of the romantic and transcendentalist deification of nature. If scenery was to reveal the hand of God, then the scene itself should incorporate the elemental forces of creation. Great chasms, thundering waterfalls, towering peaks, and geysers and other thermal phenomena were deemed sublime and awe inspiring—and thus worthy of preservation—because they showed the forces by which the divine plan was carried out. Mere forests were more transient. Except perhaps for the redwoods and giant sequoias of California, forests spoke of lesser things when they spoke at all. Some forested tracts might be saved as an incidental result of efforts to protect scenic wonders, but as yet there was little concern for preserving forests in more ordinary locations. Distance and rugged terrain provided what protection most forests got.[7]

The old Jeffersonian concept of the yeoman farmer as the backbone of the ideal society was at least as influential as romantic and transcendentalist thought in shaping American attitudes toward the forest. Society, it was argued, would draw strength from a citizenry whose members, working their own small farms, had a personal stake in the economic and political affairs of the nation. Their interested, informed participation would make the nation safe from despots and plutocrats. This political ideology was not new with Thomas Jefferson, but he articulated it brilliantly. Jacksonian politicians, repeating the refrain on countless occasions, reinforced it to the point of dogma and helped it spread. The goal of universal landholding had nonpartisan appeal, for Americans defined their national self-image in anti-European, antifeudal terms. The United States represented the democratic wave of the future; European feudalism, in which the few engrossed the land for their own benefit, represented the dead hand of the past. Both Whigs and Democrats came to repeat this Jeffersonian litany.[8]

Reflecting this idea, many in Congress had by midcentury come to believe that insofar as the public domain was concerned, the primary responsibility of the legislative branch was to devise means to transfer it quickly and easily to smallholders. The land policies that resulted were based on agrarian assumptions and designed to meet agrarian needs. That much of the land was ill suited for farming and could not be economically managed as small family farms was denied when it was not ignored. Laws affecting forestland reflected the general agrarian belief that the best thing one could do with a forested tract was to clear and farm it.[9]

The Preemption Act of 1841 marked a major turning point in the history of the public domain. Earlier legislation had been designed so that the disposal of public lands would generate funds for the government; the Preemption Act, by contrast, gave priority to encouraging agricultural settlement. Under its terms, actual settlers could purchase up to 160 acres of surveyed land in the public domain for $1.25 per acre. In so legislating, Congress was at last recognizing that settling on public land before purchase was not illegal. The bill was a signal victory for the West, which wanted farming encouraged, but it was of limited value to lumbermen. Purchase was limited to settlers—that is, farmers. In any case, 160 acres was too small a tract on which to base any significant timber operation.

The Homestead Act of 1862 made land even more readily available to agriculturists, but it did little to make timber more accessible to lumbermen. Operators of sawmills could purchase logs from farmers who had acquired land under the Preemption and Homestead laws and wished to generate some income from clearing their land. But such sources were inadequate to meet the needs of the growing lumber industry and the public dependent upon it.

Since 1820 land, once surveyed, had been offered at auction at a minimum price of $1.25 per acre. Many acres of timberland passed to lumbermen by this route, but again not enough to meet demand. Most of the nation's forests had not been surveyed, and Congress's niggardly appropriations for the work showed its lack of concern for lumbermen, who could not legally acquire timber on unsurveyed land, though they needed it desperately.

Timber could, however, be acquired legally in other ways. At various times between 1842 and 1856, Congress passed donation acts giving homesteads to citizens in Florida, Oregon, Washington, and New Mexico to encourage settlement of those frontier territories. The government also issued land scrip or warrants in satisfaction of a variety of obligations. Much of the forested land that passed into private hands as a result of these warrants was sold to lumbermen; when the land itself was not sold, the timber from it frequently was. The federal government also gave sizable tracts to the states to help finance education and for other purposes. Many states sold these lands to private citizens, thus providing other sources of logs for lumbermen. Land grants to corporations to encourage the building of railroads, canals, and wagon roads yielded additional logs for the nation's mills.

Although all these laws benefited lumbermen, none had been designed to do so. They had been intended either to aid and encourage farmers or to generate funds for education, transportation, and various other public purposes. Not until the Timber and Stone Act of 1878 did Congress pass legislation allowing for the disposal of timberlands in the public domain that had no value for agriculture or mining. Still, this act reflected the same agrarian bias in favor of smallholders that had shaped earlier land laws: no individual could claim more than 160 acres. The Timber and Stone Act and other legislation then in force resulted in precisely what one would anticipate: a fragmented pattern of timberland ownership that made little economic sense; the barring of legitimate logging operations from vast areas that had few, if any, other potential uses; and frequent bending and breaking of the laws to make them serve purposes for which they were not intended.[10]

Ironically, most lumbermen did not want land per se, only stumpage— trees. Federal law contained no provision for separating title to the land from title to the trees that grew on it. Therefore if one wanted the security of a legal, reliable source of logs for his mill, he had little choice but to obtain title to land.

For lumbermen the easiest method of dealing with this incongruous body of law was timber trespass. Loggers working either independently or for sawmill operators would simply go into the woods and cut the trees they wanted. The amount of such cutting is impossible to gauge, but it was extensive, especially in the Lake States. The commissioner of the General Land Office complained that the insatiable midwestern demand for lumber led to timber trespass on a scale unmatched anywhere in the country. For example, through the end of 1849, land sales by the federal government in Manistee County, Michigan, totaled only 852 acres, yet John Stronach had been operating a sawmill in Manistee since 1841, and by 1850 there were at least four others nearby. All must have depended heavily upon sawlogs obtained through trespass. A state land agent investigating the situation in northeastern Michigan about this time found that all of the previously granted school and university lands within two or three miles of waterways fit for log drives had been stripped of their salable timber. Thieves had taken the trees and left the then-valueless land to the state.[11]

Frequently those involved in timber trespass used a tract of their own, strategically located in the midst of federal or state land, as a base to work from. Some operators were relatively restrained. They estimated the boundaries of their tract generously or, if it had actually been surveyed, were not particularly careful to ensure that their logging crews did not cut beyond the property lines. Others were more blatant, cutting in all directions as far as greed, competitors, government myopia, and the terrain would allow. From such practices came the tongue-in-cheek term "round forty," a euphemism for a forty-acre tract to which one held title or cutting rights and around which one cut illegally in public timber or that of other landowners. One owner, despairing of the number and aggressiveness of the thieves, wrote "timber can only be protected by standing on the land with a rifle and shooting the trespassers." Only luck and isolation could protect an absentee landowner, public or private.

Not surprisingly, independent loggers seem to have been the most extreme offenders. As a group they were little respected. Sawmill operators generally considered them irresponsible or worse; most freed themselves from relying on logs from independents as soon as it was financially feasible to do so. The independent logger had little to lose if caught in timber trespass and thus little to restrain him. His assets were generally limited, his fixed investments negligible. Not tied to any given locality, he could easily transfer his activities to areas beyond the reach of any zealous protector of public interests who might appear on the scene.

Millowners had to be more cautious. They could not avoid government officials so readily and had more to lose. Most might well have preferred to obey the law, but financial pressures drove them to do otherwise. Operating in an intensely competitive industry and generally short on investment capital, mill-men long felt compelled to put what funds they had into manufacturing facili-ties rather than timberlands. To do otherwise seemed guaranteed to ensure that one could not long stay abreast of competitors. Indeed, acquiring suf-ficient timberland to sustain long-term operations was so far beyond the realm of possibility that most millowners gave it little if any consideration. They sim-ply assumed continued dependence upon public timberland, whose future availability they took for granted.

But remaining competitive in a cutthroat industry demanded more than concentrating one's capital in production; it also required that expenses be kept low. As one of the largest items in the cost of production, logs had to be obtained cheaply. Whenever a millowner purchased timberland, he strove to get the maximum yield from it, even if that meant cutting some trees beyond his property lines. When one purchased logs from an independent, one did not inquire too closely into their origins so long as they were cheap.

There were other illegal means of obtaining timber. As time passed, false entries became more and more common. Supposed settlers entered claims under the Homestead Act, Timber and Stone Act, and other acts and promptly signed them over to lumbermen who coveted the timber. Sometimes these dummy entrymen were workers—or even real farmers—who saw a chance to earn a few easy dollars; at other times they were lumber company employees dutifully following their employers' wishes. Firms even appeared that made a business of locating dummy entrymen—for a price. Whole crews from mer-chant ships visiting Puget Sound were marched down to the local land office to sign affidavits that they were actual settlers on land that in fact had been pre-selected for them by company timber cruisers and on which they had never set foot. Congress may not have provided adequate means by which lumbermen could have legal access to timber on federal land, but enterprising citizens were undeterred. They developed their own means of access, and millions of board feet of sawlogs soon found their way to the mills.

There was a considerable measure of both public support and official understanding—even sympathy—for lumbermen who had to break the law if they were to supply the quantities of wood products the nation demanded. When government officers tried to crack down on illegal cutting on federal land, they aroused strong resentment and even outright opposition. The citizenry of lumbering communities believed the timber ought to be harvested, that the laws passed by Congress barring such harvest were ill advised, and that strict enforcement of the timber laws served only to harass those who provided the community with jobs—indeed, with a reason for being. Moreover, Congress and federal officials were outsiders; as a Fourth of July orator noted in a speech in one lumber town, the United States is the land of the people: "we are the people; ergo, the land belongs to us." Local residents, rather than distant politicians and government officials, had the right to decide how best to use the resources of their area. The idea that in America the people were truly sovereign was more than empty rhetoric; in many a region it was a fact, and "the people" was taken to mean local residents, not the minions of government.

The result of the thinking that lay behind all this was predictable. As a federal judge noted, a thief is banned from "respectable social intercourse," but in regard to "timber, which renders valuable the public lands . . . a different sentiment exists, and many, openly, and without concealment, engage in a systemized business of timber plundering" without losing social standing. Indeed, as they built up fortunes and expanded their activities, they were applauded.[12]

Perhaps so many lumbermen bent and broke the law simply because they shared their townsmen's attitudes. Most lumbermen of the Gilded Age had risen from common origins. The education of three-quarters was limited to elementary school; the parents of over half had been farmers. It is perhaps no coincidence that justifications for timber trespass rested on the same sort of thinking that had made squatting on the public domain an accepted way of acquiring a frontier farm decades before Congress finally legitimized the practice in the Preemption Act of 1841. In addition, it is clear that the lumbermen saw their activities as being in the public interest. The doctrine of progress, the idea that one had an almost sacred duty to turn resources to use so as to benefit all, was as deeply embedded in the national psyche as was the Jeffersonian faith in the yeoman farmer.

Typical lumbermen saw themselves as entrepreneurs who through hard work were turning resources into capital and in so doing were opening new areas, laying the foundations of lasting communities, and enriching the nation. To question such contributions would have seemed to them like questioning progress itself, which was something neither they nor the vast majority of their contemporaries were prepared to do.[13]

Romanticism cum transcendentalism and the Jeffersonian yeoman tradition leavened by the materialist ethic of progress were not alone in molding American attitudes toward nature in general and forests in particular. Increasingly in the late nineteenth century, science and urbanism had a shaping role as well. Of the two, science was the first to play an important part. As residents of a labor-short society, Americans from colonial times onward had valued technological advances that could maintain or increase production while reducing the need for labor. In a society where unfamiliar conditions frequently demanded novel solutions for even traditional problems, the inventive mind had always been welcomed and practical science prospered.

Similarly, on a continent where much was new, a large part of early scientific effort was aimed at describing and cataloging its plants, animals, and landforms. Acquisitive Americans approved, for taxonomic science seemed a first step toward turning resources to use—and profit. In contrast, theoretical science languished in the United States, and when first-rate theoreticians such as Josiah Willard Gibbs and Henry A. Rowland finally appeared on the scene in the 1870s, they were more appreciated in Europe than in America.[14]

But the gulf between theoretical and practical science was narrowing. The industrial expansion of the Gilded Age was made possible by a host of technological developments, many of which indirectly grew out of what a later generation would call basic research. Moreover, in the wake of Charles Darwin's *On the Origin of Species* (1859) numerous Americans for the first time developed an intense interest in a purely theoretical scientific study, though their motivation was hardly scientific.

Darwin's work not only resulted in a heated rebuttal by Christians who saw the theory of evolution as an attack on sacred truths, it also had less spectacular effects. It was first used by Herbert Spencer, William Graham Sumner, and other social Darwinists to strengthen their case against government interference with the struggle for survival in human affairs, a struggle they saw as the vehicle of progress. However, it soon led some thinkers, such as Lester Frank Ward, to a very opposite conclusion—to the position that human intelligence gave mankind the capacity to select both goals for society and appropriate means of getting there. Thus Darwin's work helped pave the way for the emergence of the active state (as contrasted with the passive state of the social Darwinists) and of the highly trained specialists—including foresters—who were to make it run.

Darwin touched American forests in other ways as well. His work increased awareness of the interrelationships of living forms. Other scientists, especially Alexander von Humboldt, had encouraged investigations in this direction, but Darwin added substantial impetus to the movement.[15] Such work resulted in greater sophistication in understanding America's forests. It helped silviculture develop as a discipline and fueled a number of controversies that marked the late nineteenth and early twentieth centuries: controversies over the effect of forest cover on streamflow; over the efficacy of afforestation of the plains to increase rainfall; over the wisdom of burning brush as a way to increase forage in the pine forests of the South and West; and over the impact of grazing sheep in forests.

The longest strides toward a scientific understanding of the nation's forests were no doubt made by George Perkins Marsh. A widely read, widely traveled Vermonter, Marsh was a lawyer, editor, farmer, businessman, congressman, and diplomat. He knew twenty languages, was an authority on Scandinavian and English linguistics, and helped inaugurate the Smithsonian Institution. Among other businesses, he engaged for a time in that of lumber dealer. But the contribution that stands out, the one that gave him a lasting reputation, was his book *Man and Nature; or, Physical Geography as Modified by Human Action,* first published in 1864.

Marsh's work grew out of years of observation and study. As a youngster he tramped the Vermont countryside and read von Humboldt's works with their discussion of the deleterious effects of deforestation; as a young businessman in Burlington, he saw the city turned from an exporter of lumber to an importer in the space of twenty years. Nowhere in the country had the forests been cut faster and the topsoil eroded more quickly than in Vermont's Green Mountains. As American minister to Turkey from 1849 to 1853, he had further opportunity to observe and reflect upon the effects of man on the land. During those years he traveled widely in the Mediterranean area, insatiably collecting data on natural conditions and phenomena. Everywhere he went in this long-lived-in area, the destructive impact of man was evident. The Sahara, the Adriatic Karst, the Roman Campagna, the valleys of Provence and Dauphine, all once fertile and populous, "now stood," as Marsh's biographer has put it, "barren and deserted monuments to human improvidence." After his return to the United States, Marsh held, among other jobs, an appointment as Vermont fish commissioner—a position in which he was charged with finding means of restoring the state's declining fish populations. After careful study, he attributed the decline to taking fish during spawning season, to water pollution from industrial and urban development, to forest clearing that resulted in extreme fluctuations in streamflow and water temperature, and to declining insect populations, a side effect of deforestation that reduced a major food source for fish. Marsh was already demonstrating awareness of the complex interrelations among living things and the effect that human activity could have on them—the very themes that were to mark *Man and Nature* when it appeared seven years later. In 1861 President Abraham Lincoln appointed Marsh United States minister to Italy. In that post he at last had the time and financial support to pull together a lifetime of observations and ideas. The result was *Man and Nature.*

In his great book Marsh took issue with those who had argued that the man-wrought changes in nature were desirable. In so doing, he was attacking the ethic of progress at its heart. Nature, Marsh contended, was remarkably stable if humans did not interfere to upset the balance that had been established over the ages. But everywhere, it seemed, mankind was indeed interfering—and in the process destroying resources that could have provided security for genera- tions to come. "Man has too long forgotten," he wrote, "that the earth was given to him for usufruct alone, not for consumption, still less for profligate waste." As a result, the earth was fast becoming unfit for civilized life; "depravation, barbarism, and perhaps even extinction of the [human] species" seemed to lie ahead unless mankind changed its ways. To those who argued that human activity was no different from that of any other animal, but merely a part of the larger scheme of natural processes, Marsh replied that there was both a quan- titative and a qualitative difference. Wild animals could not cause sudden changes in the environment, whereas man could fell whole forests in a short time. Such actions could have devastating effects:

When the forest is gone, the great reservoir of moisture stored up in its vegetable mould is evaporated, and returns only in deluges of rain to wash away the parched dust into which that mould has been converted. The well-wooded and humid hills are turned to ridges of dry rock, which encumbers the low grounds and chokes the watercourses with its debris, and . . . the whole earth, unless rescued by human art from the physical deg- radation to which it tends, becomes an assemblage of bald mountains, of barren, turfless hills, and of swampy and malarious plains.

Clearly, Marsh's travels in the Mediterranean basin had made a deep imprint on his mind, reinforcing what he had observed in his native Vermont.

The solution to these problems lay in science and civic responsibility. Marsh hoped that industry and individual citizens, operating on enlightened self- interest, would come to use resources more rationally, husbanding them care- fully. But more knowledge was needed if they were to do so successfully. Marsh called not only for the tapping of technological/scientific advances made in Europe, especially in silviculture, but for further studies in his own country as well.

Marsh's work was pivotal. A reviewer for the *Nation* called it "one of the most useful and suggestive books every published." Gifford Pinchot was to label it "epoch making," and years later Lewis Mumford would describe it as "the fountainhead of the conservation movement." All were correct enough, but the full impact of *Man and Nature* was felt only after a considerable time. Some of Marsh's more intellectual contemporaries read, pondered, and acted upon what he wrote, but most Americans continued their profligate ways. Still, *Man and Nature* did have short-run effects. It helped create an intellectual climate favorable to scientific studies of the natural environment—studies such as those of forester Bernhard Eduard Fernow, hydrologist John Wesley Powell, naturalist C. Hart Merriam, and others. In Wisconsin in 1867 a three-man state commission, headed by self-trained scientist Increase G. Lapham, drew heavily upon Marsh (as well as upon Lapham's own earlier work) in putting together the hundred-page *Report on the Disastrous Effects of the Destruction of Forest Trees, Now Going on So Rapidly in the State of Wisconsin.* By the time Gifford Pinchot set out to bring scientific management to the national forests in 1905, he had a body of scientific information to draw on. That body of knowledge was considerable in large part because of George Perkins Marsh.

The rational approach of Marsh and other scientists, both amateur and professional, was a far cry from the spiritual approach of romantic and transcendentalist thinkers. Marsh still looked to the individual rather than to the state for implementation of scientific resource management, but his thinking was very much a part of the trend toward the sort of active government directed by highly trained specialists that Lester Frank Ward championed and Theodore Roosevelt was to help introduce. At the same time, Marsh played a major role in initiating the trend toward science based on the interrelations of living forms— that is, toward the ecological understandings popularized later by Aldo Leopold.

Marsh's thinking marked a break with the romantic approach that sought sublimity and uplift in nature—that linked nature and the divine. It also marked a break with the yeoman tradition and its approach to the land, which was based not on an understanding of its capacity and limitations, but on a social and political ideal. Social theory had long molded American policies toward the forests. As Marsh's ideas gradually gained acceptance, realities came to replace egalitarian concepts as the primary shaping factor. After the turn of the century, contending interests, battling for implementation of mutually exclusive policies, found it increasingly necessary to cast their arguments in rational, scientific terms. Romantic literature and Jeffersonian concepts still had the power to move Americans, but positions on the management of natural resources had to have support from science if they were to have much chance of being adopted. The Forest Service, the Sierra Club, and timber companies large and small would all find themselves having to depend increasingly upon scientific arguments. George Perkins Marsh, more than any other American, sowed the seeds of that dependence.[16]

Scientific understanding of forests did not spring forth full grown like Athena from the head of Zeus. Changes in thinking emerged slowly and haltingly from the work of Marsh and others. Indeed, much of the science underlying debates over forest policy during that late nineteenth and early twentieth centuries was badly flawed. Nothing illustrated this better than the idea that forests increase rainfall.

The Great Plains had seemed to early explorers a scene of unbroken sterility and desolation. Agriculture was deemed impossible in this land without forests, quickly labeled the great American desert. But railroads with land grants in the area, local boosters, and settlers who had daringly pushed west of the hundredth meridian were unwilling to accept the idea that the region must remain the home of wandering Indians, bison, and herdsmen. It could, they hoped, be redeemed for agriculture. Casting about for support, they seized upon works suggesting that afforestation would increase rainfall on the plains, thus making farming there practical.

Alexander von Humboldt had noted the destructive impact of deforestation and the effects it seemed to have on climate. Others did the same. Some — such as Joseph Henry, director of the Smithsonian Institution — went even further, arguing that by planting forests it was possible "to modify the processes of nature; to cultivate the plants of the torrid zones amid the chilling winds of the northern temperate zone, and to render the climate of sterile portions of the earth congenial to the luxurious productions of more favored regions." In short, tree planting could transform the great American desert into the garden of the world. In *Man and Nature,* Marsh summarized the arguments, drawing on over two hundred works in a dozen different languages.

Marsh was typically cautious, noting evidence both pro and con; but others, drawn to the idea of remaking the plains like moths to a lamp, plucked what they wanted from his work and ignored the rest. Franklin B. Hough, appointed in 1876 to prepare the first substantial federal report on the forests of the United States, became an ardent champion of afforestation of the plains. So did Joseph Wilson, commissioner of the General Land Office, and Frederick Watts, commissioner of the Department of Agriculture. Publications emanating from the Smithsonian and other government agencies provided scientific reinforcement. Ferdinand Hayden, director of the United States Geological and Geographical Survey, noted in one such work in 1867, "the settlement of the country and the increase of timber has already changed for the better the climate of that portion of Nebraska lying along the Missouri. . . . I am confident this change will continue to extend across the dry belt to the foot of the Rocky Mountains." Regional boosters seized upon these works and gave wide circulation to their ideas.

Caught up in the enthusiasm, Congress passed the Timber Culture Act of 1873, which provided that "Any person who shall plant, protect, and keep in a healthy growing condition for eight years forty acres of timber, the trees thereon not being more than twelve feet apart each way on any quarter-section of any of the public lands . . . shall be entitled to a patent for the whole of said quarter-section." In other words, if homesteaders would plant trees, they would be rewarded with additional land.

In Nebraska, J. Sterling Morton was advocating a different but related approach. In 1872 he persuaded the State Board of Agriculture to set aside an annual day for the state's citizenry to plant trees. The idea caught on. By 1922 Nebraskans had planted an estimated seven hundred thousand acres of trees, and numerous other states had also proclaimed Arbor Days. The intent behind both the Timber Culture Act and Morton's program was clear. Trees were to be the philosophers' stone by which environmental alchemists would transmute arid wastes into arable farmland, thus preparing the way for Jeffersonian yeomen on the vast sweep of the plains.

But all this was for naught. The increased rainfall noted by Hayden and others was the result not of afforestation, but of an upswing in the region's normal climatic cycle. When the cycle turned downward in the 1890s, young trees died from drought and settlers either were driven out or hung on desperately in poverty. The idea of transforming the plains by tree planting—as well as the flawed scientific literature it rested on—withered in the sere winds of the dry years. Insofar as the area was to be changed, it would be by developing dryland farming techniques rather than modifying the climate. The only important gain from these efforts was indirect. The campaigns of Morton and other advocates of tree planting increased public awareness of the value of forests and trees, helping to create a climate of opinion in which the proposals of those who wished to husband forest resources could eventually be implemented.[17]

Protecting supplies of water for irrigation and domestic use also created an interest in forest protection, if not in afforestation. The connection between forest cover and runoff was widely accepted. Belief in the protective capacity of forests was the primary reason for the creation in 1885 of New York's huge Adirondack and Catskill preserves. These areas were more important at the time as sources of water for the Erie Canal and metropolitan areas than as producers of sawtimber or sites for outdoor recreation.

The same concern was central elsewhere. In California's San Joaquin Valley, local spokesmen agitated for the creation of Sequoia National Park to stop logging and grazing that were threatening the sources of irrigation water on which the local economy depended. Farther south, Theodore Lukens and Abbot Kinney led a vigorous campaign to protect the forests in the mountains of southern California in order to ensure recharging of vital groundwater supplies. Here, as in the Sierra, the greatest threat came from unrestricted grazing—and from fires set by herdsmen to reduce brush cover and increase grass and browse, which flourished after the land was burned over. Unfortunately, herdsmen's fires were followed by a drying up of many springs and creeks. Kinney, looking eastward past the San Gabriel Mountains to the Mojave Desert, waxed eloquent: "The desert is at our door today. It is pushed up against the mountain barrier that divides us. It is creeping up on the passes . . . and even has footings on and inside our mountain wall. . . . It is the forest that mans the rampart between our orchards, fields, flowers and cities and the frosts and fire of the glittering wastes of the desert." Elsewhere he was more prosaic: "The economic interest of the American people in their forests everywhere, and especially in the West, is to preserve the integrity and water holding power of the mountain watersheds."[18]

Technical knowledge of forestry was growing. Bernhard Fernow and Carl A. Schenck, German-trained foresters, came to the United States in the late nineteenth century to practice their professions. Fernow played a key role in public events, such as serving as chief of the United States Department of Agriculture's Division of Forestry from 1886 to 1898; Schenck, as forester on George Vanderbilt's Biltmore estate in North Carolina and head of the Biltmore Forest School, furthered knowledge of forestry in the private sector by both precept and example. Gifford Pinchot, a wellborn Pennsylvanian, went to France to study in the National Forestry School in Nancy and returned to work in the Biltmore forests, to serve on the National Academy of Sciences' forestry commission, and to succeed Fernow as head of the Division of Forestry. Although less thoroughly trained than either Schenck or Fernow, Pinchot had a greater understanding of America and Americans that, together with his dynamic personality, soon made him more important than either. In addition to Schenck's school at Biltmore, forestry schools came into being at Cornell, Yale, and elsewhere.[19]

As science became more sophisticated, the interconnections within the environment became clearer. Beginning in 1906, W J McGee, Pinchot, Roosevelt, and others sought to replace the existing fragmented approach of several agencies by bringing unified planning to entire watersheds. Their claims for the necessity of such action rested on inadequate studies of the effect of deforestation on streamflow. The Army's Corps of Engineers, in charge of flood control, saw its vested interests threatened. Led by Hiram Martin Chittenden, it counterattacked, pointing out the dearth of thorough studies and the unsubstantiated claims that its opponents were making in the name of science. For better or for worse, the corps won, thereby delaying the implementation of integrated timber/watershed management.

Actually, the corps used the same basic argument as Pinchot and his allies in the streamflow controversy: scientific understanding is prerequisite to proper decision making in resource management. Both sides pointed out the need for further study; their conflict presaged the central role science was destined to play in America's forests in years to come. In contrast to the situation when the Timber Culture Act had been enacted, it was no longer sufficient to have mere scientific window dressing for a resource-management proposal to be accepted. Increasingly, scientific support had to be sound and capable of surviving close scrutiny if one's opponents were to be disarmed.[20]

While science was growing in influence in the management of natural resources, so too were forces spawned by urbanism. Cities mushroomed during the late nineteenth century, generating massive problems. As ever larger percentages of the population came to live in urban settings for which established national ideals ill prepared them, an upswelling of interest in nature developed. With desperate earnestness scores of urban intellectuals turned to nature to buttress values supposedly being undermined by city life. Recapitulation and instinct psychology, popular at the time, helped turn them against the city; at the same time, behaviorism and environmentalism lauded moral virtues judged to be intrinsic in country life.

There were loud echoes of romanticism and transcendentalism in this new nature movement, but it was more fuzzily defined and less philosophical than its precursors. From first to last, the movement was largely a visceral response to the city. As such, it appeared in a variety of guises that were only imperfectly articulated or were even inconsistent with one another. The nature movement that resulted from this reaction to the city began later than the rise of science, but it grew more rapidly. By the first decade of the twentieth century it was in full flood, generating an outpouring of nature literature and related works that touched nearly every middle- and upper-class American. Popular literature, sermons, school textbooks, new organizations such as the Boy Scouts, and increasingly numerous summer and day camps all bespoke the importance attached to nature as a preserver of what was best in America and Americans.

This crusade for nature was no back-to-the-land movement, seeking to revive farm life with its supposed joys. Indeed, those caught up in this movement tended to look down upon rural folk, who seemed too crass and materialistic to appreciate what surrounded them. Nor was it a thoroughgoing rejection of the city. There were social, cultural, and economic advantages to urban life that nature's champions were loath to give up. Instead, it was an attempt to have the best of both worlds: living in the city but feeding spiritual needs through occasional returns to outdoor life by vacations and outings or, vicariously, through literature. The dream of a healing, soothing Arcadia lured people from the cities, but all save a few recalcitrants seem to have recognized that the day of the yeoman was gone beyond recall. Urban life had become and was destined to remain the day-to-day reality for most Americans.

The nature movement and the flood of popular literature it loosed did not focus on forests per se. Writers leaned heavily toward parables; unlike animals, which could be readily anthropomorphized, trees did not lend themselves to such treatment. Many stories dealt with a hero's struggle with natural forces, a struggle from which he emerged a stronger, better person. Deserts, mountains, and the Far North provided settings more appropriate for such tales than did the nation's forests, which had lost much of their one-time wildness as a result of logging, the end of Indian uprisings, and the disappearance of much of the more menacing wildlife. But there were some exceptions. Various of Stewart Edward White's early novels, such as *The Blazed Trail* (1902), were set in the pine forests and helped popularize the stereotype of the he-man lumberjack. Irving Bacheller's *Silas Strong* (1906) revolved around the conflict between logging and the need for wilderness. And Gene Stratton Porter's *Freckles* (1904), the biggest seller of the late nineteenth and early twentieth centuries, told of a hero who studied flowers and birds while trying to protect his forest from timber thieves.

Regardless of topic, much of the nature literature of the period was solidly grounded in firsthand observation and scientific knowledge. But nature writers viewed themselves as intermediaries in a communion between their readers and the natural world. "The nature essay," one authority has observed, "was a literary not a scientific form." In these circumstances, authors soon came to the fore who were more interested in writing dramatic narratives than works that would educate readers about nature. Increasingly, they took what purists considered outrageous liberties, attributing to animals characteristics that they never possessed in life. John Burroughs complained that such writers were "bearing false witness against the animals." He and his allies, including Theodore Roosevelt, labeled these writers "nature fakers." Burroughs charged that Ernest Thompson Seton's *Wild Animals I Have Known* should have been called "Wild Animals I *Alone* Have Known." Responding to attacks like these, William J. Long insisted that what he described was all true, or could be. In doing so, Long only revealed his own gullibility and limited capacity for observation, for his stories were replete with such farfetched accounts as tales of shorebirds that made casts of dried mud for their own broken legs. Long also defended the literary license he and other nature fakers took, arguing that it was necessary to present the natural world sympathetically and movingly in order to trigger those human reactions that would allow the rediscovery of "some beautiful and forgotten part of man's own soul." If sales figures are a measure, then Long and his cohorts were certainly successful.

The legacy of the nature fakers was mixed. They helped to popularize nature, but the tales they told were so unique and wonderful that readers could never experience them in real life. By turning the wilds into a mysterious, enchanted realm, they cut urban readers off from real understanding of the natural world and helped create attitudes and impressions that were to complicate attempts at rational discussion of resource problems for decades to come. Forests may not have played a central role in the nature literature of the period, but forestry issues were to be affected by its legacy of myth, misinformation, and romance as surely as were those involving wildlife, which did have a central place in the genre.[21]

Out of this welter of intellectual currents and crosscurrents, this mixture of varying attitudes and perceptions, there had emerged by the first decade of the twentieth century an environment in which decisions regarding natural resources were more difficult to arrive at than ever before. More viewpoints now had to be reconciled, more interests served. The problem was exacerbated because participants in the discussions and debates used widely differing vocabularies and based their reasoning on different assumptions. The problem would only grow worse as time passed. The twentieth century, with all its complexities and attendant frustrations, had arrived.

Still, ways were found to reconcile divergent views — or, when that could not be done, at least to weigh their various claims. The Minnesota Forest Reserve, established by Congress in 1902, was an early indication of the new state of affairs. Beginning in 1891, preservationists had proposed that a national park be established on Chippewa Indian lands in northern Minnesota. Slowly the idea's proponents gathered strength, led by the Minnesota Federation of Women's Clubs, a largely urban group that rallied to the call of the growing nature movement. However, as scientific forestry itself gained force, it came to dominate the campaign to save the Chippewa forests. The idea of a national park was pushed into the background: forests should be properly managed, not locked up. Although a forest reserve was hardly what the park enthusiasts wanted, they acceded to the proposal of the foresters. Neither group desired indiscriminate, uncontrolled logging in the area, and it appeared that only by acting together could that be prevented. Responding to their joint pleas, Congress made the area a forest reserve and gave joint responsibility for management to the Bureau of Forestry, Bureau of Indian Affairs, and General Land Office.[22]

In years to come such accommodation was not always possible. Bitter controversy erupted in 1901 when San Francisco sought permission to build a dam in Hetch Hetchy Valley in Yosemite National Park. The debate went on for years until San Francisco finally won. Irreconcilable differences emerged at other times and places too. Yet regardless of how these debates were finally settled, it was clear from the first decade of the twentieth century on that the new forces of science and the cities were to be as much a part of the decision-making process as the older agrarian, romantic, and transcendentalist forces, and that henceforth government was to play an active rather than a passive role in determining the outcome of their interplay.

Floodtide of an Industry

Chapter 9

While attitudes and perceptions about the forest were changing, so too was forest utilization. Between 1870 and 1910 the lumber industry went through its period of greatest growth, greatest production, and greatest destructiveness. During these years all major stands of timber in the United States felt the ax.

The accomplishments of lumbermen—bigger mills, more jobs, new communities, larger shipments to domestic and foreign markets—were a source of pride for many. At the same time, the growing specter of a coming timber famine, of valueless cutover land reverting to government ownership, and of idle mills and idle men caused increasing disquiet and the first stirrings toward remedial action. The period from 1870 to 1910, in other words, saw the floodtide of the old exploitive lumber industry and initial steps toward building a new industry—one that would accommodate itself to the various demands, old and new, that twentieth-century Americans would place on their forests; to the limited resource base of the nation's forests; and to a government that no longer simply saw itself as the protector of private property and encourager of economic development but had now assumed the position of broker among contending interests and protector of the public welfare.

Nor surprisingly, expansion of lumbering generally preceded calls for the more careful husbanding of forest resources. When those calls did come, they were first sounded in those areas where the impact of major logging activities had first been experienced. Soon after the Civil War, while operators in the Lake States, Gulf South, and Far West were still marveling at "inexhaustible" stands, newspapers in Maine were agitating for reforestation and conservative forest management, and soon after Pennsylvania's Governor John Hartranft was calling for action to save his state's rapidly disappearing stands of white pine.[1] Such appeals slowly drew supporters. Nevertheless, their spokesmen represented a view seldom implemented until after the turn of the century. For

the moment, economic expansion and the burgeoning lumber industry it demanded were the order of the day.

Circumstances could hardly have been otherwise. When new timberland
could be obtained in the West or South for as little as $1.25 an acre, it was more
profitable for operators in Maine or Pennsylvania to relocate than to stay where
they were and reforest their lands. When cheap lumber from stands in newly
tapped regions reached markets previously supplied by lumbermen in the
Northeast, the latter had no choice but to try to match the lower prices; the only
way they saw to do so was through large operations and exploitive logging. No
state or local government had the capacity to reshape this economic order, and
the federal government lacked the will to do so. Every proposal to restrict the
availability of cheap western lands was attacked as lessening opportunities for
the common man. Every proposal to raise duties on lumber, so as to reduce the
influx of cheap Canadian lumber and thereby make more careful (but costly)
utilization of forests in the United States economically feasible, was denounced
as an effort by "lumber barons" to inflate their prices and profits. William Jennings Bryan and other leaders from the lumber-short Great Plains wanted
cheap building materials for their region; they ignored the fact that duty-free
entry for Canadian lumber would, by encouraging wasteful patterns of utilization in the United States, hasten the day when timber would be exceedingly
dear in the United States.[2] In short, until changing conditions brought new tax,
tariff, and land laws, lumbermen had little choice but to engage in exploitive
lumbering if they were to stay in business.

As long as the American public demanded economic growth, cheap lumber,
and cheap land, little could be done to bring management—rather than exploitation—to the nation's forests. Only through the slow processes of public
education could the situation be changed. Progress came at a glacial rate. Still,
the public's position, if not the reasoning behind it, may have been sounder
than it appears at first glance. In the 1970s the Asian Development Bank, after
careful analysis, concluded that sustained-yield-management forestry was
appropriate for developed but not for developing nations. For the latter, the
accumulation of investment capital is essential if they are to build a diversified
economy and the infrastructure to support it. This can be achieved by turning
resources into capital at a rapid rate. According to this view, forests cut to gain
such ends might wind up depleted, but the total economy would be stronger. In
the nineteenth century the United States was a rapidly developing country. Its
growth was fueled by the very policies of natural-resource exploitation that the
Asian Development Bank was to advocate a century later. Champions of the
export-base theory of economic development have argued essentially the same

case in rather different terms. Studies of the Puget Sound area in Washington and of other places have shown that sometimes, at least, the theories have actually worked.[3]

Unaware of latter-day justifications for actions like their own, lumbermen nonetheless believed they were engaged in worthwhile and honorable activity, providing the economic foundations for thriving communities and the inexpensive materials with which to build them. The vast majority of their contemporaries apparently agreed. When a later age condemned lumber barons as selfish exploiters of the nation's resources seeking only personal aggrandizement, many lumbermen were bewildered and embittered. They had operated as their age had encouraged them to operate, within parameters they had not themselves established. They had enriched not only themselves but the nation in doing so. Why then should they be whipping boys for a later generation? Even the few among them who had an answer felt the injustice of the situation keenly.[4]

The lumber baron, as both hero and villain, blossomed in the Lake States during the last three decades of the nineteenth century. Maine, associated in the public mind with lumbering both before and since, had never seen anything so extensive as what developed in Michigan, Wisconsin, and Minnesota. In 1870 lumber production in the United States was just under thirteen billion board feet. Pennsylvania had the most sawmills, followed in order by New York, Ohio, Indiana, Michigan, Maine, Missouri, and New Hampshire. But in terms of production, Michigan was in first place, ahead of Pennsylvania and New York (which had led in the preceding two censuses). Michigan's ascendancy came not because production was falling elsewhere—it was not—but because its industry was growing faster than that of other states. In subsequent years, cutting moved steadily north and west; Wisconsin and then Minnesota took over as leading producer. Extensive cutting was under way in all three states by 1870. By the time Maine reached its all-time peak of production in 1909, it was an also-ran, far down the list of lumber producers.

Various authorities have left the impression that the lumber industry migrated from Maine to the Lake States and, as timber there ran out, moved on to the South and Far West.[5] Many in the industry, bosses and workers alike, did indeed follow this route, but the story is more complex than this schema suggests. Pennsylvania and New York contributed their share to the swelling tide of migration, and the industry moved not only west to the Lake States but in other directions as well. Many went from western Pennsylvania south along the Appalachians, where they continued to put to use their knowledge of logging in rugged, hilly terrain. Other Pennsylvania lumbermen, familiar with river-based operations from their years along the Susquehanna, transferred to the middle Mississippi (from Winona, Minnesota, downstream to St. Louis). New Yorkers, by contrast, were prominent in Michigan. Twenty-four of the thirty-nine leaders of the industry in that state were in-migrants from New York; almost half of the leaders who emigrated from New York made their first stop in Michigan. The reason is clear. The Erie Canal linked the great lumber emporium in Albany, New York, and the rising center of production along Michigan's Saginaw River. New Yorkers could continue to serve established customers and familiar markets if they could find an accessible new source of white pine. They found it in Michigan.[6]

The dominance of Maine had been exaggerated in other regards as well. Techniques and tools perfected in Maine continued to dominate as lumbermen moved across the continent—or so popular histories would have us believe. Some did. Log-driving and booming techniques had been brought to a high level of development in Maine (although New Yorkers are usually credited with having been the first to utilize drives of free-floating logs); drives and booms were later used not only in the Lake States, but beyond on streams such as Idaho's Clearwater River. Operators transferred logging-camp practices and log-skidding techniques west from Maine with few modifications. However, when the crosscut saw, long used for bucking downed trees, was turned to felling them, the change came first in Pennsylvania. Log slides, flumes, and certain other devices for moving logs in rough terrain seem to have been adopted first in Pennsylvania or in neighboring New York, just as the double-bitted ax had been earlier. Other innovations in logging appeared elsewhere, and advances in sawmill technology were made almost exclusively outside Maine. In short, the lumber industry was national, and the innovations that helped push it rapidly ahead in the Lake States and elsewhere after 1870 came from all corners. Wherever men were at work in the woods, inventive minds were seeking better, faster, easier ways of getting wood from stump to buyer.

Exaggeration of the importance of Maine is understandable. Lumber loomed large in that state's economy. A high percentage of its population did emigrate to work in the forests of other states, triggering sustained but largely unsuccessful efforts to "keep the boys home." Some of the real giants of Lake States lumbering—such as Isaac Stephenson—began their careers in Maine. In addition, many prominent historians of lumbering—including that most famous and readable of them all, Stewart Holbrook—have been New Englanders. As a result, the history of Maine's forest industries and the important contributions made there are well known. By contrast, the role of the lumber industry in Pennsylvania and New York has been largely forgotten.[7]

Regardless of where they and their tools and techniques came from, what lumbermen wrought first in Michigan and then in the other Lake States was truly impressive. Between 1870 and 1880, Michigan nearly doubled its production. Although Pennsylvania still had more mills, Michigan's output was over twice that of the former leader. By 1890 Michigan was ahead in all categories. Its 2,214 sawmills cut 4.2 million board feet of lumber during the year. Ten years later Wisconsin had taken over the lead, and Minnesota was a close third. Together the three states sawed 8.73 billion board feet, valued at over $154 million, in 1900.

Behind these statistics were huge new lumber-producing centers. Along the Saginaw River from Saginaw to Bay City there were 112 steam sawmills; in 1882 they turned out over one billion board feet of lumber and three hundred million shingles. And there were other centers, smaller but nonetheless important: Muskegon, Manistee, Eau Claire, Chippewa Falls, Oshkosh, Stillwater, Cloquet, and more. Sleepy rural villages had turned into vibrant centers of production; booming lumber towns had sprung up where there had been only unbroken forest a few years before. Drawing upon St. Anthony Falls to power sawmills and gristmills and upon the Mississippi River for inexpensive transportation, St. Paul and Minneapolis began their rise earlier than many other towns. As rail connections improved after the first tracks reached them in 1862, the Twin Cities became a major transportation hub. By 1899 Minneapolis was producing 594 million board feet a year; it had replaced Saginaw as the largest lumber-producing center and was also the leading flour producer.[8]

Rising production in the Lake States sprang not only from vast, readily accessible forests of the finest white pine, but also from technological advances that speeded logging and milling. Basic patterns did not change, but the stream of improvements now came faster than ever. The band saw was especially important. Invented in England years before, it was introduced into American sawmills in 1870 by J. R. Hoffman of Fort Wayne, Indiana. In the Lake States in the 1880s it was adapted for use as the headrig, the all-important saw that made the initial cuts on a log. During the period, steam power was being adapted to more and more tasks in more and more mills. It drove mechanisms that carried lumber from saws to graders and sorters and took waste to the boiler fires— which heated yet more steam to repeat the process endlessly. Steam was also used to heat log ponds, keeping them from freezing in winter and thus making possible year-round operation of the mills.

Year-round operations also commenced in the woods. Logging had long been done only in winter, but rising demand created pressure to log in summer too. The shift was made possible by the development of greased skids and of a device known as the big wheels. Big wheels were just that: a pair of wheels some ten feet in diameter. Logs suspended beneath the axle connecting them could be hauled over stumps and brush without difficulty. Greased skids and V-shaped log slides provided other methods for accomplishing the same task, albeit only after greater preparation. These and similar developments, together with larger sawmills, lay behind the spectacular production increases in the Lake States during the late nineteenth century.[9]

The size and number of sawmills put great demands on the forest. Although boosters labeled the area's stands inexhaustible, tracts rapidly passed into private hands and were cut. As trees were felled, the price of stumpage rose dramatically, and operators moved farther and farther north and west in quest of logs. Millowners willingly paid the going price to acquire the timber to keep their plants running and thus turn a profit on the large investment of risk capital those mills represented. The purchasers of extensive tracts of timber profited from their rising value. Indeed, some have argued that more great fortunes were accumulated through the rise in value of pinelands than through the milling of logs, profitable though that was. They are probably correct.[10]

In these circumstances, the struggle among lumbermen for survival—to say nothing of dominance—was intense. Outstanding sawmill and booming sites were even more limited than timberland. The lumberman with all three was fortunate indeed, and monumental battles sometimes developed over control of key locations. The struggles over Beef Slough and the Chippewa Dells were probably the most dramatic.

Beef Slough is a quiet side channel near where Wisconsin's Chippewa River enters the Mississippi. Wisconsin, especially the Black River drainage, had for some time been a major source of logs for the mills located down the Mississippi. As the timberlands tributary to the Black fell more and more into the hands of local entrepreneurs, millmen from as far downriver as St. Louis increasingly turned for logs to the Chippewa, where as much as one-sixth of the white pine of the United States grew. Operators at Chippewa Falls and Eau Claire did not welcome these interlopers, who they feared would drive up log prices while increasing the output of their competitors in Midwestern markets. They recognized that Beef Slough was an ideal place to store logs destined for downriver operations and to form them into rafts before sending them down the Mississippi. To keep it from being so used and to cripple their rivals' operations, a group of Chippewa Valley millmen gained title to key land near the entrance of the slough and acquired a charter to build booming and sorting works there. They apparently had no intention of using the charter but simply wanted to keep the site from falling into other hands. Led by Frederick Weyerhaeuser (who had started with a lumberyard and sawmill at Rock Island, Illinois), the downriver millmen countered with maneuvers of their own. The contest—waged on the river, in the courts, and in the legislature—dragged on for years. It was settled only after the disastrous flood of 1880 washed away an entire season's log supply of the Chippewa millmen, tipping balance so that they had no choice but to accept terms that allowed Weyerhaeuser and his associates to operate in the forests of the Chippewa drainage.[11]

Rather than pitting insider against outsider, the Dells controversy set neighbor against neighbor. Millmen at Eau Claire proposed to provide a large, safe reservoir for logs at the lower Dells of the Chippewa. Nearby Half Moon Lake furnished a good storage site, but getting logs to it from the river was difficult, and not all local mills were located so they could use it. Plans for a dam, booms, sorting pens, and associated works at the Dells, on the main stem of the river a short distance above Eau Claire, offered an alternative. But the plan was fraught with danger for those upstream at Chippewa Falls: the proposed dam could hinder downstream navigation of their lumber rafts. For all its cheap power, Chippewa Falls had long suffered from the lack of adequate log storage. To add interference with their route to market could well have driven millmen there into insolvency. Competition between the two communities was already keen. People in Chippewa Falls fought the proposals of their downstream neighbors vigorously. Not until the mid-seventies, after extended, acrimonious debates, did Eau Claire finally obtain a charter from the legislature for the proposed works. It was obtained in part by subterfuge. As Orrin Ingram recalled: "We succeeded in getting a charter for a dam, or the city of Eau Claire did, for water-works ostensibly, but really to furnish a booming place to hold logs." With its new facilities Eau Claire soon outstripped Chippewa Falls as a lumber-producing center.[12]

The struggles over key sites and between conflicting uses of waterways were repeated elsewhere. Sixty-nine cases involving lumber and log transport on Wisconsin's inland waters reached that state's supreme court during the period. Both there and in other lumbering states the source of conflict was frequently the same as it had been at the Dells: construction for power or storage that would interfere with navigation. The doctrine of reasonable use held that since some legitimate uses of waterways conflicted with other legitimate uses, such interference was not actionable under the law if held within reasonable bounds. This doctrine lent itself to a variety of interpretations and, as a result, to a host of court cases.

Lumbermen also turned to state legislatures. They repeatedly importuned their representatives for franchises and other legislation that would give them exclusive use of particular sites or protect them from those claiming damages. In Wisconsin over one hundred special statutory franchises were approved for booming alone. Various states also passed general legislation authorizing corporations to improve any stream for log driving. This authority, first granted in Wisconsin in 1876, was enlarged in 1880 to include booms. The result was further friction.

The course of this legislation and jurisprudence was tortured and complex, but the general direction was clear. The law was being shaped to encourage economic enterprise. As legal historian James Willard Hurst explained, men "employed law as a positive instrument to direct action toward the dominant objective of the time." Producers who could offer bigger facilities or more efficient methods could anticipate eventual if not immediate support in the legislatures and courts. At a time when few questioned the virtues of economic expansion and when the government regularly sought to encourage it, such expectations were indeed reasonable.[13] Still, the industry did not sweep all before it. State legislatures might respond to its desires, but federal land policy remained stubbornly resistant to the needs of lumbermen.

Canadian-American relations presented another sort of legislative tangle. As the size of sawmills and other fixed investments grew, ease of migration declined. Lumbermen turned to ever more distant sources of logs to squeeze the last possible profits from the old mills before liquidating their holdings and moving on to sites nearer the remaining forests. This tendency to hang on as long as possible led to sizable importations of sawlogs across Lake Huron from Ontario to Michigan beginning about 1890. Some Canadians, disturbed by losing jobs that would have existed had these logs been sawn in Canada, tried to prevent the commerce just as residents of the Pacific Northwest were to seek to halt the export of logs to Japan three-quarters of a century later. But until 1898, when Ontario's provincial legislature shut off exports, logs from around Georgian Bay kept sawmills in the vicinity of Saginaw active even though domestic sources were too depleted to do so. After the ban went into effect, many Saginaw lumbermen closed their mills or moved them north of the border.[14]

The Wilson-Gorman tariff of 1894 brought Canadian and American differences over trade in forest products into sharp focus. The tariff was a disappointment to champions of free trade. They had expected major reductions in duties because the Democrats, whose platform advocated low tariffs, controlled Congress and the White House for the first time since the Civil War. But by the time protectionists in the Senate and champions of special interests were done, little was left of Congressman William Wilson's original bill. Except for lumber and wool, almost nothing was still on the duty-free list. Chagrined, President Grover Cleveland let the bill become law without his signature.[15]

Lumbermen in the Lake States, foreseeing a flood of Canadian imports into their markets, had lobbied against reductions in the already low lumber schedules and predicted dire results when the bill passed in its final form. Their worries were accentuated because of the nearness of Canadian producers to prime markets in the Northeast and because the Canadians produced much low-grade lumber. Producers in the Lake States were already having trouble disposing of the increasing quantity of low-grade material that they were turning out as their log supplies declined in quality. Lumbermen of Michigan, Wisconsin, and Minnesota were only slightly mollified by the inclusion in the tariff of a retaliatory section that called for reinstating duties on lumber if Canada placed an export duty on logs. Such considerations, as much as belief in the abstract virtues of protectionism, no doubt lay behind F. C. A. Denkmann's statement that he was "a Republican, just as every good lumberman should be."

The anticipated flood of cheap Canadian lumber failed to materialize. The depression that had begun in 1893 worsened, wiping out demand for domestic and foreign producers alike. But the duty-free status of the Canadian product did remove one of the last barriers keeping American millmen south of the border. A number soon transferred operations to Canada, exacerbating unemployment in the areas they left. American manufacturers of sawmill equipment soon learned to their dismay that they could not supply the new mills to the north: a prohibitive 25 percent duty on machinery imported into Canada barred the way.

Many in the Lake States lumber districts were quick to blame both the flight of capital and jobs and, less fairly, the collapse of the lumber market during the depression on the Wilson-Gorman tariff. One congressman from West Virginia claimed that 90 percent of his state's mills were closed as result of the tariff. The Democrats paid dearly in the election of 1896, losing every seat they held in Congress from the Lake States and many seats from elsewhere. Even Congressman Wilson, in office for five terms, was not reelected. Disaffection with the low tariffs on lumber—which had been supported by both Cleveland and the Democratic standard-bearer in 1896, William Jennings Bryan—also contributed to the Democrats' losing the presidency that year.

Lumber had failed to gain protection under the Wilson-Gorman tariff in part because its champions had spoken with a divided voice. Many lumber dealers, especially in Chicago, supported duty-free entry. So did many lumbermen in the South, either reflecting the traditional Democratic position on tariffs or seeing little threat from duty-free lumber in their major markets. Indeed, since the Lake States provided their main competition, some southern lumbermen apparently believed that anything weakening the industry there would help them. Even some Lake States sawmill operators supported duty-free lumber. Foremost among them were those who had built mills north of the border or expected to soon do so.

Chastened by their failures in 1894, lumbermen opposed to duty-free entry of lumber readied themselves for the battle to get tariffs restored after the Republicans returned to power in 1897. They found new recruits among lumbermen who had thought there was no threat in the Wilson-Gorman tariff but had learned otherwise. In December 1896 industry leaders from all sections of the country met in Cincinnati. They issued a strong call for protection and organized a lobbying effort that bombarded Congress with communications from associations and individuals engaged in lumbering. Relief would probably have been forthcoming even without these efforts, for the dominant Republicans were committed to protection. In any case, Congress quickly passed and President William McKinley signed into law the Dingley tariff, which restored a duty of two dollars per thousand board feet on lumber and included provisions for additional duties if an export duty were placed on logs from Canada.

The unanimity of lumbermen in seeking the restoration of duties was more apparent than real. The call for protection that emanated from the Cincinnati meeting had come only after bitter debate and much maneuvering. Among those disenchanted with the schedules in the Dingley tariff was Frank W. Gilchrist of Alpena, Michigan. Gilchrist and his associates had invested in mills in the Thunder Bay district of Ontario, only to see the restored duties block their cut from the American market they had intended to serve. After the Spanish-American War, a group of Alpena residents approached Gilchrist for a donation toward a monument to Russell A. Alger, a local lumberman who had risen to the rank of brevet major general during the Civil War and then served as secretary of war under President McKinley. As it happened, Alger had been a major figure in the agitation for a renewal of duties on imported lumber. Gilchrist refused to contribute. Pointing to his three idle mills on Thunder Bay, he declared bitterly, "there are Alpena's monuments to Alger."

Much occurred between 1870 and 1908 that tended to focus attention on Lake States lumbering, overshadowing what was happening elsewhere. The primacy of white pine worked toward this end. In 1869 white pine made up 62.7 percent of the softwood lumber and 45.4 percent of all lumber cut in the United States. As production rose in the South and West, which cut other species, these percentages gradually declined, but throughout the period white pine was king, and— Williamsport's brief ascendancy to the contrary notwithstanding—the Lake States stood out as the greatest center of white pine production.

But much was happening in other parts of the country. Production was rising rapidly in the Gulf South as expanding rail networks opened vast areas and large quantities of investment capital flowed in from the North. Many of the rail lines built during Reconstruction had defaulted on their bonds, but construction on a more solid financial foundation quickened in the 1880s, making lumber production possible on a scale unprecedented in the region. The Nashville, Chattanooga & St. Louis Railway proudly labeled itself "the great lumber route." It and other lines brought massive changes to the southern woods, sometimes to the dismay of longtime residents. By 1900 the South had become the nation's leading lumber-producing region, generating 32 percent of the total cut (to 25 percent for the Lake States). Still, the biggest mills were yet to be built: the Gulf Lumber Company, which went into operation in Louisiana in 1906, cut 120 million board feet annually; the Great Southern Lumber Company opened at Bogalusa, Louisiana, shortly thereafter, with a capacity of a million board feet a day. Characteristically, the latter was constructed by northerners—the Goodyear brothers, who had been leading lumbermen in Pennsylvania before moving south. The production of southern pine reached its zenith in 1909: 16 billion board feet.[16]

Not just pine was cut in the South. Large quantities of cypress and hardwoods also came from its saws. The cypress industry had been devastated by the Civil War but came back strongly in the late nineteenth century as the wood's capacity for resisting rot and taking on fine finishes became widely appreciated and as machinery and techniques for handling the huge cypress logs were perfected.[17]

Hardwood manufacturers, running short of logs in the North, turned increasingly to the South in the 1880s for walnut, cherry, oak, and other deciduous species. Demand rose as hardwood flooring and ornate manufactured furniture became popular. The South's first furniture factory opened in 1888 in High Point, North Carolina; others soon followed in that state and in Georgia, increasing demand on the region's broadleaf stands. But supplying the market was not easy. The hardwood industry was highly fragmented, with a host of small producers and regional distribution centers. Differences in grades and terminology existed within as well as between regions. The National Hardwood Lumber Association emerged in 1898, in large part to bring order from this chaos.

The rise in demand for hardwood flooring was even more dramatic than that for furniture. Before the 1880s there was no flooring industry to speak of, but the invention of the flooring matcher about 1885 made one feasible. This machine cut tongues and grooves into the side of boards, thus making possible economical, tight-fitting hardwood floors. Subsequent inventions (especially an end matcher in 1898) aided the rise of the hardwood flooring industry. Until after the turn of the century, most hardwood flooring was maple from the Lake States, but gradually oak came to dominate, and Nashville, Tennessee, emerged as the industry's main center. The progress of oak was hastened in 1907 when a group of oak-flooring manufacturers formed a trade association (forerunner of the National Oak Flooring Manufacturers Association) that developed standards for grades and sizes.[18]

In the wake of white pine lumbering, other forest activities rose in importance in Maine. As pine lumber passed its peak there in 1861, many sawmill operators turned to the previously despised spruce and hemlock to keep their plants running. Other changes were under way too. The sulfite process made it practical to manufacture inexpensive paper from wood pulp. This new method came to Maine in 1883 when the Penobscot Chemical Fiber Company opened a plant at Old Town, near Bangor. At first this and other such plants depended primarily upon poplar obtained from farmers, with an admixture of some spruce. As operations grew, outstripping agrarian sources, spruce came to the fore. When the Great Northern mill in Millinocket went on line in 1900, it was the largest paper and pulp mill in the world, turning out 240 tons of newsprint per day, an equal amount of groundwood pulp, and 120 tons of sulfite pulp. Small mills supplied by farmers were clearly outdated. Problems of finance continued to plague Maine's pulp and paper industry, but by this time its structure was essentially complete. Henceforward pulpwood, not lumber, was to be the dominant product of the Maine woods.

The growth of paper production in Maine was part of a larger national development. Soda, groundwood, and sulfite processes all became practical during the 1870s and early 1880s and revolutionized papermaking. Paper made from wood pulp soon replaced rag paper in many uses, for it was far less expensive. Newspapers changed over. High-speed presses coupled with cheap paper made inexpensive reading material available as never before. The growth of the educational system created more and more customers for the pulp novels, magazines, and newspapers that rolled from the presses. The federal government, itself growing rapidly, also consumed vast quantities. All in all, paper made of wood pulp was a significant contributor to the changes, social and otherwise, that were sweeping America during the late nineteenth and early twentieth centuries.

Among those supplying the rising demand was the International Paper Company, born in 1898 with a merger of twenty mills in Maine, New Hampshire, Massachusetts, Vermont, and New York. The firm owned some 2.6 million acres of forest (over half in Canada) and used five hundred thousand cords of wood during its first year. Its huge land base and its willingness to move into new lines of production led to rapid expansion. Others such as Kimberly-Clark (started in Neenah, Wisconsin, in 1872) and St. Regis (begun on the Black River in northern New York in 1899) expanded more slowly, but they too were to join the giants of papermaking. The impact of this revolution in the manufacturing of paper was nowhere more evident than in Maine.[19]

While the decline of pine and rise of wood pulp were bringing change to the forests of Maine, other factors were at work in Pennsylvania. There white pine lumbering gave way to hemlock, albeit some two decades after the transition to spruce and hemlock in Maine. The change was accomplished through the primacy of a new means of log transportation. During the heyday of Pennsylvania's pine lumbering, water transportation — log drives — had dominated. Between 1870 and 1880, as pine stands were depleted, production fell; thereafter logging railroads came to the fore, opening new areas and tapping stands of hemlock, a species rising in value. Production recovered, reaching a peak in 1890 (or 1900 if one uses value rather than quantity as the measure) and continuing high until 1910. Unlike most early lumber-producing states, which rose rapidly to their peaks and them quickly declined, Pennsylvania had a long period of relatively steady output. Its mountainous terrain made huge mills tapping a vast hinterland impractical in all but a few locations and thus slowed depletion of the state's timber stands. The sequential harvesting of its pine and hemlock also served to prolong the industry. Even after hemlock was largely gone, production continued; in the 1970s Pennsylvania was still the nation's second largest producer of hardwood.[20]

Much of Pennsylvania's hemlock never went through the saws. The bark of eastern hemlock was often valued more than the brittle lumber it yielded. Workers peeled massive quantities of bark from downed hemlocks to provide a source of tannin for curing leather. Frequently they left the logs in the woods to rot. Until the 1870s hundreds of tiny tanneries dotted the state, but as demand for leather grew with the nation's population and the rise of industry, which used vast quantities of leather belting to run its machines, tanneries became fewer and larger. By 1890, when they reached their maximum size, there were approximately 120 large tanneries in Pennsylvania. These firms frequently owned the stands they drew on. In 1901 it was estimated that 75 percent of the hemlock in the state was controlled by tannery owners. These men often combined bark gathering with lumbering, hauling bark from the woods by railroad at night and logs by day. This combination helped to make the manufacturing of hemlock lumber profitable in places where it would otherwise have been economically marginal at best.

Tanneries also turned to industrial combination to ensure their profits. In 1893 some sixty-five tanneries joined to form the United States Leather Company (later the Central Leather Company), which soon effectively dominated the industry nationwide. By 1900 efforts were under way to find new sources of tannin, for it was clear that hemlock would not long be available in quantity. Oak offered one alternative. In the end, however, declining demand, not the disappearance of hemlock, led to the leather industry's decline. The rise of the automobile, which used less leather than did horse-drawn vehicles, the development of substitutes, and the onset of depression reduced the leather industry to a relatively minor one. Until that happened, however, American forests, and those of Pennsylvania in particular, were vital to it.[21]

As supplies of first pine and then hemlock dwindled in Pennsylvania, some of the state's lumbermen moved on rather than staying where they were and going into hardwood operations or the area's growing coal-mining industry. Logging techniques in Pennsylvania's Alleghenies—splash dams, flumes, log slides, geared locomotives—were equally useful in western Maryland and in West Virginia, and many moved south along the Appalachians to put them to use rather than transferring west to the comparatively flat Lake States, where there were already lumbermen in abundance. Others moved to the Rocky Mountain and far western states, for there too their hard-won expertise could be put to use. Pennsylvania place names such as Kinzua and Tionesta reappeared in the ponderosa pine forests of the West.[22]

Lumbering expanded rapidly in the Far West after 1870, especially during the 1880s and around 1900. Lumbermen from the Lake States and Maine as well as from Pennsylvania joined with others whose firms had been cutting in the region since the Gold Rush, sending production rapidly upward. They were starting from a small base, however; in spite of spectacular percentage increases, no western state appeared in the top ten producers until 1900, when Washington vaulted into sixth place. By 1910 the census showed the western states producing 18.4 percent of the nation's lumber, much of it in Washington and Oregon, which now stood first and third respectively among the states.

Increases in the Far West during the 1880s had different origins from those that came later. A number of railroads pushed through to Oregon, Washington, and California in the eighties. These, together with the original transcontinental link—the Central Pacific–Union Pacific line, opened in 1869—spurred rapid population growth and an unprecedented influx of outside investment capital. New sawmills sprang up, old ones expanded and then expanded again. But transcontinental rail connections opened few markets in the interior. Freight rates were too high for lumber or other inexpensive, bulky products—which made up most of what the area had to sell—to penetrate markets in and beyond the Midwest. Besides, there were other producers near-er the main points of consumption. Some lumber was shipped as far as Omaha, but the shipments were too small and sporadic to have significant impact. Most of the increased lumber production went out to sea rather than inland. South-ern California was growing rapidly; plantation agriculture was expanding in Hawaii, as was mining in Australia; railroad construction was being pushed in north China, Chile, Peru, and Mexico. These and other maritime markets, cou-pled with intraregional demand, made the eighties a prosperous decade for West Coast lumbermen.

By contrast, the first years of the twentieth century saw a flood of lumber going east by rail. James J. Hill's Great Northern Railroad had slashed freight rates on lumber in 1893; other lines followed suit. But until the waning of de-pression in 1897 the reductions made little difference. Then, with production plummeting in many parts of the Lake States, lumbermen in the Far West moved aggressively to supply buyers previously served from older centers. Producers in the South eyed these same markets, and the two struggled for dominance in the Midwest, each group seeking rail rates that would give it a competitive advan-tage. The position of far western producers was greatly strengthened in 1908 when lumbermen in western Washington won through-route privileges on the Union Pacific in spite of opposition from the railroads and lumbermen in north-ern Oregon. This broke a transportation bottleneck that had kept most Wash-ington lumber out of midwestern markets. Henceforth southerners had to face even greater competition from the Pacific Northwest.[23]

Wherever it took place, late-nineteenth-century lumbering did more than sim-ply put several billion board feet of logs through the saws. With men and equip-ment in the woods and great quantities of slash accumulating from logging operations, forest fires became both more common and more destructive. In October 1871 a fire swept through the woods of Wisconsin so rapidly that people were trapped. The town of Peshtigo was wiped out and 1,100 people were in-cinerated. Overshadowed by the burning of Chicago, which occurred at almost the same time, this blaze received less attention than it deserved. Subsequent forest fires were more widely noticed, especially the Hinckley conflagration of 1894 that destroyed five Minnesota towns and took 413 lives.

Fires had been common in the woods since colonial times, but when land was being cleared for agriculture the loss had seemed less and reminders were more transient. However, the great volume of slash generated by industrial logging provided unprecedented quantities of ground fuel. Now when fires swept through an area, they frequently burned so hot that organic matter in the soil burned along with the vegetation. The mineral soil that was left eroded easily, held moisture poorly, and provided a poor rooting medium for healing vegetation. Nowhere was the situation worse than in Pennsylvania, where bark-gathering operations left huge quantities of debris in the woods. Repeated fires so scarred this land that for decades afterward only brush, scrub oak, and other noncommercial species would grow there. At the beginning of the twentieth century, this area that had once supported a massive lumber industry was being referred to as the "desert of five million acres." Less spectacularly, with repeated burning pine forests were giving way to chapparal-covered slopes in parts of California. The pattern was most uneven, however; in some types of forest and under some conditions, the effects of forest fires were only temporary.

Understandably, what most people saw in the great fires of the period was not the environmental cost—of that they were largely ignorant—but the loss of human lives, property, and resources. However, what they could see and comprehend distressed them. As with so much else in the forests of the period, the great fires of the Lake States were the most spectacular and the most widely noticed.[24]

For all the impressive advances in the Far West and South, for all the adjustments and changes in Pennsylvania and Maine, the Lake States region provided the archetype of the old lumber industry in its heyday. Great fires, mammoth mills, huge log drives, larger-than-life leaders, aggressive pursuit of timberlands by any and all methods, and "cut out and get out" policies combined to create an indelible image that decades later continues to plague the industry's leaders, despite manifest differences in the present generation's attitudes and methods. Great changes took place in lumbering and related forest-products industries between 1870 and 1908, but nowhere was the nature of these industries or these changes more dramatically demonstrated than in the Lake States. They furnished the great illustration of the industry at its height, an illustration that made clear the great social (to the especially perceptive) environmental costs of such operations. In so doing they set in motion forces demanding change and reform, forces seeking new and better ways of dealing with the nation's forest resources. People who had once thought the country's timber inexhaustible learned, as they watched the vast stands of the Lake States disappear, that it was finite after all. With that awareness, reactions to the lumber industry's old order set in. The reactions came both from within the industry's own ranks and from without.

Responses to Change

Chapter 10

Developments in the woods and mills during the late nineteenth century trig-gered a variety of responses from Americans. Intellectual forces unleashed by the sweeping changes taking place in society helped to shape, direct, and even generate these reactions. Industry, government, and the general public began to adjust their thinking to the realities of finite forest resources. Because reac-tions varied so widely, friction over the nation's forests rose to levels not wit-nessed since the days of colonial resistance to the broad arrow policy. Not all of the reactions and controversy had to do with conservation.

It is hardly surprising that laborers were among the first to respond to the new circumstances. The conditions under which they worked were a daily real-ity, their complaints concrete. Intellectual reactions were slower to crystallize, for the concerns that spawned them were less immediately pressing and solu-tions, initially at least, more nebulous. However, by the time the lumber indus-try reached its peak of production in 1909, hardly anyone remained—in or out of the industry—who had not been affected by the new ways of looking at and treating forests that were abroad in the land.

Labor unions first made their impact felt in the 1870s. As in other industries, the advent of large-scale manufacturing resulted in conditions that invited unionization. Workers who had once done a variety of jobs now found them-selves repeating the same task over and over. Plants were mechanized suf-ficiently to drive workers relentlessly along, but not sufficiently to significantly alleviate the drudgery of sawmill labor. One worker in a "modernized" mill lat-er recalled that the sheer physical demands of his work regularly left him black and blue from shoulder to elbow. Ten- to twelve-hour days were standard. Millowners were distant figures rather than the co-workers of an earlier era. They seldom knew the workers or their problems intimately, and they paid little attention to plant safety. They argued that it was the workers' responsibility to stay out of the way of saws and other dangers; workers knew sawmills were dangerous places when they took their jobs, and if they failed to stay on guard it was their own fault. Grumblers were quickly replaced. Under such conditions, unions were soon forming in the sawmills, if not in the woods.

The first significant unionization in the industry—and the first major strike—was in Williamsport. In the years following the Civil War, Pennsylvania was a center of activity by organized labor. William Sylvis, one of those who founded the National Labor Union in 1866 and its president during the period of growth beginning in 1868, was from the Keystone State. He and other labor leaders in Pennsylvania advocated political action as a means of winning gains for workingmen. A Labor Reform party sprang from the NLU and, with its allies, succeeded in getting a law passed in Pennsylvania setting the eight-hour day as the legal standard for workers. Williamsport's lumbermen, among others, ignored the law. A local of the Labor Reform Union, also spawned by the NLU, soon organized in Williamsport, but industry leaders refused to compromise on a ten-hour day at the same wage they had previously paid for twelve hours. They insisted that twelve hours' work a day was essential if they were to saw the year's log supply in the six or seven months available between the time the drives came in and the time their plants had to close for the winter; moreover, they argued, wages in Williamsport were already as high as those paid elsewhere.

On July 1, 1872, the workmen struck, closing all mills in the city. The Lumbermen's Exchange, representing the sawmill operators, offered some small concessions, but the strike continued. Events came to a head on July 22. With negotiations at a standstill, some mills reopened with scab labor. Union members, their strike funds nearly exhausted, decided to close the operating mills by force if necessary. A pitched battle with police followed, and calls went out to the state capital for help. Governor John Geary responded by dispatching state militia. Order was quickly restored and the strike broken. A number of union leaders, found guilty of inciting a riot, were sentenced to jail, although Governor Geary eventually pardoned them after tempers cooled. Until violence took over, the strikers had enjoyed much support in the community; indeed, they were able to keep going as long as they did because of donations and credit extended to them by local merchants.

The pattern was familiar. In other industries too, strikes in relatively small communities were often sympathetically viewed during this period by much of the local populace; the strikers were friends, neighbors, and familiar customers, not strangers whose activities could be dismissed as the work of dangerous (probably foreign) agitators. Conditions that drove men to strike were easily seen in the close confines of a town such as Williamsport, and class consciousness was not strong enough to blind middle-class residents to them. But wherever they occurred, strikes lost community support when they turned violent and destructive; the sanctity of private property was too deeply ingrained in most Americans to allow them to acquiesce in assaults on it even by neighbors whose goals they looked on with sympathy.[1]

Failure of the Williamsport strike and the subsequent disintegration of the National Labor Union did not halt organizational activity in the lumber industry. Local unions formed, and wildcat strikes broke out repeatedly. In 1872 millworkers in Saginaw went out, and in 1873 those in La Crosse, Wisconsin, did so. In 1879 the Chippewa Valley Workingmen's Association organized to seek shorter hours and payment of wages in cash rather than scrip or store credits. The worst strike to hit the industry in Wisconsin came in 1881, when millworkers in Eau Claire struck. As in Williamsport, the strikers enjoyed much community support but were finally defeated when violence brought in the state militia. More successful were strikes that same year in Au Sable, Oscoda, and Muskegon, Michigan. Other strikes followed.

Sometimes workers resorted to sabotage rather than strikes. Following the Williamsport strike, lumbermen were plagued by spikes driven into logs to ruin mill saws and by fires in the woods. Grievance fires, as they were called, occurred elsewhere too. One old-timer recalled, "It happened more than once when a company foreman tried to cheat a man, for the man to reach in his pocket, get a nickel, hold it up and look the foreman in the eye and say 'that will buy a box of matches!'"

The Knights of Labor, expanding rapidly after a successful strike against Jay Gould's Wabash Railroad in 1885, moved into the lumber industry in the Lake States, South, and Far West. Many formerly independent locals affiliated with this broadly based but diffuse national union. In the Saginaw Valley, millworkers belonging to the Knights went out in 1885. A bitter, prolonged struggle ensued. In the end the strike failed, in part because Terence Powderly, head of the Knights of Labor and an opponent of the use of strikes in labor negotiations, came to Saginaw and undercut the local's efforts. In spite of the failure of this strike, within a short time the ten-hour day that the Saginaw and Bay City unionists had sought was more or less universal in the area. Knights locals were also involved in strikes in Moss Point, Pascagoula, and Handsboro, Mississippi, in 1887, 1888 , and 1889; in Ray, Alabama, in 1890; and in La Crosse, Wisconsin, in 1892.

During the same period, the Knights were active on California's redwood coast and in the Pacific Northwest. In the Far West, in addition to struggles with employers, Knights engaged in an effort to drive Chinese labor from the area, an effort that had some degree of success, especially in Tacoma and Seattle, Washington, and in Eureka, California. The union's activities were so worrisome to employers that one lumberman in Hoquiam, Washington, even saw a silver lining in the depression that struck in 1893. He wrote an associate: "So far it's been a rich man's panic, but before spring it will be a poor man's empty stomach . . . perhaps this will show the labor agitators that they can not go on bidding up the price of labor beyond its legitimate level without bringing an inevitable economic counteraction."

Subsequent strikes by Knights locals in Pensacola, Florida, in 1899 and in Pascagoula, Mississippi, in 1900 failed. Thereafter the Knights dropped quickly from sight in the industry. The *Western Watchman,* a Knights paper published in Eureka, ceased publication in 1904. The details of activity by the Knights of Labor in the lumber industry have yet to be given careful study, but enough is known to make it clear that the union remained a significant force in lumber centers in the South and Far West long after historians focusing on its national organization have argued that it had disintegrated.[2]

Nationally the Knights were being eclipsed by the American Federation of Labor after the mid-1880s, but trade unionism, which was at the heart of the AFL approach, was ill suited to the lumber industry. Some within the AFL advocated industrial unionism, but they did not dominate the organization, and its efforts to organize diversified industries such as lumbering were halfhearted and generally unsuccessful. In 1905 loggers and sawmill workers received an AFL charter as the International Brotherhood of Woodsmen and Sawmill Workers, but the organization failed to prosper and eventually disappeared.

The disintegration of the Knights and the shortcomings of the AFL left a vacuum into which the militant Industrial Workers of the World soon moved. Organized in 1905, the IWW decried capitalism and the wage system that lay at its heart. With one big union and a general strike, they hoped to usher in a new age in which workers, not capitalists, would control the means of production and through them society. But not everyone who joined the IWW shared—or even understood—its anarchosyndicalist philosophy. Many joined simply because they desperately needed a union. In an age of ever larger, ever more depersonalized industrial operations, workers without a union were vulnerable indeed.

In 1907 the IWW took over a sawmill strike in Portland, Oregon. Even though the strike failed, the union gained a reputation as the best available hope for sawmill and woods workers, and it grew rapidly in the industry there-after. The press and politicians contributed by playing up the IWW's violent language and tactics and its celebrated clashes with opponents; the union was frequently made to appear much larger and more threatening than was jus-tified by the facts. Be that as it may, down to World War I the IWW remained the strongest union in the industry.[3]

Just how much the IWW owed to the Knights of Labor is not clear. Circum-stantial evidence suggests more of a connection than just the broadly based organization and hostility to the AFL's craft unionism they shared. In the Pacific Northwest, where the Knights enjoyed some of their longest-lasting strength, the IWW had some of its earliest success. Conditions in the industry may well explain both, but there may have been some continuity of mem-bership too. Certainly, ideas espoused by the Knights (whose locals, unlike Powderly, were not opposed to strikes) paved the way for the very similar, if more militantly stated, ideas of the IWW.

Workers were not the only ones in the lumber industry who moved toward collective action between 1870 and 1908. So did owners. The industry was plagued by sweeping fluctuations in demand and prices that made long-range planning difficult. Chronically overbuilt, the industry regularly turned out products in quantities that outstripped demand. The result was cutthroat com-petition that threatened the security of investments in an even more immediate fashion than did dwindling stands of sawtimber or militant unions. Cheap pub-lic land fostered overinvestment by private operators and thus increased their need to liquidate their production under duress. In the 1870s, lumbermen be-gan moving toward combinations that would bring some semblance of order out of the industrial chaos spawned by these circumstances.

The first significant effort to solve these problems through cooperative ac-tion came in the form of the National Association of Lumbermen (NAL), founded in Williamsport in 1874. At the same time, Canadian lumbermen met at Ottawa. Faced with plummeting demand as a result of the depression that had struck the year before, both groups called for drastic reductions in output. To make their efforts at controlling prices and production more palatable to the public, the American group avowed that conservation was their main pur-pose. They professed to seek to halt the "present senseless slaughtering of pine" that sacrificed forests to "the ruthless hand of the American vandal in his search for wealth." In spite of this rhetoric, the group's basic aims were clear. As protests mounted against its efforts at controlling prices and production, the group backed down; members who had agreed to reduce output the fol-lowing year were thus freed to do as they saw fit. By 1876 the organization was dead, though a variety of local and regional combines appeared and reappeared through the 1880s and 1890s. Specialized groups, such as the National Oak Flooring Manufacturers Association, and ones with a narrow focus, such as the gathering in Cincinnati in response to duty-free entry of Canadian lumber, surfaced, but no national bodies emerged to take the NAL's place.

Perhaps it was just as well, for gentlemen's agreements and toothless organizations were inadequate solutions to the problems of overproduction and unstable prices. Agreements, no matter how honestly entered into, could not last when those bound by them were faced with questions of economic survival. Trusts and other forms of outright combination might have provided a means to the ends sought, but the resource base the industry drew on was too widely scattered, too extensive, and too costly for any lumberman or group of lumbermen to control effectively. Moreover, economies of scale were limited, largely because the bulky nature of the raw material made production near the timber stands essential; unlike iron and steel production, lumber production could not be centralized in a few locations where it could be readily controlled by a handful of dominant men. As the federal government withdrew more and more land for forest reserves after 1891, artificial as well as natural barriers to combination were raised. Although one muckraking journalist trumpeted that Frederick Weyerhaeuser was richer than Rockefeller and at least one historian had labeled Weyerhaeuser the "timber king," by 1908 it was abundantly clear that neither Weyerhaeuser nor anyone else was to provide an equivalent in the lumber industry to John D. Rockefeller in oil. Lumbermen might combine to establish uniform grades, to lobby for favorable legislation, or to advertise the advantages of wood products—and they did—but lumbering itself was then, as it has remained since, the most decentralized of America's major industries.[4]

Workers and capitalists engaged in lumbering were not the only ones who responded to the changes that came as the industry expanded during the late nineteenth century. Others were also interested in what was taking place, and their reactions varied. One of their earliest responses was essentially legalistic: a call for enforcement of existing laws and for new ones to plug loopholes or solve problems that developed as the industry grew. Ostensibly, spokesmen for this position were concerned less with ends than with means, but—however poorly it was recognized at the time—a variety of assumptions lay behind their arguments, and the implementation of what they sought would have affected patterns of land use and economic development in large sections of the country.

Some of these legalistic responses were quite narrow, seeking to protect interests or groups from the side effects of lumbering. Such responses had appeared long before 1870, but as the industry and its impact grew thereafter, they became more common. Legislation to regulate the dumping of slabs, sawdust, cull lumber, and other waste into streams was one of the earliest concerns, for this refuse was often a problem, especially when washed downstream on freshets. Flood trash, as it was called, sometimes accumulated to the point that it blocked navigation; at other times it polluted domestic water supplies, littered downstream property, hampering its use, and destroyed fish runs (especially those of shad and Atlantic salmon). Burners to eliminate such waste became common only after Maine and other states passed laws against profligate dumping. Economic factors were also at work encouraging their adoption. As a result of these dual forces, by the 1870s most of the nation's large mills had refuse burners.

Laws to alleviate other problems stemming from the growth of the lumber industry also appeared. When lumbermen built dams on the Susquehanna and other rivers to provide slack water for booming, other users of the streams responded by pushing through legislation requiring that dams be equipped with chutes to allow the downstream passage of rafts and small boats. Other laws required that booms be constructed so as to allow navigation to pass with reasonable ease. Similar legislation regulated splash dams, providing redress for those whose passage was blocked by them or whose property was damaged by floods they released. But these laws, while providing means of redress, were carefully drafted so as not to block the growth of the lumber industry. As earlier, when raftsmen had failed in their efforts to obtain a ban on log drives on the Susquehanna, those whose proposals stood in the way of industrial development found few supporters in the nation's legislative bodies.[5]

More important than these palliatives was the work of a handful of men who actively sought to establish a more rational system for handling the nation's forests. One of the first was John J. McGilvra, United States attorney for Washington Territory from 1861 to 1865. Disturbed by the illegal cutting that he recognized was necessary if the area's mills (and economy) were to be kept alive, McGilvra proposed a solution to this situation that Congress had so long ignored. He suggested that standard stumpage fees be established on unsurveyed government lands and that they be levied against those cutting thereon. Technically these fees would be in the form of fines for having "illegally" cut the timber, and as such they would be levied by the courts. But in fact charges would be set at a level that would provide fair compensation to the government for timber cut and would, at the same time, give lumbermen access to lands they could otherwise log only secretly and at some risk. This system, applied in

Washington Territory during McGilvra's tenure as United States attorney, worked reasonably well; but in the face of opposition from the General Land Office (which wished to control such things itself), the objections of local lumbermen and their political minions (who preferred not to have charges levied at all), and lukewarm support from his own superiors in Washington, D.C. (where the problems of the Civil War tended to obscure all else), the approach dropped from sight when McGilvra left his post. It is perhaps as well that it did, for it was flawed at its heart. McGilvra's system depended upon levying "fines" for illegal cutting: on the lumbermen's frontier, juries willing to convict those guilty of timber trespass were at best difficult to find.

McGilvra's approach was not entirely original. In Canada authorities had developed a system of leasing timber-cutting rights on crown lands. Ontario and Quebec first began to collect timber dues in 1826. Gradually perfected thereafter, the system rested on a recognition that some land was unsuited for agriculture and ought to be kept permanently in timber production. The leasing of cutting rights provided not only an ongoing source of income to the government but also a vehicle through which authorities would in time enforce cutting practices and timber management consistent with the public interest. In practice this system meant charging relatively uniform fees, much like what McGilvra advocated; unlike the American's approach, however, it rested upon a foundation of law rather than administrative practice and was much stronger as a result.[6]

McGilvra was not alone in protesting practices in the United States. During his tenure as secretary of the interior (1870–75), Columbus Delano repeatedly called attention to what he considered unwise policies. He proposed that forests be withdrawn from entry under the Preemption and Homestead laws. An immediate exploration should be undertaken to locate all timberlands; those found should be surveyed at once, then appraised and sold for cash at the determined value. In his report for 1874–75, Delano wrote, "depredations to an enormous extent are constantly occurring, which existing laws are powerless to prevent, and seemingly equally powerless to punish." He believed that commercial forestland sold at its true value would be carefully husbanded by owners, for, having paid a fair price, they would desire to get a good return on their investment. In other words, the best way of halting trespass on federal timber and bringing sound management to forests was for the government to rid itself of commercial forests. In an age when it was commonly held that federal land policy ought to expedite the transfer of the public domain to private farmers, such a proposal sounded sane and familiar.

Carl Schurz, secretary of the interior from 1877 to 1881, took a different tack. Schurz did not subscribe to the popular frontier belief that the land belonged to those who lived on or near it and that they had a right, even a duty, to utilize its resources. Schurz believed that Interior held lands in trust for the nation and had a moral obligation to protect them from depredation. Within a month of assuming office, Schurz made it clear that the department would no longer turn a blind eye to timber trespass. Men before him had attempted to halt such cutting or to ensure that the federal government received compensation for timber taken, but never had so high a federal official labored so hard to halt what he termed the "wicked wanton waste of the public timberlands." Schurz worked through his commissioner of the General Land Office, J. A. Williamson, to obtain energetic enforcement of the laws and through President Rutherford B. Hayes to wring from Congress greatly increased appropriations for agents to ferret out lawbreakers. The result was the seizure of huge quantities of logs, as well as hundreds of suits, civil and criminal, for timber trespass and other illegalities. In the Lake States, the South, and the West violators were brought into court. Relatively few convictions followed, however, for local juries seldom found defendants guilty; when convictions were obtained, punishments tended to be light.

The outcry in response to Schurz's actions was quick in coming. Born in Germany, Schurz was denounced as an arrogant Prussian who did not understand American ways or American needs. James G. Blaine of Maine bludgeoned him by paraphrasing the Declaration of Independence. Like the King of England, Blaine claimed, the tyrannical secretary of the interior had unleashed on the land "swarms of officers to harass our people" and was seeking to block development by "raising the conditions of new appropriations of lands."

Schurz's critics attacked with more than rhetoric. In 1878 they won passage of the Timber Cutting Act, which allowed settlers and miners to take timber from the public domain for their own use free of charge, and of the Timber and Stone Act, which was even more important. Originally applicable only in California, Nevada, Oregon, and Washington, the act was extended to all public-land states in 1892. It provided for the sale at $2.50 an acre of up to 160 acres of land that was valuable for timber or stone but unfit for cultivation. Section 5, introduced as an amendment by Senator Aaron Sargent of California, allowed trespassers to obtain relief from prosecution by paying $2.50 per acre cut. Applying to past as well as future thefts, to unsurveyed as well as surveyed lands, this section seemed a timberman's equivalent of the old Preemption Act for squatters (but without its limitations on acreage) — or, worse, an open invitation to thievery. Federal courts soon reduced the impact of section 5 by ruling that paying the fine did not fully discharge liability; trespassers still had to pay the value of the timber taken. Nevertheless, the hand of Schurz and his agents had been greatly weakened.

Nor was that the only challenge. In 1879 Congressman Hilary Herbert of Alabama introduced what one opponent labeled a "bill to license timber thieves." Herbert's proposal would have extended the principle of section 5 to all public-land states and lowered the charge for those caught to $1.25 an acre. During debate, it was claimed that no one before Schurz had made serious efforts to stop timber theft. Speakers decried the "spies and informers" the secretary had unleashed in the timber-growing regions, holding that their actions were "paralyzing the great lumber companies" and causing "poor laborers" to suffer. In a grandiloquent address, Herbert pleaded for compassion for timbermen who had stolen timber to support themselves during the hard times of the mid-1870s. In spite of his pleas, his bill was watered down so as to release trespassers who paid set fees from prosecution only in those civil suits resulting from thefts before March 1, 1879. Even in this weakened form, the bill served, like the Timber and Stone Act, to undermine the efforts of Schurz. Vigorous enforcement of laws protecting public forestland would have to wait.

Schurz was ahead of his time in denying the frontier ethic that held the land was for using and in insisting upon active enforcement of the laws, but he did not stop there. Dismayed by the rapid inroads being made into America's forests and by the threat of a timber famine, Schurz joined the handful of people calling for conservation of the nation's forests. The experience of his native Germany convinced Schurz of the wisdom of such a course, and he championed it in his public utterances, with Congress, and within the executive branch.

In the GLO's annual report of 1877, J. A. Williamson called for "regulations . . . looking to a renewal of the forest by careful preservation of the young timber"and the "perpetuation of the growth of timber" on lands unfit for agriculture. Schurz not only endorsed his subordinate's report, he went beyond it. In his own annual report he suggested that "All timber lands still belonging to the United States . . . be withdrawn" from entry and that the government "in order to satisfy the current local demand, [sell] timber from the public lands under proper regulations" and "especially to see to it that no large areas be entirely stripped of their timber, so as not to prevent the natural renewal of the forest." Schurz persuaded President Hayes to include the matter in his first annual message to Congress. A bill to bring Schurz's proposals to fruition soon appeared in Congress. Drafted by General Land Office personnel, it was the first comprehensive bill aimed at providing effective administration of the nation's forests. Congress, however, gave the bill little attention.

After four years as secretary of the interior, Schurz left office as he had entered it, pleading for action to keep timberlands in federal hands and to provide for management for continuing production. In his final report, Schurz said:

What is looked upon as everybody's property is apt to be in nobody's care. Thus, our forests are disappearing with appalling rapidity, especially in those parts of the country where they will not renew themselves when once indiscriminately destroyed. Like spendthrifts, we are living not upon the interest, but upon the capital. The consequences . . . will inevitably be disastrous, unless the Congress of the United States soon wakes up to the greatness of the danger and puts this ruinous business upon a different footing by proper legislation.

Unfortunately, not until the 1891 forest reserve amendment and subsequent developments during the administration of Theodore Roosevelt were policies implemented that would bring to pass what Schurz had pleaded for.[7]

Schurz was not alone in calling for change. In August 1873 the American Association for the Advancement of Science, encouraged by a paper presented at its annual meeting by Franklin B. Hough, passed a resolution favoring creation of a federal forestry commission. Hough prepared a memorial to Congress to this end and traveled to Washington to plead the AAAS's case with President Grant and administration officials. Hough soon won over Congressman Mark H. Dunnell of Wisconsin, a key member of the House Committee on Public Land. Dunnell arranged to have five thousand copies of the memorial from AAAS printed, and in 1874 he prepared a bill to implement its proposals. That same year, Secretary of the Interior Delano also pleaded for legislation to stem the devastation of public forests, but his proposal, like that of Hough and Dunnell, died in Congress.

Dunnell persisted and in 1876 was able to wring from his legislative colleagues an appropriation of two thousand dollars for a study of forestry. Hough, appointed to conduct the investigation, was delighted. For some five years he had been gathering data; drawing upon these materials, he was able to present a 650-page report in just over a year. Impressed by it, Congress authorized the printing of twenty-five thousand copies. Hough's volume added strength to Schurz's efforts. He denounced the pioneer mentality with its destructive approach to natural resources, the waste, greed, and thievery evident in lumbering operations, and the concept of private property rights as something so nearly sacred as to prevent government interference with destructive practices on private land.

But Hough was no Jeremiah, simply lamenting the state of affairs; he had positive proposals to make. Congress, he said, should change its approach to timberlands. Recognizing that forests would be needed in perpetuity, it should stipulate in all future sales and grants of timberland "that a certain portion when cut off shall be protected and allowed to grow up with another crop, and that this proportion of timber shall thereafter be kept up. The title should be issued only upon this condition, the neglect of which by the holder should render it liable to revert to the government." Nor did he stop there.

The custom of selling only the privilege of cutting the timber upon public forest lands, as is done in Canada, is worthy of serious consideration. . . . Should such a system of leasing timber privileges be adopted, it would be proper to fix the time that the privilege should continue, and limit the size of timber allowed to be cut, reserving the small trees for future growth. The title being still held by the government, future sales of timber from time to time on the same land, could be made, and a supply thus maintained not subject to the caprice of private owners or the fluctuations of markets.

Such a system would require careful administration by professional foresters; although there were none in America, Hough pointed to Europe to demonstrate that it was indeed possible to develop a trained cadre of the sort required. Finally, Hough noted that his proposals conflicted with the prevailing ideal of smallholders. "It is obvious," he wrote, "that such a system of leasing and supervision can best be managed in bodies of timber of considerable extent, rather than in detached parcels."

Hough reported his suggestions in two reports, one in 1880, the other in 1882, and continued to agitate for change in federal forest policies until his death in 1885. Little noticed at the time—or by historians since—Hough pointed the way toward the concept of sustained yield and the system of national forests and professional foresters that was to emerge in the twentieth century. Gifford Pinchot and others were to take most of the credit, but Hough had been the real pioneer.[8]

In 1875, in the midst of Hough's campaign, John A. Warder and a handful of others met in Chicago to inaugurate the American Forestry Association. Warder had apparently become interested in forestry while serving as United States commissioner to the international exhibition in Vienna in 1873. Inspired by congresses of European forest managers, Warder dreamed of an American counterpart. The AFA, which aimed at the "fostering of all interest of forest-planting and conservation on this continent," was the result. The group grew slowly and had little impact until it merged with the American Forestry Congress in 1882. Thereafter it became increasingly influential. It was a major force behind the passage of the 1891 forest reserve amendment (commonly known as the Forest Reserve Act)—that vital piece of legislation from which most present-day national forests have sprung—and behind much subsequent forestry legislation as well.[9]

The amendment, added in conference committee to a general land bill, was the first major step in bringing Hough's suggestions to fruition. In response to lobbying activities of the AFA and pressure from Secretary of the Interior John W. Noble, the pending bill was amended by the committee to allow the president to withdraw specified areas in the public domain for forest reserves. Congress passed the bill without debating—or apparently even noticing—section 24, the added portion.

President Benjamin Harrison soon made Congress aware of its oversight. By the end of 1892 he had withdrawn over thirteen million acres. Most were set aside to protect watersheds. His successor, Grover Cleveland, withdrew five million acres and them, shortly before leaving office, twenty-one million more. Many, especially westerners, were outraged. They saw these withdrawals as "locking up" resources needed if their states and territories were to develop. To them forest reserves sounded like vast new national parks that were to be preserved in their pristine state by keeping out logging, grazing, farming, and other commercial activities. Locking up resources was not what Hough or his successors had in mind, but that did little to placate critics of the reserves.

At about the same time, responding to a request from Cleveland's secretary of the interior, Hoke Smith, the National Academy of Sciences created a forestry commission to study the forest reserves and to make recommendations on their management and on related actions that were needed. Congress appropriated twenty-five thousand dollars to underwrite the study.[10]

Deluged with protests after Cleveland's eleventh-hour withdrawals, Congress was at last moved to conscious action on behalf of forests. Near the end of its term, Congress passed a "sundry civil appropriations" bill that contained a provision revoking Cleveland's twenty-one-million-acre withdrawal. The president pocket-vetoed the bill, leaving the incoming administration of President William McKinley without funds for the coming year. McKinley quickly called a special session of Congress to deal with the situation. After intense maneuvering, the champions of forest reserves triumphed. They succeeded in getting incorporated into the new sundry civil appropriations bill what came to be known as the Pettigrew amendment (more recently the Forest Management Act of 1897), specifying criteria for the designation of reserves—watershed protection and timber protection—and directing the secretary of the interior to make rules and regulations for their protection. He was specifically authorized to sell mature and dead timber from them. Reserves already established were to remain.

The amended bill, signed into law on June 4, 1897, was the culmination of efforts stretching back to Franklin B. Hough. But in a more immediate sense it was the work of Bernhard Eduard Fernow (chief of the Division of Forestry in the Department of Agriculture), of the American Forestry Association (which had long been lobbying for a rational program), of the National Academy of Sciences (through its report, prepared primarily by Charles S. Sargent and young Gifford Pinchot), and of several members of Congress (including Thomas C. McRae of Arkansas and Richard F. Pettigrew of South Dakota). The basic elements of a reasoned approach to the nation's forests were now in place: the government had forest reserves and the means to manage and protect them.[11]

If the late nineteenth century saw the old "cut out and get out" lumber industry at its floodtide, reaction to it came into its own during the administration of President Theodore Roosevelt (1901–9). A number of factors, beyond simply years of preparation, were responsible. Not the least was Roosevelt himself. Since his boyhood, Roosevelt had loved the outdoors. He had dreamed of becoming a naturalist. Time spent as a rancher in the Dakotas broadened his perspective and deepened his understanding of nature. A voracious reader, Roosevelt continued to keep abreast of developments in natural history and related sciences even after he turned to politics. During his years as governor of New York, Roosevelt's concern with forestry and conservation was manifest. Once in the White House, he gave it more attention than had any of his predecessors.[12]

Other factors also lay behind the surge of conservation-oriented activity after 1900. The late nineteenth century had seen a plethora of protest and reform movements, frequently working at cross-purposes. Rising concern over the power of trusts—many of which prospered while individual citizens suffered during the depression of 1893–97 and which were often blamed for the inflation that followed soon after—brought the previously fragmented reformers together at the turn of the century. Antimonopoly sentiments served as the common denominator holding diverse, sometimes squabbling element together in a working coalition that dominated the political scene for over a decade. Roosevelt was both a manipulator and a product of these forces.[13]

Changing attitudes toward nature also played a part in the rising concern for conservation. Organizations such as the Appalachian Mountain Club (founded in 1876), the Boone and Crockett Club (1887), and the Sierra Club (1892)— none of which had been established for that purpose—gradually added their voices to the rising chorus calling for forest preservation. Unlike these older groups, the Appalachian National Park Association (1899) was concerned from the first with saving forests.

In these circumstances, conservation in general and forestry in particular could hardly have avoided becoming a major concern during the Progressive Era. Much conspired toward this end, above all the record of timber frauds, waste, and devastated and abandoned forests. Reformers, convinced that monopolies were evil and must be leashed if not destroyed, found ready targets in the lumber industry and the system of laws and practices that had encouraged it to take the form it had. Others, more concerned with waste and inefficiency than with the supposed malfeasance of plutocrats, welcomed the opportunities to bring rational management to natural resources that were provided by the climate the protestors had created.

Gifford Pinchot, appointed head of the Division of Forestry in 1898, seems to have reflected both outlooks. Pinchot wished to bring efficient scientific management to the nation's forests, but he also genuinely distrusted big business. He believed business tycoons had willfully desecrated natural resources in the name of profit and could be restrained from continuing to do so only by the heavy hand of government. When Pinchot unleashed a torrent of antimonopoly rhetoric during the Ballinger-Pinchot controversy of 1910, he was not cynically arguing what he did not believe in order to rally public support (as some have suggested) but was articulating the very attitudes that earlier had brought him and Carl Schenck to a parting of the ways. Schenck had advocated working with and educating the lumber industry; he viewed Pinchot's intemperate attacks on it as unwise and counterproductive.[14]

Regardless of his private opinions, Pinchot long had no choice but to work with lumbermen. Until 1905 forest reserves remained under the General Land Office. Pinchot's Division of Forestry had no forests of its own to manage; if it were to affect forest practices, it would have to do so on private lands. Toward that end, Pinchot had the division issue circular number 21, which offered to help owners of private timberlands develop plans for management and fire protection. Owners would pay only the expenses of the foresters assigned to their lands. Numerous requests for aid came in response, including one from the Kirby Company of Texas, which sought a management plan for its 1.2 million acres of pine forests. Some fifty employees of Pinchot's division soon converged on Kirby's land to plan its use and protection. By 1905 some 11 million acres had come under cooperative planning, and more were added before the program ended in 1909.[15]

Even though the times were ripe and his personality and interests might well have led one to anticipate them, Roosevelt did not embark on crusades for conservation immediately after becoming president. With a sure political hand, he first sought to reassure conservatives in Congress and to build a power base for future actions. When he finally did move on issues pertaining to natural resources, Roosevelt's actions dealt not with forests but with irrigation, where there was a ready-made body of western supporters in Congress. Working with this group, the president succeeded in gaining passage of the Reclamation (Newlands) Act of 1902, legislation that brought water to many an acre of the arid West. Gifford Pinchot and many other foresters actively supported the drive for irrigation. The American Forestry Association publicized the irrigation movement in its pages and even renamed its magazine *Forestry and Irrigation*. But forests did not long remain in the background, nor when they did come to the fore was it simply as protective cover for watersheds.

The Bureau of Forestry (created from the old Division of Forestry in 1901) sought to bring about government and private cooperation for the control of forest fires, those scourges of timberlands that over the years had probably done more than anything else to persuade lumbermen that "cut out and get out" practices were the safest way to handle investments in timber. Now, with opportunities for moving on to new forest frontiers largely past, the prevention and control of fires began to get serious consideration—especially in the Pacific Northwest, where forest fires burned over two billion board feet of timber in the summer of 1902.

The bureau also cooperated with industry in seeking to keep tariffs on imported lumber high, for its leaders recognized that scientific forestry would be more costly than previous forest use had been. Lumbermen could afford to adopt the management practices championed by the bureau only if lumber prices were kept at profitable levels through tariffs and other means.

The bureau's greatest impact came after 1905. In that year the forest reserves were transferred to it from the General Land Office, which after years of inaction had in 1901 and 1902 made halting but largely unsuccessful efforts at managing the reserves. The bureau was raised in stature and renamed the Forest Service (two years later the forest reserves were renamed national forests). With timberland—millions of acres of it—to administer at last, Pinchot's agency worked to bring federal forests the sort of management it had long sought to persuade private landowners to adopt. And the acreage involved continued to grow. When Congress passed a measure to end presidential authority to make withdrawals, Roosevelt worked closely with Pinchot to determine what remaining land might be added to the system of national forests; just before his authority to do so ran out, Roosevelt set aside an additional sixteen million acres.

Pinchot tackled his new challenge with zeal, but the Forest Service was no one-man show. The chief's enthusiasm drew a host of bright, dedicated young foresters into the agency. The decentralized administrative system that Pinchot adopted gave them responsibility and room to grow in their profession. Many eventually moved up to fill top positions in the service. The esprit de corps that developed during Pinchot's years as head of the Forest Service continued long after he was cashiered by President Taft in 1910. Decentralization had other advantages too. Convinced that scientific management was feasible only with an intimate knowledge of local conditions, Pinchot wanted decisions made as far as possible by trained men on the scene rather than by bureaucrats and politicians in Washington. At a time when most of the nation's forests were still unmapped and unclassified, his approach was wise.[16]

In spite of this, westerners frequently accused Pinchot and others in the Forest Service of being effete eastern theorists who knew little about actual conditions in the forests of the West. These charges reached a climax after Pinchot instituted a fee-permit system in 1906 to regulate grazing in the national forests. Stockmen, accustomed to grazing their animals free of charge, protested. Colorado was a center of opposition to Pinchot's policies. When Roosevelt enlarged the national forests through his "midnight withdrawals," the clamor spread. Senators Henry M. Teller of Colorado and Weldon B. Heyburn of Idaho denounced Pinchot and Roosevelt with unrestrained bitterness, reviving charges of locking up resources and adding that Forest Service officials were arrogant, ambitious men who cared nothing for the welfare of the West. Pinchot's attempts to extend the fee-permit system to hydroelectric power sites within national-forest boundaries brought attacks from yet other quarters, as did the high-handed methods he used to protect these sites until legislation could be obtained from Congress authorizing their leasing on a fee-permit basis.

The national forests, critics argued, ought to be turned over to the states they were in. Various state officials, especially from the Rocky Mountain states, agreed. But there were others in the West who did not and who rallied to the support of Pinchot and Roosevelt. This support cut much of the ground from under Teller, Heyburn, and their allies and helped ensure both the survivial of the national forests and the continuation of Pinchot's basic policies. The Pinchot years were never quiet ones for the Forest Service, but with Theodore Roosevelt's unwavering support the chief was able to make progress in building a sound agency and implementing effective policies.[17]

Neither Pinchot nor the Forest Service focused exclusively on forests and their management. Years earlier, John Wesley Powell had pointed out that in the arid West water was the key to existence and therefore what was done at the headwaters in this region affected those downstream in the most basic ways. Much of the land administered by the Forest Service was in the arid West, which forced the agency to give careful thought to watershed protection, streamflow, and related considerations. Pinchot was an early supporter of irrigation, and it was this in large part that stimulated his efforts to protect headwaters from overgrazing.

But Pinchot was neither an original nor a systematic thinker. W J McGee, a self-made scientist and former assistant of Powell's, was the main theorist of the conservation movement. Recognizing the interrelations within the great water-sheds of the nation and wanting integrated, multiple-purpose development of water resources, McGee became a key advisor to Roosevelt, Pinchot, and Secretary of the Interior James R. Garfield. Since a number of federal agencies had responsibilities within the major watersheds, McGee proposed a new body to draw up coordinated plans for development and use. Convinced, Roosevelt created the Inland Waterways Commission in 1907 and worked assiduously to get the financial support and statutory authority to make it viable. Congress, however, failed to see the need, and the agency died a lingering death. Integrated, interagency resource planning would have to wait.[18]

The Inland Waterways Commission was not the only evidence of a broadening of conservation perspectives during the Roosevelt years. Bird refuges and international treaties to protect migratory waterfowl put in their appearance. Scenic preservationists launched what was to be a long, and eventually losing, battle to protect Hetch Hetchy Valley in Yosemite National Park from being turned into a reservoir for San Francisco's water and power supplies. New national parks and monuments were created. In 1908 Roosevelt invited the governors of all the states, together with a number of leaders in the field, to a White House conference on conservation. Pinchot funded the conference from his private fortune when Congress refused to underwrite expenses. The ostensible purpose was to encourage the creation of state conservation commissions to carry the sort of work being done at the federal level down to that of the states. Numerous state conservation commissions resulted. So too did the National Conservation Commission, an agency created to make a nationwide resource survey, essential if the sort of scientific, intergrated planning McGee advocated was to be effectively implemented. In 1908 Roosevelt also appointed a Country Life Commission to investigate conditions in rural America and recommend measures to improve them. Other groups also were operating under the conservationist flag.

The early movement to prevent forest despoliation and to control the lumber barons had, in the general crusading atmosphere of the Progressive Era, become submerged in a broad range of loosely integrated concerns. In the process, conservation had become the most nebulous of terms. As William Howard Taft observed early in his administration, no one knew what conservation was any more, but everybody was in favor of it.[19]

During Taft's presidency the crusade for conservation passed its peak. Spawned in large part by the excesses of the old lumber industry, it now fell victim to its own — and to shifting public concerns. The coming of World War I furnished the coup de grace for an already seriously weakened movement. Concern over conservation was to peak again in the 1930s and 1960s. At other times individuals and organizations worked more quietly, out of the limelight. For the moment, however, the floodtide of conservation — and forestry — had passed.

The floodtide of the old lumber industry had passed too. Although short-sighted lumbermen continued to slash through the nation's forests, less myopic operators were becoming more and more common. In 1909 the all-time peak of lumber production in the United States was reached; over 44.5 billion board feet of lumber were sawed that year. From that point on it became increasingly clear that sustained-yield forestry, not cut-and-run logging, was the only viable long-range approach for the nation and its timber owners. The story of the years that followed is in large part the story of how that approach was implemented and how it was adjusted to growing demands on the forest from outside the industry.

America's Forests and the
Modern World, 1909–76

Part 4

Decades of Decision

Chapter 11

The period from 1909 to the present contrasts sharply with the one that preceded it. Economic growth and production had dominated thinking about the American forest; now the central question was how best to reconcile contending interests, public and private, with their diverse claims on the forest. Inevitably, the quest for an acceptable answer was shaped by broader social and political currents.

From 1910 to 1930 there was a backing away from the government regulation of the Progressive Era, with its suspicion of big business, and a concentration on developing a cooperative approach in which the public and private sectors worked together. With the Great Depression, government regulation grew again, accompanied by a host of federal programs that involved direct government action. Much done in the woods was now accomplished by employees of the public rather than the private sector. That the uses involved took many forms other than commercial timber harvest was both a sign of the times and a harbinger of things to come.

After World War II, demands on the forests proliferated at a bewildering rate, conflicts among potential users multiplied, and the stridency of debate rose. In the 1960s and early 1970s, when Americans were at loggerheads over social issues and war in Southeast Asia, environmental concerns were also at a peak. Attention to the forests had gone beyond the economic focus of the late nineteenth century, the regulatory approaches of the Progressive Era, and even the social and economic concerns of the 1930s. Now less easily articulated issues—quality of life, preserving the human race by preventing carbon-dioxide buildup, and the like—entered into discussions more and more frequently.

Reconciling the approaches of people with the sort of concerns that forced their way to center stage in the 1960s with those of people primarily interested in drawing upon the forests to meet commercial and economic demands may well be impossible. Nonetheless, the period since World War II has been marked by a continuing effort to devise workable mechanisms for giving people from all positions a chance to contribute to the decision-making process — and, insofar as possible, to accommodate their conflicting demands. This quest for better means of reconciling varying demands on the forest and of providing for a multiplicity of needs is not, however, solely a product of the postwar era. It is the central thrust of the entire period since the old extractive lumber industry reached its peak of production in 1909 — a thrust obscured by depression, war, and social change, but always present.

In an even broader sense, this search for accommodation in regard to the forest is but one part of a larger quest: from the Progressive Era to the present, Americans have been steadily engaged in an effort to devise more open, democratic, and effective means of meeting the many demands of a modern, heterogeneous society. As had been true ever since colonial times, what Americans have done regarding their forests in the years since 1910 tells much about Americans' values and attitudes, hopes and fears — indeed, about their images of themselves and of their ideal society.

The years from 1910 to 1930 determined the future of the American forest. Theodore Roosevelt and Gifford Pinchot had awakened the public to the problems of conservation, while nature literature and related works had made people more appreciative of the beauty of forests and more aware of the need to protect them. But much remained to be done. Fire and wasteful methods of harvesting had decimated the virgin forests that remained in New England and the Northeast after earlier clearing for farms. The Lake States' lumber industry had begun a decline reminiscent of that in older lumbering regions. Interest shifted to the Gulf South, which by 1910 had moved into first place among lumber-producing regions. The redwood, western red cedar, spruce, Douglas fir, and pine of the Pacific Coast had attracted lumbermen's attention, and production there was increasing rapidly. In these circumstances, progress toward responsible forestry that had come during the first decade of the twentieth century could easily have been lost. Decisions made and programs consolidated during the next two decades not only preserved the advances of the Roosevelt years but resulted in further, if less spectacular, progress.

The shift in the centers of lumber production lay at the heart of the threat to gains in forest protection won during the Progressive Era. In 1900 the Lake States led in production with almost 9 billion board feet. The Gulf South produced over 5 billion board feet, the Pacific States less than 3 billion. By 1910 the Gulf South's production had risen to 9.5 billion, the Pacific States produced 7.5

billion, and the Lake States' output had dropped to 5 billion. By 1920 the Pacific Coast had taken the lead with 10 billion; the Gulf South had begun to decline, dropping to 8 billion; and the Lake States had plummeted to 2.4 billion. This trend continued to 1930, by which time the Lake States had dropped out of major production, turning out only 1.5 billion board feet. As production dropped in the areas in decline, quality fell too.

Most discussion of the logging of the American forests, and the comparative statistics cited, related to softwoods—pine, cypress, Douglas fir, spruce, redwood, and such—on which interest and commercial exploitation concentrated. Seventy-eight percent of all lumber produced in the United States in 1911 was softwood. In Louisiana it represented 93 percent of the total. Similar ratios prevailed for the other states of the Gulf South and for the Pacific Coast. Hardwood lumbering and manufacturing continued to be important, especially in Pennsylvania, Virginia, West Virginia, Kentucky, and Tennessee, but in the world of large lumber operations, conservation politics, and reforestation, the emphasis was on softwoods—and would continue to be in the years that followed.

The shift of lumber production from the Lake States to the Gulf South and then to the West Coast again raised the specter of a timber famine, a fear exacerbated because in the Far West the industry was moving onto its last major frontier in the United States—with the possible exception of Alaska. Increased production in the Far West was partially a reflection of greater cutting in places where lumbering had been taking place for decades: around Puget Sound and Grays Harbor in Washington, along the lower Columbia River and around Coos Bay and other ports on the Oregon coast, and in the coastal redwoods of California. But a significant part of the increase resulted from the rise of major lumber manufacturing activity in the pine forests of the interior. Bend and Klamath Falls, Oregon, became leading lumber centers almost overnight. At Potlatch, Lewiston, and elsewhere in northern Idaho, lumbering was also booming. If the ponderosa, sugar, and western white pine of the interior were to be cut out the way earlier pine forests had been, there were no new forests in the land to which the industry could move.

In these circumstances, a timber famine seemed more likely—and nearer— than ever. Cutting was proceeding with extraordinary speed in the interior as well as in older production areas of the Far West. The example of the Lake States—where loggers swept through the white pine belt in less than a half-century—made the activity in the Far West especially ominous. What had happened in the Lake States, and earlier in Pennsylvania, Maine, and elsewhere, led one conservationist to describe lumbering as "the great nomad among American industries, driving from one virgin forest to another like a threshing machine from one ripe wheat field to the next." Charles R. Van Hise, a noted scientist and president of the University of Wisconsin, wrote in 1910 that the American people were cutting "timber more than three times as fast as it was produced." With arguments reminiscent of George Perkins Marsh, Van Hise predicted that unless Americans took immediate steps to end waste in cutting and manufacturing as well as damage from fire, and to institute systematic conservation and reforestation, they would find themselves facing the same plight as Italy, China, and other countries that had stripped their land of forests.[1]

Professional foresters emerged to add strength to such warnings. Many prophesied a fate for the Gulf South similar to that of the Lake States. William L. Bray of the United States Bureau of Forestry had estimated as early as 1903 that the virgin pine in Texas would be exhausted within twenty years. Federal foresters in Mississippi calculated in 1908 that the supply of virgin pine in that state would be cut out in twenty-five years. In Louisiana, timber harvesting grew at such a phenomenal rate that some feared the state was rapidly being reduced to bare, cutover land.

Faced with rapidly vanishing forests, a number of public-spirited citizens joined the growing body of foresters in calling for regulation of logging practices and application of sound forest management on public and private lands alike. The White House conference of governors in 1908 had been a major effort to involve both the states and private industry more directly in the conservation crusade, focusing the eyes of the nation on the problems of the forests and stimulating interest in conservation.[2] To further encourage state participation, Congress in 1911 passed the Weeks Law, which provided matching funds to any state that set up an acceptable system of protection for forested watersheds of navigable streams. The same measure provided for federal acquisition of forestland in the eastern states. This was a major step for the Forest Service, whose previous influence in the East had been only indirect and limited.

The Weeks Law marked the beginning of extensive cooperation among the federal government, the states, and private industry to protect forests from fire and other hazards. When the law was enacted, only eleven states could qualify for federal assistance; within a decade the number had more than doubled. Following the lead of the Forest Service, state governments—previously largely indifferent—established or strengthened forestry departments, gave them broader scope, and began to fund them adequately.[3]

In Wisconsin the first forestry commission had been established under Governor Robert M. La Follette in 1903. State forester Edward M. Griffith, a disciple of Pinchot, aggressively promoted a comprehensive program including fire protection, waterpower site acquisition, reforestation, a system of state forests, and forest-taxation reform. After authorization by a somewhat irregularly passed constitutional amendment, the Wisconsin legislature of 1911 approved the Griffith program and appropriated funds to purchase cutover pine lands in the northern part of the state and to establish a state forest reserve. The same legislature enlarged and made permanent the Conservation Commission. In addition to Griffith, Charles R. Van Hise was a strong advocate of a comprehensive forestry program. His monograph *The Conservation of Natural Resources* (1910) was a standard authority for a generation.

The Wisconsin program was not without opposition. Many residents of Wisconsin's northern counties still believed that "the plow will follow the ax," that much of the cutover was suitable for farms, and that the forest reserve system would keep the northern part of the state poor and thinly settled. Furthermore, as indicated earlier, Hiram M. Chittenden and others disputed the Pinchot– Van Hise–Griffith thesis that forests exercise a strong influence on climate, streamflow, and erosion. Soon opposition succeeded in reducing legislative appropriations and eventually involved the entire program in a suit over its constitutionality.

After more than two years of litigation, the supreme court of Wisconsin declared the reforestation program unconstitutional. The court both faulted the way the amendment was approved and denied that reforestation represented "internal improvements" for a "public purpose" within the meaning of the constitution. The decision left Griffith's program in shambles; not until 1924, by which time the northern pinelands had been further devastated, was a new constitutional amendment adopted and reforestation work resumed.[4]

The states of the Gulf South faced many of the same problems. In Texas the driving force for conservation was W. Goodrich Jones, a banker from the town of Temple who had an Ivy League background. Jones appeared at first glance to be an unlikely leader of a crusade for preservation and reforestation of the state's timberlands. Contrary to popular stereotypes of Texas, the eastern portion of the state had approximately eighteen million forested acres—a region almost as large as Maine. The forest consisted principally of longleaf, shortleaf, and loblolly pine, with some hardwoods at lower elevations and along the streams. Even before bonanza lumbering had reached its height, Jones was advocating selective cutting and reforestation to perpetuate these stands.

Jones was a delegate to the White House conference in 1908 and returned home determined to form a statewide forest conservation society to push for an effective forestry department in the state. His initial attempt was abortive, but he continued his efforts. In 1914 he organized the Texas Forestry Association. The TFA was at first composed of only a few public-minded citizens, but Jones soon enlisted the support of many lumbermen, foresters, and state political leaders. In 1915 they lobbied successfully for the creation of a state department of forestry, the appropriation of funds to support it, and the appointment of a trained forester as its head.[5]

Like Gifford Pinchot, Jones was an advocate of "conservation for wise use" and urged that the forests be handled so that "one forest crop follow another, generation after generation." He knew that selective cutting and reforestation would be successful only if lumbermen were convinced that conservation was good business. To secure industrial support, Jones sought the assistance of such lumber tycoons as John Henry Kirby, J. Lewis Thompson, and Joseph H. Kurth and his son Ernest. These and a few others in the state had experimented with selective cutting even before the First World War. Kirby had invited government foresters to draw up plans under Pinchot's circular number 21, issued in 1898, thereby bringing more acres under scientific management than anyone else in the country.

The professional forester who did most to promote conservation in Texas was Eric O. Siecke, the second state forester. Appointed in 1918, Siecke served for twenty-five years and did much to develop the Texas Forest Service into a highly professional, nonpolitical organization and to stamp it with his own personality. Taking advantage of the Weeks Law and later legislation, Siecke persuaded leading timber owners, led by Thomas L. L. Temple, to augment available state and federal funds so as to provide better fire protection and pine-seedling nurseries. Through the leadership of Jones and Siecke, by the end of the twenties the Texas Forest Service had become an efficient fire-protection and conservation agency and a beginning had been made in replanting the cutover areas left by the bonanza loggers. In time the whole region would again be "forested over."[6]

The leadership and enthusiasm generated by Gifford Pinchot and the White House conference extended to the Pacific Coast. There the primary and immediate concern was protection against forest fires. In California, support for forestry programs rose and fell through the late years of the nineteenth century and the early years of the twentieth. The legislature had created a state board of forestry in 1885 but abolished it in 1893. Urged on by conservation-minded Governor George C. Pardee, the legislature in 1905 authorized a new state board of forestry. On the advice of Pinchot, Pardee appointed E. T. Allen, a United States Forest Service assistant forester, as California's first state forester. The disastrous fires of 1904, which had burned more than eight hundred thousand acres in the state, encouraged Allen to give primary attention to fire prevention and control. Toward this end, he promoted cooperative fire-protection associations throughout the state. Allen resigned in 1907 to return to the Forest Service as the first district (i.e., regional) forester in the Pacific Northwest, but his work was continued by his successors.

The election of Republican progressive Hiram Johnson to the governorship of California in 1910 brought a new effort, aimed at implementing the goals of the White House conference. As a result, the 1911 legislature created the California Conservation Commission; Johnson named Pardee chairman. The commission was charged with gathering information concerning the state's forests and other natural resources. In its report of 1912 and subsequently, the commission recommended establishing a permanent board of forestry to supervise the state forester and his department, a comprehensive forest fire-protection program supported by an annual appropriation, reform in forest taxation, and a state reforestation program. In addition, the board proposed legislation that would allow the state, through the forestry board, to regulate potentially destructive logging on private lands. Because of party splits and personal conflicts, none of these proposals were passed by the legislature. Not until 1919 did the California legislature finally create an independent board of forestry and provide it with funds to set up a statewide fire-protection force.[7]

In Oregon, efforts early in the twentieth century to pass fire-control laws and establish an effective forestry agency had not been successful. Despite the example of past fires, the legislature of 1907 budgeted only five hundred dollars for forest protection. But the White House conference led in 1909 to creation of the Oregon Conservation Commission. The commission collected information on which it based recommendations for an effective forestry program and more efficient utilization of the state's resources. The outlook of the body was so utilitarian that chairman Joseph N. Teal wrote that it could as readily be called the Oregon Development Commission. However, the development it sought to further was to be carefully planned, not the first come, first served scramble of laissez-faire. In 1911 the legislature, mindful of catastrophic fires that had swept the Northwest in the summer of 1910 and drawing upon information accumulated by Teal's commission, passed a series of laws providing for reforestation of denuded lands and establishing the office of state forester with a budget of sixty thousand dollars for the biennium.

Francis A. Elliott, Oregon's first state forester, had hardly opened his office when the Weeks Law provided the means for greater cooperation and a more comprehensive program of fire control. He took the lead in a campaign to establish a state forest in the rich timber of the Coast Range through exchanges and purchases that consolidated Oregon's fragmented timber holdings so they could be given proper management. Elliott laid the groundwork for a full-scale forestry program in Oregon. Through it, and through the activities of the Forest Service and federal funds made available by the Weeks Act, forest conservation became an important concept in a state whose forest resources were the greatest in the nation.[8]

But not all progress was a result of government actions. In 1909 E. T. Allen again left the Forest Service. This time he turned his attention to voluntary industry-oriented associations promoting fire protection on the West Coast. Allen, George S. Long of the Weyerhaeuser Timber Company, and others formed what became the Western Forestry and Conservation Association—a group embracing all the states on the Pacific Coast and the province of British Columbia. Allen became its secretary-forester, a post he held for more than two decades. He wrote a fire fighters' manual and a handbook entitled *Practical Forestry in the Pacific Northwest*. Under his direction, the WFCA gained leadership in national as well as western forest affairs. This voluntary organization, together with its fire-fighting counterparts in the several states, developed fire codes, fire-control techniques, patrol regulations, fire-fighting equipment, and standards for closed-burning seasons and slash disposal. These provided the basis for subsequent legislative action, and the firsthand experience timber owners gained in working together toward a common goal in these voluntary associations was of considerable long-range importance.[9]

The creation and strengthening of state forestry agencies, if not voluntary associations in the industry, were encouraged by Gifford Pinchot. It was Pinchot who suggested E. T. Allen for the California post and who conferred with E. M. Griffith on the reforestation of northern Wisconsin and with W. Goodrich Jones on the needs in Texas. His drive and enthusiasm infected conservationists everywhere.

Pinchot carried on his crusade for forest conservation both in and out of public office. When Roosevelt retired from the White House in favor of fellow Republican William Howard Taft in 1909, the new president appointed his own men to the cabinet. Among them was Richard A. Ballinger, a Seattle lawyer, who became secretary of the interior. Soon Ballinger, with Taft's blessing, returned to the public domain more than a million acres that had been withdrawn by Roosevelt, reduced the activities of the Reclamation Service, and proposed to transfer valuable coal lands in Alaska to a Seattle group that would then sell part of the acreage to the Morgan-Guggenheim syndicate. When General Land Office investigator Louis R. Glavis publicly protested that the claims to the coal lands were illegal and a reversal of Roosevelt-Pinchot conservation policies, Taft fired him. Alarmed, Pinchot took up the fight against the "Despoilers of the Public Lands" both in congressional and executive arenas and in the press. Exasperated by what he considered irresponsible and insubordinate behavior, Taft dismissed Pinchot too—thereby making him a martyr to the cause of conservation.[10]

In the storm of controversy, Pinchot made it appear that Taft and Ballinger were anticonservationists seeking to undo Roosevelt's work in the field. Pinchot may have lost the battle with Taft and Ballinger, but in the end he was to win the war. So great was Pinchot's influence among American foresters that Taft bowed to public and private pressure and named Henry Solon Graves as the new chief of the Forest Service. Graves, Pinchot's friend and a schoolmate at Yale, and like him an American-born, European-trained forester, was dean of the Yale School of Forestry.

Richard Ballinger soon resigned as secretary of the interior. His successor was Walter L. Fisher, another friend of Pinchot's and a supporter of forest conservation. The new secretary refused to throw on the market the Alaskan coal lands, which had been the bone of contention in the Ballinger-Pinchot feud, and the president hesitated to open more public lands or allow further major reversals of Pinchot's policies.

Through the rest of the decade, Graves cautiously steered the Forest Service past occasional hostility from Congress and frequent coolness from Taft and his successor, Woodrow Wilson. Like Pinchot, Graves subscribed to the policy of efficiency and scientific planning. He would accept no substitute for management of America's forests by trained specialists. But unlike Pinchot, Graves was no self-righteous crusader, nor did he assume evil intent in those who disagreed with him. One result was that tension gradually subsided after Pinchot's ouster. Indeed, the critics of Pinchot had only temporary influence on the development of the Forest Service. In retrospect, it is apparent that by contributing to a split in Republican ranks, the Ballinger-Pinchot controversy had a greater role in bringing down the Taft administration in 1912 than in changing the course of the American conservation movement.

Pinchot was a "utilitarian" rather than a "preservationist." He was an effective propagandist for forest management, for a sustained-yield program on federal forestlands, for required fees for forestland grazing, and for leasing of waterpower sites for limited periods. Pinchot distrusted the Department of the Interior and regularly sought to have forested tracts included in national forests rather than added to national parks. He had proposed that the national parks be transferred to the Forest Service and had unsuccessfully opposed creation of the National Park Service within the Interior Department in 1916. In all this, his position sprang from a belief that resources should be managed for production rather than "locked up" for recreation or scenic preservation.[11]

Pinchot's stress on practical use involved him in one of the bitterest controversies of the Progressive Era. Hetch Hetchy Valley lies in the northern part of Yosemite National Park. In the late nineteenth century, John Muir and the Sierra Club (founded by Muir in 1892) had successfully petitioned Congress to include the valley in the park. In 1901 the city of San Francisco requested that it be allowed to use this most valuable reservoir site for the city's water supply. A great outcry arose from preservationist groups, while Pinchot supported San Francisco's request. In so doing he alienated John Muir, who exploded: "Dam Hetch Hetchy! As well dam for water tanks the people's cathedrals and churches." Urged on by Robert Underwood Johnson, editor of *Century* magazine, Muir set out to defeat the proposal. He soon found a variety of allies, including J. Horace McFarland of the American Civic Association. But the city of San Francisco had numerous supporters too, among them Pinchot, the National Conservation Association, and former secretary of the interior James R. Garfield. When Woodrow Wilson assumed the presidency in 1913, he named Franklin K. Lane, an attorney for San Francisco in the controversy, as his secretary of the interior. The Wilson administration soon took a stand in support of the dam, and with the balance thus tipped, in 1914 Congress finally granted San Francisco permission to turn Hetch Hetchy into a reservoir.[12]

Both Pinchot and Graves were "regulationists" as well as utilitarians. That is, they proposed federal regulation of cutting practices in private as well as public forests and regulation of grazing rights, waterpower sites, watersheds, and other resources. Arguing that the "public interest must be protected," they proposed establishing uniform cutting regulations through federal laws. Others preferred state to federal regulation. All too often, however, those who favored state regulation equated it with weak regulation or none and were in fact seeking to circumvent effective federal controls. As already noted, Senators Weldon Heyburn and Henry M. Teller led in support of state control, which they promoted as a West-versus-East issue. However, many westerners (including key leaders in California and Oregon), recognizing the weaknesses of state control and the aims of some of its supporters, threw their support to Pinchot and Graves. Regulation by the federal government was not something propounded solely by eastern bureaucrats and theorists, in spite of the charges advanced by Heyburn, Teller, and their allies.[13]

Federal regulation of resource use on government land seemed necessary to almost every forester, but federal control of logging practices on private land was something else again. Some, reasoning along lines propounded by Carl A. Schenck, argued that education and cooperation would bring better results than strong-arm controls. During most of the Progressive Era the chief question was not whether foresters should support public controls, but what form those controls should take. The controversy thus fomented continued for generations and remains generally unresolved.[14]

Chief forester Graves brought William B. Greeley to Washington as assistant chief in 1911 and placed him in charge of developing cooperative programs with state forestry agencies and private landowners, an effort that was much strengthened by the newly passed Weeks Law. Through education and personal contact, Graves and Greeley worked together to promote conservation on all levels.

Foresters in state and federal forest services got most of the attention during the period, but they were not alone. E. T. Allen worked in the private sector; Carl Schenck encouraged graduates of his Biltmore Forest School in that direction; others, including J. P Kinney, labored in the Bureau of Indian Affairs to bring proper management to reservation forests. Scientific forestry was still a fledgling in the United States, but it had come far from the 1870s, when Franklin B. Hough had had to turn to Europe for examples of what professional foresters might do in and for America.[15]

Professional foresters were not the only people in the woods. Loggers and millmen also had a vital interest in the future of America's forests. Traditionally, the laborer in the lumber industry worked long hours at difficult and dangerous tasks, usually in remote places. His wages were low in comparison with those in other manufacturing occupations, and he appeared to be at the mercy of both the millowner and the vagaries of the market. As the number of immigrants working in the industry rose and nativism grew during and after World War I, he also suffered because of middle-class fears and hostility. He was notoriously independent, moving from job to job as whim or the rumor of better conditions stirred him. Many employers joked that they had three crews: one coming, one going, and one working. Circumstances were different in parts of the South, but conditions were no better: workers were tied to their employers through debts to company stores and worked under conditions much like those of poor sharecroppers.

In spite of such conditions and the promising beginnings made under the Knights of Labor, trade unions had little success in organizing woods and sawmill workers. The American Federation of Labor, concentrating on skilled laborers, made only abortive efforts to organize lumber workers. Indeed, loggers and mill laborers were for a number of years under the jurisdiction of the AFL's Carpenters Union, where they were largely ignored. Gradually, however, unions began to take on strength in the lumber industries of the South and West, reaching levels of activity not seen since the heyday of the Knights.

Before 1910 there were sporadic efforts at organizing by laborers in the southern states, principally caused by local grievances and unexpected layoffs. In 1910 the Brotherhood of Timber Workers attempted to organize lumber workers in Louisiana and Texas. The Southern Lumber Operators Association (SLOA) reacted promptly, vigorously, and effectively. Led by John Henry Kirby, owner of one of the largest lumber companies in the entire South, the operators drafted a uniform nonunion (yellow-dog) contract, reduced the work week to four days, weeded out union organizers, and responded to strikes with lockouts. Kirby was paternalistic. He had been active in reducing the hours of labor in his mills, providing Christmas gifts for the families of his employees, and funding college expenses for worthy young people; but he was strongly antiunion and determined to run his own companies without dictation from either government or the workers. In this he was typical of SLOA members.

The confrontation touched off a "lumber war" that lasted three years. Strikes, lockouts, and violence flared in both Louisiana and East Texas, culminating in the "battle of Graybow." Led by A. L. Emerson, the Brotherhood of Timber Workers determined to organize workers in mills along the Sabine River. The owners determined that they would not. The affiliation of the BTW with the Industrial Workers of the World (IWW) early in 1912 gave the owners a new weapon with which to fight the union, and they hurled charges of "Anarchist, Communist, Socialist, criminal" against the union leaders. At Graybow, Louisiana, in July, guards broke up a meeting of the brotherhood at which Emerson was to speak. In the melee that followed, three union men and one company guard were killed. The governor sent in troops, and Emerson was arrested and charged with murder. After a spectacular trial he and his associates were acquitted, but the events so drained the union that the Brotherhood of Timber Workers expired within four years. Not until the New Deal period did union labor again make a serious effort to organize lumber workers in the South.[16]

The IWW fared only slightly better on the West Coast. There the American Federation of Labor had done little; its emphasis had been on organizing skilled millworkers, such as the shingle weavers, whose union was at the time the strongest in the forest industries. For the most part, the International Union of Timber Workers existed only on paper. Before the war the total membership in AFL unions in the West Coast lumber industry was under two thousand.

Into this vacuum came the Wobblies (as IWW members were popularly known), armed with arguments of Marxist philosophy, class struggle, sabotage, worker solidarity, and direct action. It was a fertile field. Working and living conditions were primitive, and the men put in long hours for low pay. Loggers were described as "homeless, womanless, and voteless," ready for any radical adventure. That many were foreign-born made them doubly suspect. In the Pacific Northwest they were frequently referred to as bindlestiffs, a pejorative term roughly equivalent to hoboes—a term that revealed how much things had changed in the few years since Stewart Edward White's novels had popularized the image of the he-man lumberjack.

When IWW representatives moved to organize Pacific Coast sawmill and woods workers, public opinion as well as owners opposed their efforts. Local police and vigilante mobs forcibly broke up their meetings and mauled organizers. The Wobblies regarded efforts to break up their street-corner harangues as a violation of the First Amendment and staged "free speech" fights whenever they could find an audience. The running violence reached a climax in a confrontation at Everett, Washington, in November 1916. There a strike by the Shingle Weavers was joined by the IWW, which sought to take over the action. When police and guards dragged down the soapbox orators and clubbed the organizers out of town, a group of Wobblies, nearly three hundred strong, set sail from Seattle in two boats to "establish free speech" in Everett. When they attempted to land against opposition by police and vigilantes, shooting broke out. Five men from the ship and two guards were killed, and more than fifty were wounded. The ships returned to Seattle without landing the unionists, only to have the entire group arrested and seventy-four indicted and charged with murder. All were eventually acquitted, and the IWW claimed a propaganda victory. But the nationwide publicity given events at Everett hurt the union at least as much as the outcome of the trial helped it.

The year 1917 saw rising labor unrest in the Pacific Northwest. The Shingle Weavers, Timber Workers, and IWW all sought to win important concessions: shorter hours, higher wages, and improved conditions in logging camps were the most frequent demands. In July many, perhaps most, of the region's workers went out on strike. The work stoppage lasted until September. When the strikers returned to work, wages were raised and food and camp conditions improved, but no union had been recognized and hours remained the same. In the months that followed, the men resorted sporadically to slowdowns, sabotage, and absenteeism; there was a virtual work stoppage after eight hours.

The First World War brought pressure for increased deliveries from a West Coast lumber industry in the throes of crisis. The government suddenly needed hundreds of millions of feet of lumber for cantonments, crates, boxes, wooden ships, timbers, and a thousand other uses. The Aircraft Production Board determined that Sitka spruce from the West Coast was the most desirable material for the air armada with which director Howard Coffin promised to fill the European skies for the 1918 campaign. The problem was to "get out the spruce." In the face of the workers' attitude, the prospects of doing so seemed slim.

The government's solution to this impasse was to organize the Loyal Legion of Loggers and Lumbermen, an All-American patriotic union made up of both employers and employees. For an administration that solved the food shortage by volunteer "meatless, wheatless, sugarless" days and promoted war-bond sales with frequent patriotic speeches by local "four minute men," this was, in retrospect, a predictable approach. With the approval of the AFL's Samuel Gompers, the 4Ls (as the Loyal Legion was known) expanded rapidly, enrolling members of the Timber Workers and other unions. Total membership for the 4Ls during the war approximated 125,000. So successful was its recruitment that most threats from the IWW were eliminated.

Behind the Loyal Legion was Colonel Brice P. Disque, a little-known progressive who believed that major changes in the treatment of workers in the lumber industry were indeed necessary. Disque was head of the Spruce Production Division, a beefed-up unit from the Signal Corps of the United States Army. The SPD officers actively recruited members for the 4Ls, pointing out draft-deferment advantages for woods and sawmill workers. The division kept the peace and even supplied troops to work in operations that met Disque's standards for working and living conditions. Genuine improvements were made, and the mills kept running. As a result, opposition from both union organizers and millowners to the reforms that Disque pushed was muted for the duration of the war. Under the Legion and with Disque's support, the eight-hour day with time-and-a-half for overtime became standard on the West Coast, wages became more competitive with those in other war industries, and logging camps became as livable and the food as palatable as that in army camps—a considerable advance over previous conditions. Most important, the Legion got out the spruce, Douglas fir, and other wood needed in the war effort. But time ran out with the coming of the armistice on November 11, 1918; the projected clouds of spruce-built American war planes over Germany never became a reality. After the war had ended and Disque had resigned, the Loyal Legion gradually became essentially a company union. This, as much as other developments, kept real collective bargaining out of the West Coast lumber industry until the New Deal.[17]

World War I and the years that followed were a time of repeated adjustments for the lumber industry. The war itself made a variety of demands on forests and forest workers beyond those faced by Disque and the 4Ls. Most unusual perhaps were those connected with the American Expeditionary Force, the army sent to Europe by the United States. The AEF required huge quantities of lumber. Rather than ship the needed timber from America, the army organized the Tenth Engineers (later consolidated into the Twentieth Engineers), a regiment of experienced foresters and lumbermen that included William B. Greeley of the Forest Service. While in France, the regiment cut about three hundred million board feet of lumber, almost three million poles and pilings, and more than three hundred thousand cords of firewood and operated some ninety sawmills. At the end of the conflict the lumberjacks and foresters returned home with valuable experience and new respect for conservation methods long practiced in French forests.[18]

Closer to home, the Emergency Fleet Corporation of the United States Shipping Board developed a standard wooden ship that could be constructed rapidly to bolster the American merchant fleet during the war. Most of the yards where the vessels were built were on the Gulf and Pacific coasts. They experienced a rash of activity in 1917 and 1918. Heavy ship's timbers, planking, and decking brought premium prices; orders taxed the capacity of mills. Like the aircraft program, the drive to build a "bridge of boats" was only partially successful, for by the time large numbers of ships began to come down the ways the war had ended. Moreover, the vessels themselves proved slow and not very seaworthy. Had there been a campaign in 1919, American pine- and fir-built vessels might have played a significant role. As it was, the program simply represented the dying gasp of wooden merchant vessels. The Dollar Steamship Company (forerunner of the American President Lines) still shipped lumber across the Pacific in wooden sailing ships in the mid-twenties, but for all practical purposes the day of wooden merchantmen was past.[19]

The end of hostilities ushered in a painful period of adjustment. Demand for lumber plummeted. The national price index for lumber fell by 50 percent from 1920 to 1921, mills closed, and production dropped. But the setback was only temporary. By 1923 the level of activity was again high, although prices remained low.

The postwar years were quieter than the war years, but far from placid. Low prices for lumber, at times below the cost of production, put a damper on expansion as well as on efforts to modernize and integrate operations to make them more efficient. Small mills were among the hardest hit, but nearly everyone suffered. When depression came for the rest of the country in 1929, the lumber industry collapsed too. It did not have as far to fall as the decade's high flyers, but as a result of the low prices (and profits) it had long faced, many of its firms had few financial reserves to draw upon as they struggled to survive.

While lumbermen were trying to cope with the problems of low prices, they also had to deal with chronic overproduction and concerns over timber depletion. Studies by both the Forest Service and a congressional committee (the Capper Report) revealed that forest resources continued to be cut much more rapidly than they were being replaced. It was estimated that in 1920 the United States had only two-fifths as much timber as in 1800. In a single year the consumption of wood amounted to twenty-six billion cubic feet, while growth totaled only six billion. New technological advances, such as gasoline-powered tractors and logging trucks, promised to speed depletion of the forests even more. To meet this crisis, Pinchot, Graves, and their supporters called on Congress to take drastic action to regulate private cutting practices. Graves, typically, was more restrained than Pinchot; he was willing to accept state control within federal guidelines. Others, fearing that such regulations would create an adversary relationship between the government and private industry, supported the cooperative policies advocated by Greeley (and earlier by Schenck). This emotional issue became the central topic of the day in forestry circles, deeply dividing the profession.

In 1920 Henry Graves resigned as chief of the Forest Service, and two years later he returned to Yale as dean of the Forestry School. There he directed the training of hundreds of aspiring young foresters and established a reputation as one of the most influential forestry educators in America. William B. Greeley succeeded Graves as head of the Forest Service. After prolonged controversy over rival forestry bills, Greeley's philosophy of education and cooperation prevailed with the passage of the Clarke-McNary Act in 1924. The bill had the support of most of the Forest Service, the Society of American Foresters, the American Forestry Association, the state forestry bodies, and the organizations of lumbermen.

The legislation was in step with the times. It expanded the federal-state-industry program of cooperative fire protection and authorized 2.5 million dollars annually to finance it (although Congress never appropriated the full authorization). Various states passed enabling legislation and appropriated funds in order to participate in the program. The bill also authorized a federal-state system of nurseries to provide seedlings for reforestation of state and nonindustrial private lands, a study of forest taxation and its effects, and a forestry extension program. More important, it authorized federal land acquisitions in the drainages of navigable streams. This landmark change cleared the way for major expansion of national forests in areas east of the Mississippi. Nowhere did the act mention federal regulation of private forests.

Greeley faced other problems that threatened the Forest Service and the national forests, not the least of which was continuing tension between the departments of Interior and Agriculture. In 1905 when President Theodore Roosevelt had transferred the forest reserves from the Interior Department to the Forest Service in the Department of Agriculture, officials in Interior had protested. Pinchot had swept their arguments aside, saying that Interior stood convicted as corrupt, inept, and incompetent. The antagonisms that the transfer and statements like Pinchot's fueled were evident behind the scenes in 1910 during the Ballinger-Pinchot affair. They continued to plague Greeley and others in the years that followed.[20]

The election of 1920 brought Warren G. Harding to the White House. Harding had campaigned for an end to experiments and crusades and a return to "normalcy." He apparently had in mind the laissez-faire policies of the late nineteenth century. When Harding appointed the notorious anticonservationist Albert B. Fall to the post of secretary of the interior, friends of the American forest were apprehensive—and with good reason. Fall set out to gather all federal lands into his department. When he proposed that Harding transfer the national forests to Interior, Greeley staunchly opposed the measure and received invaluable support from Secretary of Agriculture Henry C. Wallace, Pinchot, and Graves. Both the American Forestry Association and the Society of American Foresters publicly denounced the proposed transfer. In the face of this opposition, Harding hesitated to go along with Fall's scheme. The entire proposal was dropped when Fall resigned from the cabinet as the Teapot Dome scandal threatened to break into the headlines. Yet had it not been for Greeley's determined opposition and his support by Secretary Wallace, Harding might well have quietly signed the already-drafted transfer, and opponents of it would have been confronted with a fait accompli.[21]

It is axiomatic that conservation flourishes when it has a friend in the White House. Presidents Harding and Coolidge had little interest in conservation. Yet contrary to commonly held opinion, the conservation movement did not deteriorate during the 1920s; it expanded and matured. In the ebb and flow of events after Theodore Roosevelt left the White House, leadership in conservation shifted from the president to the departmental level and to the states, but it did not vanish.[22]

The strong leadership Greeley exhibited in forestry was duplicated in other fields that affected the American forest. Hugh H. Bennett began to attract nationwide attention to the problems of soil erosion and ways reforestation could help solve them. Stephen T. Mather and his assistant Horace M. Albright efficiently organized the National Park Service and focused attention on the problems of preservation and management of the magnificent areas, many of them forested, within the national parks. In the Southwest, forester Aldo Leopold was formulating concepts concerning balanced wildlife populations. With his articles "The Wilderness and Its Place in Forest Recreational Policy" (1921) and "The Last Stand of the Wilderness" (1925), Leopold assumed a major share of the leadership of the wilderness movement that had previously been identified with John Muir. Another conservationist from the West, Arthur H. Carhart, joined in giving leadership to the movement. As a result of their efforts the Forest Service was eventually persuaded to set aside wilderness areas. Others, disturbed by both logging and Forest Service plans to build roads into the lake country of northeastern Minnesota and western Ontario, joined in 1927 to form the Quetico-Superior Council, a body dedicated to keeping the area wild. With these actions, the wilderness movement entered a major new phase, one whose main accomplishments would not come until years later.[23]

The Save-the-Redwoods League emerged somewhat earlier than the Quetico-Superior Council. Formed in San Francisco in 1919 by a number of prominent conservationists and local leaders, this group sought to raise funds to preserve stands of the huge coastal redwoods. Urged on by the league, California's voters in 1928 approved a bond issue for the purchase of land for state parks — provided that matching funds were forthcoming from private sources. The league successfully raised millions of dollars to match the state funds, with the result that large redwood parks came into being along the northern California coast. Two of these state parks were to form the core of the Redwood National Park when Congress finally created it a half-century later.[24]

The drive to preserve the coastal redwoods, like the campaign for Quetico-Superior and many other preservationist campaigns of the twenties, was much influenced by the burgeoning use of automobiles during the period. Tourist travel by automobile brought more Americans than ever into contact with forest scenery. The automobile resulted in an influx of visitors that swiftly democratized the national parks, opening them to people who could never before afford to visit them. Public support for parks and scenery preservation increased as a result. At the same time, the expanding network of paved roads made many forested tracts accessible to loggers for the first time. The felling of roadside timber — the very timber that gave the tourist routes much of their beauty — grew apace.

Preservationists were not long in responding. Except in a few areas, such as Quetico-Superior, most of them still welcomed the auto. They wanted more people to visit and enjoy the as yet uncrowded and untrammeled places that they themselves loved; paved highways seemed a means to that end. Stephen Mather, for example, launched a campaign for a paved park-to-park highway that would link all the national parks of the West in a giant loop and thereby increase the tourist traffic to all of them. What preservationist wanted was not to block the building of highways, but to preserve the timber that lined them. Toward this end, they sought to persuade private operators to refrain from cutting strips of roadside timber until state or federal officials could arrange to save them by purchase or exchange. On the whole, Forest Service officials gave limited support; but there were important exceptions, and major victories were won— most notably when the trees along the Columbia Gorge Highway in Oregon and the highway to Mount Rainier National Park in Washington were set aside. Eventually the champions of roadside timber were able to obtain legislation from Congress that smoothed the way for the preservation of additional strips, and numerous roadside timber stands were soon set aside in the western states.[25]

Although the automobile brought more people into contact with the nation's forests and opened tourism to the average citizen as never before, no basic changes in attitude toward the forests or nature seem to have accompanied it. What shifts occurred were relatively minor. Nature literature continued to appear, but its antiurban message became muted and less urgent. Peter B. Kyne wrote a number of popular novels about lumbering that at first glance seem only to continue earlier themes but on closer examination turn out to preach Anglo-Saxon supremacy and pioneer virtues while excoriating immigrants, radicals, mixed marriages, and other matters of concern to the nativists of the 1920s. Kyne's stories tell less about the attitudes of Americans toward nature than about those who helped make life difficult for Wobblies and bindlestiffs.[26]

American attitudes toward nature continued to be a mixture of many elements: Jeffersonian ideas, romanticism, transcendentalism, the antiurban Arcadian myth, a belief in progress and the inexhaustibility of the nation's resources, and more. As always, the particular blend varied from individual to individual. Those seeking to bring scientific management and utilization to forest resources often found themselves in conflict with those who had different priorities.

In spite of the frustrations generated by these differences, the twenties saw the maturing of forest research both in Washington and in the field. The United States Forest Products Laboratory had been established in 1910 as a small operation on the campus of the University of Wisconsin. Under Carlile P. Winslow, it became the "largest organization in the world devoted to research in the utilization of wood and related products." Its magnificent building, completed in 1932 on the shores of Lake Mendota, indicated the importance that forestry and forest-products research had assumed. With the support of Greeley, researchers Raphael Zon and Earle H. Clapp worked to expand the scientific research program of the Forest Service. The result was the passage of the McSweeney-McNary Act of 1928, which provided for a comprehensive ten-year research program, funded at a much higher level than ever before. In addition, it established a series of regional forest experiment stations. Cooperation underlay the basic assumptions of this measure, and the experiment stations became a meeting place for farmers and lumbermen as well as foresters.[27]

Such meetings did little to eliminate the diversity of views toward the forest. They were primarily vehicles for selling scientific forestry. Preservationists, seldom in attendance, continued on their own way, gathering strength by proselytizing among their own. When the two sides met, it was more often to speak for rival positions than to seek accommodation. The clashes over environmental issues that were to become so common in the 1960s and 1970s had, in a small way, already begun.

The late twenties were ominous in another way too. By the first decade of the twentieth century, the relentless march of exploitive logging had proceeded as far as the Gulf South. Midwestern lumbermen such as Robert A. Long, W. R. Pickering, William Carlisle, and William T. Joyce bought large acreages in Arkansas, Louisiana, and Texas and logged their holdings furiously. Their "cut out and get out" philosophy brought fears of devastation and desolation. It was easy for lumbermen confidently to promise that "the plow follows the ax," but in vast areas farms did *not* spring up, despite the efforts of lumbermen to attract buyers for their cutover acres. Moreover, those who did purchase farm sites often gave up after a few years and abandoned the land. Much of the pineland— North, South, and West—was better for growing trees than for anything else.

Repeatedly, surveys by the Forest Service detailed a dismal picture. One of the most thorough assessments was the Capper Report, undertaken in response to a Senate resolution in 1920. This study disclosed that at least one-half of the land cut over by the lumber industry had not been converted into farms, and one-fourth of that was left barren—without trees or people. It was estimated that this devastated land totaled about eighty-one million acres.

The migration of lumbering was accelerated during the twenties. For example, the Long-Bell Company cut out in Louisiana and Texas and moved to the Pacific Northwest. By the end of the decade, a long list of major mills had closed in the Gulf South. Lumber production fell throughout the region. Part of the decline was no doubt due to the fall in lumber prices, but a great part was the result of the number of mills that cut out, discontinued operations, and moved on.[28]

To meet the challenge of diminishing timber stands, William B. Greeley pushed for a comprehensive fire-prevention as well as fire-control program that would include both private and public lands. Uncontrolled forest fires, Greeley believed, caused more devastation than did ax or skidder. The Weeks Law had made a start in funding a program of cooperation among the United States Forest Service, the states, and private industry in combating forest fires, and the Clarke-McNary Act had expanded the work. By the twenties, many private organizations were also sponsoring programs to curb the epidemic of fires. The effort became a virtual crusade.

E. T. Allen described the menace of fire in a speech to the American Forestry Association in 1925. The annual fire bill, he stated, was well over five hundred million dollars. The United States averaged some fifty thousand fires and ten million acres burned over each year. Most of these fires, he held, were caused by humans, and a large percentage were deliberately set. He called for a program of education, policing, and prosecution to curb the destruction. Allen pointed out that although people remember the disastrous fires, such as the Hinckley fire of 1894, small fires resulted in greater aggregate loss. In California, for example, for the single year 1913 the state forester reported 1,971 fires resulting in a loss of more than five hundred thousand dollars plus unestimated damage to watersheds.[29]

Spectacular conflagrations in the North and Northwest, such as a three-million-acre fire of 1910 in Idaho and Montana, attracted public attention, but most blazes were in the South. A survey by the American Forestry Association revealed that 80 percent of the total fires from 1917 to 1927 occurred in the southern states. Logged and abandoned areas were a constant invitation to uncontrolled forest fires. During the decade covered by the survey, fires burned perhaps one-third of the South's entire pine area. Burning had a number of causes, including hunters, turpentine workers, locomotives, and farmers who sought to "green up" the grass for their livestock. Many were deliberately set, often in retaliation against a large company or absentee owner who fenced the land, eliminated scrub oaks, forbade grazing or hunting, or was held responsible for some fancied wrong. A jingle of the time reflected the attitude of poor whites toward such owners:

> You've got the money
> We've got the time,
> You deaden the hardwoods
> And we'll burn the pine.

Arson was sufficiently widespread in the woods to prove that this was no idle threat.

In a major effort to combat the intentional setting of fires, the American Forestry Association raised some $150,000 in 1928 to send a team of young foresters through the Deep South to preach fire prevention. Led by Willaim C. McCormick, former assistant state forester in North Carolina, the group was nicknamed the "Dixie Crusaders." They gave lectures, showed films, displayed exhibits, and put on skits stressing the danger and cost of uncontrolled forest fires. The program lasted three years, carrying the gospel of fire prevention and control to some three million people.[30]

The emphasis that Greeley and the state foresters gave to cooperation with the timber industry in developing management policies also began to bear fruit in the twenties. Increasingly, timber owners accepted sustained yield, selective cutting, and reforestation as good business. In Arkansas Edward Crossett, following the recommendations of Herman H. Chapman of Yale, pioneered the practice of scientific forestry designed to ensure a forest harvest year after year, generation after generation. In Louisiana Henry Hardtner preached selective cutting and tree planting and practiced them on his own lands. He regularly urged the legislature to provide more adequate support for the Forestry Commission. In California O. C. Barber of the Diamond Match Company pursued policies of selective cutting, adopted progressive logging practices, and experimented with direct seeding to reforest cutover areas. Frederick Weyerhaeuser, already prominent as a leading lumberman in Minnesota, had first bought timberland (nine hundred thousand acres) in the Pacific Northwest in 1900. George S. Long, in charge of these lands, husbanded the forest carefully. At first his efforts were directed mostly toward protection from fire, but gradually he broadened his approach. "This is not for us, nor for our children, but for our grandchildren," Weyerhaeuser would say. Unlike the "cut out and get out" lumbermen, Weyerhaeuser's enterprises had come to the West Coast to stay.[31]

Such examples could be multiplied many times. They merely illustrate that Greeley's preachment—that good forestry was also good business—was taking root in the industry. Lumbermen held their cutover lands and, with the aid of the increasingly active state forest commissions, engaged in reforestation. Revised tax laws in Washington and other states made it economically feasible for them to do so. Much had been accomplished by 1928, when Greeley resigned as chief of the Forest Service to become secretary-manager of the West Coast Lumbermen's Association. As a private citizen, he continued to work for cooperation among professional foresters, the federal government, the states, and the lumber industry. By the end of the decade, most foresters had accepted cooperation as the most fruitful approach. Restrictive regulation, where necessary, would come at the state level.[32]

The election of Herbert Hoover in 1928 brought to the presidency a person more sensitive to problems of forest management, flood control, water storage, wildlife preservation, and soil erosion than his immediate predecessors. He sought through "organized cooperation" to involve states, individuals, and the federal government in a comprehensive conservation program similar to Greeley's. But the onset of the Great Depression in 1929 hit the forest industries hard, sending already depressed prices to new lows and causing many companies to abandon operations. In the South and the Lake States, production dropped to the lowest level in fifty years. Much cutover land became tax delinquent and eventually reverted to public ownership.

To protect the American lumber market for American manufacturers, Congress included a duty on imported lumber in the Smoot-Hawley Tariff of 1931. The next year Congress added an excise tax on imported lumber. These measures were aimed primarily at Canada, which was the principal exporter to the United States and had enjoyed duty-free traffic since 1913. As could be expected, Canada retaliated, enacting a preferential tariff. American lumber shipments to Canada dropped to one-third the 1929 level. The tariff wall thus raised deprived American lumbermen of a profitable market that they had developed over the previous generation. It would remain for the next administration to remove the barrier.[33]

Hoover sought to promote conservation policies on a broad front but was hampered by his conservative and individualistic philosophy. His Commission on the Conservation and Administration of the Public Domain (1930) commanded respect but led to no legislative reforms. Nevertheless, Hoover did use public-works funds to promote conservation projects and was considering more comprehensive projects when his term ended. California, moving more rapidly, set up some twenty-eight forest camps for unemployed youth and put state foresters in charge. For two years they built firebreaks, roads, and trails and felled dead, insect-infested, and diseased trees and disposed of them. California's experience influenced the organization of the Civilian Conservation Corps under the New Deal, as did a similar program in New York.[34]

The twenty years between the retirement of Theodore Roosevelt and the Great Depression were critical for America's forests. Thanks to the Weeks Law and the Clarke-McNary Act, state conservation agencies developed increasingly effective fire-prevention systems, educational programs, and seedling nurseries. The quest for progress through cooperation rather than federal regulation advanced forest conservation on all fronts. Even the most individualistic lumbermen came to accept sound forestry practices as necessary if the future of the industry were to be made secure. After 1930 fires were on the whole fewer and better controlled, cutover areas were more frequently replanted, and improved management practices were followed in both public and private forests. And in the South, the long, warm, wet growing seasons stimulated the appearance of a vigorous second-growth forest much sooner than the prophets of a timber famine had thought possible.

The period was not one of major innovations, either in the field of forestry or in the broader realm of public attitudes toward nature and the environment; but it was one of consolidation, maturation, and development. In shifting from the government regulatory approach of the Progressive Era—with its widespread suspicion of big business—to the cooperative approach, leaders in forestry had ushered in a period in which contentious debate over issues declined. Quietly, and out of the limelight, much real progress had been made.

Depression and War: The Era
of Franklin D. Roosevelt

Chapter 12

The election of Franklin D. Roosevelt in 1932 brought to the White House a dedicated champion of conservation and the American forest. As the *New York Times* reported soon after his inauguration, the "President has long practiced forestry." Indeed, Roosevelt had been interested in trees and in protecting the land since his childhood. When he took over management of the Hyde Park estate in 1910, he noted from the records that the farm had grown prize corn in 1840. Subsequent rains and floods had washed away the topsoil and eroded gullies until the estate yielded only about half what it had before. Much of this worn-out land he planted in trees, so, he explained, "my great grandchildren will be able try raising corn again." Beginning in a small way, he regularly increased his plantings until about half of the twelve-hundred-acre estate was in forest. He chose a variety of species—Norway, white, and Scotch pine, hemlock, spruce, and poplar—more than fifteen in all, placing each species where it would have the conditions it needed. Roosevelt followed approved forest-management practices: thinning and pruning the trees, removing undesirable undergrowth, and bringing in experts from the New York State College of Forestry at Syracuse University for advice in fighting diseases that from time to time attacked the stands.

Roosevelt regularly harvested mature trees, turning a small profit in the process. However, he left uncut the timber along the steep slopes leading down to the Hudson River—trees that provided a wide-spreading root system that prevented further erosion during heavy rains. He also sold crossties to the New York Central Railroad and experimented, with success, in growing Christmas trees in plantations. He demonstrated that Christmas trees could be grown commercially on a restricted acreage by rotating the areas to be harvested.

This pattern of planting, pruning, thinning, harvesting, and planting again sprang from Roosevelt's belief in the importance of maintaining the delicate balance of nature and in the relation of well-cared-for forests to the national well-being. He enjoyed taking visitors on tours of Hyde Park, identifying the different species and pointing out their role in restoring the health of the estate. The forests, he said, "are the lungs of our land, purifying our air and giving fresh strength to our people."

Roosevelt's interest in forests carried over to his public life. As a young man he had been deeply impressed by the conservation crusade led by his cousin Theodore Roosevelt during the first decade of the twentieth century. Gifford Pinchot became a warm friend and frequent advisor. As a freshman senator in the New York legislature in 1910, Roosevelt became chairman of the Forest, Fish, and Game Committee and promptly endeavored to promote wise timber use, forest protection, and improved cutting practices. He proposed an act that would have regulated the size of trees harvested, done away with clear-cutting, and required that trees be left for seed purposes. Ahead of its time, this bill did not get out of committee; a substitute merely authorized the Conservation Commission to give "advice" on forest protection and related matters. Though he incurred the wrath of many lumbermen and farmers, Roosevelt soon established himself as a leader in the drive for the conservation of natural resources — including forests, wildlife, watersheds, and power sites. He was impatient with those who stood to gain financially from conservation but, as he said, could not see six inches beyond their noses. It would be far better for the community to preserve and regulate the forests, soil, and watershed areas than to allow a few to destroy these resources for quick profit.[1]

Even before he left Albany in 1913 to join the Wilson administration, Roosevelt had been committed to planning and management by experts in a great variety of fields — including conservation. He exhibited this commitment in even greater degree some two decades later when he became governor of New York. With considerable acumen, he combined in one project plans to reduce agricultural surpluses, take marginal land out of production, combat soil erosion, and reforest areas better suited for growing trees than crops. He instructed Henry Morgenthau, his state conservation commissioner, to purchase thousands of marginal acres and to plant them with pine seedlings that in time would produce attractive forests for camping and recreation — and eventually a timber crop. To finance the project, the state legislature passed and the voters approved a constitutional amendment, the Hewitt amendment, that provided for a bond issue of nineteen million dollars. This amendment was vigorously opposed by former Democratic governor Alfred E. Smith — an action that revealed both Smith's shift to the right and his growing hostility to Roosevelt.

Having obtained adoption of this ambitious project, Roosevelt received congratulatory letters from conservationists throughout the nation. From Iowa came the thought that "the planting of trees in the waste places of New York . . . might well be extended to all other states"; and from the governor of Utah simply, "Hurrah for Trees." In implementing reforestation under the Hewitt amendment in 1932, Roosevelt provided work for about ten thousand men taken from the local relief rolls. Some two thousand additional workers engaged in gypsy moth control and in pruning and thinning in New York's state forests.[2]

Roosevelt expressed his own creed in a speech to the New York Rod and Gun Editors Association: "Long ago, I pledged myself to a policy of conservation which would guard against the ravaging of our forests, the waste of our good earth and water supplies, the squandering of irreplaceable oil and mineral deposits, [and promote] the preservation of our wildlife and the protection of our streams. We must dedicate ourselves for our own self-protection to the cause of true conservation."

The Great Depression brought an unparalleled crisis to American forestry. The depression also brought great opportunity, though it was not recognized as such by the industry. As a result of the crash of 1929, the building industry collapsed and new housing starts fell to a mere fraction of those in 1925; lumber prices, already depressed, fell below the cost of production. The lumber industry reacted in a variety of ways. Some sawmill owners increased production in an attempt to bring their annual dollar income back up to a break-even level. This added to overproduction and depressed prices even more. Many manufacturers, nearing the end of their log supply, simply closed their mills. Not only were these companies' employees left without jobs, but local county governments found their tax base greatly reduced as cutover lands became tax delinquent and no purchasers for them materialized. In every section of the country the annual production of lumber fell dramatically. In Washington (the nation's largest producer) the annual cut dropped from more than 7 billion board feet in 1929 to just over 2 billion board feet in 1932. In other states—on the Pacific Coast, in the Lake States, and in the South—the pattern was the same. In Mississippi the annual cut plummeted from over 2.6 billion board feet to 530 million, the lowest figure since 1890. State and local governments slashed appropriations for forestry work, and many companies discontinued their forestry programs. The foresters, technicians, and laborers thrown out of work by this retrenchment swelled the nation's growing army of unemployed.

But there was much work to be done. The depressed state of the industry presented government agencies with an unprecedented opportunity to encourage good forestry practices, sustained-yield policies, and reforestation.

With millions of men out of work, the means for achieving a sound forestry program was within grasp. Roosevelt acknowledged the opportunity in his speech accepting his party's presidential nomination in 1932: "There are tens of millions of acres east of the Mississippi River alone in abandoned farms, in cutover lands, now growing up in worthless brush. . . . It is clear that economic foresight and immediate employment march hand in hand in the call for the reforestation of these vast areas. . . . In so doing employment can be given to a million men."[3]

Others glimpsed the opportunity too. Ovid Butler, executive secretary of the American Forestry Association and editor of *American Forests*, took issue with Hoover's secretary of agriculture, Arthur M. Hyde, over the practicability of Roosevelt's proposal. When Congress voted three hundred million dollars to the states in 1932 for relief work, Butler wrote urging the governors to include forest work in their programs. A little later, in an editorial in *American Forests*, Butler detailed a variety of projects that would provide jobs for masses of unemployed workers. Such activities as building roads, trails, and firebreaks through the forests, establishing forest tree nurseries and reforestation programs, controlling insects and disease, and clearing undergrowth would provide employment and advance America's forests at the same time. In Roosevelt foresters found a leader who would combine unemployment relief and conservation in bold, imaginative programs that had both immediate and long-range goals. In most cases they supported him enthusiastically.

The inspiration for the Civilian Conservation Corps has been claimed for various sources. In addition to New York's experience when Roosevelt was governor, the states of California and Washington operated forest work camps for unemployed youths. Countries in Western Europe, including Norway, Sweden, Denmark, and pre-Hitlerian Germany, had developed conservation programs for unemployed young men. Some writers even traced the idea back to the writings of philosopher William James. Yet the project was, in a peculiar way, Franklin Roosevelt's own—an idea he had been dreaming over, off and on, all his life. With it he took young men and the land, at the time often wasted resources, and attempted to save both.[4]

Once in office, Roosevelt and his party acted quickly. By the end of March 1933, Congress had passed and the president had signed a measure giving him broad powers to recruit unemployed young men and put them to work at conservation tasks on public lands. By Executive Order 6101, Roosevelt brought the Civilian Conservation Corps into existence and directed the secretaries of war, agriculture, interior, and labor to name representatives on an advisory council to supervise it. He named Robert Fechner, a lean, rawboned union leader and labor negotiator, executive director of the CCC. Partly because AFL president William Green had originally opposed the scheme as "fascist" and as "detrimental " to free labor, Roosevelt was moving to rally Green's support by appointing a union man to oversee the project. Fechner was an excellent choice and continued as director for most of the CCC's life. The administration of the corps was a hybrid arrangement: the Labor Department was responsible for recruiting and enrolling the young men; the army transported them, outfitted them, and ran the camps; and technical divisions of the Departments of Agriculture and Interior—such as the Forest Service, the National Park Service, and the Soil Conservation Service—planned, directed, and supervised their work.

Beginning with a camp at Luray, Virginia, in mid-April 1933, CCC camps sprang up in national forests, state forests, and national parks, on other public properties, and occasionally on private land. Soon young men clad in olive-drab uniforms made their appearance in more than two thousand localities through the forty-eight states and the territories. Paid only thirty dollars a month (much of which was to be sent home to aid the corpsman's family) but fed, clothed, housed, and provided with medical and dental care, the "CCC boys" gained strength, weight, and height and learned useful skills. In a voluntary educational program thousands learned to read and write, additional thousands earned high-school diplomas, some earned college credits, and a few won university scholarships. By the time the program was terminated in 1942, some 2.5 million young men had gone through the CCC. Experience in the corps had an immeasurable effect upon the enrollees, most of whom were poorly educated urban dwellers. Not only were their health, education, and job fitness improved, but so too was their understanding of America, its resources, and its future. Among the most vocal in attesting to these benefits have been former corpsmen themselves.

"Roosevelt's Tree Army" did work long needed. Perhaps most spectacular was the CCC's role in fighting forest fires. By 1942 the corps had spent more than six million man-days fighting fires. In addition it built lookout towers, strung thousands of miles of telephone lines, constructed and maintained thousands of miles of roads and trails, and built numerous firebreaks—including, in California, the Ponderosa Way, more than six hundred miles long. Whenever a fire broke out, the CCC men were ready. Not surprisingly, during the CCC years the acreage lost to fire fell to the lowest level since the beginning of record keeping.[5]

Corpsmen also did less dramatic work. They combated white pine blister rust, Dutch elm disease, bark beetles, gypsy moths, grasshoppers, and various species of weevil. They opened up more of national parks and national forests to the public by building roads, hiking trails, overnight cabins, campgrounds, and recreational lakes. By 1935 CCC crews were at work in parks in every corner of the Union. States that had never had park systems, such as New Mexico, now were able to build them; others long active in parks were able to develop them at an unprecedented pace. Much of the work involved building recreational and camping facilities, but much was protective too. Firebreaks were built, brush and downed wood were cleared, and other labor was done to ensure that the forest beauty at the heart of many a park would not go up in smoke.[6]

The CCC was also important in wildlife work. Trainees developed economically submarginal land as wildlife refuges, improved nesting areas, planted food for both birds and mammals, and built or improved pools and streams that they stocked with fish.

The CCC is remembered too for its tree planting. From the first this was one of the corps' most popular activities. The young men planted more than two million acres of trees and cleared out the undergrowth in four million more. During 1936 the CCC planted more than five hundred million seedlings on national forest lands alone. The territorial forester of Hawaii, Charles S. Judd, estimated that the CCC accomplished as much in restoring the forests of the islands during its eight years as Hawaii on its own could have accomplished in forty. The same could have been said for many of the states on the mainland. One historian has estimated that more than half of all forest planting in the United States up to 1940 was done by the Civilian Conservation Corps. These forests, now reaching maturity, provide important protection for watersheds, canopies for hikers and campers, scenic vistas in national parks and forests, and a continuing source of building materials. Though the CCC was criticized at first, most opposition withered in the face of the corps' demonstrated effectiveness in performing its myriad tasks. It was probably Roosevelt's most popular program.[7]

As prices plummeted and production declined during the early years of the depression, leaders of the nation's lumber industry looked forward with a consternation bordering on panic. There was no agreement on a workable policy and no means of enforcement had such a policy been adopted. A few companies simply closed down production; Lutcher and Moore of Texas and Louisiana settled back to manage its timberlands and "raise alligators" until the depression ran its course. Other timbermen, like T. L. L. Temple in the Gulf South and the Weyerhaeusers, whose largest interests were in the Pacific Northwest, attempted to continue sound forestry practices that would protect the future and keep their organizations together even if at a reduced level of production. Too many simply sold lumber for whatever they could get, often below the cost of production, reasoning that any return was better than none. Sound forest management was forgotten, and wages shrank to a mere token. As William B. Greeley noted, the industry "had degenerated into a struggle for survival."

Voluntary trade associations, such as the Southern Pine Association and the West Coast Lumbermen's Association (WCLA), attempted to bring some order out of this chaos. But a lack of administrative funds, the absence of any enforcement authority, and the ever-present possibility of prosecution for violation of antitrust laws doomed any trade-association action almost before it began.[8]

Into this situation stepped Roosevelt with a proposal for industrial revival and self-regulation. The National Industrial Recovery Act swiftly passed through Congress, authorizing the establishment of the National Recovery Administration (NRA). General Hugh Johnson, named to head the new agency, immediately undertook to organize the major industries through a series of codes under which each industry would pledge itself to approved trade practices, more adequate wages, shorter hours, collective bargaining, and the limitation of production. "The codes," Johnson explained, "would eliminate eye-gouging and groin-kneeing and ear-chewing in business."[9]

Johnson called representatives of the various lumber associations to meet with him at Washington, Chicago, and other central locations to hammer out a code of fair practices for the industry. Forest Service chief Ferdinand A. Silcox and his assistant Earle H. Clapp, Ovid Butler and G. Harris Collingwood of the American Forestry Association, William Greeley of the WCLA, David T. Mason of the Western Pine Association, Wilson Compton of the National Lumber Manufacturers Association, and individuals from the lumber industry attended these conferences. The last group came from all sections of the country and included John Tennant of Long-Bell, C. S. Chapman of Weyerhaeuser, and Mark E. Reed of the Simpson Logging Company. Together they developed a code that included production controls, minimum wage standards, maximum hours, abolition of child labor, safety regulations, and collective bargaining. Also included was article X, the "conservation article." The inspiration for this apparently came from Greeley, who developed the idea while en route from the West Coast to an NRA meeting in Chicago. After much discussion about the content of the proposed code, Greeley remarked, "President Roosevelt is almost certain to want something in this code on forestry. Let's beat him to the draw. It will help us get the rest."

Article X committed the lumber industry to using approved forestry practices in the management of individual owners' lands. It called for individual operators to protect against forest fires during and following logging, for systematic cooperation in extending protection against fire and other destructive agencies, for preservation of young trees during logging operations, for restocking the land after cutting, for partial cutting where the species were adapted to it, and for development of individual forest management plans ultimately leading to sustained yield. Thus the industry made good forestry practices part of the code, requiring of itself what Pinchot, Graves, and later Silcox had sought through federal regulation and what Greeley had tried to achieve through education and cooperation.

The code itself did not work well. Labor, management, and government all constantly protested, charging one another with bad faith. The provisions fixing prices and production proved unenforceable, and labor complaints ran into the hundreds within a year. Regulation of a diverse industry, with more than fifteen thousand producing mills scattered in all parts of the country, was all but impossible. Both the Southern Pine Association and the West Coast Lumbermen's Association passed resolutions calling the price-protection clauses unworkable and demanding their suspension. During its last year, probably a majority of lumber manufacturers bypassed or ignored the code. Then the issue was decided by the United States Supreme Court, which in May of 1935 declared NRA unconstitutional.

This left article X—the section on forest conservation. Though it was shorn of official sanction, most regional lumber associations adopted its principles and urged members to conform voluntarily to the forestry practices in the code. Associations compiled and distributed handbooks of approved practices, set up forestry commissions, and provided professional advisory services for their members. No doubt motivated by the rapidly dwindling supplies of virgin timber, the threat of federal regulations, and the revival of markets, timbermen accepted the dictum that good forestry was also good business. In article X they had set a standard for the industry that long outlived NRA, the depression, and World War II.[10]

The most ambitious New Deal conservation program was the Tennessee Valley Authority. The concept of an integrated, multipurpose river system was not new. W J McGee and Marshall Leighton had proposed such a program in the 1907 report of the Inland Waterways Commission, and Theodore Roosevelt had endorsed the plan. The nucleus of the TVA project was Muscle Shoals Dam, which had been erected by the government during World War I as a source of power needed to produce nitrates. All through the 1920s Congress had debated whether to sell the properties at Muscle Shoals to private interests (most notably Henry Ford) or to develop the area for public power and other uses as urged by Senator George W. Norris of Nebraska. Roosevelt saw possibilities for a great multiuse project and proposed a measure that went far beyond even Norris's ideas. After a trip through the valley as president-elect in January 1933, Roosevelt vigorously pushed for creation of the Tennessee Valley Authority.[11]

TVA provided for development on three fronts: flood control, navigation, and power. But beyond these goals was the more comprehensive dream of a regional plan for the entire valley that would restore the land and forests, harness the streams, raise the standard of living and improve the quality of life for local people. As TVA's chairman Arthur E. Morgan said, three fortunes had been taken out of the valley—forests, oil, and gas; only poverty remained. Soil conservation and reforestation were badly needed, and the means were at hand to make a beginning toward rehabilitation of the valley. Under the supervision of the Forest Service, some thirty CCC camps operated in the TVA area. By 1942 they had planted forty-four million trees, controlled 114 forest fires, and done important work in checking soil erosion. The progress continued; four decades later the eroded areas have almost all been rehabilitated. Both timber volume and timber quality have increased spectacularly. Timber sales have increased tenfold, and annual growth now exceeds the annual cut.[12]

TVA was more than trees planted and lumber cut, dams built and kilowatt hours sold; it included many intangible and noncommercial values. The handsome stands of black walnut, yellow poplar, black cherry, and red oak that it brought into being are pleasing to the eye as well as valuable. The unpredictable and often violent river rushing past worn-out soil, cutover forests, and dilapidated shacks has given way to a controlled but useful river, impressive dams, and blue water with green meadows, snug and attractive towns, and prosperous farms along the shores. Many varieties of wildlife have returned to the valley, and well-stocked lakes have made this region a favorite fishing, camping, and recreation area for the entire mid-South. The restored forests provide a pleasing backdrop to the varied activities of the valley. To many, both during the New Deal and later, TVA has stood as an impressive testimony to intelligent planning.

Despite its accomplishments, the Tennessee Valley Authority has drawn strong and continued criticism. Some conservatives defined its social planning as thinly disguised socialism that would undermine private enterprise. Others feared its regional concept would prove destructive of state government and an exercise in unauthorized federal power. Led by Wendell L. Willkie, president of Commonwealth and Southern (a giant electric holding company), business interests attacked TVA on economic grounds. They charged that the Authority's sale of cheap electricity competed unfairly with private companies already in the field and that the use of the TVA cost "yardstick" to determine fair rates for electric power was arbitrary and unfair. Their legal challenge was dismissed in 1936 when the Supreme Court upheld the government's position by a vote of eight to one. For its part, the public endorsed the TVA program and goals in election after election between 1934 and 1940. Nevertheless, conservatives have sought to restrict or dismantle TVA for more than a generation.[13]

Perhaps the most controversial of New Deal conservation programs was the shelterbelt project. The germ of this proposal dated back at least to the turn of the century and the work of Charles E. Bessey of the University of Nebraska in promoting forest reserves on the Great Plains. Apparently Roosevelt's idea of a shelterbelt, a great belt of trees to be planted along the length of the Great Plains to combat erosion, was born during his campaign trip across the Dakotas and Montana in the summer of 1932. It was brought to maturity by the dust storms of 1934 that darkened the sky as far away as the District of Columbia with millions of tons of topsoil blown from the Great Plains. Newspapers reported ten-foot-high dust drifts, homes stripped of paint by blowing sand, and people losing their way in blizzards of dust within a hundred yards of their homes. In July 1934, Roosevelt announced that the government would begin a seventy-five million dollar project to provide a forest shelterbelt on the Great Plains. Originally, the proposal was to plant strips of trees in a hundred-mile-wide belt extending more than a thousand miles — from the Texas plains to the Canadian border. In all, the program was to cover 20 million acres, including some 1.8 million acres of trees, and take ten years to complete. The shelterbelt was expected to reduce droughts, curb the effects of dust storms, protect cattle and other livestock, provide a more pleasing landscape, and give residents relief from the ever-present wind.[14]

Opponents were quick to ridicule the project. Not only conservatives and members of the Republican party, but many journalists and conservationists denounced the scheme as unworkable. Professional foresters split on the issue; some supported Forest Service chief Silcox, who repeatedly sought to explain how the project would work, while others were skeptical. For example, H. H. Chapman, then president of the Society of American Foresters, called the plan "fantastically impossible." He later polled the society's membership seeking critical comments.

Congress gave scant support. Loyal New Dealers whose constituents did not live in the Plains States showed little interest in appropriating seventy-five million dollars for such a controversial and experimental program. Though Roosevelt and Secretary of Agriculture Henry A. Wallace pushed the proposal and Forest Service staff including Silcox, director Paul Roberts, and technical director Raphael Zon testified to its practicality, Congress refused to provide funds. Moreover, the comptroller general ruled that the president could use only one million dollars out of the general relief allocation on this project, since it had only indirect relief functions and the lawmakers had the power to fund it if they wished.

Nevertheless, Roosevelt proceeded. With such funds as were available, the Forest Service began planting trees and providing nursery stock to participating farmers in the spring of 1935. By the end of the season Zon could report the planting of 125 miles (2,500 acres) of tree strips on 232 separate farms. Almost two million seedlings had been planted.

The project continued to operate in 1936 without congressional appropriation, but the Work Projects Administration provided some $1,200,000. Zon's forces planted more trees—ten times as many as in the previous year. In 1937 George Norris, who had supported the project from the beginning, joined with Congressman Walter Doxey to sponsor the Norris-Doxey Act (Cooperative Farm Forestry Act), which, without mentioning shelterbelts, authorized tree planting in terms broad enough to include them. Congress appropriated no money for this measure, but at the president's request the WPA provided funds for it over the next several years. Finally, in 1942 the president transferred the "Prairie States Forestry Project" from the Forest Service to the Soil Conservation Service. The planting of shelterbelts continued under Hugh Bennett's direction.

Ten years after the initial proposal, most investigators praised the experiment as a success. Seventy-eight percent of the trees had survived and better than three-fourths of the belts were rated good or excellent based on function. At a cost of some fourteen million dollars instead of the seventy-five million Roosevelt had anticipated, the Forest Service and Soil Conservation Service had planted and cultivated some 220 million trees—or about seventeen for each resident of the Great Plains. The program's success was demonstrated by the plains farmers themselves, who were by then buying seedlings and planting additional windrows on their own. In 1965, for example, foresters and farmers converted an additional forty-four thousand acres of plains into tree belts. As its advocates had promised back in 1934, the shelterbelts did improve the quality of life on the Great Plains. They created a buffer against the winds, retarded soil erosion, preserved moisture, protected cattle, and provided a habitat for more wildlife. The much maligned stepchild of the New Deal had developed into a valuable and continuing forestry program.[15]

As president, Roosevelt greatly enlarged the national forest system. Before the Great Depression, there were few national forests east of the Rockies, near the bulk of the nation's population. The Copeland Report had called for a multipoint program to improve American forests. Among other things, it recommended greatly extending federal ownership of forestlands and making management more intensive on all forestlands.

The opportunity to do both was at hand. In the South bonanza lumbermen had left millions of acres of cutover, often a mass of stumps and tops, with no provision for clearing or reforestation. The depression brought a collapse in prices for lumber products and greatly reduced markets at any price. These factors, plus the continuing tax burden on cutover land, made many owners eager to dispose of their holdings. Congress made funds available, and the Forest Service employed a large staff of timber appraisers, surveyors, and title lawyers to speed the process of acquisition.

In Texas eleven lumber companies gladly sold some six hundred thousand acres of badly cutover land for an average price of about $4.65 per acre to form four new national forests. Much of the work of the CCC in the state involved cleaning up, protecting, and reforesting these newly acquired federal lands.[16]

In southern Illinois a large area made up of worn-out farms, cutover hardwood forests, and abandoned coal pits also offered an opportunity for rehabilitation. Farming had been carried on in the region for more than one hundred years, but many farms had been abandoned because of soil exhaustion and erosion. The forest-products industry had flourished there after the Civil War and at one time had supported some 250 mills, but it had declined by the turn of the century; by 1930 the area was so badly cut over that timber harvests would not pay taxes. A coal boom had begun about 1903, but production declined after World War I and collapsed with the coming of the depression. In many communities in southern Illinois that were dependent on the coal industry, as much as 60 percent of the work force was unemployed. In the face of such conditions, state officials and conservation-minded citizens proposed the establishment of a national forest in the area, and the state legislature passed an act in 1931 all but begging the federal government to take action. Not until August 1933 was federal approval given and funding made available for this project. Then acquisition proceeded rapidly; more than four-fifths of the forest's eventual total had been purchased by World War II. The Shawnee National Forest, as it was called, eventually encompassed some 211,000 acres acquired at an average cost of $6.43 per acre. The work of clearing, protecting, and replanting provided employment for several thousand men, largely CCC and WPA workers. Thirty years later the forest cover of southern Illinois had regenerated, and the annual growth exceeded the yearly cut. The region had become a favorite out-door recreation area, and many types of wildlife had returned to its forests. The Shawnee had been returned to its best use.[17]

In all, Roosevelt established twenty-three new national forests, mostly in the South and East, totaling some ten million acres. Additional acres were added to existing national forests. Except for the forests reserved early in the twentieth century by Theodore Roosevelt, these new purchases represented the greatest enlargement any president had made to the federal forest holdings in the contiguous United States.

Progress of another sort took place in Alaska. There, fire had long been a problem in the vast boreal forests of the interior, where sparse populations and great distances hampered efforts to spot and extinguish blazes. Trees commonly had limbs growing almost to the ground and were heavily draped with beard lichen; long summer days and low precipitation helped ensure a plentitude of dry fuel. Nearly all the land was publicly owned, but it was little valued, the timber on it being used for steamboat fuel and local needs but little else. When forest fires started, they usually were simply left to burn themselves out. Secretary of the Interior Harold Ickes, whose aegis covered most of Alaska's forests, was appalled by the devastation being wrought there by fire, and in 1939 he began implementing changes to improve fire suppression.[18]

The Roosevelt era also saw a quickening of interest in preserving wilderness areas to ensure that they would be available for both present and future generations. From at least the time of John Muir, wilderness advocates had campaigned to preserve a portion of the nation's remaining wilderness in its natural state. By the thirties not more than thirty-five million acres were still wilderness—some 2 percent of the United States land area excluding Alaska. Most of these acres were public lands, largely under the jurisdiction of the Forest Service and National Park Service.

Among the advocates of wilderness, the leaders in the generation between the two world wars were Aldo Leopold and Robert Marshall. Leopold, who began work with the Forest Service in 1909, was one of those instrumental in having the secretary of agriculture set aside the Gila Wilderness in New Mexico in 1924. In 1933 he helped establish the Pecos Wilderness, also in New Mexico. Leopold's friend Bob Marshall was probably the leading wilderness crusader of the thirties. A man of many talents and tremendous energy, Marshall combined independent social thinking, scholarship, exploration, and government service, all of which he devoted to the cause of saving the wilderness. Never so happy as when he was backpacking in primitive backcounty, Marshall developed a deep personal knowledge of the wilderness and a great respect for it.

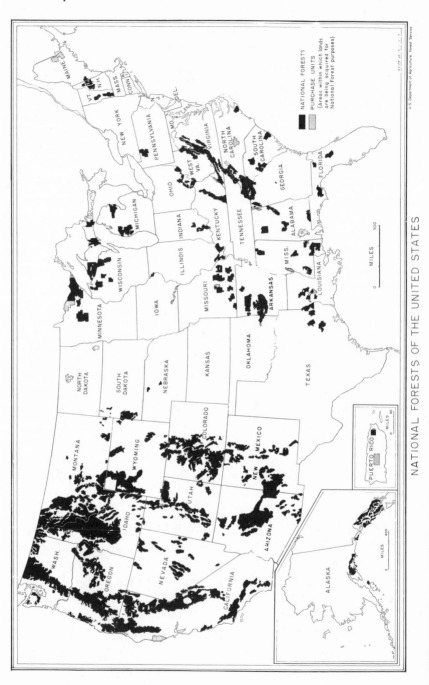

National Forests of the United States. U.S. Forest Service.

In 1935 Marshall and other wilderness advocates organized the Wilderness Society for the purposes of "fighting off invasion of the wilderness" and defending "wild country wherever it was in jeopardy."

Marshall defined true wildernesses as containing no permanent inhabitants or means of mechanical conveyance and being "sufficiently spacious that a person may spend at least a week or two of travel in them without crossing his own tracks." Marshall bombarded both Secretary of the Interior Ickes and Secretary of Agriculture Wallace with memoranda detailing the various areas that might be reserved and urging his superiors to take action. In 1937 he prevailed upon John Collier, commissioner of the Bureau of Indian Affairs, to set aside sixteen wilderness areas on Indian reservations. The same year, Marshall became head of the Division of Recreation and Lands in the Forest Service. He at once made inspection trips into remote areas to determine what additional lands could be reclassified as "primitive." As a result, more than five million acres were added to the Forest Service's primitive areas.

Marshall's influence was felt far beyond his immediate associates. Shortly before his death in November 1939, he drafted regulations for Forest Service wilderness areas. Adopted in 1940, these regulations gave stronger administrative protection to wilderness than it had ever had before. Road construction, logging, and all development were barred; boundaries could not be changed without prior public hearings and the approval of the secretary of agriculture. Until the passage of the Wilderness Act in 1964, these regulations provided the basic protective framework for America's wilderness areas, most of which were in high-mountain forests.[19]

Behind Aldo Leopold's interests in wilderness preservation lay the beginnings of the land ethic that was to make him the cult hero of environmentalists three decades later. In 1933 Leopold accepted a position at the University of Wisconsin as the first professor of wildlife management in the United States. His views on wildlife were based upon the scientific works of pioneer ecologists and on his own observations—especially on the Kaibab Plateau in northern Arizona, where, after predators were eliminated, deer multiplied rapidly, stripped the forest of food, and then died of starvation by the thousands. Game, like timber, was a crop; both were parts of an interconnected web of life. Intelligent wildlife management required knowledge of the strands of this web and of the effects that actions taken in one part might have on another. Such ideas obviously had as many implications for forest management as for wildlife management. Their full impact was to be felt only later, but Leopold and a handful of others were already preparing the way.[20]

Leopold was not alone in his interest in wildlife. Many game refuges had been established on national forests to provide protection for deer and other animals. In time they were to prove less useful in game management than were bag limits and other hunting regulations, but during the thirties and forties they stood as important testimony to rising concern for dwindling wildlife populations. Roosevelt himself took a personal interest in wildlife preservation. On the eve of World War II he rejected an army plan to establish an artillery range in Utah and incidentally destroy an important site for the endangered trumpeter swan. Roosevelt wrote, "The verdict is for the Trumpeter Swan and against the Army. The army must find a different nesting place."[21]

Although largely forgotten today, during the 1930s Stuart Chase had both a larger audience and, as a New Deal official, more immediate influence than Leopold. In *Rich Land, Poor Land,* published in 1936, Chase traced the depletion of America's natural resources over the centuries. Giving voice to the New Dealers' faith in planning, he proposed the immediate adoption of integrated resource-management plans in order "to save a continent." But Chase was no mere technocrat; man's plans, he argued, must be drawn in accordance with the rules of nature, which also "hold for man—however much he may be given to declaiming in editorials and Sunday Supplements about the Conquest of Nature by Humankind." One of Chase's chapters was a denunciation of lumber barons who had stripped the forests through "cut out and get out" lumbering.

Less impressive when taken singly, but with greater effect overall, was the steady stream of movies, pamphlets, advisors, and assorted other propaganda devices turned out by the Forest Service, Soil Conservation Service, and other government agencies to convince Americans, both on and off the land, of the necessity of changing their approach to natural resources. Cartoonist J. N. "Ding" Darling, whose work appeared from coast to coast, lent special force to the campaign.

Arguments for reshaping the nation's approach to natural resources often had moralistic and ecological overtones, but at heart most were economic. Stuart Chase devoted an entire chapter of *Rich Land, Poor Land* to demonstrating that proper resource management would generate five million new jobs—an argument he repeated in other works as well. Nor did Chase stop there. The nation, he said, was caught in an economic crisis; only through basic changes could permanent security be found. Land, the basis of all production, would have to be treated differently. Perhaps in the thirties arguments for change would not have been effective if cast in any other terms; certainly in the midst of the depression they were not apt to appear often in other forms. Nature writing, so influential and popular during the last decades of the previous century, withered during the thirties. Not until the depression had passed did it blossom once more.

Propaganda on behalf of resource-management planning may have been largely economic in content—and often in motivation as well; nevertheless, it helped to educate increasingly urbanized Americans about the land. WPA artists' and writers' projects, the TVA and CCC, and publicity about the Dust Bowl (including the Farm Security Administration's film *The Plow That Broke the Plains*) contributed. However, the impact of all this on the forests—and on concepts of forests and forest management—was less than might have been expected. Most attention was directed to agricultural lands and their problems.[22]

The old Jeffersonian yeoman ideal took on new appeal as modern social organization suddenly grew suspect during the thirties. Even while impoverished farmers who had been "dusted out" from Oklahoma and neighboring states were becoming a major social problem, a back-to-the-land movement was gaining momentum. The New Deal, in a fit of inconsistency, lent support to this movement at the same time it was trying to reduce agricultural production and get farmers off submarginal land. Later, Americans might flee to the woods to escape the frustrations of modern life, but in the thirties the farm had greater attraction. Some sought (or supported those who sought) to return to the simple, self-sufficient—and semimythical—farm life of the past. Others sought to achieve through planning and applied science a modern transmutation of the old rural life, one that would be equally secure but far less simple.

Nostalgia surfaced in other ways as well. Frightened by the present, Americans increasingly turned to the past for comfort and guidance. This led to an upsurge in historical studies, membership in historical societies, and preservation of historic buildings and sites. It also encouraged Americans (at least those who could still afford such things) to visit the nation's shrines—not just sites like Independence Hall and the Statue of Liberty, but Yellowstone, Yosemite, and the Grand Canyon as well. Visits to national parks and to lesser recreation sites, both forested and unforested, rose sharply as Americans sought contact with their country's roots. The forests were affected by all this only indirectly, but they were affected.[23]

Other factors had a more direct impact. Most notable was the quest for planning and efficiency that, ostensibly at least, was behind a new effort to get national forests moved from the Department of Agriculture to the Department of the Interior. The battle for control of federal forest lands has been a recurring theme in the history of American forests. In 1905, when Theodore

Roosevelt transferred the national forests to the Department of Agriculture, he left the national parks, the forests on Indian reservations, and unreserved public lands (some of which were forested) under the Department of the Interior. The Ballinger-Pinchot controversy reflected the conflict inherent in this division of control, as did the rumblings surrounding the establishment of the National Park Service. In the twenties Albert Fall's attempt to gain control of the national forests had been prevented by an alert Forest Service chief, by the secretary of agriculture, and by public opinion that recalled Interior's poor record as defender of the public lands. Another episode in this struggle now erupted. Secretary Ickes sought to create a department of conservation and to draw all related agencies and bureaus into his net.

Ickes—though humorless, arrogant, and irascible—was dedicated and capable, with a long record as a conservationist. Where Ballinger had been a business-oriented legalist and Fall grasping and corrupt, Ickes sincerely believed that a single department of conservation would be more efficient than the existing system—especially if the new department were under his direction. He gained Roosevelt's permission to have a bill creating a conservation department introduced in Congress. Almost at once Ickes' proposal faced opposition from the Forest Service, the secretary of agriculture, the American Forestry Association, and other conservation groups. When the measure failed in the House in 1936, Ickes vented his spleen on his opponents, especially Gifford Pinchot. Ickes assailed his former friend by writing a vindication of Richard Ballinger for a popular magazine. Pinchot answered in kind, and for a time controversy swirled.[24]

America's foresters had been advocating planned use of timberlands for years before the depression crisis brought unprecedented efforts at planning to the United States. Suddenly what foresters had long wanted seemed close at hand—and, indeed, through measures like article X of the NRA lumber code, it did draw nearer. But whatever plans were formulated would have to encompass more than the trees themselves. As Secretary of Agriculture Henry A. Wallace noted in 1939, Americans were faced not with separated problems of forestry, wildlife, soils, grazing, and farming, but with "one unified land use problem . . . which involves the whole pattern of soil, climate, topography, and social institutions; it has to do with social and economic conditions, as well as with the physical problems of crop, livestock, and timber production, and of soil and water conservation." Ironically, Ickes' plan for a department of conservation, which Wallace opposed, offered the best prospects for bringing into being plans to solve such a complex of problems. But the critics triumphed.

When the president omitted any mention of the Forest Service from the reorganization plan he put forth in 1940, Ickes' last hopes of a department of conservation with himself as its head disappeared. Those who feared that a return of national forests to the Department of the Interior (albeit under a new name) would mean a return to earlier mismanagement could breathe more easily. Integrated planning was put off once more. Such interagency cooperation as came with the Park, Parkways, and Recreation Areas Act of 1936 was but a poor substitute.

This is not to say that Roosevelt was uninterested in planning for America's forests. In the spring of 1938 in particular he turned his attention to forest problems and the need for a long-range plan of action for the nation's forests. In a message to Congress, the president outlined the importance of forests to the country's well-being, described the nature of the threats facing them, and called for a comprehensive forest policy. Defining the forest problem as one of land use, Roosevelt called for more efficient management and greater productivity on commercial forestlands. He was particularly concerned about the privately owned lands that, he said, were still only partially productive and subject to much abuse. To provide for maximum productivity and to strike a balance between present and future needs, he proposed that Congress select a joint committee to study "the forest land problem of the United States."

The president suggested that particular attention be given to such questions as the adequacy of existing methods of protecting both public and private lands from fire, insects, and disease; the measures, federal and state, that might be necessary to ensure that timber cropping on private lands be conducted in conformity with future needs; the advisability of regulatory controls to protect the many diverse interests in forestlands; the need for extended public ownership of forestlands; and the possibilities of a long-range employment program in public and private forestlands.

Chief Silcox and his assistant and successor Earle Clapp strongly supported these proposals, especially the sections regarding regulation of timber cutting on private lands. In this they followed Gifford Pinchot rather than William Greeley and others who favored cooperation and education as the best ways to improve private forestry practices. The old conflict, seemingly settled by the Clarke-McNary Act of 1924, had been resurrected. The Bankhead Report, which resulted from Roosevelt's call, appeared in 1941. Its authors recommended most of the legislation the president suggested. The congressional committee agreed that the time was ripe for "a real forest economy" in order to "put to more constructive use the American forests which occupy more than one-third of the nation's land area." Significantly, however, the committee made no proposal for direct federal regulation of cutting practices on privately owned forestlands.[25]

Not just foresters, planners, and politicians were affecting the utilization and management of the American forest during Roosevelt's presidency. Perhaps the most significant revolution in wood use during the period came via the pulp and paper industry in the South. As early as 1900 southern mills were producing kraft paper, primarily for wrapping paper and brown paper bags. But higher grades of paper and newsprint seemed impossible to develop because of the high resin content in southern pine. Paper of many types, including newsprint, had long been manufactured in the Northeast, the Lake States, and the Far West, where spruce, hemlock, and other less resinous species were common. By World War I such firms as International Paper Company, Great Northern Paper Company, Kimberly-Clark Company, and Crown-Willamette Paper Company were producing thousands of tons of newsprint daily. Hopes of a future bonanza from Alaskan pulpwood were high, but production had begun to decline in the older sections, particularly New England, as supplies grew scarce. By the 1930s Canada and the Scandinavian countries were supplying much of the newsprint for American newspapers, and prices were spiraling upward. In these circumstances many industrialists believed the South would become a major source of paper products if some way could be found to make newsprint from southern pine. The price of pulpwood was low in the region, perhaps only two-thirds the national average, and in most southern states the supply was abundant.[26]

Wood scientists had worked on this problem since the turn of the century. The Forest Products Laboratory at Madison, Wisconsin, conducted experiments that showed promise, and many southern publicists forecast a boom in the southern paper industry. About 1930 Charles H. Herty turned his attention and talents to making newsprint from southern yellow pine. Herty was an established chemist, president of the American Chemical Society, and editor of the *Journal of Industrial and Engineering Chemistry* before returning to his native South and establishing a laboratory in Savannah, Georgia. With financial assistance from both public and private sources (mainly from the pulp industry), Herty produced a successful newsprint pulp in his laboratory and tested its commercial possibilities by sending twenty-five tons to a northern newsprint manufacturer and persuading nine Georgia newspapers to print their editions of November 20, 1933, on the paper produced from it. The results were dramatic. Herty and others wrote articles publicizing the success of the experiments. Businessmen clamored for more information. The Forest Products Laboratory endorsed the results of the experiment.

In the meantime Herty interested a group of Texas industrialists, including Ernest Kurth and Arthur Temple, in erecting a plant to manufacture newsprint using his process. The company signed contracts with some thirty-five (mostly southern) newspapers to purchase the first five years' output. As a result, the Southland Paper Mills at Lufkin, Texas, began producing commercial newsprint from southern pine in January 1940. Southland quickly grew to a multimillion-dollar enterprise with specialized units making paper of many types. Other mills sprang up in a number of southern states, including Alabama, Georgia, Arkansas, and Tennessee. Since then almost as much southern pine has gone into pulp as into lumber, although most production has continued to be of kraft products rather than newsprint. The development of demand for pulpwood gave southern timber owners and tree farmers a new and profitable outlet for their young pines, and they adjusted their operations accordingly. Austin Cary, the federal forester who had been preaching the gospel of scientific forest management, sustained yield, and reforestation to a generation of southern small farmers, woodlot owners, and lumber company owners, would have felt vindicated.[27]

The entry of the United States into World War II suddenly forced the concerns of the thirties into the background. All else was quickly subordinated to winning the war. As in 1917, wood became a critical war material, used for barracks and cantonments, boxes and crates, wartime housing, airplanes (including Britain's Mosquito bomber and Howard Hughes's infamous "Spruce Goose"), ships and docks, and a hundred other purposes. According to the Forest Service, the armed forces used more tons of wood than of steel during the conflict. To coordinate efforts to get out the needed timber, Roosevelt organized the Timber Production War Project, which allocated priorities for war needs. Though civilian building declined sharply after Pearl Harbor because almost all efforts and materials went to the war, total lumber production boomed to predepression levels, reaching thirty-six billion board feet in 1941 for the first time in more than a decade. Civilian Defense volunteers provided a forest-fire-fighters service that, among other duties, patrolled West Coast forests to snuff out fires caused by Japanese incendiary bombs that were carried across the Pacific by balloons riding the prevailing winds. The Forest Service performed a variety of war-related services without entirely losing sight of the cause of conservation and necessity of taking a long-range view. Nevertheless, the larger aspects of Roosevelt's proposed "National Forest System" would have to wait until the war had been won.[28]

Before World War II was over, however, Roosevelt was dead. His plans for a long-range program to conserve and utilize the American forests remained for others to carry out—or modify. But he left a rich legacy to the American people and an example to future presidents. Six new national parks, millions of acres in newly acquired national forests, numerous national monuments, wildlife refuges, and new recreation areas were only part of the evidence of Roosevelt's continuing concern for the natural environment. CCC achievements, the TVA, the shelterbelt project, and improved fire-control programs combined to leave America's forests in the best condition in a generation. New Deal efforts raised American awareness of the need for careful stewardship of natural resources. And article X of the NRA lumber code provided a yardstick for private forest management applicable to large and small timber owners alike. Many groups of conservationists—foresters, wildlife protectors, recreationists, and wilderness lovers—rejoiced that they had had a friend in the White House for a time, and they grieved when he was gone.

The Search for Accommodation, 1945–76

Chapter 13

From the Second World War to the nation's bicentennial, only two occupants of the White House—John F. Kennedy and Lyndon B. Johnson—displayed much interest in forests and the conservation of natural resources. In spite of the less than crusading approach of most recent presidents, America's forests were in better condition and the environment more carefully protected in 1976 than they had been a generation or more earlier. Constant pressure on Congress by a variety of professional and voluntary groups including the Society of American Foresters, the American Forestry Association, the Sierra Club, the Izaak Walton League, the Wilderness Society, and the National Wildlife Federation was largely responsible. These groups, together with the Forest Service, many forest-industry organizations, and the several state forestry agencies, formed a large body of trained, informed, and concerned watchdogs of the American forests. All these groups have identified themselves as supporting the larger cause of conservation, but they have represented different and often conflicting approaches. In pursuing their respective goals they have frequently found themselves working at cross-purposes—and even denouncing one another as not true conservationists.

Since the extent of the American forest is limited and relatively fixed at any given time, public policymakers must consider all would-be users. Their search for accommodation among the many groups that have interests in the forest, and the impossibility of satisfying them all, provided the central theme in the management of timberlands of postwar America. The search grew ever more difficult as positions became more sharply delineated and issues clearer with the passage of time. Like so much else in America, views of the forests were polarized during the 1960s and early 1970s. Indeed, discussions of forests were early caught up in the larger environmental concerns of the period. Policymakers seeking to accommodate the extremes were as bedeviled as those seeking reconciliation in regard to defense, foreign policy, and economic issues. In the realm of forest policy, as in other areas, there were no easy answers for Americans looking forward to their third century of independence.

At war's end the Forest Service and the American Forestry Association undertook separate appraisals of the forest situation. The facts revealed were alarming. Their studies disclosed that the nation's timber inventory had declined some 43 percent in the preceding generation and that industry was cutting sawtimber one and one-half times faster than it grew, largely because of wartime demands. Fears of a timber famine reappeared.

The Third American Forest Congress, held in 1946, devoted most of its discussions to means of increasing timber production. An analysis of American timberlands suggested that farm forests and smallholdings would provide the chief opportunity for increasing timber stocks and annual yield. These lands were, on the whole, badly managed. In comparison, both industry-held forests and those administered by the Forest Service were well run and productive. For this reason Forest Service Chief Lyle Watts sought support for federal regulation of smallholdings and increased public ownership of forestlands. The American Forestry Association and industry spokesmen demurred, favoring William Greeley's old formula of cooperation and education to increase production on privately held lands. In the end the Forest Congress issued a call for improved fire protection of all forestlands, more intensive control of forest insects and diseases, increased funding for research in timber growing and wood uses, greater effort to reduce wood waste, and expanded tree planting. As a concession to the regulationists, delegates also called for more effective control of private timber-cutting practices by state forestry departments.[1]

Both the Forest Service and the industry promoted programs to induce forest farmers and woodlot owners to improve management and increase wood production. The tree-farm movement, begun on the West Coast in 1941 by the Weyerhaeuser Timber Company, spread through all the states after the war, encouraged by the National Lumber Manufacturers Association and other industrial groups. It was the most successful tree-growing project in the nation's history. By 1975 there were thirty-five thousand certified tree farms with a total of seventy-six million acres in forty-eight states. The American Forest Products Industries succeeded the NLMA as the nation's tree-farm sponsor and added other programs to help make the three hundred million acres of commercial forestland held by farmers and other small owners more productive. These included programs of professional assistance and instruction in self-help.[2]

The never-ending fight against forest fires continued. The "Keep Washing-

ton Green" campaign against forest fires grew into a nationwide "Keep America Green" public-relations program—with appropriate local modifications.
Because much of California consisted of grasslands that dried up in the summer, the slogan became "Keep California Green and Golden." There and elsewhere grass and brush rather than trees dominated the landscape, "Prevent
Forest Fires" became "Prevent Wildfires."

The struggle against fire received a significant ally with the appearance of
Smokey Bear in 1945. During World War II manpower was in short supply and
annual losses rose to an average of about thirty million acres, an area larger
than Pennsylvania. To cope with the problem, a number of federal and state
agencies formed the Wartime Forest Fire Prevention Campaign. With the
assistance of advertising experts and other private citizens, the Forest Service
and the Association of State Foresters created "Smokey Bear" to promote
education in forest-fire prevention. The brown bear in jeans and campaign hat
admonishing Americans to crush cigarettes, douse campfires, and report any
fires sighted became a familiar figure. The slogan "only *you* can prevent forest
fires" was a constant reminder that from year to year approximately half the
fires in the American forests (more than that in some areas) were man-caused,
and that a large portion of these were the result of carelessness. In a surge of
zeal, many posters were distributed claiming that nine out of ten forest fires
were man-caused. Those who knew the figure was inflated said little; the de-
ception served an important purpose.

The Forest Service's Branch of Cooperative Forest Fire Prevention directed
the Smokey Bear program and provided not only signs and newspaper and
magazine advertising but also picture books, games, toys, T-shirts, and similar
items. In a typical year the agency produced some thirty to forty million individual pieces that reminded the public to practice forest-fire prevention. And
the Smokey Bear campaign got a living symbol in 1950 when forest rangers
rescued a black bear cub while fighting a major fire on Capitan Mountain in
New Mexico. Though badly burned, the cub survived and grew to maturity.
Sent to live in the Washington Zoo, he attracted millions of visitors each year
and served as the symbol of Smokey the fire-preventing bear until his death in
1976.

After twenty-five years of education, the average number of forest fires per
year was cut in half, and the area burned was reduced to only one-eighth of the
pre-1945 average. Of course other innovations contributed to the improved
record too. Such developments as borate bombing, aerial spotting of fires,
smoke jumpers (begun in 1939 but with many postwar improvements), four-
wheel-drive tanker trucks that could reach many off-road fires, and improved

access roads all made fire control much more effective. But Smokey Bear caught the popular attention. As one writer put it, "that little bear has done more to make the U.S. public aware of forestry than all the Gifford Pinchots . . . put together."[3]

The Eisenhower administration came into office in 1953, bringing with it an emphasis on "partnership." President Eisenhower explained that his goal was to help develop the natural resources of a region "not as a boss, not as your dictator, but as a friendly partner, ready to help out and get its long nose out of your business as quickly as that can be accomplished." Toward this end, the president appointed knowledgeable local leaders to various boards and commissions that dealt with natural resources. He hoped thereby to create a bridge between the bureaucracies of Agriculture and Interior and the citizens they supposedly served. Although the main thrust of the Eisenhower approach was directed toward hydroelectric power development, it also affected the United States Forest Service, state forestry agencies, the forest industry, and others concerned with timberlands.

Under this program of cooperation, gains came on a number of fronts, including the reforesting of denuded areas and the protecting and improving of smaller watersheds. The important Soil Bank measure (Agriculture Act of 1956) provided funds for planting trees on reserve cropland. This act was primarily a product of the desire to reduce farm surpluses, but it had important effects on reforestation. By the end of 1957 some half a million acres were under contract for tree planting. With the additional cover that resulted, wildlife populations as well as wood production rose. Ironically, millions of these trees were removed less than ten years later so that federally subsidized soybeans and other crops could be planted.

When Alaska achieved statehood in 1959 much federal land was transferred to its control. However, an agreement was quickly worked out between the state and the federal Bureau of Land Management, Forest Service, and Fish and Wildlife Service so that coordinated fire protection was carried to state lands. The system of forest fire control in Alaska, begun under Secretary of the Interior Ickes in 1939 and strengthened by the BLM after creation of that agency in 1946, was thus continued and improved through cooperative action.

A different sort of cooperation—or compromise—was reached in the Multiple Use–Sustained Yield Act of 1960, in which Congress spelled out its intent that the national forests be administered for such varied uses as outdoor recreation, range, timber, watershed, and wildlife, with due weight being given to the relative value of resources in special areas such as wildernesses. Although the concept of multiple use had been widely accepted for years, the act itself was the subject of much debate. Some saw it as a vehicle to halt such "single-use" areas as those set aside as wilderness, while others saw it as a means of forcing the Forest Service to abandon clear-cutting or other management practices they disliked. In the end, the act was a compromise that all could live with—at least for the time being. It established government guidelines, however vague, that gave new emphasis to ends other than the production of commercial timber and grazing in the national forests.

During the same years, Eisenhower enlarged federal wildlife refuge areas by some eleven million acres, including (over the protests of many Alaskans) a nine-million-acre region above the Arctic Circle in remote northeastern Alaska. He also made modest additions to the national forest system, mostly in the Southeast, and instituted a program (known as Mission 66) to revitalize the national park system, which had been badly neglected since the beginning of World War II.[4]

Still, a great many defenders of American forests and the principles of conservation viewed the policies of the Eisenhower administration with apprehension and distrust. "Ike" himself was friendly to the general concept of conservation. Some of his advisors, such as Attorney General (later Governor) Robert Smylie of Idaho, were knowledgeable about public lands, national forests, and competition for natural resources. But the president was naive about the ramifications of environmental issues and vulnerable to the pressures of special-interest groups. Some of the local citizens he appointed to boards and commissions proved to be spokesmen for vested interests rather than the bridges between government and the people that the president wanted.

During the 1952 campaign some overzealous supporters of the general engaged in much rhetoric denouncing federal land policy, national forests, and the TVA. Such terms as nationalization, socialism, and dictatorship were used to describe Democratic conservation policies of the previous twenty years. The appointment of new heads of the two most important resource departments failed to allay conservationists' fears that such talk stirred. Secretary of the Interior Douglas McKay, former governor of Oregon, was a successful businessman whose speeches to civic and business groups stressed free enterprise, individual effort, and taxpayers' initiative. Secretary of Agriculture Ezra Taft Benson was even more conservative than McKay and known as a critic of the Forest Service and national forests. Bernard de Voto, an important voice for conservation, feared that the choices of McKay and Benson would do much damage. He was not alone in his concern.[5]

A series of incidents and proposals kept these fears alive throughout Eisenhower's terms in office. McKay chose former Montana congressman Wesley D'Ewart for the post of assistant secretary for public land management. D'Ewart had been instrumental in defeating the Columbia Valley Authority project—patterned roughly on the TVA—and had advocated turning national forests and federal grazing lands over to private interests. In his unsuccessful campaign for reelection in 1954, he or his campaign managers had attempted to use McCarthy-type smear tactics against his opponent. He was anathema to Democrats.

The Al Sarena affair was another case in point. This company had sought mining exploration rights in the Rogue River (Oregon) National Forest from the Bureau of Land Management. The Forest Service, which shared jurisdiction under special arrangements, protested that assays revealed no minerals worthy of commercial exploitation and that there was no reason to grant such a claim. After McKay took office, the Interior Department approved the application (without consulting with the Forest Service), and the Al Sarena Company moved onto the 454-acre site. A congressional hearing in 1955 revealed that although the company had not mined any ore, it had cut and marketed two million board feet of prime timber from the land. Interior officials protested that they had done nothing illegal, but Fred Seaton, who had by then replaced McKay as secretary, quickly made changes in the procedures for handling mining claims on public lands so as to prevent such an incident from happening again.[6]

And then there was Dinosaur. Spanning the Utah-Colorado border, this small national monument was a land of rugged mountains, sheer cliffs, juniper clumps, and swift streams. Western developers during the Truman administration had planned the Upper Colorado River Basin project to provide water-storage reservoirs for a three-state area. Part of the proposal included a dam and reservoir in Dinosaur National Monument that would materially alter the Green and Yampa rivers (major tributaries of the Colorado) and their spectacular canyons. When the Republicans took over, they endorsed the plan and pushed for immediate authorization. McKay had little personal knowledge of the Upper Colorado project, but he thought it was in keeping with Eisenhower's "mandate for change": it would promote local interests, encourage private enterprise, and provide practical government action in place of the meddling of bureaucrats and theorists.

A storm of protest broke. Conservationists as well as many of more utilitarian outlook objected that this was as much an invasion of the national park system as damming Hetch Hetchy had been—and far less necessary. David Brower of the Sierra Club confronted McKay personally to argue that alternative sites for water storage were available and that the decision would set a dangerous precedent. McKay repeatedly insisted that it would not. For two years letters poured in to the president, the Interior Department, and members of Congress. Finally, after the Democrats regained control of Congress in 1955, the administration won approval of the project—but with the Echo Park Dam (Dinosaur) deleted. Then, seeking to ensure that the decision would not later be reversed, Congress moved to make Dinosaur a national park.[7]

Although the area involved at Dinosaur was not forested, the central conflict over resource utilization was one that was fought, albeit less dramatically, over many forested areas. For example, proposals to build dams on the Snake River in Hells Canyon on the Oregon-Idaho border resulted in a long and bitter controversy between defenders of wildlands and proponents of development and between those favoring federal construction and those supporting private construction. In the end a series of low dams was erected by the Idaho Power Company, a private firm. Individualists in the Eisenhower administration were delighted, but others grieved at the harnessing of one of the last of the nation's long free-flowing segments of a major river. They gained but slight consolation from the fact that the low dams would be less destructive of the river's salmon runs than a high dam would have been.

Environmentalists' fears mounted further when the Forest Service proposed reducing the Three Sisters Wilderness Area in Oregon's Cascades by eliminating sections with valuable timber stands and opening them to logging. The Friends of the Three Sisters Wilderness and other groups fought a long but eventually losing battle to halt the reduction. The measures for administrative protection that Bob Marshall had drafted in 1939 now seemed inadequate, lending force to the drive for Congress to pass a bill that would give statutory protection to wilderness in place of the weaker administrative regulations then extant. Such a bill, it was thought, would permanently protect wild areas from business-oriented administrators such as Benson, McKay, and D'Ewart and offset changing emphases from administration to administration.[8]

No doubt the greatest opposition to the Eisenhower conservation policies developed over the proposed Dixon-Yates contract, which would have begun dismantling the Tennessee Valley Authority. When the near-fraudulent nature of the contract was publicized, Eisenhower himself canceled it. TVA escaped this effort at emasculation, but its funds were cut to the bone, and such programs as reforestation, erosion control, and watershed improvement had to be curtailed or delayed.[9]

Fred Seaton replaced McKay as secretary of the interior in 1956 and proved himself more receptive to conservationists' arguments than his predecessor had been. It was even suggested that Eisenhower himself had wanted to see McKay go, urging him to enter a campaign for the United States Senate as much to get him out of the cabinet as to defeat the Democratic incumbent. But conservationists had already come to regard the Eisenhower administration with a jaundiced eye, and most continued to do so.

The decade of the fifties brought profound changes to the forest-products in-dustries. The large-scale adoption of the log debarker after the war revolu-tionized sawmilling. With the log's bark peeled off before it entered the mill proper, the owner could save strips, ends, and other odd bits and run them through a chipper for shipment to pulp-and-paper or chipboard plants.Chips came to represent a significant source of manufactured wood products, such as hardboard, insulating board, and particle board; their rising importance emphasized the increased utilization of wood that had previously been value-less or in low demand.

During the war the Forest Products Laboratory at Madison, Wisconsin, had conducted intensive research in the lamination of beams, studs, and timbers for the navy, which used them primarily in large hangars for blimps. In the fifties the products of this and related industrial research became available for civilian construction and were widely adopted in both industrial and home building. These new products, light but strong, revolutionized construction.

During the 1950s the production of sawtimber fluctuated between thirty and forty billion board feet per year. In contrast to the leveling off of sawtimber production, the production of pulp and paper, plywood, and the new synthetic boards rose rapidly. By 1960 pulpwood made up one-fourth of industrial wood consumption, in contrast to 2 percent in the early 1900s. Plywood construction rose 500 percent in the fifteen years after the war; hardboard, particle board, and insulating board also showed spectacular increases.[10]

The greatest changes came in Alaska, where distance from markets, high labor costs, and problems of weather and terrain had combined since the first white settlement to keep production of wood products low and to limit their consumption to local markets. In most parts of the territory, lumber shipped north from Puget Sound undersold that sawed in Alaska. There were valuable stands of sawtimber, especially along the southeastern coast, where mixed stands of hemlock, spruce, and cedar grew. But 90 percent of the trees in Alas-ka's productive forests were considered good only for pulping. In the fifties, entrepreneurs at last moved to utilize this wood on a large scale. The Ketchikan Pulp Company opened a plant to turn out dissolving pulp for rayon and cel-lophane manufacturers, marketing most of its production on the East Coast of the United States. Japanese investors soon followed, erecting a mill at Sitka. By 1957 wood pulp had become Alaska's largest export, representing almost a third of the value of all exports. By this time 72 percent of the pulp was going to Japan. In 1959 Japanese interests established regular shipping service between Alaska and Japan. With Japanese demand expected to continue to rise, with firm transportation links, and with an ample resource base, Alaska's future as a pulp producer seemed secure. At last its forests had commercial importance. But clear-cutting and inroads into scenic areas and wildlife habitat troubled some and in time led to major confrontations.[11]

After World War II the ownership of much of America's industrial forest changed. The single-family or partnership operation, the most common lumbering pattern for a century, had largely disappeared by the seventies. The reasons were numerous, but inheritance taxes, problems of management, and the pressure to diversify were often uppermost. No longer did companies simply process logs into boards, planks, and two-by-fours. Plywood, veneer, wood fiber, pulp, packing materials, and even wood chemicals were part of the output of the modern plant. Many veteran lumbermen felt ill equipped to compete in the world of research, wood chemistry, and technology that came with the drive for "full utilization." Modernization also brought increased demand for investment capital and growing financial complexity. High interest rates, conservative banking policies, rigid state tax systems, and prospects of delayed profits helped drive family lumber companies out of business. One Forest Service official put it succinctly: "no tree can grow at twelve percent"—which was what seemed necessary if profits were to be turned with the traditional small-mill technology.

Many familiar names disappeared as the industry changed. Crossett Lumber Company of Arkansas sold its properties to Georgia-Pacific. Lutcher and Moore, the pioneer big-mill operation in southern Texas and Louisiana, became part of the Boise Cascade conglomerate. Long-Bell, one of the giants of the industry, became a subsidiary of the International Paper Company. Gone also were such well-known names as Hardtner, Vreedenburg, and Kirby. In their places one encountered large, multipurpose corporations—Louisiana-Pacific, Georgia-Pacific, Champion International, Time-Life Corporation, Owens-Illinois, Crown Zellerbach, and St. Regis Paper. Among the old family names, the Weyerhaeuser Timber Company was one of the few to change successfully, expanding and diversifying to meet new conditions. Indeed, Weyerhaeuser remained the largest single timber owner in the industry, although some surpassed it in sales and International Paper Company came to own more acres. Despite this trend toward concentration, lumbering continued to be one of the least monopolistic of major American industries. No single company's holdings approached 5 percent of the total.[12]

The geographical distribution of the American forest resulted in built-in problems and raised a variety of questions. In 1960 there were some 760 million acres of forested land, about one-third of the land area of the fifty states. Of this a little more than 500 million acres could be classed as commercial—that is, capable of continuously growing timber crops. Actually, a considerable fraction of this was not used for commercial timber production but was set aside, temporarily or permanently, for such purposes as watershed protection, recreation, grazing, wildlife, and wilderness. The area of commercial forests gained several million acres per year as old farmlands reverted to woodlands. At the same time several million acres of commercial forest were lost to airports, highways, urban development, and additions to recreation and wilderness areas. Over the years these shifts resulted in a net gain of 40 to 50 million acres in potential commercial forest.

In 1960 most of the nation's forestland was in the East and South. However, most of the salable timber was in the West. Eastern forests were almost entirely second and third growth. Though the region had 170 million acres, the volume of standing timber was only 32 billion cubic feet. In the South, timber acreage was approximately 200 million and the volume 65 billion cubic feet, almost all second and third growth. By way of contrast, western forest totaled only about 135 million acres but had over 350 billion cubic feet—more than three times the total of all other regions combined. In 1960 most of the forests in the East and South were in farm and small woodlot tracts: 128 million acres in the North and East and 145 million in the South. In the West there were only 28 million acres of such holdings. Since this is the least productive type of holding and small owners tend to be the least open to improving management practices, regional acreage figures taken alone are deceptive.

Public agencies held some 33 million acres in the Lake States and Northeast, 17 million acres in the South, and more than 90 million acres in the West. These figures are also not directly comparable, for most of the eastern and southern national forests had been acquired within the past fifty years as cutover. Though they have potential for growing large quantities of timber, they had not reached this point by 1960. In contrast, many federal forests in the West held mature, old-growth timber, by far the largest single source of wood available to the American people.

Industrial holdings showed a similar pattern. In the Lake States and Northeast, lumber and wood products companies held some 15 million acres in 1968. In the South the figure was 35 million, in the West (excluding Alaska), 14 million. But the sawtimber inventory listed 2,700 board feet per acre in the Lake States and Northeast, 3,000 in the South, and more than 16,000 in the West. Industrial holdings in the West represented the most valuable stands of large, high-quality, mature trees in private hands.

A timber-resources review by the Forest Service in the late 1950s revealed that annual sawtimber growth had increased some 9 percent during the preceding decade. The quality, however, had declined as old-growth, mature timber was cut and young stock took its place. As might be expected, management, fire-prevention practices, and reforestation were far more adequate on industrial properties and in national forests than on farms and miscellaneous small-holdings. It was in the latter that foresters and government officials hoped to markedly improve productivity through sound forestry practices so as to meet expected increases in demand in the years ahead. The Eisenhower administration announced a "Program for the National Forests" in 1959 in response to such findings. Although a useful step, it was little noticed at the time by either the administration's critics or its defenders. The Eisenhower presidency's reputation on conservation was shaped not by actions like this but by the controversies surrounding Dixon-Yates, Dinosaur, and the like.[13]

With the election of John F. Kennedy to the presidency in 1960, the White House had an occupant who considered himself the spiritual heir of earlier conservationists. His appointments of Orville Freeman as secretary of agriculture and Stewart Udall as secretary of the interior brought knowledgeable and energetic administrators to these critical positions, albeit men with very different outlooks. Kennedy gave these departments strong support, and annual appropriations for natural-resource programs and agencies increased 16 percent over the Eisenhower years. Kennedy was concerned about the environment, warning that "each generation must deal anew with the 'raiders,' with the scramble to use public resources for private profits, and the tendency to prefer short-run profits to long-run necessities." Urged on by Udall, the president called a new White House Conference on Conservation and presented to Congress a ten-year program for the long-range development of the nation's forests. In many ways it was a rehash of the Eisenhower administration's "Program for the National Forests" of 1959, but it gained new importance under Kennedy.

Secretary Udall saw the decade of the sixties as a time of decision for conservation. "America stands on a pinnacle of wealth and power," he wrote, "yet we live in a land of vanishing beauty, of increasing ugliness, of shrinking open space, of an overall environment that is diminished daily by pollution and noise and blight." Kennedy agreed, embracing the idea that the federal government must play a major role in maintaining and restoring the environment. In his introduction to Udall's book *The Quiet Crisis*, the young president said:

We must do in our own day what Theodore Roosevelt did sixty years ago and Franklin Roosevelt thirty years ago: We must expand the concept of conservation to meet the imperious problems of the new age. We must develop new instruments of foresight and protection and nurture in order to recover the relationship between man and nature and to make sure that the national estate we pass to our multiplying descendants is green and flourishing.

These brave words summarize the ultimate goal of "New Frontier" efforts to broaden the scope of recreation development, intensify timber-resource management and increase timber harvest, provide more effective protection of wildlife and wilderness, and enhance the quality and beauty of the landscape and environment.

As president, Kennedy reflected Udall's thinking when he encouraged Forest Service chiefs Richard E. McArdle and Edward P. Cliff to extend the reforestation programs of their predecessors. In 1963 the Forest Service was able to report that the annual growth of timber in the United States, both East and West, exceeded the annual cut for the first time since record keeping had begun. Although this was largely the result of factors already at work before Kennedy came to the White House, the announcement seemed to many to demonstrate the soundness of Udall's approach.

Orville Freeman, however, was pushing the president and the Forest Service in different directions from those Udall desired. Freeman sought to ensure that rangers maximized production in their districts, being sure to get out the allowable cut and to increase it whenever possible through reassessment, improved efficiency, and better management. Trained foresters found his approach easier to accept than Udall's, but conservation groups were less impressed.

Kennedy neither reconciled the alternative approaches represented by Udall and Freeman nor decided between them. The president understood the problems of the forest intellectually and recognized their importance, but he himself seldom raised issues relating to them. At one point he planned to tour the country speaking about conservation, but finding the public more interested in foreign policy, he soon scrapped the idea. International crises and the civil rights explosion encouraged him to shift his attention to other concerns. As a result of this, of conservative opposition in Congress, and of the divided voice of his advisors, accomplishments between 1961 and 1963 were modest. But Kennedy's assassination in 1963 would set off a chain reaction in conservation as in other areas of American life.[14]

In the meantime other voices abruptly intruded into the conservation dialogue. Rachel Carson published *Silent Spring* during the summer of 1962. If the crisis had been quiet until then, it suddenly became very vocal. Almost immediately environment and ecology became the center of major political, social, and moral debates. Historian Charles A. Beard once observed that occasionally there appear books that change our minds. *Silent Spring* was such a book.

Carson presented a closely reasoned critique of man's widespread use of chemical pesticides, what she called "elixirs of death." She was specifically attacking the inordinate use of pesticides, but in a larger sense she made a plea for a balanced environment and for a recognition that mankind's arrogance in wiping out everything that stands in its way, even temporarily, could end in making the planet uninhabitable. Her arguments echoed the wisdom of John Muir and Aldo Leopold that all nature constitutes a "single intricate web of life" and no one part can be destroyed with impunity. Like Muir and Leopold, Carson gloried in the infinite variety and richness of life and protested against anything that would diminish its diversity.[15]

Silent Spring started an environmental revolution. The Sierra Club, the Audubon Society, and the National Wildlife Federation joined the crusade against excessive tampering with nature. Writers such as Barry Commoner, Richard Lillard, Raymond Dasmann, and William S. Rukeyser detailed the sins of man's interference with nature as exemplified in topics ranging from phosphates in the lakes to fluorocarbons in the atmosphere and strontium 90 in food. School and university groups across the country took up the cause, and numerous others flocked to the environmentalist banner.

The new environmentalism was a mixed force. In the mood of disenchantment that dominated the sixties, arguments often took on bitter antimodern, antibureaucratic overtones. Escapism permeated much environmentalist thought, and it helped fuel an unprecedented upsurge in backpacking and rocketing memberships in the Sierra Club and similar groups. Predictions of a worldwide ecological disaster lying just ahead lent force to both a rising wave of hedonism and a concern for endangered species, with which humans, feeling threatened themselves, could identify. Thousands of "ecologists" emerged, many with little knowledge of either nature or the economy, who self-righteously trumpeted their nostrums. Yet while there was much that was negative in the movement and environmentalists were often their own worst enemy, there was also much that was positive. Concern for the quality of life increased, and issues such as a proposal for dams that would have flooded the Grand Canyon galvanized many into action. The movement had a strong element of romantic idealism, was genuinely public-spirited, and brought increased citizen involvement in policymaking. Gradually the more knowledgeable and responsible environmentalists proved themselves the most effective. Under their leadership, the environmental crusade became more rational. Significant advances followed.

Responsible environmentalists stressed ecological integrity and preservation of America's forests rather than growth and development. Individuals and societies put pressure on Congress and state legislatures to establish more wilderness areas, to protect indigenous wildlife, and to preserve native plants. At the other end of the spectrum, these groups opposed expanded commercial forestry on public lands, large-scale grazing, and power development.[16]

Among this new breed of environmentalists were a considerable number who held that plants and animals should be acknowledged to have value regardless of their usefulness to man. The new environmentalists also attacked the practice of clear-cutting in logging. Both private industry and the Forest Service had agreed that the most effective method of harvesting Douglas fir was to clear-cut a limited stand, clean up the site, and replant with selected seedlings. This was also accepted procedure on the South's even-aged pine plantations that had been replanted on cutover lands following the bonanza lumbering operations. The concept that timber is a crop to be planted, matured, and harvested like other crops was advanced by forestry leaders, both public and private. They pointed to European forests that had been grown, cut, and replanted in a regular rhythm for hundreds of years. Where clear-cutting was applicable, the result was more timber, more food for certain types of game, and a new young forest more quickly brought into being.

Led by the Sierra Club and other preservationist groups, environmentalists rejected these arguments. They protested that even-aged, monotypical stands, which clear-cutting encouraged, sacrificed variety and noncommercial assets in order to maximize timber production. Sierra Club officials accused the Forest Service of failing to provide protection for the forests in the face of the demands of industry; some of the more strident labeled it "a shill for industry." When timber was in question, they charged, "recreation, wildlife, and watershed protection are given sparse attention." They labeled clear-cutting a "scalped land policy." Only partially tongue in cheek, environmentalists predicted that all American forestlands would become as bleak and bare as North Dakota after Paul Bunyan had finished logging it. Local and regional conservation societies as well as national groups joined in demanding that clear-cutting be banned in the national forests and restricted on private holdings. They pressured the federal administration to end "multiple abuse" and ensure true multiple use of American forests.[17]

The assassination of John F. Kennedy in November 1963 brought Lyndon B. Johnson to the presidency. Born in the hill country of central west Texas, Johnson had an affinity for wide open spaces, wildlife, and free-running streams. He held trees almost in reverence and was a strong supporter of conservation in all its aspects. Because of the circumstances of Kennedy's death, Americans mourned him as a martyr and his program, hitherto largely mired in congressional committees, took on a new urgency. The new president made Kennedy's platform his own. In the field of conservation Johnson's predilections were reinforced by Stewart Udall's steady prodding. In the end his accomplishments rivaled those of the two Roosevelts.

Responding to Johnson's requests, Congress passed the Wilderness Act of 1964. This act, for which preservationists had been working for years, set aside "certain unique areas" where the "earth and its community are untrammelled by man," where man himself is a visitor but not a resident, to be forever preserved. Congress placed some 9.1 million acres in this National Wilderness Preservation System and called for study of an additional 5.5 million acres of primitive areas to determine their suitability for inclusion. It set up a ten-year program for review of areas within national forests, parks, and wildlife refuges and game ranges for possible additions to the system. The act prohibited roads, buildings, power-driven equipment and transportation devices, and other man-made creations within defined wilderness areas. Yet the importance of the Wilderness Act is easy to exaggerate: while it designated many wilderness areas, those same areas had been protected as wilderness by the Forest Service for years, and Congress did almost nothing to expand the wilderness system during the ten-year review period that followed.[18]

Johnson led a White House Conference on Natural Beauty. With the strong support of his wife, the president urged Congress to protect and restore the country's natural heritage and to foster thereby not just human welfare but spiritual dignity as well. Congress responded with some fifty conservation measures dealing with the forests, water quality and conservation, highway beautification, and fish and wildlife protection. Among them was creation of the Land and Water Conservation Fund, by which Congress provided money to assist state and local governments to plan, build, and develop parks and other scenic and recreation areas. Indeed, the Eighty-ninth Congress (elected in

1964) has been labeled the "conservation Congress" because of its extensive work in the environmental field.

Taking a leaf from the New Deal's CCC experience, Johnson requested and Congress established the Job Corps. This project placed sixty-five hundred corpsmen and forty-seven camps in national forests during its first year of operation, upgrading the environment and improving facilities. These efforts greatly enhanced opportunities for recreational use of the forests. The following year (1965) the Forest Service reported 150 million man-days of public use of its facilities, up more than 50 percent from 1960.

The Ninetieth Congress continued the concern with conservation and environment. It created two national parks, three national recreation areas, four wilderness areas, a wild rivers system (including eight scenic rivers), and a national trail system. In addition it passed the Air Quality Act of 1968 and created the National Water Commission, which would work with federal, state, and private agencies and have direct influence on the nation's watersheds. Perhaps its most significant actions in the field of conservation were the creation of Redwood National Park in northern California and North Cascades National Park in Washington. The redwood bill was the climax of a fifty-year battle over the future of the coastal redwoods, some of which were more than one thousand years old and 360 feet tall. The measure created a park of some 58,000 acres, a compromise between the 90,000-plus-acre proposal of the Sierra Club and the outright opposition of many industry and local spokemen. The North Cascades Act set aside near the Canadian border a 505,000-acre park and two recreation areas totaling almost 200,000 acres.

President Johnson attacked the problems of the American forest and the environment through massive federal funding and federal control. Toward the end of his administration, Secretary Udall assessed the record:

These have been good years for the cause of conservation. History tells us that two Presidents this century—the Roosevelts—quickened the land conscience of the nation and provided leadership that saved specific resources and established sound policies of stewardship. I believe the Johnson years will undeniably be regarded as a "third wave" of the conservation movement which quantitatively will compare very favorably with those of these two predecessor Presidents, and which qualitatively will be known for the innovations and insights.

Udall's predictions have been borne out over time.[19]

The prices of American lumber, standing timber, logs, and finished wood products took a sudden turn upward in 1968. The prices of lumber in the

United States had risen (with only minor reversals) since the beginning of record keeping, but the escalation of 1968–69 brought a variety of demands for government action. Builders demanded that the Forest Service increase the allowable cut from the national forests. Many consumers saw in the price rise a conspiracy on the part of large lumber manufacturers. Others, including some conservationists, argued that only strict federal control over growing and cutting practices on private holdings could increase the supply and stabilize prices. All joined in denouncing the export of logs to Japan from the Pacific Coast states. The Japanese had increased their purchases of logs through the decade of the sixties, which led to a clamor for action to curtail or prohibit such exports. The matter became a hot political issue on the West Coast and caused concern in Washington. At the request of an economic task force, the State Department informally asked the Japanese to reduce their log imports. Secretary Freeman limited the export of logs from the national forests in the Pacific Northwest to 350 million board feet per year. Later, Congress forbade the export of logs from federal forestlands west of the one hundreth meridian for three years. The prohibition was subsequently extended, and Japan agreed (but failed) to reduce its annual imports by 10 percent.

Though the rising tide of log exports to Japan had an adverse effect on some mills and processing plants, many writers thought the excitement over the issue excessive. They pointed out that the United States was a net importer of lumber and lumber products, mostly from Canada, and argued that many of the exports were not of a quality or species much in demand in the States. If the United States cut off the export of logs and lumber, they argued, Japan would seek supplies elsewhere, probably from Canada. The result would be a reduced Canadian supply for this country at a higher price. Moreover, the delicate nature of the overall trade balance made federal officials hesitant to restrict log exports any further.[20]

On the surface at least, government policy in the Nixon-Ford administration from 1969 to 1977 followed the pattern of the Kennedy-Johnson years. Pushed by Democratic senator Henry Jackson of Washington, Congress in 1969 passed the National Environmental Policy Act (NEPA), hailed by environmentalists (probably too hastily) as the most important piece of conservation legislation of the past seventy-five years. This measure established a full-time three-member Council on Environmental Quality (CEQ) and outlined its duties. A "sleeper" provision required that any agency proposing major federal actions significantly affecting the quality of the environment file an environmental-impact statement. The authors scarcely considered the opportunities this measure would provide for single-issue groups to delay or block federal and state projects by litigation. The same year Congress also passed a Water Quality Act that partially overlapped NEPA. Early in 1970 President Richard M. Nixon presented an environmental message to Congress in which he proposed the establishment of an independent Environmental Protection Agency (EPA) to consolidate the various aspects of environmental control. This was accomplished through executive reorganization procedures, with congressional approval, and by the end of 1970 EPA came into existence. Nixon later proposed that the various land and forest agencies be consolidated into a new Department of Natural Resources. But this scheme, like earlier proposals by Secretaries Ballinger, Fall, and Ickes, died without congressional action.[21]

The year 1970 saw Congress create the Youth Conservation Corps, which enrolled boys and girls for summer work in a conservation learn-work program. The YCC functioned well and was made permanent in 1974. Also in 1970, the Public Land Law Review Commission published its final report after almost six years of labor. Though it made numerous recommendations regarding federally owned lands, its proposals were largely ignored. When Congressman Wayne Aspinall, its sponsor and only real champion, failed to win reelection to Congress, the PLLRC became dormant. In the meantime the Forest Service, recognizing increasing public concern with the environment, in 1974 issued a comprehensive *Environmental Program for the Future*. After more than a year of discussion, Congress produced a "Forest and Rangeland Renewable Resources Planning Act" (RPA) that gave statutory authority and direction to the planning process. Described as "something for everyone," the act required the Forest Service to periodically assess the nation's renewable resources and to prepare plans based on this assessment. During this same time millions of concerned environmentalists, including large numbers of college and university students, observed "Earth Day" (first held on April 22, 1970) by engaging in a series of "teach-ins," antipollution protests, and a variety of clean-up projects.

The Environmental Pesticide Control Act, passed in 1972, empowered the director of the Environmental Protection Agency to ban highly toxic insecticides. During the next four years the agency almost completely phased out such pesticides as DDT and Mirex. For some twenty years the Forest Service, other federal agencies, state departments of forestry, and forest-industry companies had been using these chemicals to control spruce budworms, bark beetles, tussock and gypsy moths, and other pests. Sprayings kept these forest-menacing insects under control, but the pesticides often killed nontarget insects, birds, small animals, and fish. Even people in neighboring towns and villages sometimes complained of being affected. Not surprisingly, environmental groups urged the EPA to ban chlorinated hydrocarbons completely. Under pressure from Congress after an epidemic outbreak of the tussock moth in the Pacific Northwest in 1974, the EPA authorized a massive spraying of nearly five hundred thousand acres of forest, but by then much damage had been done. In view of the hostile public reaction, this may well have been the last large-scale application of such pesticides in America's forests, although more recent developments in connection with the Mediterranean fruit fly in California raise some doubts. The use of herbicides to aid in reforestation efforts also came under sharp attack during this period.[22]

Maintaining a balanced conservation program was increasingly difficult during the early seventies because of the inconsistencies of the Nixon administration. Though Nixon acknowledged the goals of multiple use and environmental protection, he tended to accept "maximization of the net economic output of the National Forests" as the principal management goal. To stimulate the economy and encourage housing starts, the administration directed that the annual cut in the national forests be increased beyond current annual growth. In many cases this meant increased clear-cutting, not only in mature stands of Douglas fir and even-aged plantations of southern pine but elsewhere as well. In some cases steep slopes, watersheds, and mixed stands were clear-cut without adequate consideration for wildlife, erosion, and regeneration. To improve the national balance of payments, the president declined to formulate a strong and consistent policy regarding the export of logs to Japan. To save money, he slashed funds needed to reforest and rehabilitate cutover areas. In these circumstances it is not surprising that neither preservationists nor the timber industry regarded Richard Nixon as a dependable friend.[23]

Large-scale timber harvests in the national forests had been an issue before Nixon became president and continued to be one after he had left the White House. Especially troubling to environmentalists were clear-cutting in the mixed forests of the Appalachians—where it seemed the intent was to replace forest diversity with even-aged, monotypical stands—and in the high-altitude forests of the Rocky Mountains—where it would take years to recover from such logging, if recovery came at all.

Clear-cutting had begun in Wyoming in the 1950s and accelerated thereafter. Observing Forest Service practices regarding harvest of the marginal low-yield, high-mountain forests of the region, one logger complained in 1968: "They're ruining our timber stands for the next three generations. They're taking out all the timber and pretty soon there won't be any more to log." The so-called Bolle Report, prepared by a group from the University of Montana's School of Forestry, was especially critical of what was being done; it followed by six months a Forest Service study of its own practices on the Bitterroot National Forest, one of the key centers of controversy, which in a muted voice included many of the criticisms found later in the Bolle Report.

Sensitized by earlier operations and the protests they had generated, conservation organizations were quick to join a diverse body of local citizens in objecting loudly when proposals came from the Forest Service to open to logging Idaho's Magruder Corridor, a steep mountain area nestled between the Selway-Bitterroot Wilderness Area and the Salmon River Breaks Primitive Area. Battles over the corridor were to continue for years, for it was highly prized by recreationists and sportsmen and supported considerable timber.

Congress and the Forest Service responded to criticisms of clear-cutting with new timber-management guidelines, but environmentalists continued to challenge policies that they thought gave timber production an unreasonable high priority in managing national forests. The climax came not in the Rockies, but in the Appalachians. Led by the Izaak Walton League and the Sierra Club, environmentalist leaders brought suit charging that the National Forest Organic Act (the Forest Management Act of 1897) prohibited clear-cutting and limited timber harvests in the national forests to "dead, physiologically mature, and large growth" trees. In the landmark Monongahela decision of 1973, the federal district court in West Virginia accepted this interpretation and enjoined the Forest Service from violating the law. In so ruling, the court rejected three-quarters of a century of professional interpretation and practice. Had this decision been applied nationwide rather than only within the court's jurisdiction, it would have reduced timber harvests in the national forests by at least 50 percent.

When the Monongahela decision was upheld by the Fourth Circuit Court of Appeals, the Forest Service and its friends determined that they should seek relief from Congress rather than pursue litigation to the Supreme Court. Working from a bill introduced by Senator Hubert H. Humphrey of Minnesota, Congress hammered out and passed the National Forest Management Act of 1976. President Gerald R. Ford signed the measure in October 1976. Called the "most constructive forestry legislation in history," the law restored essential policy control and a measure of discretion to the Forest Service. The secretary of agriculture was directed to promulgate standards and guidelines for the management of the national forests; all management decisions were to be in accord with the multiple-use policy mandated for the National Forest System. Selective cutting was encouraged where proper; clear-cutting was not prohibited but was subject to guidelines set out by the Department of Agriculture. As a result, the Forest Service regained flexibility in managing the national forests but had to operate under more specific guidelines than before.[24]

Less noted than the furor over clear-cutting, but in some ways similar, was the struggle set off by amendments to the Federal Water Pollution Control Act that were passed in 1972. Portions of the amended act threatened severe disruption of logging. For example, section 404 required a permit from the Corps of Engineers each time a road crossed a stream; since the building of logging roads involved some 180,000 new stream crossings each year, the costs and administrative delays promised to be overwhelming. Neither the Forest Service nor the lumber industry welcomed these regulations, but environmentalists sought to force the EPA to apply them to woods operations. Congress had apparently enacted these amendments, like much other environmental legislation, with urban and semiurban areas rather than wildlands in mind. When the EPA clumsily applied them to forests, it provided industry and its allies with an opening to convince congressmen of their earlier excesses. In 1977 Congress responded by exempting forestry from the restrictions of the Federal Water Pollution Control Act. This, as surely as Congress's action in legalizing clear-cutting (however restricted), suggested that by the latter half of the seventies the momentum of the environmental movement was waning.

To a large degree both the National Forest Management Act and the exemptions from the Federal Water Pollution Control Act were a limited vote of confidence in the Forest Service. That agency, said Congress, has "both a responsibility and an opportunity to be a leader in assuring that the Nation maintains a natural resource conservation posture that will meet the requirements of our people in perpetuity." With both Congress and environmentalists looking over its shoulder, the Forest Service retreated from clear-cutting as a forest harvesting technique and in other ways showed a greater concern for noncommercial values than it had generally demonstrated in the past. Only on some private holdings has truly intensive management for timber production come near to achievement.[25]

Among large timber companies, a constant drive for greater efficiency, more complete wood utilization, and where possible a larger degree of self-sufficiency has been much in evidence since World War II. The Weyerhaeuser Company and Long-Bell, among others, built large new mills in the Pacific Northwest to harvest their old-growth Douglas fir stands. These mills, with a capacity of some 350,000 board feet a day, computer-controlled and largely automated, were a great advance over earlier sawmills, including those of the immediate post–World War II era. Subsidiary plants used timber not suitable for lumber, turning it into other wood products. For example, Weyerhaeuser reported that in contrast to 1950, when it had 21 percent timber utilization per acre, by 1975 the company was converting 28 percent of the harvested timber into lumber, 10 percent into plywood, 9 percent into particle board, and 32 percent into paper—for a total of 79 percent utilization. Some of the remaining 21 percent was used for fuel.

Because of the uncertainty of supply from individual timber owners (who control 59 percent of the commercial forests) and the continuing controversy over harvesting timber from federal, state, and local holdings, the larger industrial companies have sought to free themselves of dependency on outside timber sources insofar as possible. Weyerhaeuser has been the leader, achieving some 90 percent self-sufficiency; Boise Cascade, Champion International, Georgia-Pacific, and Crown Zellerbach have all become more than 50 percent self-sufficient.

In pursuit of self-sufficiency, large timber companies have acquired large tracts of forestlands—in many cases millions of acres. Though a million acres might appear to the layman to be a vast holding, in 1975 the timber industry collectively held only 13 percent of the commercial forestland in the United States (excluding Alaska). Perhaps more meaningful is that individual commercial forest owners (who held 59 percent), the various types of federal, state, and local forests (with 28 percent), and the forest-products industry (which owns 13 percent) each supplied about one-third of the nation's timber harvest in a given year. The largest strides toward self-sufficiency came on the Pacific Coast, where stands were larger and ownership less fragmented than in the South.[26]

Special local and regional projects supported by voluntary groups regularly reduced the total acreage available for commercial timber production. The Big Thicket National Preserve, established by Congress in 1974, provides an example. Situated deep in East Texas where flora and fauna of East, West, North, and South meet, the Big Thicket has one of the most complex ecological systems in the world. Conservationists sought for nearly half a century to have this area set aside. It was not truly a wilderness, for it had been logged before 1930, but the long, warm, damp growing seasons of the Gulf South speeded reforestation. By the sixties it was a de facto wilderness providing a home for many endangered species of wildlife, including the nearly extinct ivory-billed woodpecker. Large lumber companies that owned most of the area observed a cutting moratorium while conservationists fought among themselves about the size and nature of the preserve. Eventually Congress set aside eighty-four thousand acres as a national preserve.[27]

In the national forests the prospects are that pressures will increase for a more balanced multiple-use program emphasizing noncommercial activities. Ralph Nader, the well-known consumer advocate, in 1972 released a report accusing the Forest Service of concentrating on timber production at the expense of recreation, wildlife, wilderness, and grazing. He urged a multipoint program to reverse the trend. In anticipation of such criticism, the Forest Service developed plans for a variety of recreational and aesthetic uses that would put the national forests to the greatest possible use—sometimes, as in the Big Thicket, at the expense of commercial lumbering.

As Americans approached their bicentennial, they continued to rely on their forests for most of their wood products. It was clear that any considerable increase of the annual cut in the United States would of necessity put greater pressure on the national forests, especially in the West, for only there did considerable reserves of overmature timber exist. In 1976 the forest industry was already cutting all of its timber that a sound rotating policy would allow, and the owners of smallholdings appeared unlikely to produce significantly more than they already were.[28]

It seemed probable, however, that the most intensive pressures during the last decades of the twentieth century would be for less timber cutting rather than more. Environmentalists could be expected to continue to challenge the goals of more housing starts, increased economic growth, and an ever larger gross national product. In place of the passion for expansion—bigger, faster, farther, more—the environmentalist would practice restraint, moderation, and balance. By 1976 it seemed that Americans would have to learn to live more with their environment and less upon it.[29]

At the bicentennial, the problem was one of accommodation. There were more claimants for the limited resources of the American forest than ever before. Lumber manufacturers, plywood producers, paper-mill owners, wood-products consumers, hunters, canoeists, campers, hikers, fishermen, skiers, grazing lessees, bird-watchers, wilderness enthusiasts, watershed protectors, landscape preservationists, and many others were beginning to learn that a given acreage of forest could not accommodate simultaneous conflicting uses. But all, according to the legislation of Congress and the pledge of the Forest Service, should have an opportunity to enjoy forever, in their own way, some part of the American forest.

Epilogue

As the United States began its third century, commercial pressures on America's forests were expected to continue and indeed increase. Even assuming a slowed growth in population, the nation would have approximately three hundred million people by the year 2000, with demand for wood products at least doubled. Forest specialists estimated that by intensive management, establishment of a clear priority of timber production, and an investment of approximately fifteen billion dollars, a balanced, sustained-yield program could be achieved by that time. Without such major changes in forest management, the removal of sufficient timber to meet projected demand would cause the commercial forest base to shrink by some 6 percent, and the pattern of cutting exceeding growth would become increasingly hard to reverse.

However, in light of the many noncommercial demands on America's forests, the intensive management necessary for significant long-term increase in commercial production will be difficult to achieve. Alternatives include a shortage of wood products and consequent price inflation, greatly increased imports (especially from Canada), and a shift to other (often more expensive) materials. For a variety of reasons, it does not seem likely that imports from tropical rain forests will make up the shortfall, even though increasingly sophisticated tapping of these stands will surely come.

In the climate of self-congratulation called up by the bicentennial and the waning of the divisive issues of the sixties, it seemed that Americans might at last be able to engage in rational, open-minded exchanges that would lead to equitable solutions to the problems of competing claims on the nation's forests. Subsequent events have shown this to be a false hope. Instead of arriving at mutual accommodation, policies and actions have veered from one extreme to another, and exchanges between factions have grown increasingly acerbic and accusatory. Litigation over environmental issues has increased.

President Jimmy Carter, elected in 1976, reportedly considered naming

Michael McCloskey of the Sierra Club as secretary of the interior. He settled instead on Governor Cecil Andrus of Idaho and on Rupert Cutler as undersecretary of agriculture to oversee the Forest Service. Both took actions that environmentalists applauded and conservatives condemned. The Carter administration's most notable action on the conservation front came in 1980. After extended hearings, Carter signed into law the Alaska National Lands Conservation Act (d-2 lands bill) in spite of the objections of many of that state's officials and citizens. This measure set aside more than 130 million acres of land for conservation purposes and doubled the size of both the national park and the national wildlife refuge systems. Major portions of this land were forested, though most did not have stands with commercial potential.

The pendulum soon swung back. When Ronald Reagan was elected president in 1980, environmentalists were uneasy. Among other things, Reagan had once allegedly dismissed the drive for Redwood National Park with the comment: "If you've seen one redwood, you've seen them all." When the president-elect named James Watt, an outspoken opponent of environmental causes, as his choice for secretary of the interior, he reinforced those fears. Subsequent events demonstrated that they were not unfounded. Watt set about to maximize commercial production on federal lands under his purview and to reverse what he saw as the excessive environmentalist gains of the preceding two decades. Less flamboyant than Watt, but no less dedicated to maximizing commercial output, was John Crowell, assistant secretary of agriculture in charge of the Forest Service. Charges and countercharges mounted, and tempers flared. Not since the Ballinger-Pinchot controversy had Americans appeared so deeply split over the management of their natural resources. The replacement of Watt by William Clark in 1983 lessened tension but failed to heal the breach.[1]

Other developments added to the growth of controversy after 1976. Much debate during the late 1970s centered on the definition and implementation of RARE I (Roadless Area Review and Evaluation) and RARE II, outgrowths of the drive for wilderness preservation. Forestry leaders from both the public and the private sectors held "forums"in which they sought to assess the impact of federal regulations on forestry and their cost to the consumer in increased prices for forest products.

Equally heated were debates triggered by the so-called Sagebrush Rebellion. Even before the election of President Reagan, local champions had emerged demanding a "return" of federal lands to the states. Dusting off arguments used earlier by Weldon Heyburn and Henry Teller, these champions of local control argued that westerners knew how to manage forests and rangelands better than did the Forest Service, Bureau of Land Management, and other branches of the federal bureaucracy. James Watt first came to public notice as one of their spokesmen.

Private enterprise as well as public agencies was caught up in controversies. Frequently the protagonists were bureaucrats and businessmen, which led one corporate executive to comment that the recent history of the forest has consisted of a cycle: policymakers plan, hold hearings, legislate, litigate, and plan and legislate again. Sometimes, however, the controversies assumed a different form. In 1975 the Weyerhaeuser Company proposed to further the export of wood products from the Puget Sound area by building major new port facilities near Tacoma, Washington. Exports, company president George Weyerhaeuser argued, represented the future of the forest-products industries in the Pacific Northwest: the South, with its longer growing seasons, less rugged terrain, and relative closeness to the nation's main markets, could be expected to dominate in most domestic outlets in the years ahead. But environmentalists objected to the proposed project. Some expressed fear of what it would do to the fragile ecosystem of nearby Nisqually Delta; others, more extreme, attacked the need for exports and commercial growth in terms reminiscent of the 1960s. Hearings, suits, proposals, and counterproposals ground on, and after a decade the facilities still remained on paper only.[2]

But if the vituperative exchanges of the Carter and Reagan years served to temper the rosy predictions of the bicentennial about a future of cooperation and accommodation in resource management, surveys at the same time suggested that Americans were less divided than the rhetoric of opposing camps would lead one to believe. They seemed united in treasuring their forests and other natural resources and in wanting protection for what foresters call their amenity values as much as — perhaps even more than — for other commercial values, and whether cooperation or confrontation would best serve to bring it about were questions on which opinion seemed more divided.[3]

Many components of Americans' attitudes toward their forests after the bicentennial were familiar: squabbles over policies; contests between utilitarians and those who put a higher priority on aesthetic values; and the exploitive states'-rights arguments of the Sagebrush Rebellion. From colonial times on Americans not only had used their forests extensively but had wrestled continually with the challenges they posed. Only the details seemed to vary over time. But by 1976 genuinely basic changes, largely unappreciated, were afoot in the land. From the time of the first settlements, Americans had been moving into new forest areas, tapping them and being changed by them as they went. America's lumber industry had come into being by mining centuries of accumulated forest growth. This was changing. In 1982 Georgia-Pacific moved its corporate headquarters from Portland, Oregon, to Atlanta, Georgia. The South, company officials were convinced, was the place of future promise. They were turning their backs on the West and returning to second- and third-growth forests cut long before. Others agreed. Major dependence on newly opened stands of old-growth timber would soon be over.

New conditions would demand new solutions. With the center of lumbering shifting back to the South, the importance of federal policies and public lands promises to wane, and the decisions of private landholders loom larger, for the region not only has strong traditions of individualism and states' rights but is also one where most forestland is privately held. This will inevitably have far-reaching effects on future forest use and policy debates. A new age is dawning not only for the lumber industry, but for all Americans in their use of the forests. Often-repeated old debates may at last become irrelevant—and be recognized as such. More than ever, it appears, the future of the American forest will depend on education, vision, and leadership.

Under the new conditions increasing leadership can be expected to come from the private sector, but the federal Forest Service will surely continue to play a major role. The Forest Service has, thanks to Gifford Pinchot, Henry Graves, William Greeley, and their successors, developed a strong professional, nonpartisan corps of experts. It should provide sound thinking and planning for the many and varied uses of the forest. But the Forest Service is itself divided, however much that fact may be clouded by official policy statements. Its ranks include people of widely differing outlooks, and it is thus hampered in its efforts to provide clear, consistent leadership. In these circumstances, some would argue, leadership will have to come from the president of the United States, for he is the ultimate custodian of the American environment and its resources. The examples of the great conservationist presidents—the two Roosevelts, Lyndon Johnson, and perhaps Jimmy Carter—should point the way for the use, conservation, and preservation of the American forest in the third century of the nation's independence.

Yet even this solution is incomplete. A president can provide only that leadership which the times, and the people, will allow. In a participatory democracy, if the forests are to be truly protected and cherished, the people themselves must take responsibility. Presidents, Congress, educators, foresters, and environmentalists can help to teach and inspire the public; they can lend vision and leadership. Still, in the end, it there is to be wise and equitable accommodation of contending demands on the forest, the impetus must come from the American citizens themselves. If America's forests are wasted and despoiled,

Americans will have no one but themselves to blame. But with vision and the perspective gained from more than three centuries of experience, informed citizens should be able to make wise decisions about the nation's forests. If they do, coming generations can continue to enjoy the matchless variety and productiveness that has characterized this well-wooded land throughout its history.

Statistical Appendix

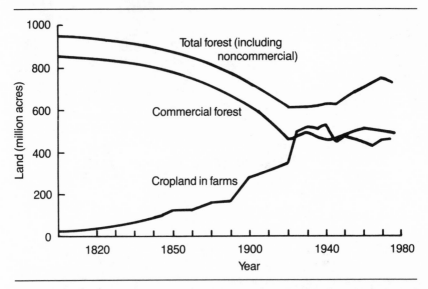

Figure 1. Land in all forests, commercial forests, and cropland in farms in the United States, 1800 to 1975. From *Science* 204 (June 15, 1979): 1171. © AAAS. Reprinted by permission.

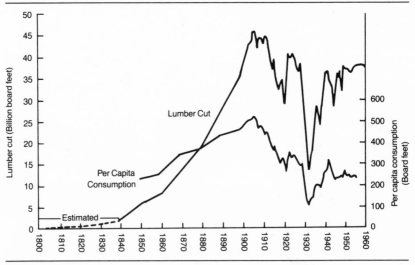

Figure 2. Lumber cut and per capita consumption, 1800 to 1960. © AAAS. Reprinted by permission.

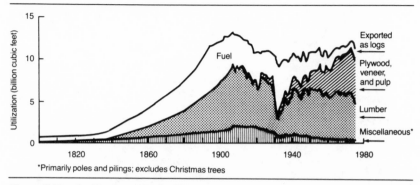

Figure 3. Total utilization of United States–grown wood (in roundwood equivalent), by major form of use, 1800 to 1975. From *Science* 204 (June 15, 1979): 1171. © AAAS. Reprinted by permission.

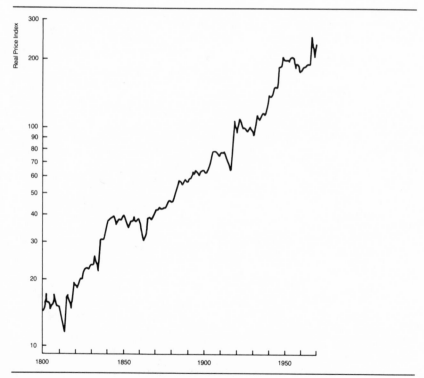

Figure 4. Lumber prices, United States, 1800 to 1971. From William A. Duerr, *Timber! Problem, Prospect, Policy.* © Iowa University Press, 1973. Reprinted by permission.

Notes

Introduction

1. Ernst C. Griffin and Larry R. Ford, "Tijuana: Landscape of a Culture Hybrid," *Geographical Review* 66 (1976): 435–47.

2. Alice Benson Allen, *Simon Benson: Northwest Lumber King* (Portland, Oreg., 1971); Thomas R. Cox, "Pacific Log Rafts in Economic Perspective," *Forest History* 15 (July 1971): 18–19.

3. Walter M. Kollmorgen, "The Woodsman's Assault on the Domain of the Cattleman," *Annals of the Association of American Geographers* 59 (1969): 215–39. Kollmorgen was not the first to recognize this clash of cultures. Herbert E. Bolton built a distinguished academic career on the foundations it provided. See John F. Bannon, "Herbert Eugene Bolton—Western Historian," *Western Historical Quarterly* 2 (1971): 261–82.

4. The historical literature on land and water laws in the West is vast. Especially valuable are Paul W. Gates with Robert W. Swenson, *History of Public Land Law Development* (Washington, D.C., 1968), and Norris Hundley, Jr., *Water and the West* (Berkeley, Calif., 1975).

5. Roughly half of what was to become the forty-eight contiguous states of the United States was originally timbered. Approximately one-third remains so today.

6. On the shaping of the material culture of settlers by the forest see Richard G. Lillard, *The Great Forest* (New York, 1948); Brooke Hindle, ed., *Material Culture of the Wooden Age* (Tarrytown, N.Y., 1981); and Charles van Ravensway, "America's Age of Wood," *Proceedings of the American Antiquarian Society* 80 (1970): 49–66. See also David M. Potter, *People of Plenty: Economic Abundance and the American Character* (Chicago, 1954).

7. Consult Clinton Rossiter, *The First American Revolution: The American Colonies on the Eve of Independence* (New York, 1956); Clarence L. Ver Steeg, *The Formative Years, 1607–1763* (New York, 1964); and Frank Thistlethwaite, *America and the Atlantic Community: Anglo-American Aspects, 1790–1850* (New York, 1963).

8. Bernard De Voto, "The West: A Plundered Province," *Harper's* 169 (1934): 355–64; Gene M. Gressley, "Colonialism: A Western Complaint," *Pacific Northwest Quarterly* 54 (1963): 1–8; Earl Pomeroy, "Toward a Reorientation of Western History: Continuity

and Environment," *Mississippi Valley Historical Review* 41 (1955): 579–600. See also the series of articles on "The American West as an Underdeveloped Region," *Journal of Economic History* 16 (December 1956).

Chapter 1

1. For descriptions, region by region, of the types of trees and extent of the woods at the time of the first European settlements, see Charles S. Sargent, *Report on the Forests of North America,* Tenth Census of the United States, vol. 9 (Washington, D.C., 1884), esp. pp. 3–6, 494–512, and James Elliott Defebaugh, *History of the Lumber Industry of America,* 2 vols. (Chicago, 1906–7), 1: 7–45. Local diversity is well described in William Cronon, *Changes in the Land: Indians, Colonists, and the Ecology of New England* (New York, 1983), pp. 19–33.

2. Oddvar K. Hoidal, "Norsemen and the North American Forests," *Journal of Forest History* 24 (1980): 200–203.

3. A number of works bear on this theme. For examples see Terry L. Anderson and Robert Paul Thomas, "White Population, Labor Force, and Extensive Growth of the New England Economy in the Seventeenth Century," *Journal of Economic History* 33 (1973): 634–67; Richard Hofstadter, *America at 1750: A Social Portrait* (New York, 1971), pp. 3–32; and James T. Lemon, *The Best Poor Man's Country: A Geographical Study of Early Southeastern Pennsylvania* (Baltimore, 1972), pp. 1–41 and passim.

4. Samuel Eliot Morison, *Admiral of the Ocean Sea: A Life of Christopher Columbus* (Boston, 1942), pp. 232–66 and passim. For discussions of the effects of wishes-become-images, see J. Wreford Watson and Timothy O'Riordan, *The American Environment: Perceptions and Policies* (New York, 1976), pp. 29–36, 63–75; R. L. Bruckberger, *Image of America,* trans. C. G. Paulding and Virgilia Peterson (New York, 1959), pp. 3–17; James Oliver Robertson, *American Myth, American Reality* (New York, 1980), pp. 19–53; and H. Roy Merrens, "The Physical Environment of Early America: Images and Image-Makers in South Carolina," *Geographical Review* 59 (1969): 530–56.

5. Carl Ortwin Sauer, *Sixteenth Century North America: The Land and the People as Seen by the Europeans* (Berkeley, Calif., 1971); Durand Echeverria, *Mirage in the West: A History of the French Image of American Society to 1815* (Princeton, N.J., 1957). See also Alfred W. Crosby, Jr., *The Columbian Exchange: Biological and Cultural Consequences of 1492* (Westport, Conn., 1972), pp. 3–34.

6. Perry Miller, *The New England Mind: The Seventeenth Century* (New York, 1939, 1954); Peter N. Carroll, *Puritanism and the Wilderness: The Intellectual Significance of the New England Frontier, 1629–1700* (New York, 1969), pp. 61–86; Alan Heimert, "Puritanism, the Wilderness, and the Frontier," *New England Quarterly* 26 (1953): 361–82; Peter A. Fritzell, "The Wilderness and the Garden: Metaphors for the American Landscape," *Forest History* 12 (April 1968): 16–21; and Roderick Nash, *Wilderness and the American Mind* (rev. ed., New Haven, Conn., 1973), pp. 33–38.

7. A host of works touch on early dependence on the forest, among them Fred B. Kniffen and Henry Glassie, "Building in Wood in the Eastern United States: A Time-Place Perspective," *Geographical Review* 56 (1966): 40–66; Carl Bridenbaugh, "Yankee Use and Abuse of the Forest in the Building of New England, 1620–1660," *Proceedings of the Massachusetts Historical Society* 89 (1977): 3–35; Curtis P. Nettels, *The Roots of American Civilization: A History of American Colonial Life*, 2d ed. (New York, 1963), pp. 145–61, 229–37; and Cronon, *Changes in the Land*, pp. 34–53.

8. The literature on colonial agriculture, especially tobacco cultivation, is vast. Useful accounts include Lyman Carrier, *Beginnings of Agriculture in America* (New York, 1923); Lewis C. Gray, *History of Agriculture in the Southern United States to 1860* (Washington, D.C., 1933), vol. 1; Percy W. Bidwell and John I. Falconer, *History of Agriculture in the Northern United States, 1620–1860* (Washington, D.C., 1941).

9. For a good summary of contrasting approaches to land use and clearing, see John R. Stilgoe, *Common Landscape of America, 1580 to 1845* (New Haven, Conn., 1982), pp. 43–83, 170–82. See also Cronon, *Changes in the Land*, pp. 108–46.

10. Naval stores—pitch, tar, turpentine, and rosin—were vital in the age of wooden-hulled sailing ships; they caulked the hulls, protected and preserved the lines to the sails, and so on. When colonial reports referred to turpentine, they normally meant the crude gum (oleoresins) extracted from the tree, not distilled spirits of turpentine—at the time a product of minor importance. On colonial naval stores production, see Harry B. Weiss and Grace M. Weiss, *Some Early Industries of New Jersey: Cedar Mining, Tar, Pitch, Turpentine, Salt Hay* (Trenton, N.J., 1965); G. Melvin Herndon, "Naval Stores in Colonial Georgia," *Georgia Historical Quarterly* 52 (1968): 426–33; Sinclair Snow, "Naval Stores in Colonial Virginia," *Virginia Magazine of History and Biography* 72 (1964): 75–93. Somewhat broader is Thomas Gamble, *Naval Stores: History, Production, Distribution and Consumption* (Savannah, Ga., 1921).

11. For accounts of this shift, see Thomas Jefferson Wertenbaker, *The Puritan Oligarchy: The Founding of American Civilization* (New York, 1947), pp. 183–207; Louis B. Wright, *The Atlantic Frontier; Colonial American Civilization, 1607–1763* (1947; Ithaca, N.Y., 1964), pp. 98–160; David M. Roth, *Connecticut: A History* (New York and Nashville, 1979), pp. 62–65.

12. The iron industry is traced in John B. Pearse, *Concise History of the Iron Manufacture of the American Colonies up to the Revolution and of Pennsylvania up to the Present Time* (1876; New York, 1970); William Thomas Hogan, *Economic History of the Iron and Steel Industry in the United States*, 5 vols. (Lexington, Mass., 1971).

13. Wertenbaker, *Puritan Oligarchy*, pp. 13–16, 106–27; Carl W. Condit, *American Building: Materials and Techniques from the First Colonial Settlements to the Present* (Chicago, 1968), pp. 2–38; Wayne D. Rasmussen, "Wood on the Farm," and Dell Upton, "Traditional Timber Framing," in Hindle, *Material Culture*, pp. 15–34, 35–93; C. A. Weslager, *The Log Cabin in America: From Pioneer Days to the Present* (New Brunswick, N.J., 1969); Rolla M. Tryon, *Household Manufactures in the United States, 1640–1860: A Study in Indus-*

trial History (Chicago, 1917); Mary Earle Gould, *Early American Woodenware and Other Kitchen Utensils* (Rutland, Vt., 1962); Lillard, *Great Forest,* pp. 13–33, 76–79; van Ravenswaay, "America's Age of Wood."

14. On the Old World background and shifting visions in the New, see Clarence J. Glacken, *Traces on the Rhodian Shore: Nature and Culture in Western Thought from Ancient Times to the End of the Eighteenth Century* (Berkeley, Calif., 1967); and Louis B. Wright, *The Dream of Prosperity in Colonial America* (New York, 1965).

Chapter 2

1. Information on colonial roads is fragmentary. However, see Jeremy Belknap, *History of New Hampshire,* 3 vols. (Dover, N.H., 1812–13), 3:58–60; Don H. Birkebile, "Wooden Roads," in Hindle, *Material Culture,* esp. pp. 129–34; Joseph Austin Durrenberger, *Turnpikes: A Study of the Toll Road Movement in the Middle Atlantic States and Maryland* (1931; Cos Cob, Conn., 1968), pp. 9–44; Seymour Dunbar, *A History of Travel in America . . .* (New York, 1937), pp. 16, 52–54, 84–96.

2. On early lumbering, see Defebaugh, *Lumber Industry,* 2:6–9, 50–52, 126, 271–78, 305–14, 556–58; Harry B. Weiss and Grace M. Weiss, *The Early Sawmills of New Jersey* (Trenton, N.J., 1968); and Nathan Rosenberg, "American's Rise to Woodworking Leadership," in Brooke Hindle, ed., *America's Wooden Age: Aspects of Its Early Technology* (Tarrytown, N.Y., 1975), pp. 37–62.

3. Richard H. Schallenberg, "Charcoal Iron: The Coal Mines of the Forest," in Hindle, *Material Culture,* esp. pp. 271–82; Joseph E. Walker, *Hopewell Village: A Social and Economic History of an Iron-Making Community* (Philadelphia, 1966), pp. 120–36; Stilgoe, *Common Landscape,* pp. 282–300.

4. Robert P. Multhauf, "Potash," in Hindle, *Material Culture,* pp. 227–40; W. I. Roberts III, "American Potash Manufacture before the American Revolution," *Proceedings of the American Philosophical Society* 116 (1972): 383–95; and Harry Miller, "Potash from Wood Ashes: Frontier Technology in Canada and the United States," *Technology and Culture* 21 (1980): 187–208.

5. G. Terry Sharrer, "Naval Stores, 1781–1881," in Hindle, *Material Culture,* esp. pp. 241–49; Joseph J. Malone, *Pine Trees and Politics: The Naval Stores and Forest Policy of Colonial New England, 1691–1775* (Seattle, 1964), pp. 28–46; Harry Roy Merrens, *Colonial North Carolina in the Eighteenth Century* (Chapel Hill, N.C., 1964), pp. 85–92, 102–7; Snow, "Naval Stores in Colonial Virginia," pp. 75–93; Robert G. Albion, *Forests and Sea Power: The Timber Problem of the Royal Navy, 1652–1862* (1926; Hamden, Conn., 1965), pp. 139–99 and passim.

6. While the origins of slavery in British North America remain clouded with uncertainty, it has been suggested that southern naval stores production played a key role in its emergence. See Clarence L. Ver Steeg, *Origins of a Southern Mosaic: Studies of Early Carolina and Georgia* (Athens, Ga., 1975), pp. 120–32.

7. Herndon, "Naval Stores in Colonial Georgia," pp. 426–33; Herndon, "Forest Products of Colonial Georgia," *Journal of Forest History* 23 (1979): 130–35.

8. Merrens, *Colonial North Carolina*, pp. 149–55; Lawrence Lee, *The Lower Cape Fear in Colonial Days* (Chapel Hill, N.C., 1965), pp. 145–81; Hugh T. Lefler and William S. Powell, *Colonial North Carolina* (New York, 1973), pp. 151–74.

9. The cooperage industry is mentioned in a host of works; one of the few detailed studies is Franklin E. Coyne, *The Development of the Cooperage Industry in the United States, 1620–1940* (Chicago, 1940).

10. For a fuller discussion, see Thomas C. Cochran, *Pennsylvania: A Bicentennial History* (New York and Nashville, 1978), pp. 16–17, 20–45.

11. Less auspicious for the future of the colony's woodlands was the presence among the settlers of a number of Finns, whose penchant for forest clearing through burning and other destructive practices had led to their transfer from Sweden to America in order to protect valuable timber stands in the mother country. See Christopher Ward, *The Dutch and Swedes on the Delaware, 1609–64* (Philadelphia, 1930), pp. 102–6; Stilgoe, *Common Landscape*, pp. 175–77.

12. For a discussion of the impact of the rise of major towns, see Carl Bridenbaugh, *Cities in the Wilderness: The First Century of Urban Life in America, 1625–1724* (1938; New York, 1964).

13. Defebaugh, *Lumber Industry*, 2:485–93, 496–596.

14. Ibid., 2:302–8; William F. Fox, *A History of the Lumber Industry of the State of New York* (1902; Harrison, N.Y., 1976), pp. 7–20.

15. Charles F. Carroll, *The Timber Economy of Puritan New England* (Providence, R.I., 1973), develops this thesis in detail.

16. The literature on shipbuilding is vast. Especially useful are Joseph A. Goldenberg, "With Saw and Axe and Augur: Three Centuries of American Shipbuilding," in Hindle, *Material Culture*, pp. 97–128, and William Armstrong Fairburn, *Merchant Sail*, 6 vols. (Center Lovell, Maine, 1945–55), 1:142–317.

17. George Francis Dow, *The Arts and Crafts in New England, 1704–1775* (1927; New York, 1967), pp. 105–31 and passim; Alex W. Bealer, *The Tools That Built America* (Barre, Mass., 1976), pp. 47–203.

18. Tied as the subject is to the coming of the American Revolution, every textbook devotes considerable space to the question of British controls over colonial trade and development, and scholars continue to produce works on the subject. Good places to start are still Nettels, *Roots of American Civilization*, esp. chaps. 11, 20–23, and Oliver M. Dickerson, *The Navigation Acts and the American Revolution* (Philadelphia, 1951). A recent view emphasizing economic rather than political ramifications is Gary M. Walton and James F. Shepherd, *The Economic Rise of Early America* (Cambridge, 1979), pp. 153–77.

19. Warren J. Gates, "The Broad Arrow Policy in Colonial America" (Ph.D. diss., University of Pennsylvania, 1951); Malone, *Pine Trees and Politics*, pp. 47–143.

20. Ronald L. Pollitt, "Wooden Walls: English Seapower and the World's Forests,"

Forest History 15 (April 1971): 6–15; Albion, *Forests and Seapower,* pp. 95–138. See also Jean R. Birrell, "The Medieval English Forest," *Journal of Forest History* 24 (1980): 78–85; John Croumbie Brown, *The Forests of England and the Management of Them in Bye-Gone Times* (Edinburgh, 1883).

21. Joseph J. Malone, "The Baltic Naval Stores Trade in the Seventeenth and Eighteenth Centuries," *Mariner's Mirror* 57 (1972): 375–95; Albion, *Forests and Seapower,* pp. 139–230.

22. Walter A. Knittle, *Early Eighteenth Century Palatine Emigration: A British Government Redemptioner Project to Manufacture Naval Stores* (1937; Baltimore, 1965).

23. Textbooks and specialized studies alike abound with discussions of these factors. Especially useful are Malone, *Pine Trees and Politics,* esp. pp. 28–56, 124–43; Justin Williams, "English Mercantilism and Carolina Naval Stores, 1705–1776," *Journal of Southern History* 1 (1935): 169–85; Gordon E. Kershaw, "John Wentworth vs. Kennebeck Proprietors: The Formation of Royal Mast Policy, 1769–1778," *American Neptune* 33 (1973): 95–119; Lawrence H. Gipson, *Jared Ingersoll: American Loyalist* (1920; New Haven, Conn., 1971); and Arthur R. M. Lower, *Great Britain's Woodyard: British America and the Timber Trade, 1763–1867* (Toronto, 1973), pp. 35–43.

Chapter 3

1. J. P Kinney, *The Essentials of American Timber Law* (New York, 1917), pp. 26–49.

2. Stilgoe, *Common Landscape,* pp. 58–76; Darrett B. Rutman, *Husbandmen of Plymouth: Farms and Villages in the Old Colony, 1620–1692* (Boston, 1967), pp. 52–62; Avery O. Craven, *Soil Exhaustion as a Factor in the Agricultural History of Virginia and Maryland, 1606–1860* (Urbana, Ill., 1926); Aubrey C. Land, "The Tobacco Staple and the Planter's Problems: Technology, Labor, and Crops," *Agricultural History* 43 (1969): 69–82; Harold B. Gill, Jr., "Wheat Culture in Colonial Virginia," *Agricultural History* 52 (1978): 380–93.

3. For further discussions of the agriculture-forests connection, see Wayne D. Rasmussen, "Wood on the Farm," in Hindle, *Material Culture,* pp. 15–34; Lillard, *Great Forest,* pp. 76–94; G. Melvin Herndon, "The Significance of the Forest to the Tobacco Plantation Economy of Antebellum Virginia," *Plantation Society* 1 (1981): 430–39.

4. Warren C. Scoville, "Did Colonial Farmers 'Waste' Our Land?" *Southern Economic Journal* 20 (1953): 178–81; Roger W. Weiss, "Mr. Scoville on Colonial Land Wastage," *Southern Economic Journal* 21 (1954): 87–90.

5. For further discussion of the settlers' attitudes toward the forest see below, chapter 4. See also Hans Huth, *Nature and the American: Three Centuries of Changing Attitudes* (1957; Lincoln, Nebr., 1972), pp. 1–13; Joseph M. Petulla, *American Environmental History: The Exploitation and Conservation of Natural Resources* (San Francisco, 1977), pp. 31–33, 50–59; Leo E. Oliva, "Our Frontier Heritage and the Environment," *American West* 9 (January 1972): 44–47, 61–63.

6. Stilgoe, *Common Landscape,* pp. 43–58; Carroll, *Puritanism and the Wilderness,* pp. 181–97; Yasuhide Kawashima and Ruth Tone, "Environmental Policy in Early

America: A Survey of Colonial Statutes," *Journal of Forest History* 27 (1983): 168–69. See also above, chapter 1.

7. Albert Bernhardt Faust, *The German Element in the United States with Special Reference to Its Political, Moral, Social, and Educational Influence*, 2 vols. (Boston, 1909), 1:129–39; Richard H. Shryock, "British versus German Traditions in Colonial Agriculture," *Mississippi Valley Historical Review* 26 (1939): 39–54.

8. Cronon, *Changes in the Land*, pp. 34–53, 90–107, 127–56; Peter O. Wacker, *Land and People: A Cultural Geography of Preindustrial New Jersey: Origins and Settlement* (New Brunswick, N.J., 1975), pp. 57–119; Stephen J. Pyne, *Fire in America: A Cultural History of Wildland and Rural Fire* (Princeton, N.J., 1982), pp. 45–83; Gordon M. Day, "The Indian as an Ecological Factor in the Northeastern Forest," *Ecology* 34 (1953): 329–46; Calvin Martin, *Keepers of the Game: Indian-Animal Relationships and the Fur Trade* (Berkeley, Calif., 1978); Shepard Krech III, ed., *Indians, Animals, and the Fur Trade: A Critique of Keepers of the Game* (Athens, Ga., 1981; J. Baird Callicott, "Traditional American Indian and Western European Attitudes toward Nature: An Overview," *Environmental Ethics* 4 (1982): 293–318.

Attempts have been made, some highly romanticized, to depict the Indians as the first American ecologists. Whether they were or not, the fact remains that their social and economic systems took less of a toll of the forests than did those of the invading whites. See J. Donald Hughes, *American Indian Ecology* (El Paso, Tex., 1983); Wilbur R. Jacobs, *Dispossessing the American Indian: Indians and Whites on the Colonial Frontier* (New York, 1972, pp. 19–30, 151–52; and Calvin Martin, "The American Indian as Miscast Ecologist," *History Teacher* 14 (1981): 243–52.

9. Cronon, *Changes in the Land*, pp. 139–70; Wilbur R. Jacobs, "The Great Despoliation: Environmental Themes in American Frontier History," *Pacific Historical Review* 47 (1978): 1–26; Craven, *Soil Exhaustion;* A. Phillip Muntz, "The Changing Geography of the New Jersey Woodlands, 1600–1900" (Ph.D. diss., University of Wisconsin, 1959). Cronon's study analyzes environmental changes in New England in detail; more such works are needed.

The weakness of ties between coastal areas and the interior and friction between the two have been touched upon in many studies and used to explain a host of events, both in the colonial period and later. For an introduction, see Nettels, *Roots of American Civilization*, pp. 537–42.

10. So reduced were New Jersey's cedar stands that, after the discovery about 1812 of quantities of still usable cedar logs buried in the swamps, an industry quickly rose that retrieved them and split them into shingles. See Defebaugh, *Lumber Industry*, 2:493–95.

11. Huth, *Nature and the American* pp. 7–13; Nash, *Wilderness and the American Mind*, pp. 38–40; Beatrice Ward Nelson, *State Recreation: Parks, Forests and Game Preserves* (Washington, D.C., 1928), pp. 3–5; Wertenbaker, *Puritan Oligarchy*, pp. 160–72; Bridenbaugh, *Cities in the Wilderness*, pp. 21, 169–70, 325; Frederick B. Tolles, *Meeting House and Counting House: Quaker Merchants of Colonial Philadelphia, 1682–1763* (New York, 1948), pp. 135–39; Jane Carson, *Colonial Virginians at Play* (Williamsburg, Va.,

1965), pp. 134–49. See also Louise Andrews Kent, *Village Greens of New England* (New York, 1948). The Great Ponds Act remains in effect in Maine and is the basis for access to fishing, and by extension hunting, on private land.

12. Kawashima and Tone, "Environmental Policy in Early America," pp. 168–79; J. P Kinney, *Forest Legislation in America prior to March 4, 1789*, Department of Forestry Bulletin no. 30 (Ithaca, N.Y., 1916), pp. 363, 381, and passim. On the communitarian impulse and patterns, see Wertenbaker, *Puritan Oligarchy*, pp. 41–77; Benjamin W. Labaree, *Colonial Massachusetts: A History* (Millwood, N.Y., 1979), pp. 47–65; Page Smith, *As a City upon a Hill: The Town in American History* (New York, 1966), pp. 3–16.

13. Kinney, *Forest Legislation*, pp. 359–405; Lillian M. Willson, *Forest Conservation in Colonial Times* (St. Paul, Minn., 1948); Kawashima and Tone, "Environmental Policy in Early America," pp. 168–79.

14. J. P Kinney, *The Development of Forest Law in America*...(New York, 1917), pp. 20–22; Kinney, *Forest Legislation*, pp. 363–70; Defebaugh, *Lumber Industry*, 2:96; Pyne, *Fire in America*, pp. 45–83.

15. Kinney, *American Timber Law*, pp. 96–97; Kinney, *Forest Legislation*, pp. 372–74 and passim. The extent to which the woods of old England and hunting rights in them were off limits to commoners is detailed in John Manwood, *A Treatise of the Laws of the Forest* (1615; Amsterdam, 1976), and in E. P. Thompson, *Whigs and Hunters: The Origins of the Black Act* (London, 1975).

16. Charles E. Clark, *The Eastern Frontier: The Settlement of Northern New England* (New York, 1970), esp. pp. 36–51, 121–43.

Chapter 4

1. Among the many accounts of the difficulties of waging warfare in the forests of early America are Lillard, *Great Forest*, pp. 43–64; Dale Van Every, *Forth to the Wilderness: The First American Frontier, 1754–1774* (New York, 1961); and John K. Mahon, "Anglo-American Methods of Indian Warfare, 1676–1794," *Mississippi Valley Historical Review* 45 (1958): 254–75.

2. For discussions see A. Whitney Griswold, *Farming and Democracy* (New York, 1948), pp. 18–46; Lewis J. Carey, *Franklin's Economic Views* (Garden City, N.Y., 1928), pp. 168–98; and Henry Nash Smith, *Virgin Land: The American West as Symbol and Myth* (1950; Cambridge, Mass., 1970), pp. 123–32. Jeffersonian agrarianism has sometimes been exaggerated. See Stuart Bruchey, *The Roots of American Economic Growth, 1607–1861* (New York, 1965), pp. 114–22; and Merrill D. Peterson, *The Jefferson Image in the American Mind* (New York, 1960), pp. 24–25.

3. For the larger context, see Lillard, *Great Forest*, pp. 65–94; John A. Jakle, *Images of the Ohio Valley: A Historical Geography of Travel, 1740–1860* (New York, 1977). For useful firsthand accounts, see Kate Milner Rabb, ed., *A Tour through Indiana in 1840: The Diary of John Parsons of Petersburg, Virginia* (New York, 1920); *Indiana as Seen by Early Travellers*, ed. Harlow Lindley (Indianapolis, 1916); Ulysses P. Hedrick, *Land of the Crooked Tree*

(New York, 1948); and William Nowlin, *The Bark Covered House; or, Back in the Woods Again,* ed. Milo M. Quaife (Chicago, 1937).

4. See William S. Osborne, *Caroline M. Kirkland* (New York, 1972), and Paxton Hibben, *Henry Ward Beecher* (New York, 1927). These works stress literary, social, and religious, not environmental, views. Kirkland's most relevant work is *A New Home—Who'll Follow? or, Glimpses of Western Life* (New York, 1839); Beecher's views are found in scattered sources.

5. See James K. Folsom, *Timothy Flint* (New York, 1965); Stilgoe, *Common Landscape,* pp. 192–93. Other observers also noted that girdling was used only in certain areas, rather than being universal on the frontier as has often been implied. When Europeans decried the American practice of girdling trees and then leaving them standing, they usually reflected not so much concern for the waste of wood that was involved as a reaction against the disorderliness and sloth that they thought they saw revealed in the practice. Coming from a labor-abundant region, they almost always overlooked the labor saving that was involved and the need for it. See also J. S. Otto and N. E. Anderson, "Slash and Burn Cultivation in the Highlands South: A Problem of Comparative Agricultural History," *Comparative Studies in Society and History* 24 (1982): 131–47.

6. Jane L. Mesick, *The English Traveller in America, 1785–1835* (New York, 1922); Max Berger, *the British Traveller in America, 1836–1860* (New York, 1943). For a discussion of what Europeans "saw" in America, particularly in the transmississippi West at a later time, see Ray Allen Billington, *Land of Savagery, Land of Promise: The European Image of the American Frontier* (New York, 1981).

7. Recent accounts decrying such historical approaches to the environment are numerous. For example, see Wilbur R. Jacobs, "Frontiersmen, Fur Traders, and Other Varmints: An Ecological Appraisal of the Frontier in American History," *American Historical Association Newsletter* 8 (November 1970): 5–11.

8. A thorough study of efforts at forest conservation in the early national period is needed; however, see Gilbert Chinard, "The American Philosophical Society and the Early History of Forestry in America," *Proceedings of the American Philosophical Society* 89 (1945): 444–88.

9. Even in remote frontier communities there were residents with the education and sensitivity to appreciate what was being lost as well as gained through rapid development. For correctives to the standard overemphasis on the ignorant, exploitive frontiersman's influence, see Pomeroy, "Toward a Reorientation of Western History," pp. 579–600; Louis B. Wright, *Culture on the Moving Frontier* (1955; New York, 1961); Ray Allen Billington, *America's Frontier Culture: Three Essays* (College Station, Tex., 1977), pp. 51–73. See also Moore, *Frontier Mind,* pp. 139–58; Potter, *People of Plenty,* pp. 128–41; and Lynn White, Jr., "The Historical Roots of Our Ecological Crisis," *Science* 155 (1967): 1203–7. White's work both oversimplifies and overstates; it should be used with caution.

10. The idea of waves of settlement was implicit in the work of Frederick Jackson Turner and explicitly developed in that of his best-known successor in the field of western history, Ray Allen Billington. For an overview of Turner and his aftermath, see Billington, *The American Frontier Thesis: Attack and Defense* (Washington, D.C., 1971).

11. Robertson, *American Myth, American Reality,* pp. 135–46; Potter, *People of Plenty,* pp. 91–110; George W. Pierson, "The M-Factor in American History," *American Quarterly* 14 (1962): 275–89.

12. On Cooper, see Nelson Van Valen, "James Fennimore Cooper and the Conservation Schism," *New York History* 62 (1981): 289–306. For broader summaries of the romantic influence, see Arthur A. Ekirch, Jr., *Man and Nature in America* (New York, 1963), pp. 22–34, and Huth, *Nature and the American,* pp. 30–53.

13. Roy Harvey Pearce, *The Savages of America: A Study of the Indian and the Idea of Civilization,* revised ed. (Baltimore, 1965), esp. pp. 58–75, 199–212, and Francis Paul Prucha, "American Indian Policy in the 1840's: Visions of Reform," in *The Frontier Challenge,* ed. John G. Clark (Lawrence, Kans., 1971), pp. 81–110, are useful; the literature on shifting attitudes toward the Indians and on their environmental values is extensive, growing, and still often highly romantic.

14. Chinard, "The American Philosophical Society," pp. 467–70; Rodney H. True, "François André Michaux, the Botanist and Explorer," *Proceedings of the American Philosophical Society* 78 (1938): 313–27.

15. Donald Culcross Peattie, *Green Laurels: The Lives and Achievements of the Great Naturalists* (New York, 1936), pp. 248–49 and passim; Palmer C. Ricketts, *Amos Eaton, Author, Teacher, Investigator . . .*(Troy, N.Y., 1933); Ethel M. McCallister, *Amos Eaton: Scientist and Educator* (Philadelphia, 1941), esp. pp. 212–62. See also William Martin Smallwood, *Natural History and the American Mind* (New York, 1941). Like Eaton, Virginia planters Edmund Ruffin and John Craven also tried to bridge the gap between science and land use, but they focused more exclusively on agricultural practices than did Eaton.

16. On the evolution of stoves and wood as fuel, see Chinard, "American Philosophical Society," pp. 451–52; Arthur H. Cole, "The Mystery of Fuel Wood Marketing in the United States," *Business History Review* 44 (1970): 339–59; William A. Hoglund, "Forest Conservation and Stove Inventors—1789–1850," *Forest History* 5 (Winter 1962): 2–8; and R. V. Reynolds and Albert H. Pierson, *Fuel Wood Used in the United States, 1630–1930,* U.S. Department of Agriculture, Circular no. 641 (Washington, D.C., 1942). Ample coal deposits had long been known, but they were little developed. As Robert Beverley had explained in 1705: "as for Coals, it is not likely they should ever be used there in any thing, but Forges and great Towns, if ever they happen to have any. . . . They have very good Pit-Coal . . . but no Man has yet thought it worth his while to make use of them, having Wood in Plenty, and lying more convenient for him."

17. Roger Burlingame, *Machines That Built America* (New York, 1953), pp. 72–82; Henry J. Kauffman, *American Axes: A Survey of Their Development and Their Makers* (Brattleboro, Vt., 1972), pp. 23–51.

18. Defebaugh, *Lumber Industry,* 2:475–501; Louis C. Hunter, *A History of Industrial Power in the United States, 1780–1930,* vol. 1, *Waterpower in the Century of the Steam Engine* (Charlottesville, Va., 1979), pp. 16–18; William T. Langhorne, Jr., "Mill Based Settlement Patterns in Schoharie County, New York: A Regional Study," *Historical Archaeology* 10 (1976): 73–92.

19. For the development of the saws and sawmill equipment, consult John O. Curtis, "The Introduction of the Circular Saw in the Early Nineteenth Century," *Bulletin of the Association for Preservation Technology* 5, no. 2 (1973): 162–89; Robert Grimshaw, *Saws: The History, Development, Action, Classification and Comparison of Saws of All Kinds* (Philadelphia, 1880); George Hotchkiss, *History of the Lumber and Forest Industry of the Northwest* (Chicago, 1898), pp. 649–60; and Bryan Latham, *Timber: Its Development and Distribution* (London, 1957), pp. 207–23.

20. The story of the application of steam to sawmills may be found in many of the works noted above that trace the development of sawmills. Also useful are M. Powis Bale, *Saw-Mills: Their Arrangement and Management . . . ,* 6th ed., rev. and ed. A. Powis Bale (London, 1924), and Grenville and Dorothy Bathe, *Oliver Evans: A Chronicle of Early American Engineering* (Philadelphia, 1935).

21. David E. Schob, "Woodhawks and Cordwood: Steamboat Fuel on the Ohio and Mississippi Rivers, 1820–1860," *Journal of Forest History* 21 (1977): 124–33.

22. Don H. Birkebile, "Wooden Roads," in Hindle, *Material Culture,* pp. 129–88; Durrenberger, *Turnpikes,* pp. 144–52; Condit, *American Building,* pp. 52–63; Stilgoe, *Common Landscape,* pp. 111–15, 128–32.

23. See Goldenberg, "With Saw and Axe and Auger," pp. 117–28; Robert G. Albion, William A. Baker, and Benjamin W. Labaree, *New England and the Sea* (Middletown, Conn., 1972); B.W. Bathe, "The Clipper's Day," in *The Great Age of Sail,* ed. Joseph Jobé (Lausanne, 1967), pp. 191–228; Howard I. Chapelle, *The Search for Speed under Sail* (New York, 1967); and John G. B. Hutchins, *The American Maritime Industry and Public Policy, 1788–1914* (Cambridge, Mass., 1941).

24. Kenneth Wiggins Porter, *John Jacob Astor, Business Man* (Cambridge, Mass., 1931); Glenn Porter and Harold C. Livesay, *Merchants and Manufacturers: Studies in the Changing Structure of Nineteenth-Century Marketing* (Baltimore, 1971); Foster Rhea Dulles, *The Old China Trade* (Boston, 1930); and Tyler Dennett, *Americans in Eastern Asia: A Critical Study of the Policy of the United States with Reference to China, Japan, and Korea* (1922; New York, 1941, 1963), pp. 1–65, 115–27; all provide additional information on the development of trade.

25. Samuel Eliot Morison, *The Maritime History of Massachusetts* (Boston, 1941); Mary Ellen Chase, *Donald McKay and the Clipper Ships* (Boston, 1959); Fairburn, *Merchant Sail,* vols. 3 and 5, passim.

26. On balloon-frame construction see Carl W. Condit, "Building and Construction," in *Technology and Western Civilization,* ed. Melvin Kranzberg and Carroll W. Pursell, Jr., 2 vols. (New York, 1967), 1:367–74; Walker Field, Jr., "A Re-examination into the Invention of the Balloon Frame," *Journal of the Society of Architectural Historians* 2 (1942): 3–29; Paul E. Sprague, "The Origin of Balloon Framing," *Journal of the Society of Architectural Historians* 40 (1981): 311–19; and Stilgoe, *Common Landscape,* pp. 320–22.

27. See Rosenberg, "America's Rise to Woodworking Leadership," in Hindle, *America's Wooden Age,* pp. 43–44, 48–55, and J. H. Mansfield, "Woodworking Machinery: History of Its Development from 1852–1952," *Mechanical Engineering* 74 (1952): 983–95.

Chapter 5

1. Information of the development of the lumber industry in Maine may be found in Albion, *Forests and Sea Power;* Defebaugh, *Lumber Industry,* vol. 2; Wood, *Lumbering in Maine, 1820–1861;* Philip T. Coolidge, *History of the Maine Woods* (Bangor, Maine, 1963); and David C. Smith, *A History of Lumbering in Maine, 1861–1960* (Orono, Maine, 1972).

2. See also Graeme Wynn, "'Deplorably Dark and Demoralized Lumberers': Rhetoric and Reality in Early Nineteenth-Century New Brunswick," *Journal of Forest History* 24 (1980): 168–87.

3. Stewart Holbrook, *Holy Old Mackinaw: A Natural History of the American Lumberjack* (1938; Sausalito, Calif., 1979), pp. 13–20; David C. Smith, "Bangor—The Shipping and Lumber Trade," in James Vickery, ed., *A History of Bangor* (Bangor, Maine, 1969), pp. 23–37; Wood, *Lumbering in Maine, 1820–1861,* pp. 36, 74–82. See also Ray Allen Billington, "The Origin of the Land Speculator as a Frontier Type," *Agricultural History* 19 (1945): 204–12.

4. Henry D. Thoreau, *The Maine Woods,* ed. Joseph J. Moldenhauer (Princeton, N.J., 1972), pp. 5, 82–83; Nash, *Wilderness and the American Mind,* pp. 90–95.

5. A climax forest is that self-perpetuating, nearly permanent type of forest that develops in an area after various transient plant communities have come and gone, each in its turn, in the process of reforesting a burned or cleared area. For discussions of the development of this ecological concept see Donald Worster, *Nature's Economy: The Roots of Ecology* (1977; Garden City, N.Y., 1979), pp. 205–20, 235–52, and Ronald C. Tobey, *Saving the Prairies: The Life Cycle of the Founding School of American Plant Ecology, 1895–1955* (Berkeley, Calif., 1982).

6. Thomas Le Duc, "The Maine Frontier and the Northeastern Boundary Controversy," *American Historical Review* 53 (1947): 30–41. On the ton timber trade, see Donald McKay, "The Canadian Logging Frontier," *Journal of Forest History* 23 (1979): 4–17; Graeme Wynn, *Timber Colony: A Historical Geography of Early Nineteenth Century New Brunswick* (Toronto, 1981), pp. 26–86; and Lower, *Great Britain's Woodyard,* pp. 159–70 and passim.

7. Wood, *Lumbering in Maine, 1820–1861,* pp. 86–95; Robert E. Pike, *Tall Trees, Tough Men* (New York, 1967), pp. 64–101, 116–28. There are useful eyewitness descriptions in John S. Springer, *Forest Life and Forest Trees* (1851; Somersworth, N.H., 1971); Isaac Stephenson, *Recollections of a Long Life, 1829–1915* (Chicago, 1915); Theodore Winthrop, *Life in the Open Air and Other Papers* (New York, 1876); and Thoreau, *Maine Woods.*

8. Wood, *Lumbering in Maine, 1820–1861,* pp. 83–95; Pike, *Tall Trees,* pp. 73–147; Stewart Holbrook, *Yankee Loggers: A Recollection of Woodsmen, Cooks, and River Drivers* (New York, 1961), pp. 42–62.

9. Descriptions of log drives may be found in Springer, *Forest Life,* pp. 129, 155–65; Defebaugh, *Lumber Industry,* 2:44–47; Holbrook, *Holy Old Mackinaw,* pp. 51–68; Pike, *Tall Trees,* pp. 192–200, 211–26; and Wood, *Lumbering in Maine, 1820–1861,* pp. 96–127.

10. Nelson Courtland Brown, *Logging: The Principles and Methods of Harvesting Timber*

in the United States and Canada (New York, 1934), pp. 356–63; Wood, *Lumbering in Maine, 1820–1861,* pp. 116–19; and Smith, *Lumbering in Maine, 1861–1960,* pp. 63–64.

11. Wood, *Lumbering in Maine, 1820–1861,* pp. 97–98; Smith, *Lumbering in Maine, 1861–1960,* pp. 65–66.

12. A discussion of log brands may be found in Wood, *Lumbering in Maine, 1820–1861,* pp. 65–66.

13. Springer, *Forest Life,* pp. 162–64. See also Holbrook, *Holy Old Mackinaw,* pp. 53–56.

14. On booms, see Defebaugh, *Lumber Industry,* 2: 54–55; Alfred G. Hempstead, *The Penobscot Boom and the Development of the West Branch of the Penobscot River for Log Driving* (Orono, Maine, 1931); Wood, *Lumbering in Maine, 1820–1861,* pp. 128–29; and *Argyle Boom,* ed. and largely written by Edward D. Ives, *Northeast Forklore,* vol. 17 (Orono, Maine, 1977).

15. Additional verses to this song may be found in Smith, *Lumbering in Maine, 1861–1960,* p. 29. See also Edward D. Ives, *Joe Scott: The Woodsman Songmaker* (Urbana, Ill., 1978), and Fannie H. Eckstorm and Mary Winslow Smyth, *Minstrelsy of Maine: Folk Songs and Ballads of the Woods and Coast* (Boston, 1927).

16. Defebaugh, *Lumber Industry,* 2:72–73, and Wood, *Lumbering in Maine, 1820–1861,* pp. 140–41. For further discussions of attempts at ocean rafting, see D. M. Williams, "Bulk Carriers and Timber Imports," *Mariner's Mirror* 54 (1968): 373–83, and Kramer Adams, "Blue Water Rafting: The Evolution of Ocean Going Log Rafts," *Forest History* 15 (July 1971): 16–27.

17. Hempstead, *Penobscot Boom,* pp. 49–51; Wood, *Lumbering in Maine, 1820–1861,* p. 145. As elsewhere, mixed rafts of hardwood and pine had been built in Maine. Rafts containing valuable birch came to be common on the St. John.

18. Wood, *Lumbering in Maine, 1820–1861,* p. 221; William H. Rowe, *The Maritime History of Maine: Three Centuries of Shipbuilding and Seafaring* (New York, 1948), pp. 168–70; Brian A. Smalley, "Some Aspects of the Maine to San Francisco Trade, 1849–1852," *Journal of the West* 6 (1967): 593–603.

19. Defebaugh, *Lumber Industry,* 2:55; Smith, *Lumbering in Maine, 1861–1960,* pp. 6–7. Both works discuss the period after 1860 in detail.

Chapter 6

1. Defebaugh, *Lumber Industry,* 2:230, 322–454; Fox, *History of the Lumber Industry of New York,* pp. 23–24. See also Evelyn M. Dinsdale, "Spatial Patterns of Technological Change: The Lumber Industry of Northern New York," *Economic Geography* 42 (1965): 252–75.

2. Defebaugh, *Lumber Industry,* 2:387–407; Robert W. Harrison, *History of the Commercial Waterways and Ports of the United States,* vol. 1, *From Settlement to Completion of the Erie Canal* (Washington, D.C., 1979); Frank Graham, Jr., *Adirondack Park: A Political History* (New York, 1978), pp. 3–11.

3. Hunter, *Waterpower*, pp. 15–21 and passim; White, *Beekmantown*, pp. 29–70, 355–62.

4. Fox, *Lumber Industry*, pp. 25–40; Defebaugh, *Lumber Industry*, 2:315–21; Dunbar, *A History of Travel in America*, pp. 282–84, 295–96, 308.

5. The development of lumbering in Pennsylvania is traced in Defebaugh, *Lumber Industry*, 2:530–655.

6. Ibid., 2:562–74, 591–607; Thomas R. Cox, "Transition in the Woods: Log Drivers, Raftsmen, and the Emergence of Modern Lumbering in Pennsylvania," *Pennsylvania Magazine of History and Biography* 104 (1980): 345–64.

7. Nollie W. Hickman, *Mississippi Harvest: Lumbering in the Longleaf Pine Belt, 1840–1915* (University, Miss., 1962); Thomas C. Croker, Jr., "The Longleaf Pine Story," *Journal of Forest History* 23 (1979): 32–43.

8. See also John F. H. Claiborne, "A Trip through the Piney Woods [1841]," *Mississippi Historical Society Publications* 9 (1907): 487–538; Frank L. Owsley, "The Pattern of Migration and Settlement on the Southern Frontier," *Journal of Southern History* 11 (1945): 147–76; and Thomas D. Clark, "The Lasting Heritage: Land and Trees," in *The Cultural Legacy of the Gulf Coast, 1870–1940*, ed. Lucius F. Ellsworth and Linda V. Ellsworth (Pensacola, Fla., 1976), pp. 17–22.

9. Hickman, *Mississippi Harvest*, pp. 29–56.

10. James M. McReynolds, "Family Life in the Borderland Community: Nacogdoches, Texas, 1779–1861" (Ph.D. diss., Texas Tech University, 1978), pp. 3–4, 13–14, 41–86, 111, and passim; Robert S. Maxwell and Robert D. Baker, *Sawdust Empire: The Texas Lumber Industry, 1830–1940* (College Station, Tex. 1983).

11. See Percival Perry, "The Naval-Stores Industry in the Old South, 1790–1860," *Journal of Southern History* 34 (1968): 509–26.

12. John Hebron Moore, *Andrew Brown and Cypress Lumbering in the Old Southwest* (Baton Rouge, La., 1967); Rachel Edna Norgress, "The History of the Cypress Lumber Industry in Louisiana," *Louisiana Historical Quarterly* 30 (1947): 979–1059. On the difficulty in logging this tree, see Ervin Mancel, "Pullboat Logging," *Journal of Forest History* 24 (1980): 135–41.

13. Howard I. Chapelle, *The History of the American Sailing Navy: The Ships and Their Development* (New York, 1949); Emilie B. Knipe and Alden A. Knipe, *Story of Old Ironsides: The Cradle of the United States Navy* (New York, 1928); Virginia Steele Wood, *Live Oaking: Southern Timber for Tall Ships* (Boston, 1981).

14. William R. Adams, "Florida Live Oak Farm of John Quincy Adams," *Florida Historical Quarterly* 51 (1972): 129–42.

15. Cameron, *Development of Governmental Forest Control*, pp. 28–67; William F. Keller, "Henry Marie Brackenridge: First United States Forester," *Forest History* 15 (January 1972): 12–23.

16. Moore, *Andrew Brown*, pp. 8–9, 22–59, 98–111.

17. On the development of the lumber industry in the South, see John A. Eisterhold, "Lumber and Trade in the Lower Missisippi Valley and New Orleans, 1800–1860,"

Louisiana History 13 (1972): 71–91; Eisterhold, "Savannah: Lumber Center of the South Atlantic," *Georgia Historical Quarterly* 57 (1973): 526–43; and Eisterhold, "Lumber and Trade in Pensacola and West Florida: 1800–1860," *Florida Historical Quarterly* 51 (1973): 267–80. See also Hunter, *Waterpower*, esp. pp. 132–33.

18. Nollie W. Hickman, "Logging and Rafting Timber in South Mississippi, 1840–1910," *Journal of Mississippi History* 19 (1957): 154–72.

19. The South's rail network was still in an early stage of development, however. See George Rogers Taylor, *The Transportation Revolution, 1815–1860* (New York, 1951), esp. pp. 84–86.

20. For a discussion of the multifaceted consequences of the development of logging in the southern forests, see Clark, "The Impact of the Timber Industry on the South," pp. 141–64, and Clark, "Lasting Heritage," pp. 17–35.

21. David C. Smith, "The Logging Frontier," *Journal of Forest History* 18 (1974): 96–106; Wood, *Lumbering in Maine, 1820–1861*, pp. 226–35.

22. See George B. Engberg, "Lumber and Labor in the Lake States," *Minnesota History* 36 (1959): 153–66; Engberg, "Who Were the Lumberjacks?" *Michigan History* 32 (1948): 238–46; and Fred W. Kohlmeyer, "Northern Pine Lumbermen: A Study in Origins and Migrations," *Journal of Economic History* 16 (1956): 529–38.

23. Michael Williams, "Products of the Forest: Mapping the Census of 1840," *Journal of Forest History* 24 (1980): 4–23; Williams, "Clearing the United States Forests: Pivotal Years, 1810–1860," *Journal of Historical Geography* 8 (1982), esp. pp. 23–25; Williams, "Ohio: Microcosm of Agricultural Clearing in the Midwest," in *Global Deforestation and the Nineteenth-Century World Economy*, ed. Richard P. Tucker and J. F. Richards (Durham, N.C., 1983), pp. 3–13; Donald A. Hutslar, "Ohio Waterpowered Sawmills," *Ohio History* 55 (1975): 5–56. For a contemporary assessment, see Rabb, *Tour through Indiana in 1840*, pp. 328–40.

24. On the difficulties of bringing prairie land into cultivation see David E. Schob, *Hired Hands and Plowboys* (Urbana, Ill., 1975), pp. 21–42. See also Richard N. Current, *The History of Wisconsin*, vol. 2, *The Civil War Era, 1848–1873* (Madison, Wis., 1976), pp. 90–95; Allan G. Bogue, *From Prairie to Cornbelt: Farming on the Illinois and Iowa Prairies in the Nineteenth Century* (Chicago, 1963), pp. 123–29; and Margaret Beattie Bogue, *Patterns from the Sod: Land Use and Tenure in Grand Prairie, 1850–1900* (Springfield, Ill., 1959), pp. 115–37.

25. Cf. Ralph W. Hidy, Frank Ernest Hill, and Allan Nevins, *Timber and Men: The Weyerhaeuser Story* (New York, 1963); Fred W. Kohlmeyer, *Timber Roots: The Laird, Norton Story, 1855–1905* (Winona, Wis., 1972); and Charles E. Twining, *Downriver: Orrin H. Ingram and the Empire Lumber Company* (Madison, Wis., 1975).

26. The rise of lumbering in the Lake States is examined in Robert F. Fries, *Empire in Pine: The Story of Lumbering in Wisconsin, 1830–1900* (Madison, Wis., 1951); Barbara E. Benson, "Logs and Lumber: The Development of the Lumber Industry of Michigan's Lower Peninsula, 1837–1870" (Ph.D. diss., Indiana University, 1976); and Agnes M. Larson, *History of the White Pine Industry in Minnesota* (Minneapolis, Minn., 1949). On

Chicago's role, see George Barclay, "Chicago—the Lumber Hub," *Southern Lumberman* 193 (December 15, 1956): 177 ff.

27. Bernhardt J. Kleven, "Rafting Days on the Mississippi," *Proceedings of the Minnesota Academy of Science* 16 (1948): 53–56; William G. Rector, *Log Transportation in the Lake States Lumber Industry, 1840–1918* (Glendale, Calif., 1953); Walter A. Blair, *A Raft Pilot's Log: A History of the Great Rafting Industry on the Upper Mississippi, 1840–1915* (Glendale, Calif., 1930).

28. In addition to Benson, "Logs and Lumber," see Hotchkiss, *History of the Lumber and Forest Industry*, pp. 36–141.

29. Alice E. Smith, *The History of Wisconsin*, vol. 1, *From Exploration to Statehood* (Madison, Wis., 1973), p. 528 and passim; Margaret Walsh, *The Manufacturing Frontier: Pioneer Industry in Antebellum Wisconsin, 1836–1860* (Madison, Wis., 1972), pp. 98–140.

30. Larson, *White Pine Industry*, pp. 25, 86–104.

31. Ibid., pp. 32–36; Hunter, *Waterpower*, pp. 233–42.

Chapter 7

1. The literature is voluminous, the interpretations are varied. See Taylor, *Transportation Revolution;* Paul H. Cootner, "The Role of Railroads in United States Economic Growth," *Journal of Economic History* 23 (1963): 477–521; and Albert Fishlow, *American Railroads and the Transformation of the Antebellum Economy* (Cambridge, Mass., 1965).

2. For the econometric view, see Robert W. Fogel, "A Quantitative Approach to the Study of Railroads in American Economic Growth: A Report of Some Preliminary Findings," *Journal of Economic History* 22 (1962): 153–97, and Fogel, *Railroads and American Economic Growth: Essays in Econometric History* (Baltimore, 1960). Fogel's interpretations have been sharply criticized. See Derek H. Aldcroft, "Railways and Economic Growth: A Review Article," *Journal of Transport History*, n.s. 1 (1972): 238–49.

3. Sherry Hessler Olson, *Depletion Myth: A History of Railroad Use of Timber* (Cambridge, Mass., 1971); Thomas R. Cox, *Mills and Markets: A History of the Pacific Coast Lumber Industry to 1900* (Seattle, 1974), pp. 199–207.

4. Walter Casler, Benjamin F. G. Kline, Jr., and Thomas T. Taber III, *The Logging Railroad Era of Lumbering in Pennsylvania: A History of the Lumber, Chemical Wood and Tanning Companies Which Used Railroads in Pennsylvania*, 14 vols. (Williamsport, Pa., 1970–78), 8:804–11, 10:1082–91; Warren Ormsby, "Peeling the Tanoak," *Forest History* 15 (January 1972): 6–10.

5. Richard H. Schallenberg, "Evolution, Adaptation, and Survival: The Very Slow Death of the American Charcoal Iron Industry," *Annals of Science* 32 (1975): 341–58; Hutchins, *American Maritime Industries and Public Policy*, pp. 456–62. For a further discussion, see Peter Temin, *Iron and Steel in Nineteenth Century America: An Economic Inquiry* (Cambridge, Mass., 1964), pp. 51–85.

6. Basil Lubbock, *The Down Easters: American Deep-Water Sailing Ships, 1869–1929* (Boston, 1929); Lubbock, *Last of the Windjammers*, 2 vols. (Glasgow, 1927–29); Hutchins,

American Maritime Industries, pp. 257–324. See also Charles Carroll, "Wooden Ships and American Forests," *Journal of Forest History* 25 (1981): 213–15.

7. Arthur M. Johnson and Barry E. Supple, *Boston Capitalists and Western Railroads* (Cambridge, Mass., 1967); Porter and Livesay, *Merchants and Manufacturers.*

8. Edwin T. Coman, Jr., and Helen M. Gibbs, *Time, Tide and Timber: A Century of Pope & Talbot* (Stanford, Calif., 1949), pp. 3–89; Cox, *Mills and Markets,* pp. 46–70.

9. Bogue, *From Prairie to Cornbelt,* pp. 1–85; Everett Dick, *The Sod-House Frontier, 1854–1900: A Social History of the Northern Plains from the Creation of Kansas and Nebraska to the Admission of the Dakotas* (1937; Lincoln, Nebr., 1979); Edward E. Dale, "Wood and Water: Twin Problems of the Prairies," *Nebraska History* 29 (1948): 87–104; Terry Jordan, "Between Forest and Prairie," *Agricultural History* 38 (1964): 205–16; C. Howard Richardson, "The Nebraska Prairies: Dilemma to Early Territorial Farmers," *Nebraska History* 50 (1969): 359–72.

10. Barclay, "Chicago—the Lumber Hub," 177 ff.; Constance McLaughlin Green, *American Cities in the Growth of the Nation* (1957; New York, 1965), esp. pp. 100–115.

11. Hidy, Hill, and Nevins, *Timber and Men,* pp. 1–102; Twining, *Downriver,* pp. 35–186; Kohlmeyer, *Timber Roots,* pp. 21–116. Other accounts of such operations exist.

12. Defebaugh, *Lumber Industry,* 1:489–505; Williams, "Clearing the United States Forests," pp. 21–25. See also Walter Havighurst, *The Heartland: Ohio, Indiana, Illinois,* rev. ed. (New York, 1974), pp. 115–25.

13. Defebaugh, *Lumber Industry,* 2:408–65; Robert G. Albion, *The Rise of New York Port, 1815–1860* (1939; New York, 1970), pp. 76–94 and passim.

14. Defebaugh, *Lumber Industry,* 2:165–77; William G. Gove, "Burlington, the Former Lumber Capital," *Northern Logger and Timber Processor* 19 (May 1971): 18 ff. David Lowenthal notes in *George Perkins Marsh, Versatile Vermonter* (New York, 1958), pp. 248–53, that Marsh's environmental thinking (described below in chap. 8) was shaped in part by his experiences in the lumber business in Burlington during its heyday as a center for the industry.

15. Cox, "Transition in the Woods," pp. 345–64; Defebaugh, *Lumber Industry,* 2:591–607.

16. William G. Gove, "Glens Falls—the Queen City Built by the Lumber Industry," *Northern Logger and Timber Processor* 24 (April 1976): 8 ff.; Defebaugh, *Lumber Industry,* 2:315–17; Fox, *History of the Lumber Industry in New York,* pp. 35–51.

17. Rector, *Log Transportation in the Lake States Lumber Industry,* pp. 115–46; Frederick Merk, *Economic History of Wisconsin during the Civil War Decade* (1916; Madison, Wis., 1971), pp. 69–70.

18. Smith, *Lumbering in Maine, 1861–1960,* pp. 6–7, 145–55; Defebaugh, *Lumber Industry,* 2:55–59.

19. Eisterhold, "Lumber and Trade in Pensacola and West Florida," 267–80; Eisterhold, "Charleston: Lumber and Trade in a Declining Southern Port," *South Carolina Historical Magazine* 74 (1973): 61–73; Eisterhold, "Lumber and Trade in the Lower Mississippi Valley and New Orleans," pp. 71–91; Hickman, *Mississippi Harvest,* passim.

20. Porter and Livesay, *Merchants and Manufacturers*, esp. pp. 116–30; Wilson M. Compton, *The Organization of the Lumber Industry, with Special Reference to the Influences Determining the Prices of Lumber in the United States* (Chicago, 1916); Merk, *Economic History of Wisconsin*, pp. 72–75; Wood, *Lumbering in Maine, 1820–1861*, pp. 29, 42–47.

21. Lonn Taylor and David B. Warren, *Texas Furniture: The Cabinetmakers and Their Work, 1840–1880* (Austin, Tex., 1975), pp. 3–37.

22. Carl Abbott, "Plank Roads and Wood-Block Pavements," *Journal of Forest History* 25 (1981): 216–18; Current, *History of Wisconsin*, vol. 2, *Civil War Era*, pp. 24–29; Don H. Birkebile, "Wooden Roads," in Hindle, *Material Culture*, pp. 129–58; Oscar Osburn Winther, "The Roads and Transportation of Territorial Oregon," *Oregon Historical Quarterly* 41 (1940): 40–42.

23. Thomas R. Cox, "The Passage to India Revisited: Asian Trade and the Development of the Far West, 1850–1900," in *Reflections of Western Historians*, ed. John A. Carroll (Tucson, Ariz., 1969), pp. 85–103; Cox, *Mills and Markets*, pp. 71–100; Coman and Gibbs, *Time, Tide and Timber*, pp. 62–89. Cf. Ivan M. Elchibegoff, *United States International Timber Trade in the Pacific Area* (Stanford, Calif., 1949).

24. Current, *History of Wisconsin*, vol. 2, *Civil War Era*, pp. 237–59; Twining, *Downriver*, pp. 35–68; Moore, *Andrew Brown and Cypress Lumbering*, pp. 98–111, 149–52.

25. An extensive literature exists on the economic impact of the Civil War. Nearly every work on the lumber industry of the period discusses it. On the larger question, see Thomas C. Cochran, "Did the Civil War Retard Industrialization?" *Mississippi Valley Historical Review* 48 (1961): 197–210, and Ralph Andreano, ed., *The Economic Impact of the American Civil War* (Cambridge, Mass., 1962).

26. Jerrell H. Shofner, "Negro Laborers and the Forest Industries of Reconstruction Florida," *Journal of Forest History* 19 (1975): 180–91; Clark, "Lasting Heritage," pp. 17–35.

27. Cox, *Mills and Markets*, pp. 227–44; Holbrook, *Holy Old Mackinaw*, pp. 97–102; Twining, *Downriver*, pp. 22–24; James Willard Hurst, *Law and Economic Growth: The Legal History of the Lumber Industry in Wisconsin, 1836–1915* (Cambridge, Mass., 1964), pp. 454–55 and passim.

28. Hidy, Hill, and Nevins, *Timber and Men*, pp. 77–102 and passim; Twining, *Downriver*, pp. 187–235; Anita Shafer Goodstein, *Biography of a Businessman: Henry W. Sage, 1814–1897* (Ithaca, N.Y., 1962), pp. 66–77, 93–111. The industry has continued to be more decentralized than most others and marked by a complex web of controlling interests to the present day.

29. Engberg, "Who Were the Lumberjacks?" pp. 238–46; Kohlmeyer, "Northern Pine Lumbermen," pp. 529–38; Defebaugh, *Lumber Industry*, 2:445–65; Rector, *Log Transportation*, pp. 147–70, 215–48; Stewart H. Holbrook, *Yankee Exodus: An Account of the Migration from New England* (New York, 1950), pp. 77–96, 108–30, 166–86.

30. For a discussion of such operations, see Thomas R. Cox, "William Kyle and the Pacific Lumber Trade: A Study in Marginality," *Journal of Forest History* 19 (1975): 4–14. See also Edmond S. Meany, Jr., "A History of the Lumber Industry in the Pacific Northwest to 1917" (Ph.D. diss., Harvard University, 1935).

Chapter 8

1. Huth, *Nature and the American*, pp. 30–53, 71–86; Ekirch, *Man and Nature in America*, pp. 22–34, 57–69; Barbara Novak, *Nature and Culture: American Landscape Painting, 1825–1875* (New York, 1980), esp. pp. 3–17; Roland Van Zandt, "The Catskills and the Rise of American Landscape Painting," *New-York Historical Society Quarterly* 49 (1965): 257–81; Perry Miller, "The Romantic Dilemma in American Nationalism and the Concept of Nature," *Harvard Theological Review* 48 (1955): 239–53.

2. Edward S. Hyams, *Capability Brown and Humphrey Repton* (New York, 1971); Laura Wood Roper, *FLO: A Biography of Frederick Law Olmsted* (Baltimore, 1973); Elizabeth Stevenson, *Park-Maker: A Life of Frederick Law Olmsted* (New York, 1977); Leo Marx, *The Machine in the Garden: Technology and the Pastoral Ideal* (New York, 1964), pp. 141–44.

3. Nash, *Wilderness and the American Mind*, pp. 90–95. The work on Thoreau is voluminous. Good introductions are provided in Douglas H. Strong, *The Conservationists* (Menlo Park, Calif., 1971), pp. 13–20; Worster, *Nature's Economy*, pp. 57–111; and Kurt Kehr, "Walden Three: Ecological Changes in the Landscape of Henry David Thoreau," *Journal of Forest History* 27 (1983): 28–33.

4. Huth, *Nature and the American*, pp. 54–70, 105–28; John F. Reiger, *American Sportsmen and the Origins of Conservation* (New York, 1975), pp. 25–49; Earl Pomeroy, *In Search of the Golden West: The Tourist in Western America* (New York, 1957), pp. 31–72.

5. For further discussion see Alfred Runte, *National Parks: The American Experience* (Lincoln, Nebr., 1979), pp. 33–47, and Huth, *Nature and the American*, pp. 148–64.

6. Roland Van Zandt, *The Catskill Mountain House* (New Brunswick, N.J., 1966); Pomeroy, *In Search of the Golden West*, pp. 16–30.

7. Alfred Runte, "Beyond the Spectacular: The Niagara Falls Preservation Campaign," *New-York Historical Society Quarterly* 57 (1973): 30–50; Huth, *Nature and the American*, pp. 171–73; Pomeroy, *In Search of the Golden West*, pp. 48–57. For further ramifications, see Novak, *Nature and Culture*, pp. 157–65.

8. For discussions, see Lee Benson, *The Concept of Jacksonian Democracy: New York as a Test Case* (Princeton, N.J., 1961); Marx, *The Machine in the Garden*, pp. 88–144; Marvin Meyers, *The Jacksonian Persuasion: Politics and Belief* (1957; New York, 1960), pp. 253–75; Edward Pessen, *Jacksonian America: Society, Personality, and Politics* (Homewood, Ill., 1969), pp. 93–96 and passim; and Robert A. Lively, "The American System: A Review Article," *Business History Review* 29 (1959): 81–96.

9. Paul Wallace Gates, "The Homestead Law in an Incongruous Land System," *American Historical Review* 41 (1936): 652–81; Smith, *Virgin Land*, pp. 190–200; Roy M. Robbins, *Our Landed Heritage: The Public Domain, 1776–1970*, 2d ed. rev. (Lincoln, Nebr., 1976), pp. 72–116.

10. Defebaugh, *Lumber Industry*, 2:342–94; Aaron M. Sakolski, *Land Tenure and Land Taxation in America* (New York, 1957); Wilson B. Sayers, "The Changing Land Ownership Patterns in the United States," *Forest History* 9 (July 1965): 2–9; Gates with Swenson, *History of Public Land Law Development*, pp. 463–94 and passim.

11. George M. Blackburn and Sherman L. Ricards, "The Timber Industry in Manistee County, Michigan: A Case History in Local Control," *Journal of Forest History* 18 (1974): 14–21.

12. There are numerous descriptions of timber trespass and fraud, most more impressionistic than analytic. See Lillard, *Great Forest,* pp. 156–208; Lucile M. Kane, "Federal Protection of Public Timber in the Upper Great Lakes States," *Agricultural History* 23 (1949): 135–39; Everett Dick, *The Lure of the Land: A Social History of the Public Lands from the Articles of Confederation to the New Deal* (Lincoln, Nebr., 1970), pp. 179–98; and Ise, *United States Forest Policy,* pp. 62–118. See also Eugene Hargrove, "Anglo-American Land Use Attitudes," *Environmental Ethics* 2 (1980): 121–48.

13. Kohlmeyer, "Northern Pine Lumbermen," pp. 529–38. See also Blackburn and Ricards, "Manistee County," pp. 16–17; D. C. Everest, "A Reappraisal of the Lumber Barons," *Wisconsin Magazine of History* 36 (1952): 17–22; and Charles E. Twining, "Plunder and Progress: The Lumbering Industry in Perspective," *Wisconsin Magazine of History* 47 (1963): 116–24.

14. Paul F. Boller, Jr., "The New Science and American Thought," in *The Gilded Age,* ed. H. Wayne Morgan, rev. ed. (Syracuse, N.Y., 1970), pp. 239–57; Russel Blaine Nye, *The Cultural Life of the New Nation, 1776–1830* (New York, 1960), pp. 54–96; Nye, *Society and Culture in America, 1830–1860* (New York, 1974), pp. 236–82; Arthur M. Schlesinger, Jr., "An American Historian Looks at Science and Technology," *Isis* 36 (1946): 162–66; John C. Greene, "Science and the Public in the Age of Jefferson," *Isis* 49 (1958): 13–25.

15. Gertrude Himmelfarb, *Darwin and the Darwinian Revolution* (1959; New York, 1968); Worster, *Nature's Economy,* pp. 113–98. See also Keir B. Sterling, *Last of the Naturalists: The Career of C. Hart Merriam* (New York, 1974), pp. 257–313.

16. Lowenthal, *George Perkins Marsh;* Robert F. Leggett, "A Prophet of Conservation," *Dalhousie Review* 45 (1965): 34–42; Strong, *Conservationists,* pp. 29–37; Stewart L. Udall, *The Quiet Crisis* (New York, 1963), pp. 81–94.

17. Howard W. Lull, "Forest Influences: Growth of a Concept," *Journal of Forestry* 47 (1949): 700–705; Charles R. Kutzleb, "American Myth: Can Forests Bring Rain to the Plains?" *Forest History* 15 (October 1971): 14–21; David M. Emmons, "Theories of Increased Rainfall and the Timber Culture Act of 1873," *Forest History* 15 (October 1971): 6–14; James C. Olson, "Arbor Day—a Pioneer Expression of Concern for the Environment," *Nebraska History* 53 (1972): 1–13; Henry Clepper, "The Man Who Gave Us Arbor Day," *American Forests* 88 (1982): 50–53, 60–62.

18. Douglas H. Strong, "The Sierra Forest Reserve: The Movement to Preserve the San Joaquin Valley Watershed," *California Historical Society Quarterly* 46 (1967): 3–17; Ronald F. Lockmann, "Forests and Watershed in the Environmental Philosophy of Theodore P. Lukens," *Journal of Forest History* 23 (1979): 82–91; C. Raymond Clar, *California Government and Forestry from Spanish Days until the Creation of the Department of Natural Resources in 1927* (Sacramento, Calif., 1959), pp. 97–99 and passim. An extended study of Kinney's activities is needed.

19. Harold T. Pinkett, "Forestry Comes to America," *Agricultural History* 54 (1980):

4–10; Pinkett, *Gifford Pinchot, Private and Public Forester* (Urbana, Ill., 1970); Rogers, *Bernhard Eduard Fernow;* Carl Alwin Schenck, *The Birth of Forestry in America: Biltmore Forest School, 1898–1913,* ed. Ovid Butler (Santa Cruz, Calif., 1974); M. Nelson Mc-Greary, *Gifford Pinchot, Forester-Politician* (Princeton, N.J., 1960).

20. Gordon B. Dodds, "The Stream-Flow Controversy: A Conservation Turning Point," *Journal of American History* 56 (1969): 49–69; Samuel P. Hays, *Conservation and the Gospel of Efficiency: The Progressive Conservation Movement, 1890–1920* (1959; New York, 1969), pp. 199–218.

21. For analyses, see Peter J. Schmitt, *Back to Nature: The Arcadian Myth in Urban America* (New York, 1969), and Russel Blaine Nye, *This Almost Chosen People: Essays in the History of American Ideas* (East Lansing, Mich., 1966), pp. 282–89. See also H. Wayne Morgan, "America's First Environmental Challenge, 1865–1920," in *Essays on the Gilded Age,* ed. Margaret Francine Morris (Austin, Tex., 1973), pp. 87–108; Eugene Hargrove, "The Historical Foundations of American Enviromental Attitudes," *Environmental Ethics* 1 (1979): 209–40.

22. R. Newell Searle, "Minnesota National Forest: The Politics of Compromise, 1898–1908," *Minnesota History* 42 (1971): 243–57.

Chapter 9

1. Smith, *Lumbering in Maine, 1861–1960,* pp. 333–36. The attitudes of Hartranft and his contemporaries have been little studied; most writers assign a later date to the beginning of conservation in Pennsylvania. See Henry Clepper, "Forest Conservation in Pennsylvania, the Pioneer Period: From Rothrock to Pinchot," *Pennsylvania History* 48 (1981): 41–50.

2. Lillard, *Great Forest,* pp. 243–49, provides an account sympathetic to the low-tariff champions.

3. Asian Development Bank, *Asian Agricultural Survey* (Seattle and Tokyo, 1969), pp. 445–511, esp. pp. 473–74. See also Peter Sartorius and Hans Henle, *Forestry and Economic Development* (New York, 1968), pp. 197–253, and Earl Pomeroy, "The West and New Nations in Other Continents," in Carroll, *Reflections of Western Historians,* pp. 237–61.

4. Kohlmeyer, "Northern Pine Lumbermen," pp. 529–38, esp. p. 538.

5. Holbrook, *Holy Old Mackinaw,* pp. 74–80 and passim; Holbrook, *Yankee Exodus,* pp. 77–96, 108–30, 166–86, and passim; Smith, "Logging Frontier," pp. 96–106; Wood, *Lumbering in Maine, 1820–1861,* pp. 226–35.

6. Kohlmeyer, "Northern Pine Lumbermen," pp. 534–36; Engberg, "Who Were the Lumberjacks?" pp. 238–40; Casler, Kline, and Taber, *Logging Railroad Era of Lumbering in Pennsylvania,* 5:574–80 and passim.

7. David C. Smith, "Toward a Theory of Maine History—Maine's Resources and the States," in *Explorations in Maine History: Miscellaneous Papers,* ed. Arthur Johnson (Orono, Maine, 1970), pp. 45–64. For an example of recent obliviousness to the importance of lumbering, see Cochran, *Pennsylvania: A Bicentennial History.*

8. Holbrook, *Holy Old Mackinaw*, pp. 81–89; Lucile M. Kane, *The Waterfall That Built a City: The Falls of St. Anthony in Minneapolis* (St. Paul, Minn., 1966); Hunter, *Waterpower*, pp. 233–42.

9. Technological innovation and its dispersion in the lumber industry have been little studied; however, see Loehr, "Saving the Kerf," pp. 168–72; Holbrook, *Holy Old Mackinaw*, pp. 46–47, 97–102; Smith "Logging Frontier," pp. 101–3; Rector, *Log Transportation in the Lake States Lumber Industry;* and Fries, *Empire in Pine*, pp. 101, 124, 125–27, 172.

10. For example, see Twining, *Downriver*, p. 169, and Lillard, *Great Forest*, p. 272.

11. For accounts of Beef Slough, see Hidy, Hill, and Nevins, *Timber and Men*, pp. 45–76; Twining, *Downriver*, pp. 105–15; and Kohlmeyer, *Timber Roots*, pp. 82–116.

12. Twining, *Downriver*, pp. 172–79; Hurst, *Law and Economic Growth*, pp. 172, 244, 253, 268–69.

13. Hurst, *Law and Economic Growth*, esp. pp. 143–70, 534–59.

14. Arthur R. M. Lower, "A History of the Lumber Trade between Canada and the United States," in Arthur R. M. Lower, W. A. Carrothers, and A. A. Saunders, *The North American Assault on the Canadian Forest*, ed. Harold A. Innis (1938; New York, 1968), pp. 1–223; Defebaugh, *Lumber Industry*, 1:172–78; Robert C. Johnson, "Logs for Saginaw: The Development of Raft Towing on Lake Huron," *Inland Seas* 5 (1949): 37–41, 83–90.

15. There are no adequate accounts of the impact of the Wilson-Gorman tariff and related events on the lumber industry. However, see Defebaugh, *Lumber Industry*, 1:450–61; Robert C. Johnson, "Logs for Saginaw: An Episode in Canadian-American Tariff Relations," *Michigan History* 34 (1950): 213–23; Fries, *Empire in Pine*, pp. 113–21; Hickman, *Mississippi Harvest*, pp. 206–11; and Lower, Carrothers, and Saunders, *North American Assault*, pp. 152–59. See also Thomas R. Tull, "The Shift to Republicanism: William L. Wilson and the Election of 1894," *West Virginia History* 37 (1975): 17–33.

16. Michael Curtis, "Early Development and Operations of the Great Southern Lumber Company," *Louisiana History* 14 (1973): 347–68; Rendigs Fels, *Wages, Earnings, and Employment: Nashville, Chattanooga, & St. Louis Railway, 1866–1896* (Nashville, 1953); Thomas D. Clark and Albert D. Kirwan, *The South since Appomattox: A Century of Regional Change* (New York, 1967), pp. 136–43 and passim.

17. Ervin Mancel, "An Historical Geography of Industrial Cypress Lumbering in Louisiana" (Ph.D. diss., Louisiana State University, 1972); Anna C. Burns, "Frank B. Williams, Cypress Lumber King," *Journal of Forest History* 24 (1980): 127–33; Norgress, "History of the Cypress Lumber Industry in Louisiana," pp. 979–1059.

18. James W. Silver, "The Hardwood Producers Come of Age," *Journal of Southern History* 55 (1957): 427–53; David H. Thomas, "Getting Started at High Point," *Forest History* 11 (July 1967): 22–32; National Hardwood Lumber Association, *A Half Century of Progress, 1898–1947* (Chicago, 1947); Henry H. Williams, "The History of Oak Flooring," *Southern Lumberman* 193 (December 15, 1956): 200–203; Jean Worth, "Hermansville: Echoes of a Hardwood Empire," *Michigan History* 65 (March–April 1981): 17–28.

19. David C. Smith, *History of Papermaking in the United States (1691–1969)* (New York,

1970); Eleanor Amigo and Mark Neuffer, *Beyond the Adirondacks: The Story of the St. Regis Paper Company,* ed. Elwood R. Maunder (Westport, Conn., 1980); John R. Kimberly, *Four Young Men Go in Search of a Profit: The Story of Kimberly-Clark Corporation, 1872–1957* (New York, 1957).

20. Casler, Kline, and Taber, *Logging Railroad Era,* 1:vi–viii. See also Defebaugh, *Lumber Industry,* 2:530–655.

21. Casler, Kline, and Taber, *Logging Railroad Era,* 2:1082–91 and passim. See also Craig A. Newton and James R. Sperry, *A Quiet Boomtown: Jamison City, Pa., 1889–1912* (Bloomsburg, Pa., 1972).

22. No systematic study of the migrations of Pennsylvania lumbermen has been done.

23. Cox, *Mills and Markets,* pp. 199–226, 284–96; Coman and Gibbs, *Time, Tide and Timber,* pp. 149–62, 174–209, 210–20; John H. Cox, "Organizations of the Lumber Industry in the Pacific Northwest, 1899–1914" (Ph.D. diss., University of California, Berkeley, 1937), pp. 142–51.

24. Stewart H. Holbrook, *Burning an Empire: The Story of American Forest Fires* (New York, 1943), pp. 12–30, 62–76; Richard White, *Land Use, Environment, and Social Change: The Shaping of Island County, Washington* (Seattle, 1980), pp. 78–79, 89–91, 106–10; Pyne, *Fire in America,* pp. 181–218; Thomas R. Cox, "Trade, Development, and Environmental Change: The Utilization of North America's Pacific Coast Forests to 1914 and Its Consequences," in Tucker and Richards, *Global Deforestation,* esp. pp. 25–27. For a summary of attitudes, see Franklin B. Hough, *Report upon Forestry,* vol. 3 (Washington, D.C., 1882), pp. 128–30.

Chapter 10

1. There is no full study of the Williamsport strike. However, see Nancy Lee Miller, "Sawdust War: Labor Strife in Lumbermills," *Pennsylvania Forests* 72 (March–April 1982): 6–8, 13. Cf. Herbert G. Gutman, "The Workers' Search for Power," in Morgan, *Gilded Age,* pp. 31–53.

2. Jeremy W. Kilar, "Community and Authority Response to the Saginaw Valley Lumber Strike of 1885," *Journal of Forest History* 20 (1976): 67–79; Richard W. Massey, "Labor Conditions in the Lumber Industry in Alabama, 1880–1914," *Journal of the Alabama Academy of Science* 37 (1966): 172–81; Vernon H. Jensen, *Lumber and Labor* (1945; New York, 1971), pp. 58–63, 86–87. For the standard treatment of the Knights of Labor, see Gerald N. Grob, *Workers and Utopia: A Study of Ideological Conflict in the American Labor Movement, 1865–1900* (1961; Chicago, 1969).

3. Jensen, *Lumber and Labor,* pp. 114–24; Robert L. Tyler, *Rebels in the Woods: The I.W.W. in the Pacific Northwest* (Eugene, Oreg., 1967). The literature on the IWW is extensive.

4. Cox, *Mills and Markets,* pp. 255–83; Cox, "Organizations of the Lumber Industry"; James E. Fickle, *The New South and the "New Competition": Trade Association Development in the Southern Pine Industry* (Champaign, Ill., 1980); Fries, *Empire in Pine,* pp. 128–31.

5. Hurst, *Law and Economic Growth*, pp. 143–270 and passim; Kinney, *Essentials of American Timber Law*, pp. 210–40.

6. Ivan C. Doig, "John J. McGilvra and Timber Trespass: Seeking a Puget Sound Timber Policy, 1861–1865," *Forest History* 13 (January 1970): 6–17; Frances Whitton, "Evolution of Forest Policies in Canada," *Journal of Forestry* 76 (1978): 563–66; Robert Edgar Cail, *Land, Man, and the Law: The Disposal of Crown Lands in British Columbia, 1871–1913* (Vancouver, B.C., 1974).

7. Most works on Schurz give little attention to his efforts on behalf of conservation. However, see Jeannie S. Peyton, "Forestry Movement of the Seventies in the Interior Department, under Schurz," *Journal of Forestry* 18 (1920): 391–405; James B. Trefethen, "Carl Schurz: Forestry's Forgotten Pioneer," *American Forests* 67 (September 1961): 24–27; Udall, *Quiet Crisis*, pp. 95–108.

8. Harold K. Steen, *The U.S. Forest Service: A History* (Seattle, 1976), pp. 9–21; Edna L. Jacobsen, "Franklin B. Hough, a Pioneer in Scientific Forestry in America," *New York History* 15 (1934): 311–25.

9. Steen, *Forest Service*, pp. 7–37; Henry Clepper, *Crusade for Conservation: The Centennial History of the American Forestry Association* (Washington, D.C., 1975), pp. 2–18.

10. Among the many accounts of these events are Steen, *Forest Service*, pp. 22–46, and Frank E. Smith, *The Politics of Conservation* (New York, 1966), pp. 55–70.

11. Steen, *Forest Service*, pp. 22–37; Joseph A. Miller, "Congress and the Origins of Conservation: Natural Resources Policy, 1865–1900" (Ph.D. diss., University of Minnesota, 1973), pp. 230–38 and passim; Rogers, *Bernhard Eduard Fernow*, pp. 154–252; Ise, *Forest Policy*, pp. 119–42.

12. G. Wallace Chessman, *Governor Theodore Roosevelt: The Albany Apprenticeship, 1898–1900* (Cambridge, Mass., 1965); R. L. Wilson and G. C. Wilson, *Theodore Roosevelt, Outdoorsman* (New York, 1971).

13. Hays, *Conservation and the Gospel of Efficiency*; David P. Thelen, "Social Tensions and the Origins of Progressivism," *Journal of American History* 56 (1969): 323–41; William Henry Harbaugh, *Power and Responsibility: The Life and Times of Theodore Roosevelt* (New York, 1961), pp. 149–65 and passim.

14. Schenck, *Birth of Forestry*, pp. 121–22, 142–44, and passim; J. Leonard Bates, "Fulfilling American Democracy: The Conservation Movement, 1907–1921," *Mississippi Valley Historical Review* 44 (1957): 29–57. However, compare Hays, *Conservation and the Gospel of Efficiency*, p. 2, and Pinchot's many admirers in and out of the Forest Service who chose to play down his antibusiness statements.

15. Steen, *Forest Service*, pp. 52–56; Hays, *Conservation and the Gospel of Efficiency*, pp. 29–30.

16. The literature on the early Forest Service is extensive. For a useful summary, see Steen, *Forest Service*, pp. 69–102. Lawrence Rakestraw, "A History of Forest Conservation in the Pacific Northwest, 1891–1913" (Ph.D. diss., University of Washington, 1955), provides valuable insights into operations at the regional and local levels.

17. Richardson, *Politics of Conservation*, pp. 86, 104; Hays, *Conservation and the Gospel of*

Efficiency, pp. 147–74 and passim; McCarthy, *Hour of Trial*, pp. 82–93, 175–77, and passim; Harold T. Pinkett, "Western Perceptions of Forest Conservation," *Journal of the West* 18 (1979): 72–74.

18. Whitney R. Cross, "W J McGee and the Idea of Conservation," *Historian* 15 (1953): 148–62; Hays, *Conservation and the Gospel of Efficiency*, pp. 5–26, 100–121, 199–240, and passim.

19. Literature on these diverse activities and events is scattered in a host of studies, but none catches their spirit as well as Taft's own statement.

Chapter 11

1. Studies of these years primarily focus on individual firms and states. However, see William B. Greeley, *Forests and Men* (Garden City, N.Y., 1951); Hidy, Hill, and Nevins, *Timber and Men*, pp. 248–89; and William G. Robbins, *Lumberjacks and Legislators: Political Economy of the U.S. Lumber Industry, 1890–1941* (College Station, Tex., 1982), pp. 1–74.

2. Gifford Pinchot, *Breaking New Ground* (New York, 1947), pp. 347–55; Hays, *Conservation and the Gospel of Efficiency*, pp. 127–30, 138–41.

3. Clepper, *Crusade for Conservation*, pp. 21–25; George T. Morgan, Jr., *William B. Greeley, a Practical Forester, 1879–1955* (St. Paul, Minn., 1961), p. 30; Steen, *Forest Service*, pp. 122–31.

4. See Vernon R. Carstensen, *Farms or Forests: Evolution of a State Land Policy for Northern Wisconsin, 1850–1932* (Madison, Wis., 1958). In a separate decision in 1912, the state's waterpower supervision authority was also declared void by the Wisconsin high court. Cf. Norman Schmaltz, "The Land Nobody Wanted: The Dilemma of Michigan's Cutover Lands," *Michigan History* 67 (January–February 1983): 32–40; Charles Gordon Mahaffey, "Changing Images of the Cutover: A Historical Geography of Resource Utilization in the Lake Superior Region, 1840–1930" (Ph.D. diss., University of Wisconsin at Madison, 1978).

5. Robert S. Maxwell, "One Man's Legacy: W. Goodrich Jones and Texas Conservation," *Southwestern Historical Quarterly* 77 (1974): 355–80.

6. Maxwell and Baker, *Sawdust Empire;* David Lane Chapman, "An Administrative History of the Texas Forest Service, 1915–1975" (Ph.D. diss., Texas A & M University, 1981).

7. Clar, *California Government and Forestry*, pp. 328–440.

8. Ralph W. Widner, ed., *Forests and Forestry in the American States: A Reference Anthology* (Washington, D.C., 1968), pp. 161–71; Morgan, *William B. Greeley*, pp. 20–23; Rakestraw, "Forest Conservation in the Pacific Northwest," pp. 280–330 and passim.

9. Eloise Hamilton, *Forty Years of Western Forestry: A History of the Movement to Conserve Forest Resources by Cooperative Effort, 1909–1949* (Portland, Oreg., 1949); Clyde S. Martin, "History and Influence of the Western Forestry and Conservation Association on Cooperative Forestry in the West," *Journal of Forestry* 43 (1945): 165–70.

10. See Pinchot, *Breaking New Ground*, pp. 391–490; Hays, *Conservation and the Gospel*

of Efficiency, pp. 165–74; Henry Clepper, "The Forest Service Backlashed," *Forest History* 11 (January 1968): 6–15; James L. Penick, Jr., *Progressive Politics and Conservation: The Ballinger-Pinchot Affair* (Chicago, 1968); Pinkett, *Gifford Pinchot*, pp. 114–29; Richardson, *Politics of Conservation*, pp. 51–84 and passim.

11. Bates, "Fulfilling American Democracy"; Hays, *Conservation and the Gospel of Efficiency*, pp. 196–97; Samuel P. Hays, "Gifford Pinchot and the Conservation Movement," *Living Wilderness* 44 (June 1980): 4–9; Alan B. Gould, "'Trouble Portfolio' to Constructive Conservation: Secretary of the Interior Walter L. Fisher, 1911–1913," *Forest History* 16 (January 1973): 4–12.

12. Eric Seaborg, "The Battle for Hetch Hetchy," *Sierra* 66 (November–December 1981): 61–65; Nicholas Roosevelt, *Conservation: Now or Never* (New York, 1970), pp. 30–38; Hays, *Conservation and the Gospel of Efficiency*, pp. 192–98; Holway Jones, *John Muir and the Sierra Club: The Battle for Yosemite* (San Francisco, 1965); Elmo R. Richardson, "The Struggle for the Valley: California's Hetch Hetchy Controversy, 1905–1913," *California Historical Society Quarterly* 28 (1959): 249–58.

13. Cook, "Senator Heyburn's War against the Forest Service," pp. 12–15; McCarthy, *Hour of Trial*, pp. 46–74; Pinkett, "Western Perceptions of Forest Conservation," pp. 72–74; Richardson, *Politics of Conservation*, pp. 88–110 and passim.

14. Morgan, *William B. Greeley*, pp. 39–44; Richardson, *Politics of Conservation*, pp. 139–59; Steen, *Forest Service*, pp. 227–37, 256–71, and passim; Clepper, *Crusade for Conservation*, pp. 58–65.

15. Clepper, *Crusade for Conservation*, pp. 21–25; Schenck, *Birth of Forestry in America*, pp. 136–37. 141–44, and passim; J. P Kinney, *Indian Forest and Range: A History of the Administration and Conservation of the Redman's Heritage* (Washington, D.C., 1950); Rakestraw, "Forest Conservation," pp. 214–36.

16. Jensen, *Lumber and Labor*, is the standard account. On clashes in Texas and nearby, see Ruth A. Allen, *East Texas Lumber Workers: An Economic and Social Picture, 1870–1950* (Austin, Tex., 1961); George T. Morgan, Jr., "No Compromise—No Recognition: John Henry Kirby, the Southern Lumber Operators' Association, and Unionism in the Piney Woods, 1906–1916," *Labor History* 10 (1969): 193–204; and James E. Fickle, "The Louisiana-Texas Lumber War of 1911–1912," *Louisiana History* 16 (1975): 59–85.

17. Harold M. Hyman, *Soldiers and Spruce: Origins of the Loyal Legion of Loggers and Lumbermen* (Los Angeles, 1963), pp. 48, 323–41; Hidy, Hill, and Nevins, *Timber and Men*, pp. 332–51; Robert L. Tyler, "The Government as Union Organizer: The Loyal Legion of Loggers and Lumbermen," *Mississippi Valley Historical Review* 47 (1960): 434–51; Tyler, *Rebels in the Woods*.

18. For American foresters in France during World War I, see *Journal of Forest History* 22 (October 1978).

19. Edward N. Hurley, *The Bridge to France* (Philadelphia, 1927); W. C. Mattox, *Building the Emergency Fleet: A Historical Narrative of the Problems and Achievements of the United States Shipping Board Emergency Fleet Corporation* (Cleveland, Ohio, 1920); Gregory

Charles O'Brien, "The Life of Robert Dollar, 1844–1932" (Ph.D. diss., Claremont Graduate School, 1968).

20. Donald C. Swain, *Federal Conservation Policy, 1921–1933* (Berkeley, Calif., 1963), pp. 1–15; Greeley, *Forests and Men*, pp. 101–10; Steen, *Forest Service*, pp. 142–95.

21. Donald L. Winters, *Henry Cantwell Wallace as Secretary of Agriculture: 1921–1924* (Urbana, Ill., 1970), pp. 162–84; Greeley, *Forests and Men*, pp. 95–101; Clepper, *Crusade for Conservation*, pp. 40–44; David H. Stratton, "Two Western Senators and Teapot Dome: Thomas J. Walsh and Albert B. Fall," *Pacific Northwest Quarterly* 65 (1974): 52–65.

22. Swain, *Federal Conservation Policy*, develops this theme in detail.

23. See Robert Shankland, *Steve Mather of the National Parks* (New York, 1951); Nash, *Wilderness and the American Mind*, pp. 182–99; Susan Flader, *Thinking Like a Mountain: Aldo Leopold and the Evolution of an Ecological Attitude toward Deer, Wolves, and Forests* (Columbia, Mo., 1974), pp. 14–16, 79–81; Holway R. Jones, "John Muir, the Sierra Club, and the Formulation of the Wilderness Concept," *Pacific Historian* 25 (July 1981): 64–78; R. Newell Searle, *Saving Quetico-Superior: A Land Set Apart* (St. Paul, Minn., 1977); and Donald Nicholas Baldwin, *The Quiet Revolution: Grass Roots of Today's Wilderness Preservation Movement* (Boulder, Colo., 1972).

24. Susan R. Schrepfer, "Conflict in Preservation: The Sierra Club, Save-the-Redwoods League, and Redwood National Park," *Journal of Forest History* 24 (1980): 60–76; Schrepfer, *The Fight to Save the Redwoods: A History of Environmental Reform, 1917–1978* (Madison, Wis., 1983); Joseph H. Engbeck, Jr., *State Parks of California from 1864 to the Present* (Portland, Oreg., 1980), pp. 41–55.

25. Thomas R. Cox, "The Crusade to Save Oregon's Scenery," *Pacific Historical Review* 37 (1968): 179–99; Pomeroy, *In Search of the Golden West*, pp. 125–31.

26. Carl Bode, *The Half-World of American Culture* (Carbondale, Ill., 1964), pp. 125–40; Schmitt, *Back to Nature*, pp. 177–89.

27. Charles A. Nelson, *A History of the U.S. Forest Products Laboratory (1910–1963)* (Madison, Wis., 1971); Steen, *Forest Service*, pp. 131–41; Norman J. Schmaltz, "Raphael Zon: Forest Researcher," *Journal of Forest History* 24 (1980): 24–39, 86–97; Lida W. McBeath, "Eloise Gerry: A Woman of Forest Science," *Journal of Forest History* 22 (1978): 128–35. The name Charles L. McNary appears frequently in the literature of conservation legislation during this period. The liberal Republican from Oregon was a personal friend of both William Greeley and E. T. Allen and was a dependable supporter of forestry and conservation measures in the Senate. A good biography of him is needed.

28. On these shifts, see George P. Ahern, *Forest Bankruptcy in America: Each State's Own Story* (Washington, D.C., 1933); Inman F. Eldridge, "Southern Forests Then and Now," *Journal of Forestry* 50 (1952): 182–85; and Nelson C. Brown, *The American Lumber Industry . . .* (New York, 1923).

29. E. T. Allen, "50,000 Firebrands," *American Forests and Forest Life* 31 (1925): 142 ff.; Clar, *California Government and Forestry*, pp. 365–68; George T. Morgan, Jr., "The Fight against Fire: The Development of Cooperative Forestry in the Pacific Northwest," *Idaho*

Yesterdays 6 (Winter 1962): 20–30; Morgan, "Conflagration as a Catalyst: Western Lumbermen and American Forest Policy," *Pacific Historical Review* 47 (1978): 167–88; Pyne, *Fire in America*, esp. pp. 260–72.

30. Clepper, *Crusade for Conservation*, pp. 45–51; William F. Jacobs, "The Dixie Crusade," *American Forests* 84 (December 1974): 18–21, 38–46; Edward F. Kerr, "Southerners Who Set the Woods on Fire," *Harper's Magazine* 217 (July 1958): 28–33; Holbrook, *Burning an Empire*, pp. 121–41; Betty G. Spencer, *The Big Blowup* (Caldwell, Idaho, 1956); Pyne, *Fire in America*, pp. 143–60.

31. E. L. Denmon, "Twenty Years of Forest Research in the Lower South," *Journal of Forestry* 40 (1942): 33–36; William H. Hutchinson, *California Heritage: A History of Northern California Lumbering* (1958; Santa Cruz, Calif., 1974); Hidy, Hill, and Nevins, *Timber and Men*, pp. 212–16 and passim. Sustained yield, at heart simply the idea that forests should be managed for continuing production, gradually evolved and matured as a concept. See Thomas B. Perry, Henry J. Vaux, and Nicholas Dennis, "Changing Conditions of Sustained-Yield Policy on the National Forests," *Journal of Forestry* 81 (1983): 150–54.

32. Morgan, *William B. Greeley*, pp. 59–65. See also Thomas R. Cox, "The Stewardship of Private Forests: The Evolution of a Concept in the United States, 1864–1950," *Journal of Forest History* 25 (1981): 188–96.

33. Swain, *Federal Conservation Policy*, pp. 160–62; William G. Robbins, "Voluntary Cooperation vs. Regulatory Paternalism: The Lumber Trade in the 1920s," *Business History Review* 56 (1982): 358–79; Robert E. Ficken, *Lumber and Politics: The Career of Mark E. Reed* (Seattle, 1980), pp. 157–81; Edwin M. Fitch, *The Tariff on Lumber* (Madison, Wis., 1936).

34. C. Raymond Clar, *California Government and Forestry*, vol. 2, *During the Young and Rolph Administrations* (Sacramento, Calif., 1969), pp. 189–216.

Chapter 12

1. Edgar B. Nixon, ed., *Franklin D. Roosevelt and Conservation, 1911–1945*, 2 vols. (Hyde Park, N.Y., 1957), 1:3–134, shows Roosevelt's prepresidential interest in conservation through his correspondence. See also Joseph P. Lash, "I'm an Old Conservationist," *Amicus Journal* 4 (Winter 1983): 14–21; Kenneth S. Davis, *FDR, the Beckoning Destiny, 1882–1928: A History* (New York, 1972), pp. 257–69; Whitney R. Cross, "Ideas in Politics: Conservation Policies of the Two Roosevelts," *Journal of the History of Ideas* 14 (1953): 421–38.

2. Bernard Bellush, *Franklin D. Roosevelt as Governor of New York* (New York, 1955), pp. 94–98.

3. Clepper, *Crusade for Conservation*, pp. 52–57; Ficken, *Lumber and Politics*, pp. 182–210.

4. Henry Clepper, "The Birth of the C.C.C.," *American Forests* 79 (March 1973): 8–11; John A. Salmond, *The Civilian Conservation Corps, 1933–1942: A New Deal Case Study* (Durham, N.C., 1967), pp. 3–9.

5. Numerous accounts of the CCC exist, including many focusing on single areas of limited fields of activity. For useful analyses, see Salmond, *The Civilian Conservation Corps;* Percy H. Merrill, *Roosevelt's Forest Army: A History of the Civilian Conservation Corps, 1933– 1942* (Montpelier, Vt., 1981); and Frank Freidel, *Franklin Delano Roosevelt,* vol. 4, *Launching the New Deal* (Boston, 1973), pp. 255–66.

6. Salmond, *Civilian Conservation Corps,* pp. 123–25. Elmo Richardson, "The Civilian Conservation Corps and the Origins of the New Mexico State Park System," *Natural Resources Journal* 6 (1966): 248–67, is a good case study.

7. Calvin W. Gower, "A Continuing Public Youth Work Program: The Drive for a Permanent Civilian Conservation Corps, 1933–1942," *Environmental Review* 5 (Fall 1981): 39–51; Elmo R. Richardson, "Was There Politics in the Civilian Conservation Corps?" *Forest History* 16 (July 1972): 12–21; Robert W. Dubay, "The Civilian Conservation Corps: A Study of Opposition, 1933–1935," *Southern Quarterly* 6 (1968): 341–58. In a letter to the president, director Fechner detailed the work completed by the CCC from its beginning to June 1936. The list of accomplishments is most impressive. See Robert Fechner to Roosevelt, October 24, 1936, in *FDR and Conservation,* 1:591–93.

8. Schlesinger, *Coming of the New Deal,* pp. 88–102; Fickle, *New South,* pp. 117–21; Steen, *Forest Service,* pp. 222–26.

9. William G. Robbins, "The Great Experiment in Industrial Self-Government: The Lumber Industry and the National Recovery Administration," *Journal of Forest History* 25 (1981): 128–32; *FDR and Conservation,* 1:213–16, 259–62; Ellis Lucia, *Head Rig: Story of West Coast Lumber Industry* (Portland, Oreg., 1965); pp. 168–77.

10. Greeley, *Forests and Men,* pp. 137–38; Rodney C. Leohr, ed., *Forests for the Future: The Story of Sustained Yield as Told in the Diaries and Papers of David T. Mason, 1907–1950* (St. Paul, Minn., 1952), pp. 95, 177–79, and passim; Robbins, "Great Experiment," esp. pp. 132–43; James E. Fickle, "The S.P.A. and the N.R.A.: A Case Study of the Blue Eagle in the South," *Southwestern Historical Quarterly* 79 (1976):253–78.

11. The literature on the TVA is extensive. For general accounts, see Wilmon H. Droze, *High Dams and Slack Waters: TVA Rebuilds a River* (Baton Rouge, La., 1965), and David E. Lilienthal, *TVA—Democracy on the March* (New York, 1944).

12. John C. Allen, "A Half Century of Reforestation in the Tennessee Valley," *Journal of Forestry* 51 (1953): 106–13; James O. Artman, "Trees for the Tennessee," *American Forests* 61 (April 1955): 8–12.

13. Wendell Willkie, "Political Power," *Atlantic Monthly* 160 (August 1937): 210–18; William E. Leuchtenberg, *Franklin D. Roosevelt and the New Deal, 1932–1940* (New York, 1963), pp. 54–55, 164–65.

14. Wilmon H. Droze, *Trees, Prairies, and People: A History of Tree Planting in the Plains States* (Denton, Tex., 1977); Allan J. Soffar, "The Forest Shelterbelt Project," *Journal of the West* 14 (July 1975): 95–107.

15. For example, see E. N. Munns and Joseph H. Stoekeler, "How Are the Great Plains Shelterbelts?" *Journal of Forestry* 44 (1946): 237–57. See also Richard W. Tinus, ed., *Shelterbelts on the Great Plains: Proceedings of the Symposium, Denver, Colorado, April*

20–22, 1976, Great Plains Agricultural Council, Publication no. 78 (Lincoln, Nebr., 1976). Critics have tended to see the shelterbelts as inappropriate meddling by man with the Great Plains environment. For a discussion of the broader issue, see Worster, *Nature's Economy*, pp. 221–53.

16. Henry Clepper and Arthur B. Meyer, eds., *American Forestry: Six Decades of Growth* (Washington, D.C., 1960), pp. 11 ff.; Steen, *Forest Service*, pp. 196–221; U.S. Department of Agriculture, Forest Service, *Highlights in the History of Forest Conservation*, rev. ed. (Washington, D.C., 1976), pp. 50–51.

17. Fred W. Soady, Jr., "The Making of the Shawnee," *Forest History* 9 (July 1965): 10–23.

18. Lawrence Rakestraw, "Forest History in Alaska: Four Approaches to Two Forest Ecosystems," *Journal of Forest History* 23 (1979): 66–69. Rakestraw, *A History of the United States Forest Service in Alaska* (Anchorage, 1981), pp. 83–116, provides a good view of New Deal forestry programs in Alaska. Cf. Pat Lawler, "Harold Ickes: The Man Alaskans Loved to Hate," *Alaska Journal* 13 (1983): 100–107.

19. Bernard Frank, *Our National Forests* (Norman, Okla., 1955), pp. 91–96; Roderick Nash, "The Strenuous Life of Bob Marshall," *Forest History* 10 (October 1966): 19–23; Richard E. McArdle with Elwood R. Maunder, "Wilderness Politics: Legislation and Forest Service Policy," *Journal of Forest History* 10 (1975): 166–79; David A. Bernstein, "Bob Marshall: Wilderness Advocate," *Western States Jewish Historical Quarterly* 13 (1980): 26–37.

20. Flader, *Thinking Like a Mountain;* Strong, *Conservationists*, pp. 139–54; Nash, *Wilderness and the American Mind*, pp. 187–99; Paul Brooks, "The Wilderness Ideal," *Living Wilderness* 44 (September 1980): 4–12.

21. James B. Trefethen, *An American Crusade for Wildlife* (New York, 1975), pp. 195–236; Ira N. Gabrielson, *Wildlife Refuges* (New York, 1942), pp. 15–31; Worster, *Nature's Economy*, pp. 258–90.

22. Worster, *Nature's Economy*, pp. 221–35; David L. Lendt, *Ding: The Life of Jay Norwood Darling* (Ames, Iowa, 1979).

23. Pomeroy, *In Search of the Golden West*, pp. 212–15; Alfred Kazin, *On Native Grounds: An Interpretation of Modern American Prose Literature* (New York, 1942), pp. 485–518; John Ise, *Our National Park Policy: A Critical History* (Baltimore, 1961), pp. 355–64, 429–31.

24. Clepper, *Crusade for Conservation*, pp. 52–57; Smith, *Politics of Conservation*, pp. 264–66; Richard Polenberg, "The Great Conservation Contest," *Forest History* 10 (January 1967): 13–23.

25. Steen, *Forest Service*, pp. 199–213; Wellington R. Burt, "Forest Lands of the United States: Report of the Joint Congressional Committee on Forestry," *Journal of Forestry* 39 (1941): 349–54.

26. Smith, *History of Papermaking*, pp. 219–87, 391–410. New England's papermaking experienced a revival after World War II when the industry turned more to specialized and high-quality papers; see ibid., pp. 545–46.

27. Jack P. Oden, "Charles Holmes Herty and the Birth of the Southern Newsprint Industry, 1927–1940," *Journal of Forest History* 21 (1977): 76–89; Nelson, *History of the U.S. Forest Products Laboratory,* pp. 117–20.

28. Philip F. Cashier, "Natural Resource Management during the Second World War, 1939–1947" (Ph.D. diss., State University of New York at Binghamton, 1980); *FDR and Conservation,* 2:491–648; Hidy, Hill, and Nevins, *Timber and Men,* pp. 451–69; Fickle, *New South,* pp. 349–67.

Chapter 13

1. Clepper, *Crusade for Conservation,* pp. 58–65; Steen, *Forest Service,* pp. 256–71.

2. Richard Lewis, "Tree Farming: A Voluntary Conservation Program," *Journal of Forest History* 25 (1981): 166–69; Paul F. Sharp, "The Tree Farm Movement: Its Origin and Development," *Agricultural History* 23 (1949): 41–45.

3. Mal Hardy, "The Legend of Smokey Bear," *National Parks Magazine* 43 (January 1969): 18–20; Clepper, *Crusade for Conservation,* pp. 71–74; James F. Stevens, "The Greenskeepers," *American Forests* 71 (December 1965): 20–21, 44–45; Roosevelt, *Conservation: Now or Never,* pp. 84–96.

4. Elmo Richardson, *Dams, Parks, and Politics: Resource Development and Preservation in the Truman-Eisenhower Era* (Lexington, Ky., 1973), pp. 71–87; Franklyn D. Mahar, "The Politics of Power: The Oregon Test for Partnership," *Pacific Northwest Quarterly* 65 (1974): 29–37; George Van Dusen, "Politics of 'Partnership': The Eisenhower Administration and Conservation, 1952–1960" (Ph.D diss., Loyola University of Chicago, 1973).

5. Wallace E. Stegner, "De Voto's Western Adventures: A Great Historian's Search for the West of Lewis and Clark and How It Transformed Him into an Ardent Conservationist," *American West* 10 (November 1973): 20–27.

6. Richardson, *Dams, Parks, and Politics,* pp. 71–87, 166–78; A. Robert Smith, *The Tiger in the Senate: The Biography of Wayne Morse* (Garden City, N.Y., 1962), pp. 322–25.

7. Richardson, *Dams, Parks, and Politics,* pp. 129–52; Nash, *Wilderness and the American Mind,* pp. 209–20.

8. Richardson, *Dams, Parks, and Politics,* pp. 116–26; Smith, *Tiger in the Senate,* pp. 304–7, 328–31, 340–41. The controversy over the Three Sisters Wilderness has yet to receive extended analysis.

9. Smith, *Politics of Conservation,* pp. 231–39; Herbert S. Parmet, *Eisenhower and the American Crusades* (New York, 1972), pp. 466–68; Aaron Wildavsky, *Dixon-Yates: A Study in Power Politics* (New Haven, Conn., 1962); David A. Frier, *Conflict of Interest in the Eisenhower Administration* (Ames, Iowa, 1969), pp. 54–77.

10. Nelson, *A History of the U.S. Forest Products Laboratory,* pp. 138–59.

11. Rakestraw, *United States Forest Service in Alaska,* pp. 127–28; David C. Smith, "Pulp, Paper, and Alaska," *Pacific Northwest Quarterly* 66 (1975): 61–70; John Edward George Boyman, "Alaska's External Trade, 1951–58: Some Characteristics and Developments" (M.A. thesis, University of Washington, 1963), pp. 1–3, 57–63, 115–66, and passim.

12. Walter J. Mead, *Mergers and Economic Concentration in the Douglas-Fir Lumber Industry* (Portland, Oreg., 1964); Dennis C. LeMaster, *Mergers among the Largest Forest Products Firms, 1950–1970* (Pullman, Wash., 1977); William A. Duerr, ed., *Timber! Problems, Prospects, Policies* (Ames, Iowa, 1973), pp. 63–77. As of 1978, the picture was as follows:

	Sales (billion)	‰ of Industry Total	Acres (million)	Land Value (billion)
Georgia-Pacific	$4.4	3.6	4.1	$3.4
International Paper	4.1	3.5	7.1	3.9
Weyerhaeuser	3.8	3.4	5.9	9.5
Champion International	3.6	3.4	3.0	2.1

The top seventeen companies owned 58 percent of the industry total, or approximately 16 percent of all commercial forestland.

13. Duerr, *Timber*, pp. 22–29, 74–75; John W. Bartlett, ed., *Regional Silviculture of the United States*, rev. ed. (New York, 1980); Clepper, *Crusade for Conservation*, pp. 78–80.

14. On Udall see Barbara Laverne Blythe Leunes, "The Conservation Philosophy of Stewart L. Udall, 1961–1968" (Ph.D. diss., Texas A & M University, 1977), and James L. Sundquist, *Politics and Policy: The Eisenhower, Kennedy, and Johnson Years* (Washington, D.C., 1968), pp. 345–61.

15. Donald Fleming, "Roots of the New Conservation Movement," *Perspectives in American History* 6 (1972): 7–14, 25–34; Paul Brooks, *The House of Life: Rachel Carson at Work* (Boston, 1972); Thomas R. Dunlap, *DDT: Scientists, Citizens, and Public Policy* (Princeton, N.J., 1981), pp. 98–125.

16. Fleming, "Roots," esp. pp. 40–91; U.S. Department of the Interior, *The Third Wave: America's New Conservation*, Conservation Yearbook no. 36 (Washington, D.C., 1963), pp. 81 ff.; Timothy O'Riordan, "The Third American Conservation Movement: New Implications for Public Policy," *Journal of American Studies* 5 (1971): 155–71; Frank Graham, Jr., *Since Silent Spring* (Boston, 1976); Samuel P. Hays, "The Environmental Movement," *Journal of Forest History* 25 (1981): 219–21; Hays, "The Structure of Environmental Politics since World War II," *Journal of Social History* 14 (1981): 719–38; Allan K. Fitzsimmons, "Environmental Quality as a Theme in Federal Legislation," *Geographical Review* 70 (1980): 314–27.

17. Hidy, Hill, and Nevins, *Timber and Men*, pp. 490–93; Nancy Wood, *Clearcut: The Deforestation of America* (San Francisco, 1971), pp. 19, 23–24, 89–92; Jack Shepherd, *The Forest Killers: The Destruction of the American Wilderness* (New York, 1975), esp. pp. 113–72, 345–64; Duerr, *Timber*, pp. 235–36.

18. Nash, *Wilderness and the American Mind*, pp. 220–26; Craig W. Allin, *The Politics of Wilderness Preservation* (Westport, Conn., 1982), pp. 102–42; Sundquist, *Politics and Policy*, pp. 336–40, 358–61; Ronald G. Strickland, "Ten Years of Congressional Review

under the Wilderness Act of 1964: Wilderness Classification by 'Affirmative Action'" (Ph.D. diss., Georgetown University, 1976).

19. Sundquist, *Politics and Policy,* pp. 361–81; John P. Crevelli, "The Final Act of the Greatest Conservation President," *Prologue* 12 (1980): 173–91; Lyndon Baines Johnson, *The Vantage Point: Perspectives of the Presidency, 1963–1969* (New York, 1971), pp. 336–39; Schrepfer, *Fight to Save the Redwoods;* Joel Ray Dickinson, "The Creation of Redwood National Park: A Case Study in the Politics of Conservation" (Ph.D. diss., University of Missouri, Columbia, 1974).

20. Duerr, *Timber,* pp, 15, 19, 60; Forest Service, *Highlights in the History of Forest Conservation,* pp. 41–46. The log export controversy awaits full historical study.

21. John C. Whitaker, *Striking a Balance: Environmental and Natural Resource Policy in the Nixon-Ford Years* (Washington, D.C., 1976), passim.

22. Duerr, *Timber,* pp. 38, 60–61; Dunlap, *DDT,* pp. 231–45; Shepherd, *Forest Killers,* pp. 219–27; Samuel Trask Dana and Sally K. Fairfax, *Forest and Range Policy: Its Development in the United States,* 2d ed. (New York, 1980), pp. 323–27; Paul W. Gates, "Pressure Groups and Recent American Land Policies," *Agricultural History* 55 (1981): 103–27, esp. 110–19.

23. No full study exists. However, see Marion Clawson, *Forests, for Whom and for What?* (Baltimore, 1975), pp. 80, 156, and Shepherd, *Forest Killers,* pp. 28, 68, 114, and passim.

24. Paul J. Calhane, *Public Lands Politics: Interest Group Influence on the Forest Service and the Bureau of Land Management* (Baltimore, 1981), pp. 110–32, 274–85. Also, compare Eleanor C. J. Horwitz, *Clearcutting: A View from the Top* (Washington, D.C., 1974), with Wood, *Clearcut,* and Shepherd, *Forest Killers,* pp. 113–72, 242–44, 274–76.

25. *The National Forest Management Act of 1976,* U.S. Department of Agriculture, Current Information Report no. 16 (Washington, D.C., 1976). See also Phillip Martin, "Conflict Resolution through the Multiple Use Concept in Forest Service Decision Making," *Natural Resources Journal* 9 (1969): 228–36, and William C. Siegel, "Environmental Law—Some Implications for Forest Resource Management," *Environmental Law* 4 (Fall 1973): 115–34.

26. A full study of the lumber industry of recent years is needed. A useful beginning is James O. Howard and Bruce A. Hiserote, *Oregon's Forest Products Industry, 1976* (Portland, 1978).

27. Pete Addison Y. Gunter, *The Big Thicket: A Challenge to Conservation* (Austin, Tex., 1971); James Joseph Cozine, Jr., "Assault on a Wilderness: The Big Thicket of East Texas" (Ph.D. diss., Texas A & M University, 1976).

28. Duerr, *Timber,* pp. 92–108; U.S. Department of Agriculture, Forest Service, *Environmental Program for the Future: A Long-Term Forestry Plan* (Washington, D.C., 1974) 4:1–9; Stephen Spurr, *American Forest Policy in Development* (Seattle, 1976), pp. 59–82.

29. See E. F. Schumacher, *Small Is Beautiful: Economics as If People Mattered* (New York, 1973); Rice Odell, *Environmental Reckoning: The New Revolution to Protect the Earth* (Cambridge, Mass., 1980), pp. 253–76; Fleming, "Roots," pp. 64–91.

Epilogue

1. Neither adequate source material nor the perspective of time is as yet available to allow full historical analysis of the Carter and Reagan years. To date nearly all analyses are journalistic or partisan or both. Among them, see William K. Wyant, *Westward in Eden: The Public Lands and the Conservation Movement* (Berkeley, Calif., 1982); William Tucker, *Progress and Privilege: America in the Age of Environmentalism* (New York, 1982); and Elizabeth Drew, "A Reporter at Large: Secretary Watt," *New Yorker* 57 (May 4, 1981): 104–36. See also Charles E. Hewitt and Thomas E. Hamilton, eds., *Forests in Demand: Conflicts and Solutions* (Boston, 1982).

2. Useful, if not disinterested, introductions to the Sagebrush Rebellion and Weyerhaeuser's port proposal are provided by John Strohm, "What's Behind the Sagebrush Rebellion? Interview with Cliff Young," *National Wildlife* 19 (August–September 1981): 30–34, and Daniel Jack Chasan, "A Matter of Blind Opposition?" *Audubon* 82 (January 1980): 98–104. On RARE, see Culhane, *Public Lands Politics*, pp. 59–60 and passim, and Forest Service, *Roadless Area Review and Evaluation: Final Environmental Statement* (Washington, D.C., 1979).

3. George B. Lowe, Thomas K. Pinhey, and Michael D. Grimes, "Public Support for Environmental Protection: New Evidence from National Surveys," *Pacific Sociological Review* 23 (1980): 423–45; Samuel P. Hays, "From Conservation to Environment: Environmental Politics in the United States since World War II," *Environmental Review* 6 (Fall 1982): 14–41; and Hays, "Structure of Environmental Politics since World War II."

Bibliographical Essay

The field of forest history has burgeoned in the United States over the past two and a half decades. Both a cause and a reflection of this has been the Forest History Society (formerly Forest Products History Foundation), founded in 1946 by Theodore C. Blegen, Frederick K. Weyerhaeuser, and others disturbed by inattention to the role of forests in American history. Apart from government reports, there were at the time only a handful of broad-gauged studies. One of the first was James Elliott Defebaugh, *History of the Lumber Industry in America*, 2 vols. (Chicago, 1906), but it covers in detail only the Northeast and eastern Canada. Stanley F. Horn, *This Fascinating Lumber Business* (Indianapolis, 1943), was broader, but only partially historical. Jenks Cameron, *Development of Governmental Forest Control in the United States* (Baltimore, 1928), and John Ise, *United States Forest Policy* (New Haven, Conn., 1920), reflected the interest in government land policy strong in scholarly circles during the twenties and thirties but showed concern with little else. Stewart H. Holbrook's *Holy Old Mackinaw: A Natural History of the American Lumberjack* (New York, 1938), was a delightful, larger-than-life account that had to be used with care. A much more solid, but still readable and broadly conceived work was soon forthcoming: Richard G. Lillard, *The Great Forest* (New York, 1948). Strongly influenced by the dominant progressive historical school of the time, Lillard's work presents a view markedly different from that contained in this volume.

Since *The Great Forest*, works have tended to be narrowed in scope, dealing only with subdivisions of the story (whether defined topically or geographically). Useful exceptions are Marion Clawson, "Forests in the Long Sweep of American History," *Science* 204 (1979): 1168–74; Joseph M. Petulla, *American Environmental History: The Exploitation and Conservation of Natural Resources* (San Francisco, 1977); and W. G. Youngquist and H. O. Fleischer, *Wood in American Life, 1776–2076* (Madison, Wis., 1977). As his title suggests, Petulla covers far more than forests.

The reader wishing to ferret out works on specialized topics should begin with Ronald J. Fahl's invaluable *North American Forest and Conservation History: A Bibliography* (Santa Barbara, Calif., 1977). Items published since 1976 can be found in the Biblioscope section of *Journal of Forest History*, the quarterly journal of the Forest History Society. Richard C. Davis, ed., *Encyclopedia of American Forest and Conservation History* (New York, 1983), has entries on a host of topics and lists of further readings on them. For unpublished sources, consult Davis's *North American Forest History: A Guide to Manuscripts and Archives in the United States and Canada* (Santa Barbara, Calif., 1977).

Forest use and policy receive coverage in some general studies of the colonial economy, trade policies, and society. Among the most useful are Curtis P. Nettels, *The Roots of American Civilization: A History of American Colonial Life* (New York, 1939, 1954); Bernard Bailyn, *The New England Merchants in the Seventeenth Century* (Cambridge, Mass., 1955); and Richard Pares, *Yankees and Creoles: The Trade between North America and the West Indies before the American Revolution* (Cambridge, Mass., 1956).

For early perceptions of the forest, see Carl Ortwin Sauer, *Sixteenth Century North America: The Land and the People as Seen by the Europeans* (Berkeley, Calif., 1971); Henry Savage, Jr., *Discovering America, 1700–1875* (New York, 1979); Peter N. Carroll, *Puritanism and the Wilderness: The Intellectual Significance of the New England Frontier, 1629–1700* (New York, 1969); Hans Huth, *Nature and the American: Three Centuries of Changing Attitudes* (Berkeley, Calif., 1957), chaps. 1 and 2; and Peter A. Fritzell, "The Wilderness and the Garden: Metaphors of the American Landscape," *Forest History* 12 (April 1968): 16–21. Indian impact on the forest is discussed in J. Donald Hughes, *American Indian Ecology* (El Paso, Tex., 1983); Stephen J. Pyne, *Fire in America: A Cultural History of Wildland and Rural Fire* (Princeton, N.J., 1982), esp. pp. 71–83; and Calvin Martin, "The American Indian as Miscast Ecologist," *History Teacher* 14 (1981): 243–52. Contrasting economic and land-use patterns are delineated in William Cronon, *Changes in the Land: Indians, Colonists, and the Ecology of New England* (New York, 1983).

The importance of forests to the American colonies is shown in Charles F. Carroll, *The Timber Economy of Puritan New England* (Providence, R.I., 1973), and, somewhat differently, in Brooke Hindle, ed., *Material Culture of the Wooden Age* (Tarrytown, N.Y., 1981), and Charles van Ravenswaay, "America's Age of Wood." *Proceedings of the American Antiquarian Society* 80 (1970): 49–66. More narrowly focused works emphasizing economic aspects are Carl Bridenbaugh, "Yankee Use and Abuse of the Forest in Building New England, 1620–1660," *Proceedings of the Massachusetts Historical Society* 89 (1977): 3–35; Sinclair Snow,

"Naval Stores in Colonial Virginia," *Virginia Magazine of History and Biography* 72 (1964): 75–93; Arthur C. Bining, *Pennsylvania Iron Manufacture in the Eighteenth Century* (Harrisburg, Pa., 1938); W. I. Roberts III, "American Potash Manufacture before the American Revolution," *Proceedings of the American Philosophical Society* 116 (1972): 383–95; Harry B. Weiss and Grace M. Weiss, *The Early Sawmills of New Jersey* (Trenton, N.J., 1968); and Joseph A. Goldenberg, *Shipbuilding in Colonial America* (Newport News, Va., 1976). The related issue of technology during the colonial and early national periods is traced in Brooke Hindle, ed., *America's Wooden Age: Aspects of Its Early Technology* (Tarrytown, N.Y., 1975).

Of the works dealing with British policies affecting the forests, Robert G. Albion's *Forests and Sea Power: The Timber Problem of the Royal Navy, 1652–1862* (Cambridge, Mass., 1926), is the indispensable classic. It should be supplemented by Joseph J. Malone, *Pine Trees and Politics: The Naval Stores and Forest Policy of Colonial New England, 1691–1775* (Seattle, 1964); Walter A. Knittle, *Early Eighteenth Century Palatine Emigration: A British Government Redemptioner Project to Manufacture Naval Stores* (Philadelphia, 1937); Justin Williams, "English Mercantilism and Carolina Naval Stores, 1705–1776," *Journal of Southern History* 1 (1935): 169–85; Warren J. Gates, "The Broad Arrow Policy in Colonial America" (Ph.D. diss., University of Pennsylvania, 1951); and Gordon E. Kershaw, "John Wentworth vs. Kennebeck Proprietors: The Formation of Royal Mast Policy, 1769–1778," *American Neptune* 33 (1973): 95–119.

For studies of colonial efforts to protect forests and regulate their use, see J. P Kinney, *Forest Legislation in America prior to March 4, 1789,* Department of Forestry Bulletin no. 30 (Ithaca, N.Y., 1916)—reprinted with other material as *Development of Forest Law in America prior to March 4, 1789* (New York, 1972)— and Lillian M. Willson, *Forest Conservation in Colonial Times* (St. Paul, Minn., 1948).

For the period following independence, the literature is more extensive. Perceptions of the forests and land are traced in Ray Allen Billington, *Land of Savagery, Land of Promise: The European Image of the American Frontier* (New York, 1981), and John A. Jakle, *Images of the Ohio Valley: A Historical Geography of Travel, 1740–1860* (New York, 1977). The impact of nature, including forests, on thought is analyzed in Henry Nash Smith, *Virgin Land: The American West as Symbol and Myth* (Cambridge, Mass., 1950); David M. Potter, *People of Plenty: Economic Abundance and the American Character* (Chicago, 1954); Arthur A. Ekirch, Jr., *Man and Nature in America* (New York, 1963); and Barbara Novak, *Nature and Culture: American Landscape and Painting, 1825–1875* (New York, 1980). The works by Smith and Potter are seminal.

A number of studies deal with natural sciences. Especially relevant are Gilbert Chinard, "The American Philosophical Society and the Early History of Forestry in America," *Proceedings of the American Philosophical Society* 89 (1945): 444–88; Susan Delano McKelvey, *Botanical Exploration of the Trans-Mississippi West, 1790–1850* (Jamaica Plains, N.Y., 1955); and William Martin Smallwood, *Natural History and the American Mind* (New York, 1941).

The effect of agricultural expansion is skillfully traced by Michael Williams in "Clearing the United States Forests: Pivotal Years, 1810–1860," *Journal of Historical Geography* 8 (1982): 12–28, and in "Ohio: Microcosm of Agricultural Clearing in the Midwest," in *Global Deforestation and the Nineteenth-Century World Economy,* ed. Richard P. Tucker and J. F. Richards (Durham, N.C., 1983) pp. 3–13, 179–80. The interplay of forest use and farming is discussed in Philip L. White, *Beekmantown, New York: Forest Frontier to Farm Community* (Austin, Tex., 1979), and Richard White, *Land Use, Environment, and Social Change: The Shaping of Island County, Washington* (Seattle, 1980).

The story of fuel wood has proved illusive. However, see Arthur H. Cole, "The Mystery of Fuel Wood Marketing in the United States," *Business History Review* 44 (1970): 339–59; William A. Hoglund, "Forest Conservation and Stove Inventors—1789–1850," *Forest History* 5 (Winter 1962): 2–8; and David E. Schob, "Woodhawks and Cordwood: Steamboat Fuel on the Ohio and Mississippi Rivers, 1820–1860," *Journal of Forest History* 21 (1977): 124–33. Waterpower, by contrast, has been exhaustively analyzed; the definitive work is Louis C. Hunter, *A History of Industrial Power in the United States, 1780–1930,* vol. 1, *Waterpower in the Century of the Steam Engine* (Charlottesville, Va., 1979). Suggestive, but more narrowly focused, are William T. Langhorne, Jr., "Mill Based Settlement Patterns in Schoharie County, New York: A Regional Study," *Historical Archeology* 10 (1976): 73–92, and Donald A. Hutslar, "Ohio Water-powered Sawmills," *Ohio History* 55 (1975): 5–56.

On the adoption of steam and circular saws, see M. Powis Bale, *Saw-Mills, Their Arrangement and Management . . .,* 6th ed., rev. and ed. A. Powis Bale (London, 1924); Greville Bathe and Dorothy Bathe, *Oliver Evans: A Chronicle of Early American Engineering* (Philadelphia, 1935); and John O. Curtis, "The Introduction of the Circular Saw in the Early Nineteenth Century," *Bulletin of the Association for Preservation Technology* 5 (1973): 162–89. Additional studies of early mill technology are needed.

The use of wood in America during the early national period has been more thoroughly studied. Carl W. Condit, *American Building: Materials and Techniques from the Beginning of the Colonial Settlements to the Present* (Chicago, 1968), and other works by the same author are solid. Also useful is Paul E. Sprague, "The

Origin of Balloon Framing," *Journal of the Society of Architectural Historians* 4 (1981): 311–19. Shipbuilding has been the subject of numerous studies. Robert G. Albion, *Naval and Maritime History: An Annotated Bibliography*, 3d ed. (Mystic, Conn., 1963), lists book-length works. Among the most useful studies are Samuel Eliot Morison, *The Maritime History of Massachusetts* (Boston, 1941); Mary Ellen Chase, *Donald McKay and the Clipper Ships* (Boston, 1959); John G. B. Hutchins, *The American Maritime Industry and Public Policy, 1788–1914* (Cambridge, Mass., 1941); Virginia Steele Wood, *Live Oaking: Southern Timber for Tall Ships* (Boston, 1981); and, for a later era, Basil Lubbock, *The Down Easters: American Deep-Water Sailing Ships, 1869–1929* (Boston, 1929). Hindle's works, cited above, contain essays on other aspects of wood use in the period.

Many general works touch on the era of pine lumbering in Maine. More specifically focused are Richard G. Wood, *A History of Lumbering in Maine, 1820–1861* (Orono, Maine, 1935), and Philip T. Coolidge, *History of the Maine Woods* (Bangor, Maine, 1963). John S. Springer's classic, *Forest Life and Forest Trees . . .* (New York, 1851), continues to be a must. Also useful is William H. Rowe, *The Maritime History of Maine: Three Centuries of Shipbuilding and Seafaring* (New York, 1948).

The growth of forest industries elsewhere has been examined in various studies, but the coverage is uneven and gaps remain. Holbrook, cited above, makes migration of the lumber industry his central theme. More reliable for the movement west are David C. Smith, "The Logging Frontier," *Journal of Forest History* 18 (1974): 96–106, and Fred C. Kohlmeyer, "Northern Pine Lumbermen: A Study of Origins and Migrations," *Journal of Economic History* 16 (1956): 529–38. For a comparison of production in the various regions, see Michael Williams, "Products of the Forest: Mapping the Census of 1840," *Journal of Forest History* 24 (1980): 4–23.

Pennsylvania and New York have been little studied since Defebaugh's pioneer work, cited above. On New York, see also William F. Fox, *A History of the Lumber Industry of the State of New York;* originally published in the Sixth Annual Report of the New York Forest, Fish, and Game Commission in 1901, this work was printed separately in Washington, D.C., in 1902 and reprinted in Harrison, N.Y., in 1976.

Coverage of the South is better, but far from complete. Useful are the early chapters of Nollie W. Hichman, *Mississippi Harvest: Lumbering in the Longleaf Pine Belt, 1840–1915* (University, Miss., 1962), and Percival Perry, "The Naval Stores Industry of the Old South, 1790–1860," *Journal of Southern History* 34 (1968): 509–26; John Hebron Moore, *Andrew Brown and Cypress Lumbering in the Old Southwest* (Baton Rouge, La., 1967): John A. Eisterhold, "Lumber and

Trade in the Lower Mississippi Valley and New Orleans, 1800–1860,"
Louisiana History 13 (1972): 71–91; and "Lumber and Trade in the Seaboard
Cities of the Old South, 1607–1860" (Ph.D. diss., University of Mississippi,
1970).

The spread of forest industries into the upper Lake States has been thor-
oughly traced, as have later developments there. Basic works are Robert F.
Fries, *Empire in Pine: The Story of Lumbering in Wisconsin, 1830–1900* (Madison,
Wis., 1951); Agnes M. Larson, *History of the White Pine Industry in Minnesota*
(Minneapolis, Minn., 1949); and Barbara E. Benson, "Logs and Lumber: The
Development of the Lumber Industry of Michigan's Lower Peninsula, 1837–
1870" (Ph.D. diss., Indiana University, 1976). The pioneer work, still valuable,
is George W. Hotchkiss, *History of the Lumber and Forest Industry of the Northwest*
(Chicago, 1898). Also important are Margaret Walsh, *The Manufacturing Fron-
tier: Pioneer Industry in Antebellum Wisconsin, 1836–1860* (Madison, Wis., 1972);
Charles E. Twining, "The Lumbering Frontier," in *The Great Lakes Forest: An
Environmental and Social History*, ed. Susan L. Flader (Minneapolis, Minn., 1983)
pp. 121–36; and William G. Rector, *Log Transportation in the Lake States Lumber
Industry, 1840–1918* . . . (Glendale, Calif., 1953).

Studies of forest industries are much more numerous for the period after
1850. Solid scholarly accounts exist for all major regions. Among the more
valuable, in addition to works cited in the two preceding paragraphs, are David
C. Smith, *A History of Lumbering in Maine, 1861–1960* (Orono, Maine, 1972);
Thomas R. Cox, *Mills and Markets: A History of the Pacific Coast Lumber Industry to
1900* (Seattle, 1974); Edmond S. Meany, Jr., "A History of the Lumber Industry in the Pacific Northwest to 1917" (Ph.D. diss., Harvard University, 1935);
and Robert S. Maxwell and Robert D. Baker, *Sawdust Empire: The Texas Lumber
Industry, 1830–1940* (College Station, Tex., 1983). A number of excellent stud-
ies of individual firms also need to be consulted. Among them are Ralph W.
Hidy, Frank Ernest Hill, and Allan Nevins, *Timber and Men: The Weyerhaeuser
Story* (New York, 1963); Charles E. Twining, *Downriver: Orrin H. Ingram and the
Empire Lumber Company* (Madison, Wis., 1975); and Edwin T. Coman, Jr., and
Helen M. Gibbs, *Time, Tide and Timber: A Century of Pope & Talbot* (Stanford,
Calif., 1949). More disjointed but nonetheless useful is Fred W. Kohlmeyer,
Timber Roots: The Laird, Norton Story, 1855–1905 (Winona, Minn., 1972). Bio-
graphical studies provide further insights, especially Anita Shafer Goodstein,
Biography of a Businessman: Henry W. Sage, 1814–1897 (Ithaca, N.Y., 1962);
Richard W. Current, *Pine Logs and Politics: A Life of Philetus Sawyer, 1816–1900*
(Madison, Wis., 1950); and Robert E. Ficken, *Lumber and Politics: The Career of
Mark E. Reed* (Seattle, 1979). Also important is Lucile M. Kane, *The Waterfall*

That Built a City: The Falls of St. Anthony in Minneapolis (St. Paul, Minn., 1966). On papermaking, the basic work is David C. Smith, *History of Papermaking in the United States (1691–1969)* (New York, 1970); also useful is Eleanor Amigo and Mark Neuffer, *Beyond the Adirondacks: The Story of the St. Regis Paper Company,* ed. Elwood R. Maunder (Westport, Conn., 1980).

Nearly all the works in the paragraph above contain some material on technology; but except for studies of logging railroads, few studies of logging or sawmill technology per se have appeared for the post-1850 years. Useful exceptions are Rodney C. Loehr, "Saving the Kerf: The Introduction of the Band Saw Mill," *Agricultural History* 23 (1949): 168–72; Robert C. Johnson, "Logs for Saginaw: The Development of Raft Towing on Lake Huron," *Inland Seas* 5 (1949): 37–41, 83–90; and Ervin Mancil, "Pullboat Logging," *Journal of Forest History* 24 (1980): 135–41. The results of a shift in basic technology are traced in Thomas R. Cox, "Transition in the Woods: Log Drivers, Raftsmen, and the Emergence of Modern Lumbering in Pennsylvania," *Pennsylvania Magazine of History and Biography* 104 (1980): 345–64. On railroads, see Michael Koch, *Steam and Thunder in the Timber: Saga of the Forest Railroads* (Denver, Colo., 1979).

The crucial years of the early twentieth century have received considerable attention from scholars. The traditional view of the progressive conservation movement is presented in J. Leonard Bates, "Fulfilling American Democracy: The Conservation Movement, 1907–1921," *Mississippi Valley Historical Review* 44 (1957): 29–57. The major revisionist work is Samuel P. Hays, *Conservation and the Gospel of Efficiency: The Progressive Conservation Movement, 1890–1920* (1959; New York, 1969). One ignores Hays's work at one's own peril. Also vital are Elmo R. Richardson, *The Politics of Conservation: Crusades and Controversies, 1897–1913* (Berkeley, Calif., 1962), and G. Michael McCarthy, *Hour of Trial: The Conservation Conflict in Colorado and the West, 1891–1907* (Norman, Okla., 1977).

Good specialized studies on the period abound. Among them are Harold K. Steen, *The U.S. Forest Service: A History* (Seattle, 1976); Lawrence Rakestraw, *A History of Forest Conservation in the Pacific Northwest, 1891–1913* (New York, 1979); James L. Penick, Jr., *Progressive Politics and Conservation: The Ballinger-Pinchot Affair* (Chicago, 1968); and Norman J. Schmaltz, "Cutover Land Crusade: The Michigan Forest Conservation Movement, 1899–1931" (Ph.D. diss., University of Michigan, 1972). Works by principals continue to be of value, especially Gifford Pinchot, *Breaking New Ground* (New York, 1947); Carl Alwin Schenck, *The Birth of Forestry in America: Biltmore Forest School, 1898–1913* (1955; Santa Cruz, Calif., 1974); and William B. Greeley, *Forests and Men* (Garden City, N.Y., 1951). Henry Clepper puts the works of these and others in the larger context in his *Professional Forestry in the United States* (Baltimore, 1971).

Organized labor during the early twentieth century is traced in Vernon H. Jensen, *Lumber and Labor* (1945; New York, 1971); Harold M. Hyman, *Soldiers and Spruce: Origins of the Loyal Legion of Loggers and Lumbermen* (Los Angeles, 1963); and Robert L. Tyler, *Rebels in the Woods: The IWW in the Pacific Northwest* (Eugene, Oreg., 1967). Working conditions are treated in Ruth A. Allen, *East Texas Lumber Workers: An Economic and Social Picture, 1870–1950* (Austin, Tex., 1961); Andrew Mason Prouty, "More Deadly Than War! Pacific Coast Logging, 1827–1961" (Ph.D. diss., University of Washington, 1982); Richard W. Massey, "Labor Conditions in the Lumber Industry in Alabama, 1880–1914," *Journal of the Alabama Academy of Science* 37 (1966): 172–81; and Jerrell H. Shofner, "Forced Labor in the Florida Forests, 1880–1950," *Journal of Forest History* 25 (1981): 14–25.

Organization efforts of lumbermen are recounted in James E. Fickle, *The New South and the "New Competition": Trade Association Development in the Southern Pine Industry* (Champaign, Ill., 1980); William G. Robbins, *Lumberjacks and Legislators: Political Economy of the U.S. Lumber Industry, 1890–1941* (College Station, Tex., 1982); and John H. Cox, "Organizations of the Lumber Industry in the Pacific Northwest, 1899–1914" (Ph.D. diss., University of California, Berkeley, 1937).

Shifting environmental perceptions and the rise of preservationism are the focus of a host of studies. Especially good are Donald Worster, *Nature's Economy: The Rise of Ecology* (1977; Garden City, N.Y., 1979); Peter J. Schmitt, *Back to Nature: The Arcadian Myth in Urban America* (New York, 1969); and Stephen Fox, *John Muir and His Legacy: The American Conservation Movement* (Boston, 1981). More narrowly focused and popular works abound.

Developments during the twenties are ably sketched in Donald C. Swain, *Federal Conservation Policy, 1921–1933* (Berkeley, Calif., 1963). The wilderness movement, which took solid form during the decade, has been the subject of several studies. Roderick Nash, *Wilderness and the American Mind*, 3d ed. (New Haven, Conn., 1982) is a good overview. More specific, but still broadly suggestive, are Donald C. Swain, *Wilderness Defender: Horace M. Albright and Conservation* (Chicago, 1970); Susan Flader, *Thinking Like a Mountain: Aldo Leopold and the Evolution of an Ecological Attitude toward Deer, Wolves, and Forests* (Columbia, Mo., 1974); R. Newell Searle, *Saving Quetico-Superior: A Land Set Apart* (St. Paul, Minn., 1977); Donald N. Baldwin, *The Quiet Revolution: Grass Roots of Today's Wilderness Preservation Movement* (Boulder, Colo., 1972); and Craig W. Allin, *The Politics of Wilderness Preservation* (Westport, Conn., 1982).

Forest and wood products research made great strides during the twenties. There is no good overall work, but aspects are traced in Charles A. Nelson, *A History of the U.S. Forest Products Laboratory (1910–1963)* (Madison, Wis., 1977); Robert W. Merz, *A History of the Central States Forest Experiment Station, 1927– 1965* (St. Paul, Minn., 1981); Norman J. Schmaltz, "Raphael Zon, Forest Researcher," *Journal of Forest History* 24 (1980): 24–39, 86–97; Jack P. Oden, "Charles Holmes Herty and the Birth of the Southern Newsprint Industry, 1927–1940," *Journal of Forest History* 21 (1977): 76–89; and Stephen J. Pyne, "Fire Policy and Fire Research in the U.S. Forest Service," *Journal of Forest History* 25 (1981): 64–77 (also in Pyne, *Fire in America*, cited above).

Appropriately, works on the New Deal era tend to focus on federal agencies and key government officials. Major studies include John A. Salmond, *The Civilian Conservation Corps, 1933–1942* (Durham, N.C., 1967); Wilmon H. Droze, *High Dams and Slack Waters: TVA Rebuilds a River* (Baton Rouge, La., 1965); Droze, *Trees, Prairies, and People: A History of Tree Planting in the Plains States* (Denton, Tex., 1977); Marion Clawson, *New Deal Planning: The National Resources Planning Board* (Baltimore, 1981); and Clayton R. Koppes, "Oscar L. Chapman: A Liberal at the Interior Department, 1933–1953" (Ph.D. diss., University of Kansas, 1974). Not to be overlooked is the correspondence in Edgar B. Nixon, ed., *Franklin D. Roosevelt and Conservation, 1911–1945*, 2 vols. (Hyde Park, N.Y., 1957).

Sound, scholarly studies of the post–New Deal period have already begun to appear. For the period of the war itself, see Philip F. Cashier, "Natural Resources Management during the Second World War, 1939–1947" (Ph.D. diss., State University of New York at Binghamton, 1980). On the Truman-Eisenhower years, see Elmo R. Richardson, *Dams, Parks, and Politics: Resource Development and Preservation in the Truman-Eisenhower Era* (Lexington, Ky., 1973); George Van Dusen, "Politics of 'Partnership': The Eisenhower Administration and Conservation, 1952–1960" (Ph.D. diss., Loyola University of Chicago, 1973); and Aaron Wildavsky, *Dixon-Yates: A Study in Power Politics* (New Haven, Conn., 1962).

The ascendancy of environmental concerns during the Kennedy-Johnson years resulted in a spate of studies, not all polemic. Samuel P. Hays offers a broad, theoretical framework in "The Structure of Environmental Politics since World War II," *Journal of Social History* 14 (1981): 719–38. Nearly as useful are Donald Fleming, "Roots of the New Conservation Movement," *Perspectives in American History* 6 (1972): 7–91, and Timothy O'Riordan, "The Third American Conservation Movement: New Implications for Public Policy," *Journal of American Studies* 5 (1971): 155–71. Among more narrowly focused works, see Barbara Laverne Blythe Leunes, "The Conservation Philosophy of Stewart L. Udall, 1961–1968" (Ph.D. diss., Texas A & M University, 1977); Thomas R. Dunlap, *DDT: Scientists, Citizens, and Public Policy* (Princeton, N.J., 1981); and John P. Crevelli, "The Final Act of the Greatest Conservation President," *Prologue* 12 (1980): 173–91. Beginning earlier but climaxing during the period at hand is Susan R. Shrepfer's even-handed *The Fight to Save the Redwoods: A History of Environmental Reform, 1917–1978* (Madison, Wis., 1983).

As yet most studies of forests and environmental activity during the post-Johnson era are only faintly historical. Still, useful insights can be gained from John C. Whitaker, *Striking a Balance: Environmental and Natural Resource Policy in the Nixon-Ford Years* (Washington, D.C., 1976); Paul J. Culhane, *Pubic Lands Politics: Interest Group Influence on the Forest Service and the Bureau of Land Management* (Baltimore, 1981); Allan K. Fitzsimmons, "Environmental Quality as a Theme in Federal Legislation," *Geographical Review* 70 (1980): 314–27; and Samuel Trask Dana and Sally K. Fairfax, *Forest and Range Policy: Its Development in the United States,* 2d ed. (New York, 1980).

Studies of forest industries during the postwar years are few. Useful starting points are Dennis C. LeMaster, *Mergers among the Largest Forest Products Firms, 1950–1970* (Pullman, Wash., 1977); David C. Smith, "Pulp, Paper, and Alaska," *Pacific Northwest Quarterly* 66 (1975): 61–70; and portions of such company studies as W. J. Reader, *Bowater: A History* (Cambridge, 1981); Jeffrey M. LaLande, *Medford Corporation: A History of an Oregon Logging and Lumber Company* (Medford, Oreg., 1979); and John R. Ross, *Maverick: The Story of Georgia-Pacific* ([Portland, Oreg.], 1980). Also worthwhile is John A. Zivnuska, *U.S. Timber Resources in a World Economy* (Washington, D.C., 1967).

Most other areas of study remain virtually untouched for the postwar era. Indeed, in view of the volume of source materials, the rapidity of social and technological change, and the complexities of the world economy, it may take decades for historical scholarship to reach the level for the period that it already has arrived at for earlier years. Fortunately, a host of scholars are at work trying to speed the advent of improved understanding.

Index